A HISTORICAL GEOGRAPHY OF CHRISTOPHER COLUMBUS'S FIRST VOYAGE AND HIS INTERACTIONS WITH INDIGENOUS PEOPLES OF THE CARIBBEAN

This book offers a unique account of Christopher Columbus's first voyage, the most consequential voyage in world history. It provides a detailed day-by-day account of the explorer's travels and activities, richly illustrated with thematic maps.

This work expands our understanding of Columbus's first voyage by mapping his sea and land experiences, offering both a historical and geographical exploration of his first voyage. Traveling chronologically through events, the reader builds a spatial insight into Columbus's perspectives that confused and confirmed his pre-existing notions of Asia and the Indies, driving him onward in search of new geographic evidence. Drawing from a diverse range of primary and secondary historical resources, this book is beautifully adorned with illustrations that facilitate an in-depth exploration of the connections between the places Columbus encountered and his subsequent social interactions with Indigenous people. This methodology allows the reader to better understand Columbus's actions as he analyzes new geographic realities with pre-existing notions of the "Indies." Attention is given to Columbian primary sources which analyze how those materials have been used to create a narrative by historians. Readers will learn about the social and political structures of the Lucayan, Taíno, and Carib peoples, achieving a deeper understanding of those pre-Columbian cultures at the time of contact.

The book will appeal to students and researchers in the disciplines of history, geography, and anthropology, and the general reader interested in Colombus.

Al M. Rocca is a Professor Emeritus at Simpson University and is currently serving as Adjunct Research Professor at California State University, Monterey Bay.

Routledge Research in Historical Geography

This series offers a forum for original and innovative research, exploring a wide range of topics encompassed by the sub-discipline of historical geography and cognate fields in the humanities and social sciences. Titles within the series adopt a global geographical scope and historical studies of geographical issues that are grounded in detailed inquiries of primary source materials. The series also supports historiographical and theoretical overviews, and edited collections of essays on historical-geographical themes. This series is aimed at upper-level undergraduates, research students and academics.

Empire, Gender and Bio-Geography
Charlotte Wheeler-Cuffe and Colonial Burma
Nuala C Johnson

Dissertating Geography
An inquiry into the making of student geographical knowledge, 1950–2020
Mette Bruinsma

Urban Planning During Socialism
Views from the Periphery
Edited By Jasna Mariotti and Kadri Leetmaa

A Historical Geography of Christopher Columbus's First Voyage and His Interactions with Indigenous Peoples of the Caribbean
Al M. Rocca

For more information about this series, please visit: https://www.routledge.com/ Routledge-Research-in-Historical-Geography/book-series/RRHGS

A HISTORICAL GEOGRAPHY OF CHRISTOPHER COLUMBUS'S FIRST VOYAGE AND HIS INTERACTIONS WITH INDIGENOUS PEOPLES OF THE CARIBBEAN

Al M. Rocca

Routledge
Taylor & Francis Group

LONDON AND NEW YORK

Designed cover image: Peoples Pictorial Press Ltd / Alamy

First published 2024
by Routledge
4 Park Square, Milton Park, Abingdon, Oxon OX14 4RN

and by Routledge
605 Third Avenue, New York, NY 10158

Routledge is an imprint of the Taylor & Francis Group, an informa business

© 2024 Al M. Rocca

British Library Cataloguing-in-Publication Data
A catalogue record for this book is available from the British Library

Library of Congress Cataloging-in-Publication Data
Names: Rocca, Al M., author.
Title: A historical geography of Christopher Columbus's first voyage and his interactions with indigenous peoples of the Caribbean / Al M. Rocca.
Description: Abingdon, Oxon ; New York, NY : Routledge, 2024. | Series: Routledge studies in historical geography | Includes bibliographical references and index.
Identifiers: LCCN 2023055811 (print) | LCCN 2023055812 (ebook) | ISBN 9781032734248 (hbk) | ISBN 9781032734262 (pbk) | ISBN 9781003464143 (ebk)
Subjects: LCSH: Columbus, Christopher--Travel--Caribbean Area. | Caribbean Area--Discovery and exploration--Spanish. | Caribbean Area--History--To 1810. | Indians of the West Indies--History--15th century.
Classification: LCC E118 .R64 2024 (print) | LCC E118 (ebook) | DDC 970.01/5--dc23/eng/20231213
LC record available at https://lccn.loc.gov/2023055811
LC ebook record available at https://lccn.loc.gov/2023055812

ISBN: 978-1-032-73424-8 (hbk)
ISBN: 978-1-032-73426-2 (pbk)
ISBN: 978-1-003-46414-3 (ebk)

DOI: 10.4324/9781003464143

Typeset in Times New Roman
by SPi Technologies India Pvt Ltd (Straive)

CONTENTS

FIGURES

FOREWORD

By Ronald H. Fritze

In the early summer of 2023, *Choice: Reviews of New Books* sent me a book to review. It was *Mapping Christopher Columbus: An Historical Geography of His Early Life to 1492* by Al M. Rocca. There is a vast number of books about Christopher Columbus—biographies, life and times, and various specialized studies. Some Columbus books are classics or future classics, some are good, some mediocre, and a few sadly awful. I was not familiar with Professor Rocca's work, so I wondered where his book would fall in the spectrum. As I paged through *Mapping Christopher Columbus*, I noticed that it contained a large number of maps—92 maps in a 244-page book. Most of them were quite specialized as to what they depicted. How they depicted the information was clear and readily understandable. Rocca had done a fine job designing them.

Columbus lived in a world where Europeans were preoccupied with finding a feasible route to Asia's spices and other riches that were not fettered by Islamic dominion. Chapter by chapter, Rocca detailed how Columbus gained knowledge of how winds and currents operate in the Mediterranean and parts of the Atlantic Ocean. Columbus's goal was to determine a feasible route for sailing to Asia that would get him back home safely. Using primary sources and maps, Rocca shows how step by step, Columbus gathered the information that he needed. Rocca presents a convincing explanation and I gave his book a positive review.

Professor Rocca and I are both members of the Society for the History of Discoveries. Shortly after I submitted the review to *Choice*, Professor Rocca contacted me. It was unconnected to my review as it was not yet published and Professor Rocca had no way of knowing that I reviewed his book. He asked if I would be willing to evaluate his new book *A Historical Geography of Christopher Columbus's First Voyage and His Interactions with Indigenous Peoples of the Caribbean*. He was submitting it to Routledge. His email started a scholarly conversation and friendship that still continues.

If you are reading this, you have the book in hand and you can see it is a study of Columbus's first voyage that focuses on tracing his route as far as possible. Again, as with his first book, Professor Rocca takes the reader through a step-by-step calculation of Columbus's itinerary through a close reading of the primary sources and his maps. As with his previous book, Rocca has provided 50 maps to illustrate his narrative. Themes included in these maps are "The World of Columbus," "Columbus in the Eastern Atlantic-departure and return." "Columbus in the Western Atlantic-arrival and departure." "Columbus in the Canary Islands," and "Columbus's course change on 8 October." All of them enhance the narrative. The major source that Rocca uses is Columbus's *Diario* or logbook. It is not Columbus's actual ship's log. Instead, it is a combined transcription and paraphrase prepared by the Dominican missionary and historian Bartholeme de Las Casas as research for his own history of Colombus's career and the Spanish colonization of the Caribbean islands. Sadly, the original *Diario* and any copies of it have been lost.

I won't go into details and get in the way of Professor Rocca's account. What I will say, however, is that I found his account to be quite persuasive and I think other readers will agree. What is special about Rocca's account is that it is the most detailed attempt to reconstruct the route of Columbus's first voyage since Samuel Eliot Morison's *Admiral of the Ocean Sea* (1942). Professor Rocca's account stands up well in comparison to the patrician Morison's classic authoritative account. While Rocca does not supersede Morison, he supplements him with an equally credible narrative based on new sources. Both accounts are worth reading.

Another issue that Professor Rocca deals with is where Columbus first made landfall in 1492. It has been a long-standing and ultimately unresolved controversy among scholars of the Columbian voyages. The first landfall obviously took place on one of the islands of the Bahamas, but which one? The problem is that Columbus moved on in short order to find the larger lands that his native informants were telling him about. After all, his goal was to find Asia or at least the island of Cipangu. The natives pointed him south and he quickly found Cuba and Hispaniola. After that, Columbus never went back to his first landfall. All of his remaining three voyages took more southern approaches to reach Hispaniola and Cuba and never came near the Bahamas. As a result, the exact location of the first landfall was never firmly established. Later, the so-called landfall controversy arose and intensified during the twentieth century and beyond. Various scholars of Columbus have suggested a variety of possibilities. Professor Rocca bravely joined the fray and has reached his own convincing conclusion. But I am not going to spoil it for the reader.

With *A Historical Geography of Christopher Columbus's First Voyage and His Interactions with Indigenous Peoples of the Caribbean*, you can expect to experience an armchair adventure as you sail along with Columbus and Professor Rocca. It will be a fascinating voyage as well as a great lesson as to how a good historian can construct a coherent and convincingly sourced narrative out of a variety of sources. So, take up the book and read. You won't be disappointed.

PREFACE

As Christopher Columbus prepared for his first voyage of discovery, geography dominated his thoughts. Despite having spent years working out the general geographic look of the world and the width of the great *Ocean Sea*, he could not be sure of his calculations until he actually completed a crossing. Call it courage or stupidity, he was determined to do it. Thus was his imagination for discovery lit, kindled by tradition, biblical and secular, not so much for one over the other, but for truth, a geographic truth, subtly revealed here and there, a never-ending search for clues in documents, maps, and stories told. At the latitude he was proposing for the crossing, 28 degrees north latitude, this effort called for, in Columbus's estimation, an extended ocean crossing of approximately 2,400–3,000 miles. To do this in a westerly direction, sailing without deviation into the vastness of the Atlantic appeared to most who heard his theory, an exercise in maritime suicide.

My previous book on Columbus investigated how he conceived and implemented his *Enterprise to the Indies*. This new book will take an extensive historical and geographical look at his first voyage, the most consequential voyage in world history. The purpose of this book is to extend our understanding of Columbus's first voyage by mapping his sea and land experiences. These maps, hopefully, will inform the reader concerning Columbus's specific route across the great stretches of open water in the mid-Atlantic Ocean, alternative theories for the first landfall, detailed locational maps of his activities on each island visited, and authenticated and suggested Indigenous village sites; no previous Columbus's studies have mapped the inland expeditions of the first voyage nor presented a comprehensive mapping summary of known native villages. In this sense, my work is a historical geography of the 1492 voyage, presenting, for the most part, a day-by-day journal account of his experiences, moving from the perspective of the Europeans to the reactions of the Indigenous peoples encountered, and interpreting key events through a historical and geographical lens.

A major purpose for writing this book centers on looking more deeply into the lives of the Indigenous peoples Columbus and his crew encountered. For example, as events unfold, readers will learn about the social and political structures of the Lucayan, Taíno, and Carib (Kalinago) peoples, achieving a deeper understanding of those pre-Columbian cultures at the time of contact.[1] Previous books have focused predominately on Columbus's first voyage using European written sources, with minimal inclusion of work by anthropologists and archaeologists describing the Indigenous cultures: Lucayan, Taíno, and Carib. Irving Rouse, an anthropologist, provided insights (1992) into the migration background of Indigenous groups into the Caribbean, the natural setting into which they settled, and the state of the cultures at the time of contact. More recent (2007) is William F. Keegan's *Taíno Indian Myth and Practice*, revealing time and space systematics between the Lucayans of the Bahamas and the Taíno of the Greater Antilles. Keegan uncovers valuable evidence to suggest the background of cacique (chief) Caonabó, a key figure who lived and impacted Columbus's exploration and conquest of Hispaniola. Along the way, Keegan investigates Taíno's political economy, the rise of caciques, and their hierarchical structure; he also takes on the interesting discussion of the Caribs and the suggestion of their cannibalism. Most recently (2022), a group of scholars published an investigation on the population history of Indigenous Bahamian islanders using DNA tracing technology; their work has revealed trends in island migration.[2] In addition, new research (2019) has studied the material encounters and exchanges between Indigenous islanders and the Spanish colonizers, suggesting that negotiation and choice played an important role in illuminating native traditions and values.[3] Of significant note on the Carib peoples, formerly believed to live, for the most part, in the Lesser Antilles, is a ground-breaking study (2021) titled "Faces Divulge the Origins of Caribbean Prehistoric Inhabitants," supporting "evidence for an ongoing Carib invasion of the Greater Antilles around AD 800."[4] Columbus reported Caribs during his first landings on islands in the Bahamas, believing them to be raiders from other islands to the south, as gestured by natives on San Salvador and other Bahamian islands, but little evidence has come forward until now linking a permanent Carib presence on Hispaniola and Jamaica.[5] This is a significant finding, as Columbus later rationalizes the continuing Carib threat against Taino tribes as a justification to use military force on later voyages.

Karen Anderson-Córdova, in 2017, supported the concept of a broad Carib invasion of the Antilles, Greater and Lesser. In her book, *Surviving Spanish Conquest*, she noted that the Caribs were "more mobile and hostile" than their Taíno neighbors. Anderson-Córdova cites one study that looked at the ceramic traditions emanating from northwest Guinea, estimating that Caribs entered the Antilles "around AD 1250."[6] Rouse commented on the observed size of Indigenous villages from his archaeological digs and their relationship to survival in the face of incessant pre-contact Carib raids. He compartmentalized small villages, from 12 to 15 houses, comprising 120–225 individuals, existing in the Bahamian Islands and within eastern Hispaniola, suffering near or complete extinction by Carib raiders.[7] Lynne Guitar and Jorge Estevez estimated that by AD 1200, Carib tribes and Taíno villagers had become "bitter enemies, fighting for the islands' resources."[8]

On the historical side, several key primary sources will be utilized, including Columbus's letter to King Ferdinand and Queen Isabella of Spain announcing his return and findings. One version of the letter addressed to Luis de Santángel, an official at the Spanish court, became widely circulated, and a Latin version addressed to Gabriel Sánchez appeared in publication soon afterward. The letter holds a unique historical significance as a first-level primary source (from the central character under investigation).[9] Also of importance are the second-level primary resources of Columbus's son, Ferdinand. Ferdinand, too young to participate in the first voyage, did subsequently sail with Columbus on his fourth voyage to the Indies and was privy to personal interactions with his father about the events of 1492. Ferdinand's biography of his father, *The Life of the Admiral Christopher Columbus* (referred to henceforth as *Historie*), recounts key events from the first voyage.[10] Likewise, another important second-level primary source used in this investigation is Fray Bartolomé de Las Casas's *Historia de las Indias* (referred to henceforth as *Historia*). In writing *Historia*, Las Casas drew upon his abridged version of Columbus's logbook, known today as the *Diario*. As with Ferdinand, Las Casas did not participate directly in the events of 1492, but he came to Hispaniola (La Española) on a later voyage and possibly interacted with Columbus in 1502.[11]

Ferdinand Columbus, born on August 15, 1488, was the result of Christopher Columbus's encounter with Beatriz Enríquez de Arana, Christopher's first wife, who had died a few years earlier. Raised by Beatriz in Cordoba, Spain, alongside his brother, Diego, the earlier legitimate son of Christopher Columbus, both sons later served as pages in the Spanish royal court. There, Ferdinand found access to books and scholarly training in a wide variety of subjects, including history and philosophy, which later became among his favorite writing topics. In 1502, Ferdinand accompanied his father on the fourth voyage to the Caribbean, the most dangerous adventure the Columbus family encountered. Savage storms, shipwrecks, and near starvation plagued the trip. Upon returning to Spain, Ferdinand cared for his father; Christopher Columbus's death on May 20, 1506, saw Ferdinand take the lead in ongoing legal discussions with the Spanish crown over promised titles and rewards.[12] As the years moved on, Ferdinand engaged in scholarly writing, collecting volumes of European monographs, books, unpublished manuscripts, letters, and memoranda, eventually accumulating more than 15,000 volumes or papers that "included many of Columbus's manuscripts and annotated books," becoming one of the largest private libraries in Europe, open to scholars and serious researchers.[13]

Ferdinand's *Historie*, described by Benjamin Keen as "A mass of narrative and descriptive details etches in a convincing literary portrait of the Hero...We are told of the superb seaman whom his admiring sailors called 'diving,' underscores the inherent bias in much of the book."[14] Anticipating future readers to respond exactly as Keen has done, Ferdinand explained, "I promise to tell the story of the Admiral's life only from his own writings and letters and what I myself observed."[15] Noted Columbus scholar Ilaria Caraci, who has dedicated many years to investigating the content and form of the *Historie*, concludes that the work leads one to believe "that the book is excluded from being composed by a single author, Ferdinand or anyone else; instead, it is a product of a complex drafting, extended over time."[16] Caraci's work is recognized as some of the most intensive and productive on this subject of Ferdinand's biography, and therefore, the reader is strongly urged to understand the possible prejudice and partiality displayed in references to his work.

Bartolomé de Las Casas (1484–1566) grew up in Seville, Spain, under the tutelage of his father, Pedro de las Casas, a local merchant. The younger Las Casas remembered watching Columbus enter the city with several *Indios* (Indigenous Lucayans and Taínos), and subsequently, his father joined Columbus's second voyage.[17] Bartolomé joined his father on a journey to the Americas in 1502, eventually participating in overseeing an *encomienda*, a land grant that included, more or less, the forced participation of any Indigenous peoples living within the boundaries of the legal contract; in a sense, he became a willing slave owner.[18] However, in a few years, a religious metamorphosis transformed him into a vigilant defender, or "Protector of the Indians."[19] From 1511 onward, he traveled and wrote extensively, including the books noted above, working diligently from 1527 until 1559, although *Historia* remained unpublished until after his death.

Las Casas vowed to document, write, and advertise an honest, full-throated defense of the Indigenous peoples. It was during these years that Las Casas investigated and transcribed Ferdinand's copy of the journal, known as the Barcelona copy, into its final form. While admiring Columbus for his religious zeal and commitment to Christian evangelism, Las Casas viewed suspicious actions or apparently exploitative incidents by the explorer as cruel and unforgivable. Switching back and forth from the third person to the first person, Las Casas wrote the *Diario*, describing many incidents from a viewpoint firmly establishing despicable Spanish actions in the New World, including certain events during Columbus's first voyage.[20] Put simply, we do not know the degree to which Las Casas modified or changed the actual reported events in the *Diario* and thus into his *Historia*. Any scholar writing on the subject is expected to examine the sources, consider differing historical opinions, and contemplate the preponderance of the evidence, eventually opting to make a judgment or not; it is not mandatory to make that judgment, thereby allowing the reader to render a decision.[21]

For secondary translated accounts, this author began with the earliest known English version of Las Casas's manuscript, Samuel Kettell's *Personal Narrative of the First Voyage of Columbus to America*.[22] Published in 1827, Kettell translated this directly from the early Spanish edition by Don Martín Fernandez de Navarrete of 1825. In addition, the acclaimed log translation by Robert Fuson (1992) and Cecil Jane's *The Journal of Christopher Columbus* are referenced as checks on the 1827 version. Clements Markham's *The Journal of Christopher Columbus and Documents Relating to the Voyages of John Cabot and Gaspar Corte Real* provides a late-19th-century translation that is interesting.[23] As a final check on the above resources, I referenced Oliver Dunn and James E. Kelley, Jr.'s excellent computer translation, *The Diario of Christopher Columbus's First Voyage to America, 1492–1493*. Of special recognition is the *Synoptic Edition of the Log of Columbus's First Voyage*, edited by Francesca Lardicci in 1999. This well-regarded translation is the scholarly standard, combining excerpts from Las Casas's *Diario*, Columbus's letters from *Historia de las Indias*, and Ferdinand Columbus's *Historie*; Spanish and English versions allow the researcher to make detailed analyses.[24] I was pleasantly surprised that the early versions of Navarrete's translation, such as the books by Kettell and Markham, proved helpful in obtaining a historical perspective from American translators; their work aligned quite well with the modern 20th-century versions.[25]

As the reader might imagine, a voluminous assortment of articles and books, both scholarly and for general consumption, have emerged following the events of 1492. It is this author's wish to draw upon secondary accounts from the Americas (Latin America and the United States) and the significant contributions of authors from Italy, Portugal, and Spain. For the purposes of this book, most of the basic log quotes dealing with directions, distances sailed, flora, and fauna are from American authors unless otherwise noted.

As already noted, a unique feature of this investigation will be to map in detail the key moments of the first voyage. Thanks to the cooperation of the United States Geological Survey (USGS) and California State University, Monterey Bay, I obtained permission to access appropriate base maps from the *National Map—Advanced* mapping program (USGS) and ArcGIS online mapping program (Full Caribbean Terrain, CSUMB) and received publishing permission to construct highly accurate island configurations that will help readers follow Columbus's paths through the waters of the Caribbean Sea and, for the first time, depict cartographically the location of native villages and Columbus's land experiences. It is my hope that these maps and the ensuing discussions help readers link the events with a geographic connection. In this way, one may see the impact that location and place have on ensuing developments. *Location* is where a place is located on the Earth's surface, whereas *place* describes the physical and social characteristics of that location. The sequential presentation of events is chronological, allowing the reader to build a regional geographic understanding and replicating Columbus's perspectives that confused and confirmed his pre-existing notions of Asia and the Indies, driving him onward in search of new geographic evidence. Thematic maps will provide a geographic context (*location*) for the event and hopefully engage the reader to analyze suspected connections between the geography (*place*) encountered and the events experienced, helping the reader to consider a deeper understanding of Columbus's actions, reactions, and overall experience.

Notes

1 The term *Lucayans* refers to those Indigenous peoples living in the Bahamas at the time of Columbus's visit. Archaeologically, they are known as the Palmetto people, a subgroup of the Taíno. To ethnohistorians, they are called Lucayan Taíno. Rouse, *The Taínos*. The use of the word *Taíno* reverts to the name the Indigenous people of Cuba and Hispaniola gave to the Europeans; it purportedly means "good people." See Deagan & Cruxent, "Reluctant Hosts," 23–24. For the most recent work on the Kalinagos (Carib) migration into the Caribbean, see Ann Ross et al., "Faces Divulge the Origins of Caribbean Prehistoric Inhabitants," (2020).
2 Forbes-Pateman et al. "A population history of indigenous Bahamian islanders: Insights from ancient DNA," *American Journal of Biological Anthropology*, January 2022, 1–14.
3 Rojas, Roberto Valcárcel. "European Material Culture in Indigenous Sites in Northeastern Cuba." In *Material Encounters and Indigenous Transformations in the Early Colonial Americas: Archaeological Case Studies*, edited by Corinne L. Hofman and Floris W.M. Keehnen, 9:102–23.
4 Ross, A.H., Keegan, W.F., Pateman, M.P. *et al.* "Faces Divulge the Origins of Caribbean Prehistoric Inhabitants." *Sci Rep* 10, 147 (2020). https://doi.org/10.1038/s41598-019-56929-3
5 These findings validate Columbus's claims that a pervasive, geographically extensive Carib presence did, in fact, exist on Hispaniola. According to Ferdinand Columbus, his father named the first island encounter San Salvador "for the glory of God who had revealed it to him and saved him from many perils." Lardicci, *A Synoptic Edition, Historie*, FH 34, sections 4–5.
6 Anderson-Córdova, *Surviving Spanish Conquest*, 26–27. She mentions studies by archaeologists Arie Boomert in 1995 and Michael Hoff in 1995 as supporting the invasion hypothesis. For a historiographic review of the use of the term Carib to describe hostile peoples from the Lesser Antilles, see page 25. For information on how Spanish authorities used the term *Carib* for specific social and political purposes, see Dubois & Turits, *The Indigenous Caribbean*, 33–34.
7 Rouse, *The Taínos*, 17–18.
8 Guitar & Estevez, "Taínos," 1015.
9 It should be noted that Columbus's original letter to the Spanish monarchs is lost; the surviving printed copies circulated throughout Europe in Spanish and Italian. A copy of the letter sent to Ferdinand and Isabella did survive and was published in 1989 by Antonio Rumeu de Armas. This transcription, one of several of the Columbus letters, was discovered in a copybook in 1985 and authenticated by Spanish scholars Juan Gil and Consuelo Verla. The book, owned by the Spanish government, remains in the General Archive of the Indies in Seville. This major find is known today as the *Libro Copiador de Cristóbol Colón*, comprising nine documents; document 1 is dated March 4, 1493. For more information on Columbus's letters to

the Spanish monarchs and to read an English translation, see Wadsworth, *Columbus and His First Voyage*, 79–94.

10 It is recognized that Ferdinand Columbus brought family bias into his writings concerning his father's adventures, as was recognized early on by Martín Fernandez de Navarrete in his publication, *Coleccion de Los Viages y Descubrimientos*, 8. Fernandez wrote, "We note the sagacity [cunning] and caution with which he omitted some facts, and with which he adulterated others of the early days of his father in Spain when he was not yet born or was a child and cannot be considered a witness." The above quote is translated by this author. Ferdinand Columbus was born on August 15, 1488, making him 4 years old at the time of his father's first voyage.

11 Las Casas labored from 1527 until 1563 to compile material and compose the *Historia*, attributing his 1547 return to Spain as the beginning of when he dedicated his time to writing. Lardicci, *A Synoptic Edition*, 8.

12 These legal disagreements and enacted lawsuits were recorded and are known as the *pleitos colombinos*, lasting until 1536.

13 Delaney, *Columbus and the Quest for Jerusalem*, 249. Sadly, after Ferdinand's death in 1539, Luis Columbus, Ferdinand's nephew, acquired control of the library and the library quickly fell into disrepair, even abandonment. Thousands of precious volumes disappeared. The remaining books and manuscripts, about 2,000 in number, reside at the Biblioteca Colombina, in the El Archive de la Caterdral, Seville, Spain.

14 Keen (editor), *The Life of the Admiral Christopher Columbus*, vi. There is evidence that suggest Ferdinand may not have completed his father's biography before his death in 1539. Also see Taviani, "Fernando Colón," 136. Taviani noted that the book is "apparently a posthumous compilation, based on a writing of Fernando's, but substantially changed by the insertion of false or imprecise statements." Italian scholars have written extensively on the concerns over the authenticity of Ferdinand Columbus's *Historie*, believing that a "manipulator, or shrewd editor" had a hand in the final composition. See Caraci, *The Puzzling Hero*, 147–149, 191. Also, Lardicci summarizes her concerns over Ferdinand's *Historie* in her introduction to the log, *A Synoptic Edition of Columbus's Log*, 6–7.

15 Keen, *The Life of the Admiral*, lxxi. Further anticipating that readers might assume bias, he wrote, "And whoever suspects that I have added something of my own invention may be certain that I know such a thing would profit me nothing..." Ibid.

16 Caraci, *Colombo Vero e Falso*, Chapter 3, *The Birth of the Historie*, 417 (translated by the author). Caraci believes Ferdinand started his father's biography accurately, describing various aspects of Columbus's voyages, but that much of his father's early life may have been written later by a "compiler." For an in-depth analysis, see Caraci as noted above, 412–420.

17 Columbus first encountered the name *Taino* during his second voyage, as captured persons on Guadeloupe Island tried to explain they were not Caribs. According to the account, the people explained they were *Tayno*, meaning good people. See Anderson-Córdova for more information, *Surviving Spanish Conquest*, note 2, page 186. Also, see Curet, *The Taíno*, 470.

18 Sale, Kirkpatrick. *The Conquest of Paradise*, 156–57. It is interesting to note that no account, primary or secondary, accuses Columbus of ever owning a slave. His one long-time Indigenous guide and interpreter, Diego, became Columbus's godson and volunteered to continue participating in later voyages, despite the opportunity to return to his home island during the second voyage.

19 For a thorough explanation concerning Las Casas's change of heart and ongoing religious devotion for defending Indigenous "natural rights" see Griffin, *Las Casas on Columbus*, 3–4.

20 For a summary of the writing style revealed in the logbook, see Lardicci, 9–11. Lardicci believes Columbus maintained a "positive, assertive, and reassuring" approach to describing events encountered, including contact with Indigenous peoples. When encountering troubles or difficult situations, Lardicci noted that Columbus found a guiding hand in "comforting new signs… from God."

21 The reader should recall that most of the key original writings of Columbus are lost, including the logbook and his first letter to the Spanish monarchs. All extant transcriptions and translations may contain errors of content or language.

22 For readers who are interested in perusing the entire document, Kettell's book is available at the *Internet Archive* (archive.org). See the bibliography for a hyperlink.

23 Markham made use of Navarrete's 1825 original translation. He held the position of President of the Hakluyt Society in 1893, at the time when the Hakluyt Council voted to issue a translation of Columbus's logbook on the "four hundredth anniversary of that momentous expedition." *The Journal of Christopher Columbus*, i.

24 Interestingly, this author discovered that Kettell's 1827 translation is quite effective in defining the tone and intent of the textual content when compared to Dunn and Kelley's computer rendition and Lardicci's advanced 1999 effort. Much can also be said for Clement Markham's translation; I have found most of the critical passages discussing European encounters with Indigenous Peoples to mirror more modern accounts. For example, see October 14, 1492, when Columbus declares "As your Highnesses will see from the seven that I caused to be taken, *The Journal of Christopher Columbus*, 41. Compare this to Lardicci's "As your Highnesses will see from the seven that I have had taken," A Synoptic Edition, 50.

25 For an interesting introspection on the use of historical translations, see Henige, *Historical Evidence and Argument*, 97–100.

ACKNOWLEDGMENTS

As with my first book on Christopher Columbus, this work owes tremendous credit to Italian scholar Ilaria Caraci for her ongoing support of my research. She reviewed early drafts, recommending additional European resources, especially Italian and Spanish. As one of Europe's most knowledgeable Columbus intellectuals, Caraci helped me refocus sections of the manuscript and limit other areas. Her book, *The Puzzling Hero*, provides an outstanding analysis of Columbus, fifteenth-century culture, and rationale for his thinking and actions. Likewise, University of Rome professor, Carla Masetti, reviewed the entire draft copy, making specific suggestions for the work of other Italian scholars. Caraci and Masetti encouraged me to include more research interpretations from recent European professors working in the field of historical geography.

William D. Phillips, an American scholar whose book *The Worlds of Christopher Columbus* was co-authored with his wife Carla Rahn Phillips, served as an excellent general resource for my work. William Phillips read my manuscript and provided helpful feedback that caused me to revise important sections dealing with how Columbus interacted with the Indigenous people. I also wish to thank Ronald Fritze, Professor of History at Athens State University for his intensive review in the manuscript stages of my research, prompting me to take a deeper look into the actions by Portuguese navigators in understanding the system of winds and currents in the eastern Atlantic region.

During my research, I was fortunate to have two helpful librarians that acquired rare monographs and other resources that allowed me to sequentially investigate, from the late nineteenth century onward, translations and transcriptions from European and American authors. Karen Wagner, at California State University, Monterey Bay, regularly helped me acquire materials through the inter-library loan system. The same goes for Heather McCulley, librarian at Simpson University in Redding, California. I want to recognize the United States Geological Survey Map Division for allowing me to use their National Map (Advanced Viewer) to create base maps, measure nautical miles accurately, and print digital high-resolution files.

A special thanks goes to Faye Leerink, Commissioning Editor for Routledge Publishing for her encouragement, from the start, that my work would complement Routledge's ongoing series on historical geography.

Al Rocca, September 2023

INTRODUCTION

The monumental first voyage logbook of Christopher Columbus is unique in that it remains the earliest detailed day-by-day account of the explorer's travels and activities available in print form.[1] To account for his discoveries, Columbus, early in the voyage, decided to commit to paper his experiences during the trek across the *Ocean Sea*, his observations of flora and fauna, and his contact with Indigenous people on lands encountered. This extraordinary effort provides readers of his journal with a unique look at the physical and social geography of the Americas at first contact in 1492.[2] On another level, author Robert Fuson states, "It is, in essence, a singular, documentary link between the Middle Ages and the Renaissance."[3]

The history of the Columbus logbook is confusing and amazing, confusing because the original is lost, and amazing because, in many ways, it is a "mirror of the man. It shows his failings and his virtues."[4] Most scholars agree that Columbus dutifully entered summaries of his daily activities, whether at sea or on land, to give a full account later to Queen Isabella and King Ferdinand, his sponsors. On the return voyage from the "Indies," he encountered a severe storm. Fearing the worst and desiring to save the logbook manuscript, Columbus placed it, or a summary of it, in a cloth covering, sealed it with wax, placed it in a barrel, and tossed it overboard.[5] Apparently, by the time he returned to Spain and presented himself to the monarchs in Barcelona, Columbus had provided a letter and a new official log of his journey; reportedly, he had finished while waiting for an audience with the king and queen. How this "official" log differed from the document tossed overboard is unknown. Isabella ordered a copy drawn up for Columbus, purportedly commanding scribes to accurately transcribe the log; this copy was given to Columbus as he prepared for his second voyage—it is known as the Barcelona copy. Again, we are not sure if the

DOI: 10.4324/9781003464143-1

copy was an exact transcription. The Barcelona copy, considered a derivative record like the original given to the Spanish monarchs, is lost to history.[6]

Columbus's copy legally moved to his oldest son, Diego, after the explorer died in 1506. Most researchers believe that Ferdinand, Columbus's illegitimate son, later acquired the remaining Barcelona copy and placed it in his large personal library, a repository used by scholars of the time. However, this is not certain. In writing his father's biography, Ferdinand, commonly known as the *Historie*, refers to using the logbook (journal) when summarizing key events of the first voyage.[7] Evidence suggests that he did not finish the manuscript before his death and that others contributed significant portions of the work.[8]

Fray Bartolomé de Las Casas somehow gained access to Columbus's copy of the journal, either on Hispaniola or in Spain, and spent considerable time transcribing it in a summarized form, presenting a limited number of purportedly direct quotes from Columbus's Barcelona copy, the majority of the *Diario* consisting of the Dominican friar's abridged subjective interpretation. Concerning the *Diario*, Columbus scholar David Henige explains:

> About 20 percent of the Diario is not a paraphrase of some original, at least not by Las Casas, who presented it as "the very words" of Columbus. This portion of the text is characterized by being in the first person and the present tense. The degree to which the remaining four-fifths of the *Diario* departs from any original source is unknown. Nor do we know whether it was Las Casas, an earlier copyist, or both who changed the text.[9]

For purposes of this book, all direct Columbus quotes are stated as such; the remaining text information is quotes or my interpretations of Las Casas's abridgment.[10] Las Casas wanted to include Columbus's writing as research content for his comprehensive *Historia de las Indias* (*Historia*).[11] Las Casas did go to the Indies on a later voyage and was in Santo Domingo (Hispaniola) at the same time Diego Columbus resided there. It is possible that Las Casas gained access during this time, access that allowed him sufficient time to read, analyze, and paraphrase the explorer's daily journal, adding first-person quotes at key points in the voyage. Described as an abstract of the Barcelona copy, Las Casas's manuscript disappeared until 1789, when Spanish naval officer Don Martín Fernandez de Navarrete discovered the work at the Royal Library in Madrid. Soon, various translations appeared as scholars examined the Las Casas manuscript or translated new language documents from Navarrete's work.

The first English version came out in 1827, when Samuel Kettell published his translation. While Kettell's book titled *Personal Narrative of the First Voyage of Columbus to America*, is rarely used by scholars today, I wanted to see how it compared to later translations. The book alludes to the fact that Las Casas's work is only an abstract of an original, self-professed by Las Casas, while at the same time preserving some actual quotes from Columbus. Kettell believed that Las Casas left out "uninteresting particulars and repetitions."[12] A natural question to immediately ask is: What did Las Casas leave out or change? This is difficult to answer without recovering at least one of the two original copies of the journal. Yet, as many Columbus scholars have said, the Las Casas abstract is the most complete written source of the original journal; other sources present partial components of the log.[13] Margarita Zamora wrote, "Thus, much of our understanding of the Discovery, much of what we know of what Columbus thought or [actually] said, as well as what we do not, is the result of Las Casas's intervention in the transmission of the Columbian texts."[14] This statement summarizes the concern historians and social scientists face when the preponderance of primary resource evidence is interpreted only by a few people.[15] On the other hand, Samuel Eliot Morison, who wrote the 1942 Pulitzer Prize-winning biography of Columbus, noted, "The charge that he [Las Casas] or anyone else garbled the Journal is false." Morison does admit that Las Casas, unfamiliar with nautical terms, "doubtless omitted some nautical detail that we should wish to have and interpolated some stupid remarks of his own that are easily detected."[16]

However, it is vital that readers understand the context in which Las Casas decided to undergo decades of research and writing to report publicly the devastating impact of the Spanish occupation and colonization of New Spain, including the Caribbean, and North and South America. Las Casas admitted he never saw the original copy of the *Diario*, claiming later that he used a scribe's (Barcelona) copy. There is a strong possibility that Las Casas referenced all his *Diario* accounts, including first-person quotes, in his *Historia* between 1527 and 1539, decades after the events he describes.[17] Helen Nader, in summarizing the accuracy of the *Diario*, wrote, "These and other instances suggest that it is not inappropriate to suspect that the *Diario* written by Las Casas in about 1552 differed in many respects from any shipboard log that Columbus kept."[18]

He began working on the *History of the Indies* in 1527 after numerous failed attempts to stop Indian slave trading while still acquiescing to the introduction of African slaves. He continued to travel throughout Central and South America, the Caribbean, and Spain, writing and encouraging Spanish authorities to halt, or at least limit, the *encomienda* system, where local Spanish officials in the Americas established land grants in return for money or favors. Any Indigenous peoples residing within the boundaries of the *encomienda* became vassals, virtual slaves, of the *encomendero* (grantee).[19] In 1552, he published *Brevísima relación de la destrucción de las Indias* (*A Short History of the Destruction of the Indies*). He wrote much of this book during the 1540s as he traveled and amassed damning evidence from a variety of geographical regions.[20] Finally, in 1561, he completed his monumental manuscript, *A History of the Indies*.

Using various translations of the Las Casas *Diario* as well as his other writings and other more recent historical sources, this author proposes including a historical and geographical investigation of Columbus's first voyage. This work will explore the physical and social geography of the adventure from the day-to-day viewpoint of Columbus by employing intense mapping of each leg of the voyage while also exploring the pre-contact Caribbean world. Christopher Columbus was primarily a geographer of the land and sea. Prior to 1492, he traveled extensively in the Mediterranean Sea as a lad and the Eastern and Northern Atlantic Ocean as a young man; these experiences provided a vital school of maritime learning.[21] All his underlying ambitions and long-term goals—social recognition, accumulation of wealth, hereditary rights, and religious evangelism—depended on understanding the natural world of the 15th century. Geography provided the tools and skills necessary for unlocking the mysteries of unknown places in the east and west of Europe. Along with his passion for achievement, Columbus desired organization and control, gaining these traits as he rose in ship-handling ability and responsibility as a trading representative for Genoese merchants. Marrying his love for the sea with a passion for understanding the physical world, he understood that mastering the sea and all its meteorological mysteries (winds and currents) helped organize his thoughts for a transatlantic voyage.[22]

In this book, the regional culture and village traditions of the Indigenous peoples living in the Caribbean at the time of European contact, as represented in archaeological and anthropological studies, are juxtaposed alongside unfolding encounters with Columbus as the expedition moves from the Bahamas to Cuba and Hispaniola (Haiti). Existing in an uncompromising, harsh equatorial climate, Lucayan (Bahamas), Taíno, and Carib (Eastern Cuba and Central and Eastern Hispaniola) people struggled but succeeded in developing their economies and political structures. Columbus's first encounter changed everything, and never again would the Caribbean region remain isolated from Europe and the rest of the world.

The pre-Columbian Caribbean boasted a large, industrious population consisting of three major cultures: Lucayan, Taíno, and Carib.[23] Migration pressure brought these peoples from mainland sites in Central and South America to new locations in the Lesser Antilles and the Greater Antilles.[24] By 1492, they may have numbered in the millions, with demographic estimates running from 200,000 to more than three million people.[25] A 2002 report announced that the increased "archaeological database on village size and distribution of the Taíno population suggests a figure (for Hispaniola) closer to the higher estimates might be more accurate."[26] The "population debate" has raised spirited disagreement, with one writer noting, "At the heart of the High Counters' [scholars promoting a high population] enterprise is an ensemble of assumptions, each of which must be true if their conclusions are to be accepted."[27]

The pre-Columbian settlement of the Caribbean reveals a series of distinct waves of migration emanating from Central and South America, beginning as early as 5000–4000 BC. Paddling in seaworthy canoes of various sizes, these people, known as Guanahatabeys, made their way to the western side of Cuba. At the same time, Ortoiroid natives from the Orinoco River in what is now Venezuela leapfrogged the Lesser Antilles north to Puerto Rico. Other waves of migrants arrived in the Lesser Antilles around 2000–500 BC, some of them agriculturalists, conquering or "pushing out" previous Indigenous settlers. It is believed that the Eastern part of Hispaniola attracted, peoples we now call the *Classic Taíno*, forced the Guanahatabeys to relocate to the extreme western parts of the island, achieving this through conquest, with some of the population intermarrying the newcomers. Taíno's mastering of agricultural knowledge and skills allowed their population to grow, thus forcing emigration outward in all directions, "settling Cuba, the Bahamas, the Turks and Caicos, and Jamaica."[28]

The Lucayan culture, a sub-group of the Tainos, moved in small groups from Cuba and Hispaniola northward; they settled on the small islands strung out along the Bahama archipelago, eventually developing different cultural traditions as they erected their small, clan-based villages.[29] Their extant pottery reveals unique techniques, and they were more reliant on inter-island trade with their neighbors to the south. The Tainos and Lucayans shared the Arawakan language, with distinct dialects noticeable on Bahamian islands further from Hispaniola, such as San Salvador.[30]

The last pre-contact group to migrate in large numbers from South America were the Carib people (Kalinagos), aggressively subjugating villages and then entire islands of the Lesser Antilles beginning around 1000 AD. Hilary Beckles said in a 2008 article that when the Caribs arrived in the Greater Antilles, they already "found the Tainos to some extent already on the defensive [fighting each other]" but later encountered Kalinagos [Caribs], who they described as more prepared for aggression."[31] Beckles adds that when Columbus arrived on the scene in 1492, the Caribs were "in the process of establishing control over territory and communities occupied by Tainos in the Lesser Antilles and parts of the Greater Antilles." Columbus had referred to a Carib presence based on the crude communication from his Lucayan and Taino interpreters and other contacts on Cuba and Hispaniola, but until recently, little archaeological evidence sustained this argument.[32] Confirming Beckles's ideas of large-scale incursions by Caribs into islands of the Greater Antilles, forensic anthropologist Ann Ross and her team investigated the facial morphology of the pre-Columbian inhabitants of Hispaniola and Cuba, and compared them to the Lucayan skulls of the Bahamas islands. The team's summary results, announced in 2020, included supporting evidence to indicate a "Carib invasion of the Greater Antilles around AD 800,"[33] validating Columbus's claim of a large Carib presence on Hispaniola and possibly eastern Cuba.[34]

Thus, the three Indigenous groups existed, along with a few remaining Guana-hatabeys, in the Caribbean region, living a challenging life with limited resources, building social connections and political affiliations, trading successfully within an intra- and inter-island commercial tradition, unaware that outsiders approached,

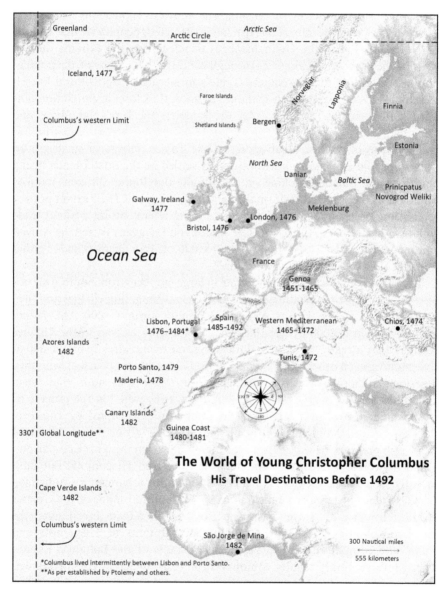

FIGURE 0.1 The World of Christopher Columbus: His Travel Destinations before 1492

people never seen before, strangers in their appearance and mannerisms; everything was about to change. No one knows how the date of contact was understood by these Indigenous peoples, but one of the strangers coming to their homeland, Christopher Columbus, recorded the date as October 12, 1492, as noted on the Julian calendar.[35]

It is amazing to consider the combined sailing experience Christopher Columbus logged during his pre-1492 years. From the frigid north, almost to the Arctic Circle, to just a few degrees of latitude above the Equator. While it is true that many 15th-century Portuguese, Spanish, Genoese, French, English, and Basque sailors sailed parts of the vast eastern Atlantic waters, few, if any, could boast of traversing such a large latitudinal breadth of the known *Ocean Sea*.

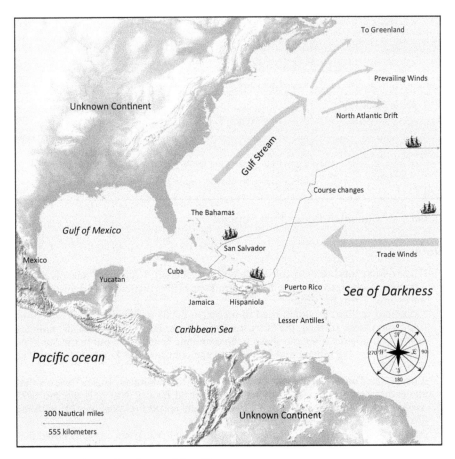

FIGURE 0.2 Columbus Route: First Voyage

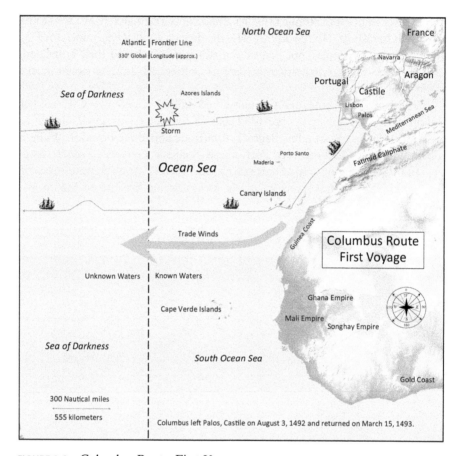

FIGURE 0.3 Columbus Route: First Voyage

Notes

1 The explorer was born Cristoforo Colombo [Genoese], "Colombo," meaning *dove*; however, he changed his name to accommodate his Portuguese and Spanish experiences into "Cristóbal Colón."
2 Columbus realized he would need to report, in detail, as he noted, to King Ferdinand and Queen Isabella, the latter needing substantial verification of his findings before granting the titles and sharing the economic benefits laid out in the *Santa Fe Capitulations*, the official and binding voyage contract. See Dunn & Kelley, *The Diario*, 2021.
3 Fuson, *The Log of Christopher Columbus*, I. By this comment, Fuson believes that the events described changed the course of world history. Not only did the 1492 voyage link historic periods, but it geographically linked the "New World" with the Old World.
4 Markham, *The Journal of Christopher Columbus*, viii. Markham correctly noted that the journal "records his lofty aims, his unswerving loyalty, his deep religious feelings, his kindliness and gratitude." As for the document's overall importance, Markham wrote, "The journal is the most important document in the whole range of the

history of geographical discovery, because it is a record of the enterprise which changed the whole face, not only of that history, but of the history of mankind."

5 Ibid., Columbus did this on the night of February 14, 1493, thinking it might float eastward toward the Azores; the strong flowing North Atlantic Drift winds and currents have and continue to transport physical objects in a steady easterly direction, 186. See also Dunn & Kelley, *The Diario*, 371. Lardicci, DB Entry120: Note 32, 126.

6 The original copy, probably the one left with the Spanish monarchs, disappeared sometime after Isabella died in 1504. The Barcelona copy vanished sometime when Diego's son, Luis, retained possession of the document. See Fuson, pp. 1–12, for an in-depth explanation of the history of the Barcelona copy and subsequent transcriptions and translations. Another concern is the fact that Columbus's command of the Spanish written language by 1492 retained Portuguese and Genoese idioms. Also, one needs to consider to what degree the scribe or scribes changed key verbs that show the intent of action or nouns describing people, places, or things Columbus experienced. Thus, historians consider all extant documents concerning Columbus's logbook as derivative records, therefore requiring one to contemplate and correlate its accuracy and usability.

7 Columbus, Ferdinand. *The Life of the Admiral Christopher Columbus*, 45–46. Ferdinand wrote the biography late in his life; he died in 1539. It is important to look for prejudgment in Ferdinand's interpretations of events as much as it holds for Las Casas.

8 Ibid., see Editor's Preface, xiii. Also see Caraci, *The Puzzling* Hero, 227–8.

9 Henige, *Journal*, 738. It is assumed that Las Casas did transcribe Columbus's actual words. The only caveat here is that Columbus used a hybrid of languages that confounded Las Casas. See Fuson, *The Log of Christopher Columbus*, 8–11, and Dunn & Kelley, *The Diario*, 5–11, for more on the transcription and translation problems in Las Casas's abridged version of the log.

10 For a deeper understanding of the origins and subsequent transcriptions and translations, see Henige, *Journal*, 738–43. Henige praises Dunn & Kelley's computer-created translation, noting that it "is the most literal yet, in any language, as they abandoned the fluid prose of most translations in favor of fidelity to the original text," 739. Many scholars also use Francesca Lardicci's *A Synoptic Edition of the Log of Columbus's First Voyage*, Volume VI of *Repertorium Columbianum* with an English version available (1999).

11 On a discursive note, Fuson argued that the summarized copy of the journal was probably used only as a reference as he wrote *Historia*. Las Casas wrote his abridgment of the journal in the lexicon of early 16th-century Castilian Spanish. Fuson estimates Las Casas may have acquired access to the Barcelona copy from Diego Columbus while residing in Santo Domingo, Hispaniola, at the same time. Two dates appear most likely as the best candidates, either in 1514 or later in 1522, the latter date being when Las Casas entered Dominican service as a novice friar and when Diego supported Las Casas's effort to obtain a protective land grant in Venezuela, helping Indigenous tribes.

12 Kettle, Personal Narrative, vi. Kettle and subsequent scholars appear to suggest that Las Casas's main concern was to use only important material for his reference notes in his *Historia*. In addition to Kettle's transcription, the Italian government in the mid-1890s released *Raccolta*, edited by Cesare de Lollis, providing an excellent Italian-language account of Las Casas's journal. During the 20th century, various other transcriptions have appeared, including a computer-assisted transcription by Oliver Dunn and James Kelley, Jr., and the Lardicci translation.

13 The other contemporary sources with material or references to the journal are Ferdinand Columbus's biography, *Historie*, and Las Casas's *Historia*. Columbus's

writing skills blended Castilian Spanish with some Portuguese; with Caraci noting that Columbus possessed a "halting and disjointed Latin," able to write in Spanish but displaying a "lexical and syntactical simplicity" along with "Portuguese idioms." *The Puzzling Hero*, 148. Helen Nader goes further, explaining, "His Castilian, however, was heavily mixed with other languages: Portuguese, Latin, Italian, and the Mediterranean sailors' pidgin, 'Levantisca.'" Nader, "Writings: An Overview," 737–38. Nader references Consuelo Varela's "Prólogo edición, y notas" in *Christopher Columbus, Textos y documentos completos: Relaciones de viajes, cartas, y memorials* (1984) for a more complete understanding of Columbus's writing knowledge and skills.

14 Zamora, *Reading Columbus*, 6. Zamora noted the concern for the problems occurring from errors made by the scribe or scribes that attempted to decipher Columbus's original logbook, but she adds a deeper worry surrounding Las Casas's possible editorial interventions.

15 For more on the concerns about the actual author or authors of the *Diario*, see Elise Bartosik-Vélez, "The First Interpretations of the Columbian Enterprise," 322–23.

16 Morison, *Admiral of the Ocean Sea*, 156. Morison did not believe that Las Casas manipulated any of the material concerning Spanish and Indigenous interactions.

17 Fuson, based on geographic references in *Historia*, 12. See Nader, "Writings: Journal," 738–42 for a sampled analysis of the concerns historians have over the accuracy of Las Casas's" paraphrased, perhaps abridged," published *Diario*.

18 Nader mentions that the *Diario* may have been "the product of a dynamic text that both influenced and was influenced by the events that surrounded its genesis, a process that took sixty years to complete." "Writings: Journal," 742. The "events" Nader references included the ongoing subjugation and colonization of the Indigenous peoples that Las Casas came to criticize.

19 For more on the *encomienda* system and how it evolved from the straightforward trade and barter practice of Columbus during the first voyage, see Roberto Valcárcel Rojas, "European Material Culture in Indigenous Sites in Northeastern Cuba," 103–5.

20 Las Casas compiled *Brevísima*, it is believed, as supporting evidence during the Council of Valladolid (1550–1551) as a *junta* of 14 theologians investigated the appropriateness of Spain's New World colonial laws and administration. Las Casas argued that the birthright of freedom that all Indigenous peoples possessed within the "natural order," despite extensive direct evidence of ongoing human sacrifice practices that contradicted Christian orthodoxy. See "Introduction" by Anthony Pagden in *Las Casas on Columbus*, 3–19.

21 Morison, *The Admiral of the Ocean Sea*, 18–26. Morison makes special note of the dead-reckoning skills Columbus learned, including how to "hand, reef, and steer, estimate distances by eye, to let go and weigh anchor properly, and all the other elements of seamanship," 23.

22 Morison noted that Christopher Columbus's joint chart-making business in Lisbon with his brother, Bartholomew, allowed him to be privy to the then-expanding Portuguese demand for local portolan sea charts, and regional sea-to-land maps. *Admiral of the Ocean Sea*, 35–36. A large Genoese community existed in Lisbon at that time, supporting a strong commercial partnership between Genoese merchants and Portuguese sea-going commercial interests.

23 The Lucayan and Taíno peoples spoke the Arawakan language; the Carib language appears to have morphed during the early Spanish contact, see Douglas R. Taylor and Berend J. Hoff, "The Linguistic Repertory of the Island-Carib in the Seventeenth Century: The Men's Language: A Carib Pidgin?", 310–2.

24 The Lesser Antilles today extend from the U.S. & British Virgin Islands to Grenada.

25 Sale, *The Conquest of Paradise*, 160. See also: Cook. *Born to Die*, 21–24; Anderson-Córdova, Surviving Spanish Conquest, 74–76.

26 Deagan, "The Taínos of Hispaniola," 24. The author goes on to consider a high figure of one million Indigenous peoples living on the large island of Hispaniola at the time of contact. See Lynne Guitar et al. for an explanation of where the name Taíno originated, "*Taínos*," 1014. Also, see Anderson-Córdova for population estimates for Hispaniola via studies from the late 1960s onward, 81–83. She noted that more recent studies have moved the estimates toward lower values, such as Arranz Márquez's calculation of 200,000 to 300,000 individuals.

27 Henige, *Numbers from Nowhere: The American Indian Contact Population*, 6.

28 Guitar, "*Taínos*," 1014–5. Laurent Dubois and Richard Lee Turits, in The Indigenous Caribbean (2019), agree with Guitar that the Guanahatabeys and the Ciboney people are one in the same. Other scholars believed the Ciboney to be early migration people who occupied central Cuba at the time of Spanish contact.

29 On Hispaniola and, to some extent, Cuba, Taíno villages averaged 500–1,000 inhabitants, based on a well-established fishing and agricultural economy. See Guitar, 1015. Guitar cites the reports of Las Casas and Peter Martyr as sources for these estimates. Columbus, in his journal, does describe several encounters with large villages ruled by regional caciques; see Dunn & Kelley, see December 23, 1492, 331.

30 Columbus's Lucayan interpreters had difficulty with much of the language exchanges once the fleet reached the northern shores of Hispaniola. For an example of the difficulty with Lucayans understanding Taíno people see Dunn & Kelley, *The Diario*, January 12, 1493, 331. For more information on the diversity of languages and attempts by Europeans to communicate with Indigenous peoples of the Americas see *The Language of Encounter in the Americas, 1492–1800: A Collection of Essays*, edited by Edward G. Gray and Norman Fiering. The first use of the term Arawak came in 1540, used by a Spanish bishop in the Americas, referenced the Indigenous peoples of northern South America, see Dubois & Turits, *The Indigenous Caribbean*, 15.

31 Beckles, "Kalinago (Carib) Resistance to European Colonization of the Caribbean," 77.

32 Ibid., 78. Beckles believes that the Taínos and Caribs competed for island dominance against each other, and then against Spanish aggression "as part of their natural, ancestral, survival environment."

33 Ross Ann H., William F. Keegan, Michael P. Pateman, and Collen B. Young, "Faces Divulge the Origins of Caribbean Prehistoric Inhabitants," *Scientific Reports (Nature Research)*, Abstract.

34 Ross and her team urge future migration studies to include "Carib influences, [warning, if not] they will produce incomplete results. The recommendation suggests Carib migration, at the time of contact, may have included other parts of the Greater Antilles such as eastern Cuba and Jamaica.

35 September 30 on the Gregorian calendar, as commanded by Pope Gregory XIII in 1582.

PART I

Planning the Transatlantic Voyage and Setting the Physical Geography of the Caribbean

Call him determined, stubborn, or obsessed, or perhaps all three, Columbus, after years of tirelessly presenting his ideas for a voyage to the Indies, finally received tentative approval of his plans from the Spanish monarchs. Now, the nitty-gritty of working out the details for the practical implementation of that plan became Columbus's main concern; collectively, the finalized agreement known as the *Santa Fe Capitulations* and the subsequent *Granada Accords* officially set responsibility and guidelines for both parties. In Part I of this work, we will look at the agreements, analyzing each article and its economic and political ramifications. The question next centered on the practical matters of acquiring the ships and men needed to make the Atlantic crossing, and we will see how the Pinzón brothers, Martín Alonso and Vicente Yañez, helped Columbus encourage local participation from the port of Palos de la Frontera.[1] For those readers who might not be familiar with the early years of Columbus's life, a section is inserted to review how the master navigator conceived of his *Enterprise of the Indies*, synthesizing his comprehensive sailing experiences as a Genoese trading representative in the Mediterranean Sea and Eastern Atlantic Ocean, leading to his conception of a North Atlantic system of winds and currents—a gyre. Assured of the consistency of westward flowing winds and currents (Trade Winds)[2] and an easterly flowing northern version of that same system (North Atlantic Drift), Columbus gained confidence in his plan; now he only needed to verify the extent of the *Ocean Sea*.[3] Eventually, Ferdinand and Isabella decided to risk a little money with the hope that the brash Genoese might prove right and open up new economic and political vistas and opportunities for expansion, recently initiated successfully with the reconquest (*Reconquista*) of southern Spain.

DOI: 10.4324/9781003464143-2

The key to understanding Columbus's conceptual development lies in investigating his prior sequential sailing experiences and how each geographic region provided how the Atlantic gyre worked. We will explore how he fused methodologies for calculating important geographic distances and directions and determining, accurately, miles sailed. For reference, he brought several custom-drawn maps with him on the *Santa Maria*, and the reader will learn how Columbus used them, hypothetically, to organize a system of navigation called *dead reckoning*.[4]

Finally, we will begin the actual journey, discovering how the fleet of three ships made their way to the launching point for the transoceanic voyage, the Canary Islands, Spain's only Atlantic colony, or *factoria*—extended trading posts. The reader learns of the extant journal manuscripts, including those by 15th- and 16th-century sources such as Bartolomé de Las Casas, Peter Martyr, and Gonzalo Fernández de Oviedo, and from subsequent translations of Columbus's journal, usually referred to as the *Diario*, with special emphasis on the work of Francesca Lardicci, Oliver Dunn and James E. Kelley, Jr., Robert Fuson, Cecil Jane, Samuel Morison, Clements Markham, and Samuel Kettell. The voyage itself is summarized on a day-to-day basis, with highlights subjectively discussed along with leagues (mileage) and directions stated.

Notes

1 For more information on the Pinzon brothers, see Navarrete, *Coleccion de Los Viages y Descubrimientos*, 558, 578, 604. See Morison, *Journals and Documents*, 24–25, to read an eyewitness account of the preparations by Fernando Valeinte; this is a deposition account taken as part of the *Pleitos de Colón* [trial or litigation of Columbus] many years later.

2 The Trade Winds do vary seasonally, extending further south in the winter months and reversing to the north in the summer. For more information on the Trade Winds and their influence on Columbus, see Nunn, "The Geographical Conceptions of Columbus," 36–38.

3 See my previous book, *Mapping Christopher Columbus*, which contains over 90 maps depicting how Columbus built his transoceanic plan. Of particular interest on how he may have referenced previous maps, see chapter 8 "Columbus Builds his Cartographic Support."

4 Columbus sent one of his custom sea charts to Martín Pinzon on the *Pinta* on September 25, 1492, in anticipation of sighting islands. Fuson, *The Log of Christopher Columbus*, 67. Columbus evidently had drawn several islands he expected to be in the current sea zone, approximately at 46 degrees west longitude today. These islands may have been deduced from his reference to the Henricus Martellus 1491 *mappa mundi*. See Rocca, *Mapping Christopher Columbus*, 165–9.

1

THE TRANSATLANTIC PROPOSAL AND PREPARATION FOR THE VOYAGE

For, the islands wait for me, and the ships of the sea in the beginning: that I may bring thy sons from afar, their silver and their gold with them, to the name of the Lord thy God.

—Isaiah 60:9

The *Santa Fe Capitulations*

For 8 long years, the tall Genoese merchant representative yearned to gain approval for a creative commercial proposal. His youthful maritime experience sailing in the Mediterranean Sea and the eastern Atlantic Ocean provided meteorological and oceanographic clues to solve an age-old mystery. How wide was the *Ocean Sea* and could it be crossed? For certain, other sailors pondered this question. Ship captains from western European Atlantic-facing nations such as England, France, Portugal, and the Spanish kingdoms plied the Eastern regions of the great ocean, yet rarely before 1400 did anyone dare sail far from known coastlines.[1] Rumors circulated from this time concerning the Northmen (Vikings) and their bold, extended sailing adventures west to Thule (Iceland) and Ultima Thule (Greenland), but these were considered rumors by most learned Europeans, although an ongoing trade existed between Bristol, England, and isolated settlements on Iceland.[2] Little or nothing had been written down about these far-northern, ice-encircled expeditions. No matter, the frozen wastelands of Thule remained of little interest to the monarchs and commercial investors of Middle Atlantic nations and kingdoms.

Born into a middle-income weaver's family with the name Cristoforo Colombo, the pale-faced, reddish-gray-haired man now stood before two of the most powerful European monarchs, King Ferdinand of Aragon and Queen Isabella

DOI: 10.4324/9781003464143-3

of Castile.[3] Their marriage had united both kingdoms, soon to coalesce officially into the robust nation of Spain. Driven by strong nationalistic and religious motivations, the monarchs recently succeeded in conquering the last Moorish stronghold on the Iberian Peninsula, Granada. Remaining near their military camp at Santa Fe, Isabella and Ferdinand sat poised to announce the good news to the anxious mariner. The monarchs knew their guest as Cristóbal Colón, but for anyone speaking and writing in English, the name translates to Christopher Columbus.

The date recorded on Columbus's invitation to address the monarchs is read as April 17, 1492. Waiting outside the royal quarters for summoning, one can imagine the 41-year-old Genoese recalling how this moment came to be: all his years in Portugal and all his years in Spain, waiting to be heard. All this prepared him for this time and place; there were some bright moments, but rejection and frustration ruled over many of the 8 years of waiting.[4] He passionately explained his transoceanic theory several times before to the monarchs and their advisory committees. Even at this instance of expected victory, Columbus may have remained puzzled as to why it took so long for his ideas to be accepted. What was it about his theories and plans that seemed so outside the box, so distant and unreachable? Did they not see the logic of the stated scientific facts drawn from ancient and medieval writings?[5] Why did they not recognize the brilliance of his ability to synthesize the knowledge from these maps and manuscripts and merge them with his sailing experience to explain the mysteries of the *Ocean Sea*? He must have concluded, what more can I do? Yet, through the years, he held an unbelievable level of confidence, an entrenched determination—some would say arrogance—that drove him always onward.[6] Surely, one would believe, now would be his time for the ultimate recognition that he deserved—the opportunity of a lifetime.

Columbus entered the palace of Ferdinand and Isabella, excited by the expectation of good news. He stood nervously, no doubt, at a respectful distance from the Spanish majesties, eagerly anticipating a successful conclusion to the negotiations, never suspecting the triumphs and tragedies the resulting royal contract would bring, staring first at Isabella, then at the king, the queen always appearing more favorable to his ideas than the king. Though humble at this moment in time, he was in no mood to negotiate any of the already-presented terms of acceptance. He wanted everything on the list. Negotiations continued until the end of the month, and on April 30, 1492, all parties signed the official agreement.[7] For a foreign-born dreamer with few existing financial resources, his demands seemed excessive. The agreed-upon five articles are summarized as follows:

Article One: that he should be Admiral of such islands and mainland as he or his heirs should discover or acquire with such prerogatives as belonging to the office of High Admiral of Castile.

Article Two: that he should be Viceroy and Governor-General in all those islands or mainlands he might discover or acquire, with power to name three persons for each office under him, from which three persons the Sovereign must select one.

Article Three: that he should have a tenth of the profits arising from buying, bartering, discovering, acquiring, or obtaining merchandise of whatsoever kind.

Article Four: that he should in his quality of Admiral have in himself or by deputy sole cognizance or judicial jurisdiction of any [law] suit growing out of trade or traffic in the lands and islands to be discovered.

Article Five: that whenever and as often as ships should be equipped for traffic, he should have the right to furnish one-eighth of all that should be expended in the equipment and have and enjoy one-eighth of the profits which should result from such equipment.[8]

While these demands appear extravagant, the title and economic opportunities noted in each article listed above had in one way or another been offered to prior European explorers and maritime merchants. Portugal provided the best and most recent example of power-giving with the case of Columbus's own father-in-law, Bartolomeu Perestrello. Perestrello, along with two other squires, João Gonçálves Zarco and Tristão Vaz Teixeira, explored and discovered "the archipelago of Madeira (which also includes the island of Porto Santo)."[9] The subsequent attempts at colonization moved along slowly with the explorer named *1st Capitã o-donatário*, or Captain Major, with hereditary rights. In effect, he became "Viceroy and Governor." This occurred in 1445, just before Columbus was born. The initial settlements struggled, and Perestrello left the island.

The Spanish, for their part, also retained a history of allowing foreign exploration, conquest, and official titles. In the case of the Canary Islands under Spanish conquest dating from the early 1400s, two Frenchmen sailed under the authority of Henry III of Spain. Jean de Béthencourt and Gadifer de la Salle first ventured to the large island of Lanzarote, eventually claiming rights to Fuerteventura and the small island of El Hierro.[10] For a brief time, Béthencourt claimed the title "King of the Canary Islands" and attempted to secure commercial rights on the islands.[11]

James Parsons, writing in 1983, noted that Spain used the Canary Islands as a laboratory, combining its exploratory expeditions with subsequent possession and political control.

The philosophical justification and legitimization of conquest was first faced in the Canaries as a new colonial bureaucracy sought to adapt and refine the medieval European institutions of government to the new [geographical] situation. Authority to appoint officials and to distribute land and natives in service was delegated to local governors...[12]

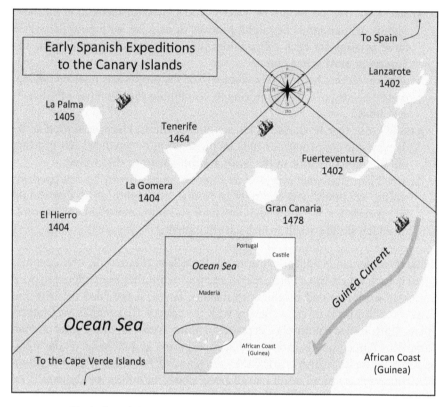

FIGURE 1.1 Early Spanish Expeditions to the Canary Islands

Beginning early in the 14th century, Portugal made an effort to extend its maritime trading zones of influence. Much of that effort reached deep into the Atlantic Ocean, then known as the *Ocean Sea*. At the same time, Castilian (Spanish) ship captains skirted the African coast along with their Portuguese counterparts, with Spain focusing on securing *factoria* (trading post) footholds in the Canary Islands.

During the time of the *Reconquista*, leaders from Castile and Aragon, including Ferdinand and Isabella, generously portioned out newly reclaimed land to loyal nobles fighting the Moors. People then occupying said areas now served as vassals to these acknowledged leaders. In this political and economic system, the vassals paid homage through regular tax payments and with the expectation that they would serve to defend the area if needed. This homage required of vassals remained distinct from the service and taxation to the regional king or queen—in this case, Castile (Isabella) and Aragon (Ferdinand). To this end, financial and royal recognition already existed as expectations for services rendered to the crown. Columbus knew this and drew upon its tenets in laying out his demands.

In such a manner, King Ferdinand and Queen Isabella inherited a tradition of granting an array of titles and authority to explorers in direct service to the crown. Accordingly, let us take a deeper look at each article to investigate Columbus's charge from the Spanish monarchs, knowing that the would-be explorer desired to be successful, success measured only by his royal patrons.

Article 1 stated that Columbus would earn the title of Admiral upon discovering heretofore unknown and unclaimed islands and the mainland in the Western Ocean. The original Spanish expression for the geographic reference is "todas aquellas islas é tierras-firmes." The literal modern translation is "all the islands and firm land." Firm land apparently references the Asian mainland adjacent to the Indies. However, Wilcomb Washburn, in 1962, published an article discussing the use, by Ferdinand and Isabella, of the plural forms "islas" and "tierras-firmes" when describing Columbus's destination. Certainly, one can understand its use in describing islands, as numerous islands existed in the Eastern Atlantic, and most European maps of Cathay and the Indies displayed many such features distributed in the western region of the *Ocean Sea*. Washburn noted how Cecil Jane, in the introduction to his *Select Documents of Columbus*, suggested and supported the idea that an *antipodean* or unknown southern continent was also a possible Columbian destination.[13]

Jane's theory on an antipodean destination is interesting, but the reference to firm land most likely is the east coast of the Asian mainland. When tying this into Article 2, one would conclude that Columbus would become governor and viceroy of the said islands he discovered. This is applied in situations where the islands are uninhabited or inhabited by small, independent tribes. However, if that mainland area resided within the boundaries of a powerful Asian king, under what authority did Ferdinand and Isabella have to assert dominion? This was the underlying presumption made by Washburn in concluding that the Spanish monarchs were referring to a different "tierra firma." As the reader will soon learn, Columbus carried a letter of introduction for presentation to the "Great Khan" of Cathay.[14] Clearly, Columbus could not claim governorship over lands ruled directly by powerful Asian leaders, so the intent must have applied to uninhabited islands or politically and militarily weak island populations, such as the case with the Canary Islands or Portugal's experiences in the Azores.

Therefore, in discussing Columbus's intentions and Ferdinand's and Isabella's directions, one can imagine three distinct outcomes. First, Columbus, after sailing west for a number of days, would "discover" one or more islands, inhabited or not. The desire here included finding the large island of Cipangu.[15] Here, his men would survey the island for exploitable resources and safe harbors and initiate friendly contact with Indigenous peoples occupying the island, if any. An option for this scenario might call for establishing a small fort, the beginnings of a future *factoria* especially for Cipangu.[16] He would return to Spain and report his findings, and then plan for a follow-up voyage to formally set up a trading post. Eventually, once established and functioning, Columbus would become viceroy and governor of the trading post community, overseeing all commercial activity and political governance. Second, since his destination was the "Indies," Columbus would set a direct course for the East Asian coastline, only stopping to resupply at any islands encountered. Here, he would seek the Great Khan of Cathay or a similar regional potentate, promote awareness of Spain and its monarchs, and suggest a commercial partnership. With a formal treaty or trading agreement, Columbus would return to Spain. The third option allowed Columbus and the monarchs to gain the most politically and commercially. He would "discover" a few islands en route to the Indies, claim sovereignty over the island for Spain, map locations of potential harbors, leave a small contingent of men to set up a fort, resupply, and continue seeking the Asian mainland.

Long discussed and written about throughout emerging nation-states in Western Europe was the concept of a southern continent, introduced by Ptolemy on maps as an imaginary continent, large and inaccessible. Columbus was aware of this geographic concept but insisted his discoveries involved Asian territories. However, medieval chronicler, Peter Martyr believed that

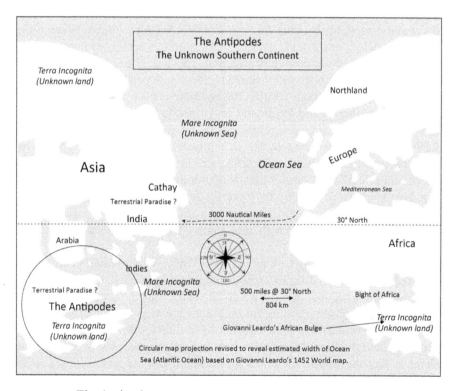

FIGURE 1.2 The Antipodes

Columbus, upon returning from his first voyage, had indeed discovered a heretofore unknown large land mass, the "Western Antipodes."

The first scenario is not what either party, Columbus or the Spanish monarchs, desired as an ultimate goal. Unless the island(s) discovered proved to be extraordinarily abundant with desired resources such as gold, spices, and pearls, the voyage's result would prove little except that the Western Atlantic Ocean contained islands similar to those found in the Eastern Atlantic Ocean. Finding the "Indies" as hoped in the second scenario might prove more profitable to Columbus, as the agreement provided a ten percent bonus for merchandise traded or "acquired." If Marco Polo wrote correctly in his famous book, *Travels of Marco Polo*, that riches abounded. In this situation, Columbus would not experience his desire to become a viceroy or governor unless Asian political leaders allowed a foreign political entity and leader to control a trading post at an Asian seaport, as the Portuguese found out in their attempt to create a trading post on the African coast among the Ashanti people of the Akan kingdom.[17]

We see the best potential case for Columbus in option three. Any or all the islands he "discovered" would immediately become Spanish possessions, with himself set up as viceroy and governor. If a successful contact on the Asian mainland subsequently occurred, then Columbus would receive ten percent of mainland trading profits and keep political control of any islands discovered, inhabited or not—the best of both worlds.

A look at Articles 4 and 5 reveals a further extension of executive power. In Article 4, the agreement gave Columbus complete authority to resolve trading disagreements and subsequent court actions. Presumably, this authority extended only to island cases under his immediate political control and/or a mainland trading post in Asia. In Article 5, the Spanish monarchs allowed Columbus to seek investments in any commercial opportunities. With his extensive contacts with Genoese merchants living in Spain, this might prove financially beneficial. We may see the *Santa Fe Capitulations* as a dual-purpose proposal. On the one hand, Columbus gained political power and recognition, and on the other, both parties, Columbus and the Spanish monarchs, gained wealth. Ferdinand and Isabella knew well the already established Portuguese gains in the Eastern Atlantic, Azores, Madeira, Porto Santo, and Cape Verde Islands, and they desired a "piece of the action" of commercial gain, political power, and international recognition.[18]

The reader will note that the *Capitulations* contained nothing concerning religion or converting "heathens." To be sure, Columbus later revealed his devout Catholic faith and shared a desire to spread Christianity, as did Isabella and Ferdinand. On subsequent voyages, after experiencing contact with the Taíno and Carib peoples, Columbus placed evangelism as an expedition priority.[19] But for now, the primary goal of the first voyage focused on the geographical quest to cross the *Ocean Sea* in a relatively short time and arrive at the fabulous Indies and east coast of Cathay, establishing a reliable transoceanic route.

Luis de Santangel, one of the kings' trusted advisors, played a vital role in Isabella's decision to go ahead and agree to Columbus's demands in the *Capitulations*.[20] From Santangel's point of view, the Genoese merchant representative might just be correct in his wild geographic ideas. And even if wrong, the minimal investment offered by the Spanish monarchs to support the voyage made the venture a reasonable risk.[21] Historical geographer D.W. Meinig believed the Spanish monarchs agreed to the "panoply of titles, authority, and rights... suggests that he [Columbus] was not expected to discover anything really extraordinary."[22] Anxiously, Santangel asked for a meeting with the queen. At one point in the discussion with Isabella, Santangel offered to help finance the expedition. Isabella relented. For years, she listened with interest to Columbus's impassioned presentations on the extraordinary commercial opportunities that awaited the first European kingdom to reach the East—the Indies. Portugal continued with its ever-longer exploration voyages down the West African coast, and now was the time to take a chance and see if the Genoese mariner could actually do what he said he could do.

Margarita Zamora, in 1993, produced a magnificent interpretive study, *Reading Columbus*, concerning the writing of Columbus, focusing primarily on documents pertaining to the first voyage. At the time of her writing, disagreements abounded over the reliability and intent of Las Casas's transcription of the *Diario*[23] and letters sent to Spanish officials. She also analyzed the *Santa Fe Capitulations*, arguing that acquisition was the goal of the first voyage, "not so much of territories or subjects, but of markets." Within this conceptual framework, the proposed voyage looked to expand Spain's commercial interests and thus was unique from the recent "reconquest of Muslim territories."[24]

Palos de la Frontera and the Acquisition of Men and Ships

With this official royal contract in hand, Columbus left Isabella and Ferdinand for a small seaport town on the southwest coast of Castile, Palos de la Frontera. This coastal community remained active in sending out commercial ships to Mediterranean and Eastern Atlantic ports. Experienced crews are what Columbus needed, and Palos seemed like a logical place to recruit his men and boys. Yes, there would be boys going on the voyage of discovery. It seems questionable today that any father or mother would allow their 12-year-old son to sign up for a voyage of multi-week duration, but extraordinary when considering the rumors of mysterious destinations expected and led by an unknown Genoese foreigner.[25]

The Spanish monarchs required the townspeople of Palos to provide two ships for Columbus. This official decree resulted in punishment for an unspecified violation. James Reston mentions the notion that a ship from Palos

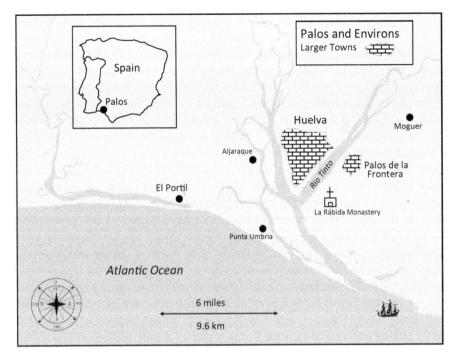

FIGURE 1.3 Palos & Huelva

cruised previously into the West African region of Guinea, thereby trespassing on ocean access legally secured for the Portuguese. Not desiring a political confrontation over the incident, Ferdinand and Isabella demanded restitution from Palos through the temporary use of men and ships.[26]

Palos de la Frontera and the larger community of Huelva provided Castile with a gateway to the Atlantic Ocean and the opportunity for reliable contact with Lisbon, Portugal, and for trading opportunities down the African coast.

Two of the most experienced and respected seamen in Palos were the Pinzón brothers, Martín and Vicente. Both brothers were born in Palos, with Vicente being the younger. The Pinzón family held deeply to a seafaring life that extended back to at least their grandfather. Martín is believed to have already completed extensive ocean experience shipping out to destinations on the west coast of Africa and the Canary Islands. When Columbus arrived in Palos, he soon discovered it was difficult to recruit men. A major concern on the part of potential sailors included their distrust of foreigners with unknown maritime experience. It was at this time that the friars at the monastery nearby in La Rábida connected Columbus to Martín. Martín, who had just returned from a voyage to Rome, was ready for a new challenge.[27] Columbus soon learned that Martín was held in high regard for his skills as a sailor and his ability to lead effectively. At some point during the early preparations, probably in late May or early June, Martín signed on to the expedition.[28] Martín immediately advised Columbus to engage two ships, the *Pinta* and the *Niña*, for the voyage, knowing that the vessels needed to cruise well in the open ocean and navigate nimbly in shallow waters. As the summer moved along, Martín visited nearby towns, recruiting men, hoping his maritime reputation, promise of substantial reward, and earning royal recognition might induce men to sign for the voyage, confident yet a little anxious. Helping garner reluctant crew members, Juan Niño, a mariner from the nearby town of Moguer, also encouraged sailors he knew to sign on for the voyage.[29] Niño owned the *Niña*, and he would serve as shipmaster of that vessel. Columbus must have made a favorable impression on Martín Pinzón, as he, Pinzón, agreed to invest half a million *maravedís* in the Enterprise to the Indies.[30] Martín also agreed to captain the *Pinta*; his younger brother, Vicente, also joined the expedition, serving as captain of the *Niña*.[31]

It should be noted here that subsequent to the first voyage of discovery, Columbus's sons, Diego and Ferdinand, pressed legal charges against the Spanish crown for not honoring the articles contained in the *Santa Fe Capitulations*. During the many-decade court battle, the crown countered the Columbus family charges, arguing that Christopher "Columbus was only the nominal head of an enterprise" approved by the crown and only succeeded due to the "energy, courage, and maritime skill of Martín Alonso Pinzón." Both sides secured crew members from the expedition, along with other local citizens, to testify; these proceedings are available for study and are known as the *Pleitos de Colón*, also known as the *Pleitos Colombinos*. By the spring of 1515, Diego Columbus believed he had proved his case only to find out months later that a former crew member on the *Pinta* declared under oath that Martín Pinzón "discovered America, and if not for Captain Pinzón, the voyage would have been a failure."[32]

In looking for a third ship, Columbus met with Juan de la Cosa. La Cosa owned a *não* [cargo ship] that contained plenty of below-deck storage and had a length of over 77 feet.[33] The three-masted ship held square sails that effectively powered the loaded vessel when the wind blew strongly from behind. Alternatively, tacking into the wind, even in small increments, proved challenging. Columbus did not want to engage the *Santa Maria* at first due to its existing hull and sail configuration. He wanted his caravels to have the ability to use a combination of lateen (triangular) and square sails. A ship's pilot effectively employing the lateen sail helped him tack successfully into the wind. This type of sail arrangement, referred to as the *caravela redonda*, found effective use during Portuguese voyages to African destinations. Columbus, realizing the sail limitations, ordered the workers to rig the *Santa Maria* with the *caravela redonda* configuration.[34]

The crew members' nationality makeup is important to consider on all of Columbus's voyages. As a Genoese, only three other non-Spanish persons served on this first voyage. Not knowing is not trusting, and so it would be with Columbus; he would need to demonstrate superior navigation skills; nothing less would be expected of his Spanish crew. While Columbus felt confident in his ability to reach the Indies safely, it boggles the imagination, by today's standards, as already noted earlier, to consider that 23 children are listed on the crew manifest, as mentioned earlier. However, Mediterranean seafaring communities held traditions of employing boys, as young as twelve, to fulfill routine tasks onboard ships. Their jobs as *grommets* varied depending on the will of each ship's captain and master. One important job they did involved turning the hourglass and ringing a bell to signify the time. This process helped the master determine the ship's speed and distance as well as alert crew members to changes in their shift.[35] It is not clear whether the parents of these children were fully aware of the proposed destination and the length of the journey. No doubt Columbus discussed his plans with the Pinzón brothers and the ships' pilots, but did the crew know the full extent of Columbus's intentions? We do not know. Credit goes to Columbus and the other officers during this path-breaking voyage to cross the Atlantic Ocean, as no fatality, for men or children, occurred at sea.[36]

Little detail survives as to the preparations for voyages prior to August 3, 1492. Columbus and his officers purchased supplies from the area surrounding Palos, carefully selecting foodstuffs for long-term storage, dickering for the lowest prices, and realizing the limited available royal funds. They calculated supplies for a round-trip voyage of approximately 1 year, and this, according to historian Samuel Morison, represented more than needed. In addition, the plan called for a stopover in the Canary Islands, a Spanish possession off the east coast of Africa, aware that waters below the Canary Islands at 28° north latitude remained off limits. The Canaries offered a final replenishment of meat, and other perishables, and drinking water before tackling a transatlantic crossing. At least, this was his plan. Let's take a look at Columbus's pre-voyage plans for crossing the *Ocean Sea* and the discovery of "islands and mainlands."[37]

The Plan

Winston Churchill, when referring to the Soviet Union under Joseph Stalin, said it was "a riddle, wrapped in a mystery, inside an enigma." The same goes for Christopher Columbus, who appeared religiously motivated yet desperate for social recognition and financial gain. In addition, he wanted to pass down this recognition and the resulting commercial profits to his children. His "plan," he believed, if successful, resulted in obtaining his life goals. The deeper you move into Columbian studies, the more difficult it becomes to discover the "real Columbus," his formation of the transatlantic concept, and his actions during his voyages. Leading Columbus scholar Ilaria Caraci devoted an entire book to investigating *The Puzzling Hero*, his transatlantic plan, and subsequent actions.[38] I laid out my ideas in a previous book, *Mapping Christopher Columbus*, on how this Genoese merchant representative conceived the Enterprise to the Indies.[39] The plan came together somewhere between 1482 and 1484 after Columbus completed voyages throughout the Mediterranean Sea and various regions of the Eastern Atlantic Ocean. His geographic ideas coalesced slowly, region by region, learning oceanographic and meteorological facts from short and extended voyages. These maritime trips included widely separated ocean regions, stretching from Iceland in the north to the Bight of Africa in the south.[40] More specifically, he traversed 60 degrees of latitude from Iceland in the north to the Portuguese trading post at São Jorge da Mina, Africa, in the south. Few sailors prior to 1492 possessed extensive northern and southern Atlantic maritime experience and sojourns to the Eastern Mediterranean Sea. For example, Portuguese explorer Bartolomeu Días grappled with the African Atlantic coastal waters before his groundbreaking voyage to the southern tip of Africa in 1488, yet he did not sail in the far North Atlantic. Columbus, ever desiring to glean new geographical knowledge and maritime skills, studied the details concerning prevailing winds and currents and talked with sailors from many nations, establishing a mental pattern of an ever-broadening oceanographic system and hoping to synthesize his reasoning, a marriage of science and hearsay.

Columbus also sailed extensively in lateral, or east and west, directions. His early voyage to the eastern Mediterranean island of Chios gave him the vital experience to complement what he already knew of the Western Mediterranean Sea, reacting to countercurrents in and around the Greek Islands, and watching anxiously for unannounced, un-flagged visiting ships, vessels ready to pirate unescorted vessels.[41] This author projected a possible extension of his Iceland experience to points west equating to approximately 30 degrees of west longitude, sailing farther west than any known southern European mariner had done.[42] He also visited that longitudinal region on his return voyage from São Jorge da Mina, as Portuguese ships swung far westward into the Atlantic, hoping to catch favorable winds, breezes that blew ships northward. This journey gave Columbus a longitudinal experience extending almost 60 degrees— equivalent to his latitudinal experience, covering almost all *Ocean Sea* waters then known.

From the above-noted geographical encounters, Columbus pondered a general system of winds and currents. I have previously postulated that he conceptualized an Atlantic Gyre—the system of winds and current circulation that moves in an anticyclonic (clockwise) direction, providing southern winds and currents to Asia and northerly winds and currents for a safe return. His ability to synthesize the bits and pieces of each sub-region's winds and currents and their movements is what provided the conceptual foundation of his unrelenting determination to sail westward; it was not some wild guesswork, but rather the disciplined, practical problem-solving application of a man merging Medieval and Renaissance concepts, ideas, and traditions.[43] Paolo Taviani noted, "In reality, he bestrode the two ages," Columbus's philosophy, theology, and even science were medieval: whereas his "keen interest in nature, and capacity for accepting phenomena previously unobserved or unexplained were peculiar to the Renaissance."[44] In this manner, Columbus pondered the *Ocean Sea* as a geographical problem, and as noted Italian historical geographer Ilaria Caraci wrote, "For Columbus the ocean was not a goal, but a barrier; not an end, but a means."[45]

Even though his global geography proved incorrect, the world was much larger than he believed, which is almost beside the point—he firmly maintained it was small. Yet, few cosmographers and philosophers sitting on Portuguese and Spanish academic councils, understanding the ocean distances to be greater, disbelieved his arguments regardless of the maps, calculations, and concepts Columbus presented. According to James Lynch, Columbus "was probably better prepared for the great event than anyone else at the time."[46] However, his frustration grew as he attempted to didactically link his scientific findings to commercial and religious (moral) goals, as we shall see later.

It is this author's contention that Columbus, with his extensive early sailing experience in the Mediterranean Sea, transferred the concept of circulatory winds and currents, an oceanographic gyre, that he observed in the Mediterranean Sea to his awareness of the eastern Atlantic Ocean, confirming the idea that reliable winds would allow him to sail to Asia and return via an equally reliable northern wind pattern.

No one knows the detailed plans Columbus carried with him to Palos. Despite the above facts, one can suggest various scenarios that involve possible island stopovers and mainland destinations. His knowledge of several widely circulated maps and books placed the large island of Cipangu (Japan) somewhere past the halfway point across the *Ocean Sea*. Cartographers taking Marco Polo's account as accurate, portrayed the island as quite large, extending ten or more degrees of latitude. Polo's *Travels* recounted exotic tales of Cipangu that excited Europeans.

Cipangu is an island to the sunrising [sic] which is on the high sea 1500 miles [Roman miles] distant from the land of Mangi [Southern China]. It is an exceedingly great island... Moreover, I tell you that they have gold in very great abundance, because gold is found there beyond measure, but no man takes gold out from that island, because the kind does not easily allow it to be taken out and no merchant goes there from the mainland because it is so far, and ships are rarely brought there from other regions.[47]

Geographer G. F. Hudson claimed that Columbus prioritized finding Cipangu, which makes geographical sense.[48] As shown on the Proposed Contact

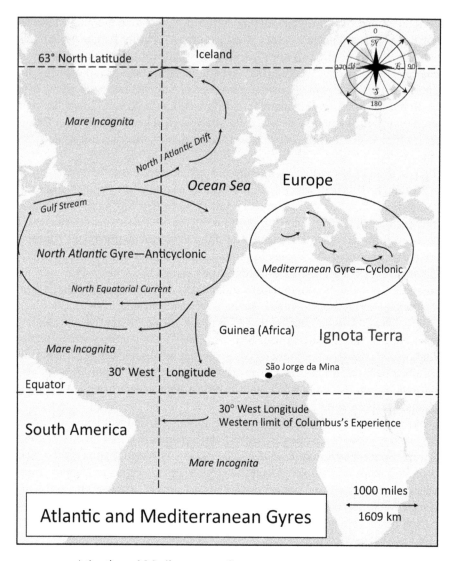

FIGURE 1.4 Atlantic and Mediterranean Gyres

Locations map, the Genoese explorer, if the maps correctly placed the island, would "discover" that island first. Being latitudinally extensive, a competent ship pilot should sight the island after a couple of weeks.[49] With Cipangu between 20 and 30 degrees north latitude, Columbus knew that steady westerly winds from the North Equatorial Current region (Trade Winds) would provide a quick and reliable voyage. It is interesting to note that Hudson remarked on Chinese stories concerning Cipangu and gold, stating those rumors were not true. The Japanese only used limited amounts of gold as gold-leaf sheeting in architectural forms. Later, as Columbus first found small amounts of gold in Cuba, he believed it to be Cipangu. Likewise, on Hispaniola (Haiti), he once again writes about Cipangu. As we shall see, Columbus remains saddled in geographic confusion as the amounts of gold he finds only trickle in, and the people he encounters do not match Polo's description.

More likely than finding Cipangu, Columbus probably reasoned his first landing sighting would be one of the hundreds, possibly thousands, of small islands that existed in the western *Ocean Sea*—off the coast of Asia. Most medieval *mappae mundi* (maps of the world) depict numerous islands, most of them small, suggesting they contained limited Indigenous populations or remained uninhabited. Columbus read Polo's book *Travels* and most assuredly paused in excitement when encountering the discussion of Polo's return trip. Marco Polo left the Chinese mainland and ventured south to the island of Java. In his description of Java, the focus is on commodities for a possible trade. The account read,

> Departing from Ziamba, and steering between south and south-east, fifteen hundred miles, you reach an island of very great size, named Java, which, according to the reports of some well-informed navigators, is the largest in the world, being in circuit above three thousand miles. It is under the dominion of one king only, nor do the inhabitants pay tribute to any other power. They are worshippers of idols. The country abounds with rich commodities. Pepper, nutmegs, spikenard [similar to Ginseng], galengal [spice root], cubebs [type of pepper], cloves, and all the other valuable spices and drugs, are the produce of the island, which occasion it to be visited by many ships laden with merchandise, that yields to the owners, considerable profit. The quantity of gold collected there exceeds all calculation and belief.[50]

No wonder Columbus became mesmerized by the commercial possibilities, and this example was from only one island. In chapter 54 of the account, the writer claims the Great Khan built and maintained 15,000 ships to secure any rebellions on a large number of islands under his control. Additionally, the ships were available to engage in "expeditions to any more distant region."[51] This information corroborated nicely with the ancient and medieval understanding that a vast number of islands existed in East Asia. Polo's sea travels mostly discussed the islands he visited, but cartographers imagined a geographic distribution of islands from the Southeast Asian mainland extending northward into the waters off Cathay (Northern China). The latitudinal spread of these islands ranged from below the Equator to 60 degrees north latitude. This matched European experiences in the Eastern Atlantic with Iceland in the north and the Portuguese discoveries of São Tomé and Príncipe on the West Coast of Africa. The geographic logic seemed obvious. If islands existed in the eastern region of the *Ocean Sea*, why not on the western side?

If these islands were under the Khan's authority, then Columbus might have presented his letter of introduction to a Chinese official, satisfying that part of the contract. But to do this, he knew his small fleet would need to penetrate and pass through the middle region of the great *Ocean Sea*. To his knowledge, though rumors abounded to the contrary, he would be the first to accomplish this feat. Columbus may have understood that traversing the *Ocean Sea*, a great watery desert that awed Western Europeans for centuries, would unlock a new era, an era of commercial, political, and social awakening—a trip of thousands of miles. One wonders if he fully contemplated how a transoceanic event would open a new future for him and for Spain, and later for Europe and the rest of the world. Of course, he had no way of knowing the devastating impact of what this voyage would unleash on two continents, North and South America.

The third option, landing directly on the East Asian mainland, would be his preference, but probably the least attainable. Columbus would need to sail an additional 1,000–1,500 miles west from Cipangu, asking his crew to endure more weeks at sea and in unknown waters. We will see this become a concern on his first voyage when the anxious crew sailed farther west from the 30-degree longitude limit in known waters.[52] Another concern about landing at any given point on the Asian mainland involved geopolitical considerations. Most medieval maps partitioned China into two major regions: Cathay, or Northern China, and Mangi, or Southern China. Were both political areas controlled and administered by the Great Khan, or would Columbus land in a region in open rebellion or ruled by some other Asian potentate? If the scenario played out to be the latter, what would he do? His letter from Ferdinand and Isabella was clearly conceived with hopes of contacting the Great Khan. However, to cover all possibilities, additional letters he carried included a blank line at the top, allowing Columbus to insert the name of any Asian leader encountered. Of course, one critical problem might arise in the lack of enthusiasm for political and commercial contact. The Chinese might not be interested in trade with Europe; after all, Polo's contact with the Khan occurred in the 13th century, and the current ruler might reject political and commercial overtures.

The third option also fundamentally decreases Columbus's opportunities for personal political authority. He must have known that Asian leaders on the mainland would never grant Columbus the right to exercise power as "viceroy and governor," as stated in the *Santa Fe Capitulations*. It is true that Columbus, on his return trip, might discover islands not under the control of the Asian mainland, but nothing was guaranteed. If the Chinese had been sailing in East Asian waters for centuries, would not most of these islands, especially the islands rich in resources, already be under mainland control?

Through his reading of Marco Polo's book, *Travels*, and his examination of contemporary *mappae mundi*, Columbus developed a geographic vision for sequencing discoveries in eastern Asia. The sequence included contact with small uninhabited or lightly inhabited islands of the western *Ocean Sea* and contact

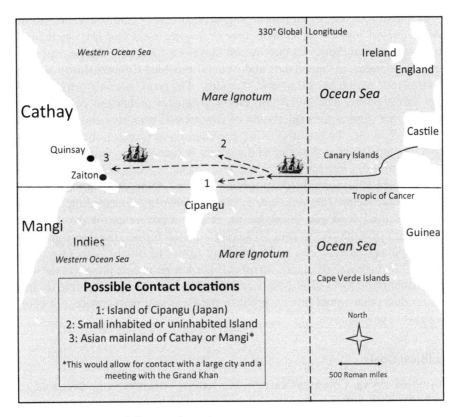

FIGURE 1.5 Proposed Contact Locations

with the large and fabled island of Cipangu (Japan). The final destination, Cathay, included diplomatic contact and the securing of trade agreements.

The *fieri potest optimus* (best possible) outcome included discovering and acquiring several uninhabited or sparsely populated islands and either Cipangu or the Chinese mainland. In that manner, most of the commercial and political requirements would be satisfied. In fact, this would lead to the Spanish monarchs fully recognizing Columbus's success while authorizing a second, more ambitious expedition to initiate the construction of trading posts on selected islands and mainland locations authorized by local Asian political administrators.

It is important for the reader to understand the geopolitical and commercial goals of the *Santa Fe Capitulations* as Columbus's travel guide and trading representative contract. There was no mention of the religious conversion of foreign heathens, although this would become apparent in later voyages. The first voyage needed only to contact established kingdoms and invite further discussions about opening up a commercial exchange. It was expected that this would be the protocol for major nation-states, such as the Spanish monarchs believed currently existed on Cipangu and the Asian mainland.

In addition to this, Columbus negotiated that other "mainlands and islands [Asian coastal zones]… he shall discover or acquire in the said seas" be thenceforth under his authority as Viceroy and Governor-General.[53] The general geographic reference to "mainlands and islands" provided Columbus with a huge transatlantic region to explore and "acquire." The term "acquire" requires further investigation. The initial impression insinuates permanent colonization. This further implies the exploitation of commercial resources and Indigenous peoples. Was this the intent of King Ferdinand and Queen Isabella? The old Castilian term used in the original document is "ganac."[54] Using modern electronic translators, one can see that the term "ganac" derives from the root word "ganar," which in Spanish today means "to win." However, using the highly acclaimed academic *Diccionario de la lengua Española* (also called the *Diccionario de la Real Academia Española*), the first level preference for the Castilian translation of ganar is "to gain."[55] Taking it a step further, the term "gain" in contemporary analysis can mean anything from "to obtain," "to earn," "to profit," "to increase," or simply "to reach." The key point here promotes the idea of a commercial focus of discovery and acquisition, or at least access to desirable products that would bring a profit to the European marketplace, not comprehensive colonization.

Political Goals

As noted above, Columbus carried two letters with him as he prepared to embark. Both letters suggest Columbus understood he had no ambition or authority to "discover and acquire" any mainland area already under a powerful Asian ruler. The first letter served to introduce Columbus to any Asian king or administrator. It reads,

> By these presents we dispatch the noble man Christoforus Colon with three equipped caravels over the *Ocean Sea*s toward the regions of India [*ad partes Indie*] for certain reasons and purposes.[56]

This does sound like an international introduction, with the suggestion of some degree of secrecy. What were the "certain reasons and purposes?"

The second letter apparently answered part of the question. It reads,

> Ferdinand and Isabella, to King _____
> The Sovereigns have heard that he and his subjects entertain great love for them and Spain. They are, moreover, informed that he and his subjects very much wish to hear news from Spain, and send therefore their admiral, Christopher Columbus, who will tell them that they are in good health and perfect prosperity. Granada, April 30, 1492.[57]

The name of the "King" was left blank, allowing Columbus to insert the name and title of whatever Asian ruler he met. There is a possibility that several copies of this letter accompanied Columbus on the voyage to accommodate multiple important political and commercial contacts. The first sentence indicating prior knowledge of Spain and its monarchs is mysterious. Various theories have come forth about Eastern travelers who arrived in various locations in Europe and learned of Spain's attempt to drive out Muslim occupation of the Iberian Peninsula. Geographically, this makes sense, as Muslim incursions into India and Central Asia had already come to the attention of Chinese authorities.[58] It is possible that the Spanish monarchs believed that a political and commercial alliance might be contracted between Spain and China, thereby limiting further Muslim expansion.

The geopolitical situation made sense for a Spanish–Chinese alliance. Both kingdom-states resided at the extreme ends of the Eurasian continent, with ever-increasing Muslim expansion. Since the sacking of Constantinople in 1453, Muslim forces advanced deep into the Balkan Peninsula. The entire Italian Peninsula, including the Papal States, remained on high alert for a possible invasion. A brief landing at Otranto in 1480 and the resulting massacre of Italians not willing to convert to Islam raised calls for a Christian crusade to repulse the "infidel" and, further, to reclaim the Holy Land (Jerusalem). Columbus was well aware of the Otranto incident as the news spread throughout Europe, and when he arrived in Portugal and, later, Spain, the Spanish *Reconquista* was in full swing.[59]

The two major subgroups of Muslim kingdoms included the Moors, based in North Africa, and the powerful Ottomans, deriving power from a geographic base in modern Turkey. By 1492, the Moors controlled North Africa and coastal zones on the western shores of the Atlantic and the eastern shores along the Red Sea, extending ever southward. Courageous Muslim traders ventured across the vast Sahara Desert in organized trading caravans, reaching southward, toward, and below the Equator, making commercial contacts and attempting the conversion of local Africans. Meanwhile, Osmon I, in the 13th century, compiled his military conquest in Anatolia into the Ottoman Empire. From their homeland, subsequent Ottoman rulers aggressively expanded in all directions. Europeans realized the growing Muslim threat but did not unite effectively in attempts to thwart advances. The fall of Constantinople in 1453 further emboldened the then-Ottoman ruler, Sultan Mehmed II. Already established in the southern Balkans, Mehmed continued to expand northward, encroaching year-by-year closer to the city-state of Venice with the goal of conquering the Italian peninsula and Eastern Europe.

With the marriage of Isabella of Castile to Ferdinand of Aragon, a new united Christian kingdom successfully completed the *Reconquista*, recovering all lands formerly lost to the Moors. In the eyes of many Europeans, especially

Mediterranean kingdoms and principalities, Ferdinand and Isabella's nation-state, later formally known as Spain, assumed the responsibility of halting further Muslim expansion. Columbus himself participated in the final days of military conquest with the taking of the city of Granada. Thus began his religious fervor, determined to assist in the fight with the goal of retaking the Holy Land.[60]

Notes

1 The 15th century saw an explosion of sailing discoveries brought about by bold Portuguese officials such as Prince Henry the Navigator and his entourage of able-bodied ship captains. These men struck out into the Atlantic, westward to the Azores Islands, and southward to the Cape Verde Islands.
2 See Bradford, *Christopher Columbus*, 35–36. Bradford believed that Bristol merchants traded their manufactured goods for fish, especially cod.
3 Italian historian Paolo Taviani completed extensive research into the Columbus family roots, noting that Christopher's great-grandfather and grandfather remained peasant farmers in the Mo\u0301conesi area, about 15 miles east of Genoa. Domenico shifted from farming to weaving wool, moving to Genoa for economic opportunities. Later, he married Suzanna Fontanarossa, which included a dowry consisting of a small home and some land in Quezzi, a short 1 mile outside the city to the northeast. As a young boy, Columbus also spent time in the nearby towns of Quinto and Savona. See Taviani, *Columbus: The Great Adventure*, Chapters 1–3, 1–14.
4 This includes his time attempting to gain approval from King João (John) II of Portugal. His problems in Spain, much like those in Portugal, centered on the rejection of crown-appointed commissions that refused to approve Columbus's transatlantic plan. However, the monarchs, King Ferdinand and Queen Isabella, did not completely ignore Columbus but remained preoccupied with the ongoing war against the Moors. See Caraci, *Three Days in May*, 228–30. Columbus, rejected by Portuguese councils investigating his proposals, decided to try Spain in June 1485, finally meeting Queen Isabella in May 1486. The Talavera committee also rejected Columbus's plans by December of that year. For a complete chronology of Columbus's movements and actions, see Morison, "The Columbus Chronology," *Journals and Other Documents*, 401. For a summary of Columbus's attempts to earn the support of King João and the reasons for rejection, see Bradford, *Christopher Columbus*, 56–61. For more on Hernando de Talavera and the Spanish commission, see Ruiz, "Hernando de Talavera," 657–58. For information on how Columbus's Portuguese experience impacted his conception of a transatlantic voyage, see Caraci, *Columbus and the Portuguese Voyages in the Colombian Sources*, 561–70.
5 Columbus borrowed ideas from Roger Bacon's (*Opus Majus*) and Pierre d'Ailly's (*Imago Mundi*). Both medieval authors quoted research from ancient philosophers and cosmographers such as Aristotle, Pliny, and the prophet Esdras, all of whom believed the distance from Europe across the *Ocean Sea* (Atlantic) to Asia remained short. Columbus copiously annotated his copy of *Imago Mundi*. Randles, "The Evaluation of Columbus's 'India Project,'" 50–51.
6 Recently, Paolo Chiesa announced highlights of his findings from his study of Galvaneus de la Flamma's *Cronica Universalis*. This 14th-century Milanese friar included an expanded geographic treatise on exo-European regions, including a tantalizing reference to land west of Greenland, called *Marckalada*. This possibly is a reference to the *Markland* noted in Viking sources before this time. Chiesa believes that Galvaneus acquired the *Marckalada* story while at residence in Genoa, Italy. The tempting connection is almost too good to be true—learned persons, possibly

Columbus himself, in Genoa knew of land existing west of Iceland 150 years before the explorer sailed.

7   The initial agreement, the *Articles of Agreement*, dated April 17 added personal titles for Columbus, known as the *titulo* [Conditional grant of titles] came on April 30, 1492. The full text of the agreements is available in Morison, *Journals and Documents*, 27–30. This former agreement allowed Columbus the opportunity to contribute one-eighth of the "total expense" and in return receive one-eighth "himself of the profit." 28. The latter letter pronounced and conveyed the official title of "Our Admiral of the said Ocean Sea" on Columbus, but only with the understanding that he must be successful in finding "islands and mainlands." 30.

8   Thacher, Vol.1 *Christopher Columbus*, 438. After final negotiations, seven legal documents comprised the agreements between Columbus and the Spanish monarchs. For this complete list and analysis, see Morison, *Admiral of the Ocean Sea*, 104–05.

9   Caraci, Personal Communication. December 26, 2022. Perestrello attempted to settle Porto Santo as early as 1428. Prince Henry recognized this discovery, honoring Perestrello with the title and authority as *capitã o-donatário* of the island. Matthew Restall noted, "Columbus had profound Portuguese connections," 7. Restall recalled the pioneering work done by previous Portuguese seafarers to explore the eastern Atlantic, including Madeira, the Azores, and the Cape Verde Islands, the point being that "Many others created and contributed to the expansion process of which Columbus became a part," 9.

10 Beasley, "The French Conquest of the Canaries in 1402–06," *The Geographical Journal*, Vol. 25, No.1 (Jan., 1905), 77–81.

11 Béthencourt's nephew, Maciot, eventually sold the inherited title of "Lordship" to Portugal's Prince Henry the Navigator, and in doing so, he set off a dispute between Castile and Portugal that was finally settled in the 1479 Treaty of Alcáçovas.

12 Parsons, "The Migration of Canary Islanders to the Americas: An Unbroken Current Since Columbus," *The Americas*, 447.

13 Washburn, "The Meaning of 'Discovery,'" 6–7. See also Jane, "The Opinion of Columbus Concerning Cuba and the 'Indies,'" 266. The concept of antipodes reaches back to Greek philosophers such as Plato, who used it to help explain the idea of a spherical Earth, with the exact opposite location from where one is standing being the antipodal position.

14 There was no "Great Khan" in China in 1492. Xiaozong, the tenth emperor of the Ming Dynasty, reigned during the years 1487–1505, the period covering all of Columbus's four voyages. Given the era title, *Hongzhi*, or *Great Governance*, Xiaozong believed deeply in Confucian philosophy, attempting to set an example for his subjects. He held only one wife, preferred no territorial expansion, and maintained good relations with Muslim traders and settlers within and on the border of Chinese provinces. The letter is presented in its entirety in Morison, *Journals and Documents*, 30–31. The focus of the letter stated, "We have learned with joy of your esteem and high respect for us and our nation, and of your great eagerness to be informed about things with us." Columbus also carried an official "passport," declaring that Christopher Columbus was sent by Spanish monarchs "over the seas toward the regions of India for certain reasons and purposes," 31.

15 Sometimes written as Cipango, Zipangu, or Cipangu(o).

16 A *factoria*, or commercial outpost, usually run by an appointed agent(s) of the Portuguese of the Spanish crown, engaged European "artisans and craftsmen employed under a rigid wage system," such as seen by Columbus on his trip to São Jorge da Mina, in Africa. According to Frank Moya Pons, Columbus used this approach when initiating the construction of La Isabella on his second voyage. However, Spanish laborers rebelled due to harsh working conditions in the humid region and the realization that Columbus would not allow them to exploit native labor. See Pons, "Caribbean Trade," 674–75.

17 Rocca, *Mapping Christopher Columbus*, 88–92.
18 For more on the commercial aspects driving the Spanish monarchs, see Varela, "The Difficult Beginnings, Columbus as a Mediator of New World Products," 38–39. Later, Ferdinand Columbus and Columbus family members brought suit against King Ferdinand over the "definitions of privileges, governmental and judicial powers, territorial extent, and economic rights and obligations." See Ursula Lamb, "Lawsuits (Pleitos Colombinos)," 413–20.
19 Columbus studied intently the teachings of Jewish, Moslem, and Christian scholars for clues to better understand the relationship between geography and cosmology, and to a degree, science. For more on this topic, see "Christopher Columbus, Lost Biblical Sites, and the Last Crusade," 521–22.
20 Morison, 102. Santangel held the position of *escribano de ración* (keeper of the privy purse).
21 Delaney, *Columbus and the Quest for Jerusalem*, 67.
22 Meinig, *The Shaping of America*, 8. I agree, as far as the benefits noted. However, Queen Isabella in particular remained enthusiastic about the possibility of Columbus making contact with an Asian potentate, opening the opportunity for an economic and possible political relationship, thereby making the concessions to Columbus appropriate.
23 The *Diario* references Las Casas's transcription account of Columbus's logbook. The Barcelona copy of Columbus's logbook was originally titled *Diario de la Bordo* (*The Onboard Log*). Las Casas's published work on the logbook was renamed *El librode la primera navegacion* (*The Book of the First Navigation*). Today, Las Casas's work is known as the *Diario*.
24 Zamora, *Reading Columbus*, 28. Zamora determined that the monarchs hoped to exploit new markets in expanding geographical regions as yet untapped. Certainly, they hoped for Asian contact, but there was no guarantee of success. Thinking along these lines, Columbus saw his voyage as opening the door to a perceived "New World" of mercantilism. Colonization, not yet a hardened, accepted socio-economic reality, despite experience in the Canary Islands, would develop from Columbus's first voyage's acknowledged success and placed as a priority by King Ferdinand and Queen Isabella.
25 However, in the 15th century, it was common practice to hire young boys onto a voyage. They served as personal servants to the ship's master and pilot and assisted deck hands with everyday chores such as turning the sand clock.
26 Morison, *Admiral of the Ocean Sea*, 109. Morison noted that the larger port of Cadiz, then crowded with Jewish families forced to leave Spain, remained congested with 8,000 refugees, making securing ships difficult. Delaney noted that "some kind of debt" was owed by the people of Palos to the crown. Delaney provides a letter sent by the Spanish sovereigns to the mayor of Palos, the letter declaring, "Because of certain acts performed and committed by you to our detriment, you were condemned by *Our Council* and obliged to provide *Us* for twelve months with two caravels equipped at your own cost and expense…" *Columbus and the Quest for Jerusalem*, 69."
27 According to the testimony of a citizen of Huelva, Spain, one Hernán Yáñez de Montiel heard a story that Martín Pinzón had just returned from a trip to Rome, carrying a shipment of sardines, when Pinzón learned of Columbus's need for men and ships. Wadsworth, *Columbus and His First Voyage*, 120–21.
28 It is believed that Martín agreed to meet with Columbus after talking with Pedro Vázquez de la Frontera, a retired ship captain known to be knowledgeable in Atlantic sailing and the costs involved. See Morison, *Admiral of the Ocean Sea*, 140–41. Laurence Bergreen, in referencing Pinzón's subsequent actions on the voyage, states, "Pinzón behaved as though he had been forced into a partnership with the hotheaded Genovese mystic named Christopher Columbus." Bergreen, *Columbus: The Four Voyages*, 33.

29 Delaney, *Columbus and the Quest for Jerusalem*, 72. An excellent summary of the sequence of events in Palos can be discerned through the 1515 testimony of Garcia Fernandez, a local doctor, revealing how Columbus arrived in town, met the Pinzón brothers, and together they prepared for the voyage. See, Wadsworth, 105–06.

30 The Spanish *maravedís* appeared as a gold coin sometime in the 12th century. Minted first as a gold coin, the *maravedís* became devalued in time and appeared as silver and, eventually, copper coins. By Columbus's time, the *maravedís* became a "unit of account," being replaced as a coin by silver *reales*. Martín's investment equaled half the sum promised by King Ferdinand and Queen Isabella. Ibid. Also see Lardicci, A Synoptic Edition, DB26 note 11, 629, for an estimate of its value.

31 Ship captains commanded all final decisions, navigation-wise or otherwise. The ship's master, in turn, next held power, responsible for seeing that the captain's commands were followed efficiently. See Morison for an extended discussion of the efforts by the Pinzón brothers and Juan Niño, *Admiral of the Ocean Sea*, 135–140.

32 Lamb, "Lawsuits (Pleitos Colombinos)," 418. Lamb provides a detailed analysis of the ongoing lawsuits and formal "decisions" and "judgments," concluding, "On the balance, the *Pleitos* are a remarkable illustration of the rise of monarchical sovereignty over private lordship," 419. See pages 413–20 for the complete article. Also see Wadsworth, *Columbus and His First Voyage*, chapter 5, for a balanced, easy-to-read, selection of testimonies. For more on Martín Pinzón and his skills and experience, see Manzano, *Los Pinzones y el descubrimiento de América*, 3 vols. Madrid: Ed. Cultura Hispánica, 1988.

33 Fuson, *The Log of Christopher Columbus*, 38.

34 Campbell, "The Lateen Sail in World History," 21.

35 Delaney, *Columbus and the Quest for Jerusalem*, 73. See Morison, *Admiral of the Ocean Sea*, chapter 10 for more information on the officers and men.

36 However, as we shall see, 39 men would remain in the "New World" and suffer death at the hands of the Indigenous peoples.

37 This was the official terminology and Columbus's direct charge used by King Ferdinand and Queen Isabella in the *Santa Fe Capitulations*.

38 Caraci wrote that Columbus has become an "enigmatic figure, certainly not an ordinary character, tenacious and determined, an exceptional sailor, but also a man of his time." *The Puzzling Hero*, back cover summary.

39 Rocca, Al M. *Mapping Columbus: A Historical Geography of Christopher Columbus's Early Life Before 1492*, McFarland Publishers, 2023.

40 Columbus voyages to Iceland are supported by Taviani, *Columbus the Great Adventure*, 28–29; Bradford, *Christopher Columbus*, 35; Catz, "Columbus in Portugal," 175, and others.

41 Bradford, *Christopher Columbus*, 25–26. Bradford noted the long-held power of the Giustiniani on Chios for over 200 years, adding that Columbus may have made several voyages to the island, thereby increasing his seamanship skills and knowledge of the Mediterranean Sea gyre, system of winds and currents.

42 The determination of longitude, or the distance east or west from a known starting point, varied among European nations, with Portugal and Spain using the Canary Islands. See Fuson, *The Log of Christopher Columbus*, 25. Ptolemy used two systems for calculating geographic coordinates overlaid on a graticule; measuring the altitude of given stars, usually the North Star, Polaris, or sun; and for the longitude, Ptolemy employed a degree system with 15 degrees equaling one hour out, or the total of 360 degrees for the Earth's full circumference. He also measured or estimated land distances east to west, compensating for latitudinal shortening. See Grabhoff, "Of paths and places: the origin of Ptolemy's Geography," *Archive for the History of Exact Sciences*, 483–508.

43 Cecil Jane argues that Columbus grew up in an environment that encouraged a "vigorous intellectual life, and since that spirit of inquiry was very active, speculation

upon almost every topic was naturally rife." *The Four Voyages of* Columbus, xxi. This spirit of inquiry was a critical component defining much of Renaissance thinking and action.

44 Taviani, Columbus: *The Great Adventure*, 254.

45 Caraci, *The Puzzling Hero*, 89.

46 Lynch, "The Maps of Discovery," 6. The unique geographical and maritime skills of Columbus were not limited to his Genoese training and experience; they were enhanced by the direct knowledge and involvement he gained while residing in Portugal and Spain.

47 Taken from Hudson, "Marco Polo," 311. The Roman mile equaled 5,000 feet.

48 Ibid., Hudson's belief that Cipangu was indeed Columbus's high priority is conjecture. The actual *Santa Fe Capitulations* do not mention Cipangu, only "islands and mainlands." During the first voyage, Columbus at one point believed he was close to Cipangu but opted to bypass the opportunity in favor of sailing on to the Asian mainland. He reasoned that on the return voyage, he might look for Cipangu.

49 The idea that Columbus thought through a series of steps is highlighted by Italian historical geographer Ilaria Caraci; she noted, "He believed he would find some islands (to allow him to divide his voyage into legs) in the latitude of his route." *The Puzzling Hero*, 89.

50 Wright, *The Travels of Marco Polo, the Venetian*, 280.

51 Ibid., 229. This is an intriguing statement, as historical accounts date ongoing Chinese sea expeditions from China into the Indian Ocean beginning as early as the 2nd century BC and onward, increasing during the Ming Dynasty. These expeditions often initiated political contact with various islands and/or conducted trade. See *The Sea in History* by Qu Jinliang, published by Boydell and Brewer, 2017.

52 Columbus and his crew did not use our modern longitudinal system of coordinates, but he calculated miles of westward passage from his starting point, in this case, the Canary Islands. This form of calculation utilizes dead reckoning for determining miles sailed. See Fuson, *The Log of Christopher Columbus*, 42–44 for a detailed explanation of 15th-century navigation and the use of dead reckoning.

53 Morison, *Admiral of the Ocean Sea*, 105.

54 Juan II Coloma drafted the original document of *The Capitulations*; he represented the Spanish monarchs. The original document is online and in the public domain from the Royal Archive of Barcelona. The above determination of the exact old Castilian spelling of the word was determined by my reading of the document.

55 Translated by the author using Babylon Translation services, recognizing historical preference for Spanish used on the Iberian Peninsula as opposed to Spanish spoken throughout Latin America.

56 Morison, *Admiral of the Ocean Sea*, 107.

57 Gillett, "The Religious Motives of Christopher Columbus," 10.

58 Muslim penetration reached north into Afghanistan and Uzbekistan. Also, strong commercial elements with Muslim influence traveled east along the Silk Road into western China.

59 The *Reconquista*, or reconquest of the Iberian Peninsula by King Ferdinand and Queen Isabella, remained a political priority. When Columbus entered Spain in 1484, the Spanish monarchs were well on their way to defeating the remaining Muslim forces located in Southern Spain--coalesced around the kingdom of Granada.

60 See Delaney, *Columbus and the Quest for Jerusalem*. See the Introduction for a summary of Columbus's dedication, some say, obsession, to reclaim the Holy Land; this also becomes a contemplated goal of Ferdinand and Isabella, although the queen dies before a plan is considered.

2

PREPARING FOR THE VOYAGE

The Columbus Map

We know that Columbus constructed maps, an essential tool for trading representatives searching out new markets to contact. On the first voyage, Columbus referenced a map he shared with Martín Alonso Pinzón, captain of the *Pinta*. That map is lost to history; if found, it would tell us much about his cartographic preparations and his trans-*Ocean Sea* understanding. Attempts have appeared from time to time to investigate maps claimed to have been drawn by Columbus.

In 1992, Italian scholar Ilaria Caraci and a team of specialists in the fields of history and geography reviewed and debated the merits of a possible Columbus map. The team looked at earlier maps and map fragments thought to be drawn by Columbus or his brother, Bartholomew.[1] One key map, discovered in France, looked authentic until Caraci recognized the content of the map legend as similar to Columbus's postils (notes) from his copy of Pierre d'Ailly's 1410 influential cosmography, *Imago Mundi*.[2] She has maintained that most, if not all, of the postils were written after the first voyage.[3] The team also recognized the lack of focus on Asia. In fact, Asia was not drawn on the map. The map instead revealed a myriad of unknown islands scattered about the western Atlantic. Proponents of the map believed the map to be real and that Columbus's planned destination was not the Asian mainland but islands off the coast of Asia.[4] In the interim time period since Caraci and her team investigated the "Columbus Map," other maps have received scientific scrutiny, but nothing has been authenticated. This includes the famous 1474 Paolo dal Pozzo Toscanelli map reportedly sent to a Portuguese official representing the

DOI: 10.4324/9781003464143-4

crown. It is thought that Columbus somehow obtained a copy of that map and corresponded with Toscanelli.[5]

The extant maps studied by historians and geographers today, including portolan charts and mappae mundi (world maps) for the 15th century, may not be representative of the map Columbus used in planning for a transatlantic voyage or the actual maps he carried with him on the *Santa Maria*.[6] Actually, Columbus may have carried several maps. It was common practice for Portuguese mariners cruising north and south along the Atlantic coastline to carry regional sea charts (rhumb line charts, also called portolans), specifically locating cities and harbors.[7] Columbus would need one or more of these maps for the first stage of his voyage, from Palos to the Canary Islands. A good example of this type of map is the 1482 portolan chart of Western Europe and the Eastern Atlantic. Drafted by expert Italian cartographer Grazioso Benincasa, the sea chart came into use in 1482—about the same time Columbus compiled his ideas for a transoceanic crossing.[8] Spain and the Canary Islands, clearly displayed along with a number of Rhumb lines for directional navigation, offer mariners insight into understanding homeport to destination directions and distance. The location of two islands not yet discovered, but assumed to lie somewhere in the *Ocean Sea*, Antilla, and Satanazes, apparently tantalizingly close yet undiscovered appeared on the map. Both islands on this map are located to the north of the Canary Islands, although other maps of the same period show Antillia farther south. At a critical point in the Atlantic crossing, Columbus believed his position remained close to Antillia as if he had planned that scenario. The Benincasa map is somewhat unique in its geographic extent, locating the exact position of seaports and coastal towns from England to Africa on the Atlantic seaboard and the coastlines of the Southern European, West Asian, and North African regions of the Mediterranean Sea.

Columbus's Methodology for Calculating Global Distances

Let us assume that in 1482, as Columbus was planning for a transoceanic voyage, he knew he needed to provide proof of the distance across the *Ocean Sea*. This distance needed to be short enough to encourage support for a permanent sea route to the fabled Indies. At that time, Europe, especially Italian city-states and kingdoms, pursued a rebirth in all things classical. This included philosophy and the sciences. Columbus grew up in the world of the Genoese Renaissance. Genoa and Venice, leaders in the Mediterranean and trans-Mediterranean commercial contacts, experienced and shared general language characteristics but with distinct dialectal differences while pursuing similar business goals in ever-growing and competitive regional realms.

In the same year, the Benincasa Map appeared, as did a new mappa mundi (map of the world). Printed in Florence, Italy, by Nicholas the German, this 1482 Ptolemy map attempts, as did some earlier versions, to depict the known world based on the mathematical coordinates laid out by Greek geographer and mathematician Claudius Ptolemy. His original work is lost, but extant copies of Ptolemy's *Geographia* date from the 13th century, signaling renewed intellectual interest in ancient studies. The Latin Italian editions with maps began appearing in the early 15th century, with Latin being the *lingua scholarium*. Depending on the edition, some copies contained maps, while others did not.[9]

This map, or one similar to it, may have provided the global foundation for Columbus's Enterprise to the Indies. The 1482 Ptolemy map is somewhat unique for its extensive latitude and longitude grid laid upon the world's land area.[10] The Canary Islands in the west are located at 0 degrees longitude, while latitude lines extend northward from the Equator to 73 degrees and southward to 28 degrees. Southern Hemisphere land configurations are more guesswork than based on reliable data. There is an absence of oceanic regions to the west and east of the Europe—Africa–Asia landmass. This reflects the known ocean areas during Ptolemy's 2nd century AD Roman geographical understanding. In the extreme eastern portion of the map, the Asian landmass is left incomplete, and the *Mare Indicvm* (Indian Ocean) is an enclosed waterbody.

The 1482 Ptolemy map exposes 180 degrees of longitudinal breadth, leaving half the globe unmapped. Yet, clues to the missing regions, water, or land can be estimated, at least in Columbus's mind, from his own experiences in the Eastern Atlantic Ocean and from his reading of manuscripts and study of earlier maps. Let us look at the western portion of the map. Columbus had sailed at least twice into longitudinal zones of between 30 and 40 degrees west longitude. The first time was on his Icelandic voyage, and the second was on his return from the coast of Africa. He knew the *Ocean Sea* was at least that wide.

In looking at the far eastern portion of the map, we see the Asian mainland extending some unknown distance eastward, clearly inferring a huge landmass several times the size of Europe. The question for an observer contemplating the overall size of Asia arises whether one would need a fixed point on the Ptolemy map to compare with other data or maps. The *Serica regio* (region) is located between 45 and 50 degrees north latitude and 150 and 170 degrees longitude on the Ptolemy map. *Serica* is an ancient Greek and Roman term used to reference the land from which silk was derived. This was an important geographic location of reference for European merchants and political advisors. A portion of the Silk Road ran through this location. Debate on its longitudinal placement is ongoing, but it is most often referred to as being part of northwestern China. Today, that might cover much of Gansu Province in western China. This places the province centered at approximately 100 degrees east longitude.[11] The Ptolemy map thus extends locations too far to the east by 50–60 degrees from current maps. Yet, there is no determination as to the full width of Asia.[12]

The Ptolemy map, designed by medieval cartographers using Ptolemy's data, laid out a vast single continent stretching from Europe in the west to

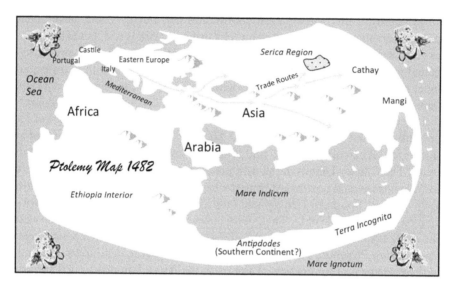

FIGURE 2.1   Ptolemy Map, 1482

Cathay and Mangi in the east. Following the ancient belief of an antipodal landmass, the cartographers presented a land bridge that encircled the *Mare Indicvm* (Indian Sea). The map left into question the width of the *Ocean Sea*, should one want to sail from Europe to Cathay.

To calculate the remaining distance east to the Asian coastline, Columbus, before 1491, may have looked at the widely circulated Fra Mauro map of 1459. The *Serica regio* (region) is shown in relation to the overall extent of the Asian landmass.[13] Estimating the longitudinal scale at the latitude of *Serica regio* would add another 50 degrees, proportionately, to reach the shoreline of the western *Ocean Sea*. Now, Columbus had enough data to estimate the width of Asia; it extended to 230 degrees. Now he could calculate the remaining breadth of the *Ocean Sea*. The Ptolemy map revealed 180 degrees, to which Columbus added another 50 degrees (proportional estimation to the Asian east coast). The figure totaled 230 degrees, leaving 90 degrees of *Ocean Sea* unexplored.

From the 90 degrees of ocean, Columbus, referencing one of the several widely circulated mappa mundi, may have estimated Cipangu at 30 degrees east of the coast of Cathay.[14] Thus, only 60 degrees of unexplored ocean lie between his known experiences on the coast of Europe and the wealth of Cipangu.

Columbus used the incorrect figure of 40 miles (Roman miles) per degree in computing his calculations.[15] This left approximately 2,400 miles of wide-open ocean from the European coast to Cipangu. To reach coastal Cathay (Quinsay),[16] one needed to sail another 1,200 miles. Voyages of this length were entirely possible, injecting confidence into the young mariner's decision-making. In fact, his trip to and from São Jorge da Mina approached this length, particularly on the

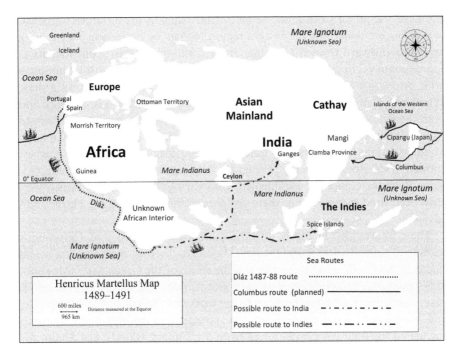

FIGURE 2.2 Martellus Map, 1489

return voyage.[17] This estimation may have been used in his 1484 presentation to King João II of Portugal; however, by 1489, another more accurate map became available on which to calculate, proportionally, the remaining East Asia distance—the Martellus map.

It is this author's belief that Columbus obtained a copy of the Martellus map or viewed it sometime during its production, which extended from 1489 to 1491. While Henricus Martellus lived within the area known as Germany today, he spent considerable time in Florence from 1480 to 1496. Columbus's Italian contacts in Genoa and Florence may have provided him with knowledge of and access to the map.

Henricus Martellus Germanus, a cartographer, probably from Nuremberg, Germany, produced another adapted version of the Ptolemy map, offering specific geographic detail. Two significant geographic conditions between the Martellus map and the Fra Mauro map possibly helped Columbus more in calculating the width of the *Ocean Sea* and in preparing maps for the 1492 voyage. First, the Martellus map reveals an extensive western *Ocean Sea* dotted with numerous islands and depicting Cipangu on the extreme eastern edge. The mapmaker intended to represent the world eastward to 270 degrees. Interestingly, the portion of the *Ocean Sea* revealed off the coast of Europe extends west about 20–30 degrees, more or less the "known waters" for European mariners, including Columbus. Second, Martellus, in his modified spherical projection, elongated the far eastern region of Asia by projecting a narrowing peninsula outward toward Cipangu. In fact, the tip of this peninsula sits at approximately 250 degrees longitude. This compares closely with Columbus's prior estimation from the Fra Mauro or similar pre-1482 map. Using these figures, the distance from Spain to the Indies worked out to 110 degrees, and from the Canary Islands, about 100 degrees. This left 80 degrees of ocean to cross before reaching Cipangu from the Canary Islands. The voyage to Cipangu would consume 3,200 Roman miles, or 1,000 leagues.[18] To reach Cathay, another 1,350 Roman miles (421 leagues) were needed. These are the approximate distances Columbus established from cartographic sources, which may have been used in presenting them to Queen Isabella and King Ferdinand's advisors.[19]

These figures also fit nicely into the more accepted theory of Columbus's reading of several ancient and medieval books to discover mathematically and calculate the Earth's circumference and the width of the *Ocean Sea*.[20] Morison, in his extensive investigation into the conception of Columbus's transoceanic plan, states that Columbus referred to the works of Ptolemy, Marinus of Tyre, and Marco Polo. After considering these sources and the idea that Columbus calculated his final voyage distances from the Canary Islands, not Spain, the young mariner arrived at a figure of 283 degrees as the geographic breadth of the Eurasian continent. This left 77 degrees of ocean. Morison states that Columbus believed Marinus's "degree was oversized," and Columbus downsized the remaining distance to 60 degrees.[21] In Roman miles, this came to 2,400 miles from the Canary Islands to Cipangu and 3,550 miles to the mainland of Cathay.

Sequence of Conception: Enterprise to the Indies

It is quite probable that Columbus used both maps and book sources to confirm his beliefs. Conversely, determining the sequence of when and how he conceived his Enterprise to the Indies is a major historical question left unanswered. Depending on the time and place of Columbus's activities, the resources available to him naturally affected his thinking and concept formation. We can roughly separate his concept development into three distinct stages of his life. The first stage occurred between the years 1451, his birth, and 1476, the year he arrived in Portugal. The second stage lasted from 1476 until 1484–1485, when he relocated to Spain. The third stage, from 1485 to 1492, occurred almost exclusively in Spain.

Columbus, as a youth, grew up in the maritime seaport of Genoa.[22] He saw early sea duty beginning as a young teen, and he quickly fostered a career as a trading representative for his father, Domenico Colombo, and other Genoese woolen weavers and merchants. During this time, he learned his basic maritime skills of navigation, reading portolan charts, and seamanship.[23] It is doubtful that he used or had an interest in any mappae mundi. However, he did learn how to measure sailing distances in leagues and miles in the Italian (Genoese) and Portuguese systems. These skills led to applying calculating daily distances during a voyage to existing portolan charts and determining the effects of winds and currents on the sailed sea route. This early period laid the foundation for maritime mastery. It is doubtful if he read any of the books later collected and archived by his son Ferdinand during these early years. Although it is possible that he did acquire or obtain access to Marco Polo's *Travels*, the book remained popular in mid-to late-15th-century Italy, particularly among merchants desiring to expand trade to eastern destinations.

This author would venture to suggest that Columbus's background in cartography provided the initial opportunity to launch his investigation by studying various mappae mundi, especially Italian maps, and reading Marco Polo's *Travels*. This applies specifically to his 1482–1484 period of concept construction and presentation to the Portuguese court. Then, when given the opportunity to access books such as Pierre d'Ailly's *Imago Mundi*, he confirmed his calculations in Spain during the period 1485–1492. During this time, he also reviewed the latest available mappae mundi, including the Martellus map.[24]

The First Voyage Maps of Columbus

This section of the book will attempt to recreate the portolan charts and mappae mundi used by Columbus on his first voyage. In the introduction to the log of his first transatlantic crossing, Columbus declared:

> Moreover, Sovereign Princes, besides describing every night the occurrences of the day, and every day those of the preceding night, I intend to draw up a nautical chart, which shall contain the several parts of the ocean and land in their proper situations; and also to compose a book to represent the whole by picture with latitudes and longitudes, on all which accounts is behoves me to abstain from my sleep, and make many trials of navigation, which things will demand much labor.[25]

Columbus intended his first voyage to provide a scientific, that is, a geographic study of the *Ocean Sea* and lands encountered. Among the introductory comments of his logbook, he writes, "I intend to draw up a nautical chart, which shall contain the several parts of the ocean and land in their proper situations."[26] This author interprets the statement "several parts of the ocean" to mean several distinct stages in his transoceanic adventure. In addition, he proposed to put it all together "to compose a book to represent the whole." Quite possibly, he intended to compile the several charts into one regional map depicting the full extent of the *Ocean Sea*. This author proposes that before he sailed, Columbus drew up preliminary charts and maps to help guide his sea route and for comparison to any new geographic findings as the expedition unfolded.

There existed four critical oceanographic regions Columbus would encounter, and he would need cartographic references for each region. Region 1: Palos to Canary Islands was the most familiar to Columbus; both locations existed on Portuguese and Spanish charts. Looking at the southwest portion of the Benincasa chart is representative of this kind of map. Columbus's version might have extended from the Portuguese coast in the north to just below the Canary Islands in the south. Region 2: Known Waters of the Eastern Atlantic: Leaving the Canary Islands, Columbus knew he would begin his westward course in longitudinal waters familiar to him and much of his crew. Region 3: Unknown Waters to Cipangu: Upon reaching the zone between 30°- and 40 degrees west longitude (320- and 330- degrees global longitude[27]) his ships entered unknown waters. At the western edge of this zone, he hoped to spot the large island kingdom of Cipangu or a smaller island nearby. Region 4 Island Clusters to the Asian Coast: If Columbus missed or decided not to land on Cipangu, he would continue west, looking for the coast of Cathay. He understood that Marco Polo reported numerous islands scattered throughout this

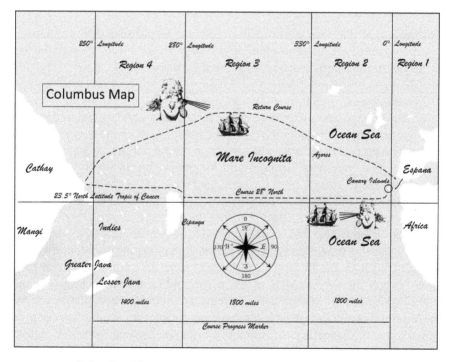

FIGURE 2.3   Columbus Map

region; he could stop here to resupply and claim sovereignty if unoccupied by a "civilized" society.[28]

We know that Columbus carried with him one or more nautical charts and probably a large hemispheric map, laying out the eastern shores of the Iberian Peninsula and islands of the eastern *Ocean Sea*, including the western coast of Cathay and a variety of mid-to-western oceanic islands, such as Cipangu. A course progress line, most likely located horizontally, allowed Columbus and his pilots to mark off the daily miles attained.

The first region covering the Palos to the Canary Islands covers waters he knew quite well. After marrying, Columbus lived on the island of Porto Santo, part of the Madeira Islands off the southwest coast of Portugal.[29] He also sailed through these waters on his trip to São Jorge da Mina and probably on several other voyages to the African coast that have not been recorded.

In Region 1, Palos to the Grand Canary Islands, Columbus may have used a portolan chart where the guiding compass rose extends from the offshore waters of the Portuguese-Spanish coastline, allowing ship pilots directional access to points in the Mediterranean Sea and all routes north and south in the Atlantic. We will discuss the actual directional headings and Columbus's experience with this region in a subsequent chapter. For reckoning miles sailed and logging the figures, Columbus used the Italian (Roman) mile of 5,000 feet per mile. Under the Italian maritime system, 4 miles equaled 1 league.[30] His projected course heading would be south, then southwest for a distance of 860 Italian miles, or 215 leagues. Following the Portuguese Current in his favor, Columbus planned 7–8 days of sailing time.[31]

Moving into Region 2, Columbus's plan called for his small fleet to follow the 28degree latitude course. This latitude offered a branching effect of the southward flowing Portuguese Current. Here, hot interior African winds helped accentuate a steady westward current—part of the already existing Atlantic gyre. Columbus had noticed this wind and current split on his African voyage and from other Portuguese mariners sailing south along the West African coast. The latitude he selected formed the bottom portion of the North Equatorial Current, later known as the Trade Winds. In addition, this latitude coincided with the northern coastal zone of Cipangu. At least that is what the Martellus map and other maps depict.[32] Politically, Columbus understood that the current Papal decree, the Treaty of Alcáçovas (1479), ensured a legal agreement between Spain and Portugal that ocean areas below the Canary Islands remained exclusively within the domain of Portugal—Columbus had to stay north of that latitude line.[33]

While Columbus never planned to turn back once he sailed, this latitude would afford the shortest route to fabled riches. This chart extended to approximately 30 degrees west longitude or, more likely, designated as 330° global longitude, as postulated on a map Columbus may have used for navigation. While he may only have sailed in these waters once or a few times, he knew this stage of the voyage might hold some challenges. Not all the crew may have sailed this far west in the *Ocean Sea*, and he would need to display confidence in his selection, of course. He planned an uneventful crossing of this region in 12–15 days.

In considering the third phase of the trip, Columbus knew major geographic and social concerns would arise. This ocean region became a true *mare incognita* (sea unknown). It would also represent the greatest distance for any stage; Columbus estimated that around 1,800 Italian miles of ocean existed between the 330 degree line and the coastline of Cipangu.[34] He understood the expectation that no land sightings might spook the crew, and so, as we shall see, it did. He no doubt harbored a fear of this region as well. For all his studies of maps and charts, along with ancient and medieval manuscripts, this part of the *Ocean Sea* was new to him. To cross this zone and hit the shores of Cipangu, it required a steady course west and a reliable pushing wind. Yet, somehow, he knew these facts and proceeded. This author has always suggested that what we know about what Columbus knew before the voyage is not sufficient to explain his decision for this route and timeframe. To display such outright audacity or stupidity is difficult to believe. It almost invites the suggestion that he acquired more oceanographic knowledge of winds, currents, and destinations than is now extant and available as documentary evidence. One may consider the social aspect as well. Upon crossing this stage to the 285 degree global longitudinal location, the crew would have been at sea for a minimum of 30 days—each day traveling farther from home and the safe haven of a known European shoreline.

Columbus expected the final stage, Region 4, to represent his crowning achievement, reaching the shores of Cathay. On the other hand, his maps indicated that the large island of Cipangu and whatever smaller islands he could encounter might be his first stop. It all depended on the accuracy of the Martellus map and Marco Polo's written description. He also understood that somewhere within this ocean region, he needed to make an important voyage decision. Three options presented a difficult course correction if Cipangu did not appear. One option called on Columbus to change course and search for Cipangu, while another option involved looking for any small island where water and food might be obtained. His third option would ask the crew to continue west until reaching the Asian coast—a hard sell for an anxious crew. Columbus was well aware that he would only need to make the call on these options once he hit this zone. The wrong decision could spell an extended delay, mutiny, or worse. Even though the Martellus map depicted numerous islands in this region, Columbus knew only too well that the depiction represented guesswork on the part of the cartographer.

In addition to the regional oceanographic charts, Columbus needed a concise mappa mundi to continually provide a strategic overview of the voyage—what was completed and what lay ahead. This map needed to depict the boundaries of each region and provide accurate latitude and longitude positions. In considering the cartographic projection affording him the best advantage, Columbus no doubt considered some of the maps already discussed. Logic concludes that he may have selected the Martellus map as the most current and adaptable map. In the hypothetical Columbus map shown above, the *Ocean Sea* becomes center stage, with Columbus eliminating much of Europe, Asia, and Africa. A progress marking line would allow him to chart the weekly distance estimated from the individual regional maps; thus, providing a strategic overview.

The Art of Navigation in the 15th Century

From his earliest days of sailing, Columbus acquired the skill of reading a compass. Compass instruments came in all sizes and designs. By the 15th century, most European pilots carried 32-point compasses with them. This allowed for precise determination of route bearings when used in conjunction with windrose (rhumb) lines depicted on accurate portolan charts. Columbus did carry a 32-point compass, and his log is chock-full of stated bearings from his first voyage.[35] For his first ocean crossing, the coastal portolan chart and compass made passage easy for the initial leg of the journey, a stopover at the Canary Islands.

Columbus understood well that no portolan chart mapped the *Ocean Sea* west of the Canary Islands, and he also knew that he would follow his own conceived windrose line, a latitude bearing west of 28 degrees north. With the compass on board, Columbus now only needed to calculate the distance sailed each day. In his mind, following the designated course for a certain number of leagues, a measurement used by 15th-century sailors to reckon sailing distances, would eventually lead him to the Indies. Finding a ship's speed involved timing the passage of a floatation device (a piece of wood) from one end of the ship to the other. A long rope was tied to the wood and tossed overboard at the bow (front) as a crew member chanted or counted the seconds. On occasion, an hourglass with minutes marked on the sides was used if the passage was expected to be slow.[36] Knowing the length of the ship, the distance covered was calculated. These readings occurred several times during the day. Later, at sunset, the pilot and captain determined the average distance covered. Using the compass heading in tandem with several distance measurements was known as dead reckoning navigation. Columbus displayed an uncanny mastery of dead reckoning techniques throughout the first voyage and on all subsequent voyages.

While Columbus felt comfortable relying on his honed skills in dead reckoning, he understood the need to verify his location with the use of celestial navigation. We know that Columbus carried at least one celestial instrument with him on board the *Santa Maria*; it was a quadrant. The quadrant measured degrees in the latitude of the "north star," Polaris, and, on occasion, the height of the sun (at noon) in relation to the observer's horizon.[37] Often, the device was made of wood in a quarter-circle shape. Degrees of latitude were engraved from 0 to 90 degrees. Using the quadrant simply required an observer to sight the target along the right edge of the device. A metal weight attached to a string hung down (plumb bob) is pulled by gravity to a perpendicular angle of 90 degrees from zero. As the observer tilted the quadrant upward, the plumb bob crossed through marked lines of degrees on the side of the quadrant, indicating the latitude. Of course, the device worked well enough on land, depending on the patience and accuracy of the observer. On the high seas, using a quadrant, presented with constant movement, even in what seemed to be calm waters; the swaying plumb bob rarely remained stationary.[38]

A focused review of the many ocean challenges faced by Columbus on all four voyages reveals a combination of outstanding seamanship and a healthy dose of good luck. When it comes to navigational skill, he uniquely possessed the ability to meet every calamity he faced—as we shall see during his epochal first voyage. Douglas Peck completed an in-depth look at Columbus's voyages before 1492 and concluded that "This study has presented viable evidence from reliable sources that Columbus was one of the most skilled and experienced seafarers of the respected Genoese captains and navigators in Europe during his lifetime."[39]

Directional Methodology

Columbus relied almost solely on the magnetic compass and dead reckoning to point the way to the Indies. Interestingly, during the voyage, Columbus reported his first encounter with the concept of magnetic variation. Sailing in the limited sea environments of the Mediterranean and the coastlines of Western Europe, he encountered unexpected small compass needle movements. However, during the first transatlantic crossing, the scientific phenomenon of magnetic variation appeared more pronounced the further westward he journeyed. Unaware of a magnetic north pole, Columbus apparently ignored its implications. However, he continued to rely solely on magnetic compass headings, with a few opportunities for celestial verification. Toward the end of the voyage, he did not realize this heading deviated from true north by as much as seven degrees or more.[40] While Morison related the impact of magnetic variation on Columbus's dramatic routing change to the southwest beginning on September 25, Robert Fuson, writing in the 1990s, disputed the effect of magnetic variation on Columbus's voyage. Much of the confusion about the impact of magnetic variation on Columbus's voyage comes from the fact that, until recently, we did not know the position of the magnetic pole in the late 15th–16th century and, thus, the resulting isogonic line patterns for the Atlantic region.[41]

Also, local magnetic fields can be affected for a variety of reasons. This usually applies on a ship if magnetized iron is present near the compass. In Columbus's time, the steering compass was usually mounted permanently away from large iron objects, such as weapons. However, small pieces of iron, if situated close to the compass, may cause a slight deviation. Morison quickly discounted this idea and confidently predicted that Columbus did not experience a magnetic deviation of this type.

Fuson did note that Columbus might have used sunrise and sunset observations to verify course direction. This is a definite possibility, especially considering the voyage began near the autumnal equinox. Taking readings on or near this date allowed for the sun's position on the horizon to point accurately in the true directions of west and east.[42] In taking these observations, a ship's pilot could plot the difference between magnetic north and true north, and he could then pinpoint a due west direction. It is true that Columbus did not mention sunrise or sunset readings in his log, but the reader should recall that we do not have the original log.

Nautical Mileage Methodology

When working with recorded sailing distances dating from the transitional period of the Middle Ages to the Renaissance, it can be difficult to secure accurate figures. Las Casas's version of Columbus's log refers to leagues sailed daily but does not quantify feet per mile, or league. Numerous studies have suggested a wide range of feet-to-mile ratios. This is important as it establishes the mathematical proportion of miles to leagues. Historical estimates vary from 4,100 English feet per mile suggested by James E. Kelley Jr. to 5,000 Roman feet (4,858 English feet) per mile, as noted in Alton Moody's "The Nautical Mile."[43]

Columbus recorded sailing distances in leagues, with 4 Roman miles equaling 1 league. In converting Roman miles to modern nautical miles, 1 league equals approximately 3.18 nautical miles.[44] The mapping measurements for this book will thus multiply the number of leagues stated in Las Casas' version of the log by 3.0 to determine each day's accrued sailing distance in nautical miles.[45] The reader will then see the nautical miles sailed along with the approximate latitude and longitude locational information presented. As explained in the section titled "Directional Methodology," magnetic variation affected the compass instruments used on all three ships. Morison noted this and attempted to adjust his daily sailing directions; accordingly, Fuson disagreed that magnetic variation impacted Columbus's route, and this may account for why Morison believes Watlings Island was Columbus's landfall, while Fuson believed it to be Samana Cay.[46] It is assumed that Columbus did not fully understand the impact of magnetic variation and thus ignored its effect. For this study, I have used a combined estimate using Morison's calculations and NOAA's National Centers for Environmental Information Historical Magnetic Declination (1590).

Notes

1 For more on Bartholomew's training and skills as a cartographer, see *L'Eredita dei Colombo: dal "Libro de Conto" de Cristoforo e da quello del Fratello Bartolomeo*, edited by Giorgio Bazzurro, Istituto Idrografico della Marina, Genoa, 2020.

2 D'Ailly presented persuasive ideas on the size of the world; Columbus mentioned the book in several of his writings. For more on D'Ailly's impact on Columbus's thinking, see Watts, "Prophecy and Discovery," 4–5.

3 For an in-depth analysis of Columbus's postils, see Caraci, "Columbus' Postilla 858c and its Chronological Value," 65–83. *The Puzzling Hero*. Many of the postils from *Imago Mundi* are translated by Samuel Morison. Morison, *Journals and Documents*, 23–24.

4 Caraci, *Puzzling Hero*, 85–87. See Chapter 2 of Caraci's book for an in-depth analysis of her ideas on an existing Columbus map.

5 Caraci and others do not believe Columbus corresponded with Toscanelli. However, they concede the original contact between a Portuguese official and Toscanelli and the probability of a map becoming part of that correspondence. For a summary of Toscanelli's life, see Dilke, "Toscanelli, "Paolo Dal Pozzo," 670–71. To obtain an understanding of the connection between Columbus and the Toscanelli map, see Caraci, *The Puzzling Hero*, 191. For an in-depth analysis of the Toscanelli letter and possible communication with Columbus, see Taviani, "The Scientific Support," Chapter XXXI, 156–63, *Christopher Columbus: The Grand Design*.

6 Ibid., 23.

7 Portolan, or Portolano, is an old Italian term for a written account describing the characteristics of seaports and possible landings. It was in the 19th century that the term *portolan* became associated with nautical charts. It is more appropriate to use the term *rhumb line charts*. Caraci, personal communication, July 22, 2023. This map is available to view online. For information on the impact of pilot books and nautical charts on stimulating navigation in the Mediterranean, a precursor to Atlantic exploration, see Simonetta Conti, *Portolano e carta nautica: Confronto toponomastico*.

8 A copy of the original map is available online at various sources, including Wikipedia. For background information on the style and content of the map, see www.maphistory.info

9 It should be noted that Ptolemy's ideas most likely originated with an earlier Greek philosopher, Marinus of Tyre. The 15th-century copies of *Geographia* contained eight books, with Book VIII containing the maps. The latitude and longitude locational calculations appear in Books II through VII. For more on the origination of Ptolemy's work, see Leo Bagrow's "The Origins of Ptolemy's Geographia," *Geografiska Annaler*, Vol. 27 (1945), 318–87, and Mark T. Riley's "Ptolemy's Use of His Predecessors' Data," *Transactions of the American Philological Association*, (1974), Vol. 125 (1995), 221–50. The 1482 Ptolemy map may be viewed at high resolution at the British Library. https://www.bl.uk/learning/timeline/large126360.html

10 The Ptolemy measurement only laid out 180 degrees of the assumed 360 degrees of the Earth's circumference. For reference in this book, the term *global longitude* will be used. To calculate global longitude from any given west longitude, simply subtract the west longitude figure, that is, degrees, from 360degrees.

11 This determination is an estimate based on the topography of the shown mountain chains and major lakes, as noted on the Ptolemy map. Latitude coordinates are incorrect, as the Ptolemy map reveals the region to be in southern Siberia.

12 See a high-resolution version of the Ptolemy map at the University of Minnesota, James Ford Bell Library, online.

13 See Wikipedia. A high-resolution map at the site is up and available, displaying its original orientation with the south up, depicting the *Serica regio* (region) on the lower left side of the map.

14 The geographic relational distance is clearly visible on the 1459 Fra Mauro map, the 1457 Genoese map (cartographer unknown), the 1453 Giovanni Leardo map, and the famous 1491 Henricus Martellus map. There is a dispute over whether Columbus may have accessed the Toscanelli map; the latter is lost, but an 1889 version is based on descriptions from a letter by Italian cosmographer Paolo da Pozzo Toscanelli to King Joao II of Portugal. The Portuguese canon, Fernam Martins, originally sent an inquiry to Toscanelli, asking for his opinion on the feasibility of sailing west to Asia.

15 Columbus used the figure of 45 Roman miles to a degree for the Equator. At 28–30 degrees north, the latitude he planned to sail, the figure would drop to 40 miles for one degree of longitude. See Morison, *Admiral of the Ocean Sea*, 68. However, he used these figures before his voyage, not during the voyage. Today, at the 28-degree north latitude line, one degree equals 53 nautical miles.

16 Hangzhou today.

17 It is true that on the Africa trip, Columbus no doubt stopped at several intermediate locations along West Africa. Nevertheless, recall that he believed that he could also stop at several islands in the western portion of the *Ocean Sea.*

18 One Spanish League is equal to roughly four Roman (Italian) miles. There is debate on which system of measurement Columbus used in his presentations in Portugal and Spain. During his first voyage, he recorded distance mainly in Spanish miles, according to Las Casas's abridged account. Fuson, *The Log of Christopher Columbus*, 11.

19 It is interesting to note that upon reaching his first landfall at Guanahani Island, Columbus calculated 3,409 miles (1,072 leagues) from the Canary Islands.

20 Columbus used the Arab calculation of 56 2/3 Italian nautical miles for the length of one degree of longitude, estimating 20,400 miles for the Earth's circumference. The correct figure is 24,855 miles at the equator. It is believed that the Arab geographer Al-Farghani's writings became the source for Columbus. George Nunn noted that "this erroneous figure was not original with him [Columbus]; if fact, it was a commonplace of medieval geography and goes back to the ninth." The Geographical Conceptions of Columbus, xvii. Nunn references the efforts by Arab geographers who working under orders from the Caliph Al-Mamûn, calculated 56 2/3 while surveying the plains of Sinjar.

21 See pp. 65–68 of Morison, *Admiral of the Ocean Sea*. Morison concludes, incorrectly, that Columbus's calculations were not "logical." However, Columbus did use logic, logic obtained by combining his Atlantic maritime experiences with limited manuscript references. Caraci believes that Columbus only acquired many of the books now residing in the Colombian Library in Seville after his third voyage as he prepared to defend his discoveries; criticism argued that Columbus's discoveries were only isolated islands in the Atlantic Ocean. Personal communication, July 17, 2023.

22 For a summary of Genoa's historical and commercial development before Columbus's birth, see Simonetta Conti, "Verso l'ignoto. Colombo e I grandi navigator," 163166.

23 See Bazzurro, *L'Eredita dei Colombo*, pp. 36–54 for an analysis of Columbus's navigational skills during his outgoing and return voyages.

24 In addition to D'Ailly's *Imago Mundi*, Columbus also owned Enea Silvio Piccolomini's *Historia rerum ubique gestarum*, Marco Polo's De consuetudanibus et conditionibus orientalium regionum, Pliny the Elder's *Historia naturalis*, Plutarch's *Las Vidas de los ilustres Varones*, and other works including a notebook of folios now compiled to form the *Libro de las profecias*. See West, "Library of Columbus," 420–22.

25 Las Casas, *First Voyage of Columbus*, 11.

26 Ibid.

27 Ancient and medieval cartographers, in calculating longitude, considered the spherical Earth to be comprised of 360 degrees of girth—that of a circle. There was no universal determination for zero degrees longitude; however, many Italian and other European scientists considered the Canary Islands the "prime meridian."

28 The author will discuss the concepts of discovery rights and subsequent sovereignty declarations based on the level of civilization later in this work.

29 Columbus, in 1479, married Felipa Moniz Perestrelo. The couple met in Lisbon, and the next year they produced a son, Diego. For more information on Felipa, see Delaney, *Columbus and the Quest for Jerusalem*, 37–38, and Morison, *Admiral of the Ocean Sea*, 54–57. For additional detail on her family background, see Catz, "Columbus in Portugal," *Christopher Columbus and the Age of Exploration*, 176–7; also see Bradford, *Christopher Columbus*, 48–49. See M. Montserrat León Guerrero, *Mujeres que ayudaron al plan descubridor de Colón*, for a detailed description of Felipa Moniz de Perestrello and the other woman in Columbus's life, Beatriz Enriquez de Arana.

30 See Fuson, *The Log of Christopher Columbus*, 48. The Spanish mile is 1,792 feet shorter than the contemporary Western figure of 6076 feet per nautical mile. Thus, the Spanish mile is approximately 70% the length of the current nautical mile.

31 Using the 1827 translation as the foundation for distances given in the log, the author will henceforth, in this work, use Spanish miles and leagues when referencing Columbus's sailing distances.

32 Cartographers designing maps earlier than 1491 located Cipangu at different latitudes. Most maps concurred that the general coastal configuration ran north-south for several hundred miles.

33 For a summary of the included articles of agreement, see O'Callaghan, 678.

34 This calculation recognized the fact that distances between longitudinal degrees increase as one gets closer to the equator. Thus, his estimates are derived from determining a sailing plot aligned near the 30-degree latitude line. In measuring longitude distances today, one can easily calculate the miles needed to sail from 20 degrees west longitude to 30 degrees west longitude; this would come to approximately 600 miles. However, moving north to the 40-degree latitude line, a ship sails only 530 miles.

35 On November 14, 1492, he used compass terms North, NW, SSW, and NW by W. Fuson, *The Log of Christopher Columbus*, 109.

36 Ibid., 44.

37 Measurements of the sun were taken at noon when the sun reached its highest point in the sky.

38 Fuson, in his excellent discussion of Columbus's navigational equipment, reminds the reader of the mariner's frustration in getting his quadrant to work correctly. Ibid., 40–41.

39 Peck, "The Controversial Skill of Columbus," 424. Morison wrote that a modern mariner, using the equipment and instruments that Columbus possessed, could not duplicate Columbus's skill. *Admiral of the Ocean Sea*, 195. For more information on Columbus's leadership and navigational skills, see Murphy and Coye, "Columbus: The Dawn of an Age," 21–22.

40 See Morison, pp. 213, 203–04. Morison discusses specific zones of magnetic variation at named longitudes. At the time of his writing in the 1940s, this would have been difficult to calculate for 1492, as today our best calculations are limited historically to 1590 forward. After Morison's book, advances in understanding occurred that explained the movement of the magnetic north pole. See also Taviani, *Columbus*, 92–94.

41 Current research by the National Oceanic and Atmospheric Administration (NOAA) traces the movement of the magnetic poles and isogonic lines as far back as 1590.

42 The autumnal equinox in 1492 occurred on September 13.

43 See Kelley, 122. See Moody, 79.

44 There is disagreement on the length of the conversion ratio of Roman miles to leagues, with low estimates ranging from 2.67 to 4.00. This study will utilize 3.0 miles per league.

45 For the purposes of this study, measurements from USGS maps will be determined in current nautical miles, in which one mile equals 6,076 feet. Each day is meant to extend from morning light through the night.

46 According to NOAA, it is impossible to know the exact isogonic line patterns occurring in 1492 due to the paucity of recorded magnetic field observations. The earliest modeled estimates begin for the year 1590. Personal communication, July 7–10, 2021.

3
THE ADVENTURE BEGINS

> God made me the messenger of the new heaven and the new earth of which
> he spoke in the Apocalypse of St. John [Rev. 21:1] after having spoken of it
> through the mouth of Isaiah; and he showed me the spot where to find it.
> —Christopher Columbus, *Book of Prophecies*, 1501

The Journal of Christopher Columbus

Columbus made it clear in his opening journal comments that his immediate
goal included "to see the said princes, people, and territories, and to learn their
disposition and the proper method of converting them."[1] In fact, much of his
introductory remarks focused on religion, not commerce or any personal
financial opportunities. He talked about being present when the last Iberian
stronghold, Granada, fell to the Christian forces of Ferdinand and Isabella. In
another section, Columbus recounts how his voyage began at the same time the
Spanish monarchs expelled Jews who refused to convert to Christianity.[2] He
does mention "great favors" granted to him by the king and queen. While
Columbus writes "from then on," indicating that at this point the "favors" are
conditional, he would first need to fulfill his part of the contract—discover
something new. These favors granted royal standing as a "Don," along with the
accompanying societal benefits.[3] In addition, Columbus received the title of
Admiral of the *Ocean Sea*, a title he felt could only be earned by discovering
new islands and continental areas of the Indies.[4] Thinking of the future, he did
mention that such titles and honors would be passed down to his eldest son,
Diego. To achieve these rewards, he had to satisfy the geographic discovery

DOI: 10.4324/9781003464143-5

requirements, find a workable route to the Indies, make contact, and suggest, maybe secure, trading agreements.

To ensure all the above contractual requirements would be met and honored, Columbus determined to keep a detailed day-to-day log containing pertinent maritime information such as course and mileage sailed, as well as reflections on the conditions of the ships and crew. As we shall see, this log became the first in recorded history to provide detailed accounts of each island visited and ensuing encounters with Indigenous peoples.[5] Within the log, he promised to draw charts detailing locations with proper coordinates (latitudes and longitudes). As a final note, Columbus recorded "that I forget sleep and pay much attention to the navigation" to complete his journal entries.[6] This last promise came true more often than not as the voyage progressed.

Moving into the journal at this time, it is good to remind the reader that Columbus's original log is lost to history; we are obliged to rely on translated and transcribed accounts written, for the most part, years after the events. These extant log entries may only be summaries of the actual content written by Christopher Columbus and, as such, may contain significant errors in historical interpretation. Most of the writings presented come from a variety of translations, including the 1827 version by Samuel Kettell, Clements Markham's 1893 work, the 1992 work of noted naval historian Robert Fuson, Cecil Jane's translation of Las Casas's abridgment of the Columbus log, the updated 1988 version, and most importantly, Francesca Lardicci's outstanding 1999 English and Spanish version in *A Synoptic Edition*. Kettell and Markham's versions, while deficient in some specific events, are otherwise quite accurate and available for publishing large, quoted sections, being in the public domain. Vital checks on specific translated words, phrases, and events are derived from the highly acclaimed computer-generated *Diario of Christopher Columbus's First Voyage to America, 1492–1493* by Dunn & Kelley. Reference checks and additional historical interpretations of Columbus's log come from his son Ferdinand Columbus's *Historie*, La Casas's *Historia de las Indias*, Columbus's 1493 letter to King Ferdinand and Queen Isabella and letters to Luis de Santángel and Gabriel Sánchez, Peter Martyr's *Decades de Orbo Novo* (*Decades*), and Andrés Bernáldez's *Historia de los reyes católicos*. Samuel Morison's authored work provides an excellent reference for questions concerning maritime navigation from his book *Christopher Columbus: Admiral of the Ocean Sea*, while leading Italian scholar Ilaria Caraci lends her expertise on the subjects of a Columbus map, documents (*Libro Copiador*), and the impact of the *encounter* from her book, *The Puzzling Hero*.

Sailing directions are arbitrarily given as abbreviations, such as NW (northwest) and SE (southeast), or spelled out for the reader.

Sabotage as the Voyage Begins, August 3 to September 5

August 3, 1492

Columbus's first log entry simply stated the time of departure, 8 o'clock in the morning, his course heading, southwest (SW) and south (S), and the total distance sailed, 15 leagues (45 nautical miles).[7] All three ships steered toward the Canary Islands, then under Spanish occupation and economic exploitation. At a distance of approximately 800 miles, this first leg of the journey was well known and traveled by young Columbus as a trading representative, encouraging a no-incident experience but proving to be a challenge.

August 4, 1492

This is the shortest account in the journal; it simply read, "They steered S.W. ¼" [by S.]. It is interesting to note that Columbus did not record his sailing progress on this day. On-ship demands with a new crew probably occupied most of his time. From the start, Columbus no doubt wanted to check every aspect of the ship's handling and his men's performance, involving setting sails correctly, maintaining course headings, and ship-board responsibilities.

August 5, 1492

Holding his course, the fleet made more than 40 leagues. The use of the term "more than" suggests Columbus was more preoccupied with the overall running of the ship than concerned about the exact mileage to the Canary Islands. Since commercial intercourse remained active at this time between Spain and the Canary Islands, it was not necessary to account for sailing details at this point. He would pay more attention to course heading and distance sailed after departing the Canaries.

August 6, 1492

Martín Alonzo Pinzón, captain of the *Pinta*, reported his ship's rudder either broken or unshipped (jumped loose) from its supporting ring. Columbus, concerned and worried about losing precious time, later thought the incident was not an accident but the "contrivance of Gomez Rascón and Christopher Quíntero, who were on board the caravel, because they disliked the voyage."[8] Pinzón, creative and energetic, worked with his crew to apply a temporary rope connection; on they sailed. Relieved, Columbus, by the next morning, reported 29 leagues covered. Las Casas also noted that Columbus heard of "heated arguments" aboard the *Pinta*, hinting at discord among certain crew members concerning the feasibility of completing the voyage successfully.[9] This is important to note, as Spanish discontent with the voyage grew as the expedition plowed west from the Canary Islands. In fact, Columbus may have

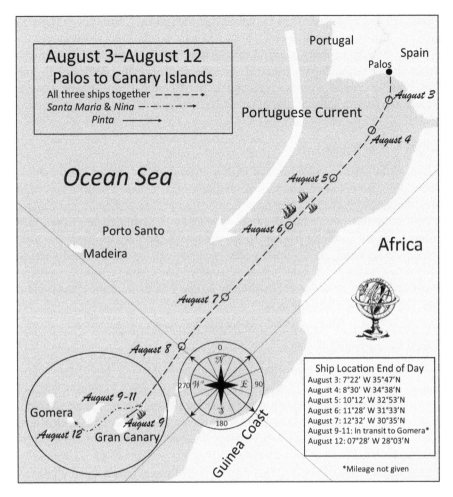

FIGURE 3.1   Palos to the Canary Islands: August 3 to August 12

already gleaned a plan for dealing with a non-compliant crew. Another translation relates that Columbus was concerned but believed that the repair to *Pinta* would be successful due to Pinzón being a "courageous and an intelligent man."[10]

Columbus carefully laid out the first segment of his journey, understanding that he wanted to sail south at first to pick up favorable winds. In this manner, he ordered the fleet to set a course for the Spanish-controlled Canary Islands. Here, he would secure supplies—water and food—for the ocean crossing.

August 7, Tuesday

Another day and the same problem—pilots on the *Pinta* notified Pinzón that the rope connection broke again. Acting quickly, men on the *Pinta*, knowing not what else to do, tied a new rope knot to secure the rudder. Columbus ordered his ship, the *Santa Maria*, alongside. Shouting over to Pinzón, he discussed the problem. Pinzón, in reply, pleaded to secure permission to change course and head for the nearest Canary Island, Lanzarote, approximately 200 miles distant. Columbus overruled Pinzón, ordering him to continue his present course. Despite the further setback, the ships made 25 leagues.

August 8, Wednesday

Again, Columbus felt discouraged with additional news today that the *Pinta* moved slowly due to substantial leaks in her hull. He made an important decision. Columbus reasoned that securing a new vessel somewhere in the Canary Islands to replace *Pinta* might be the best move. Accordingly, he issued new orders to Pinzón, telling Martín to proceed with the fleet to Gran Canaria. Pinzón understood his options: either successfully repair his ship while at anchor or abandon the vessel for another ship. The second temporary rudder repair apparently held the rest of the day, as the fleet made some progress, but they did not reach Gran Canaria.

August 9, Thursday

Columbus summarized the events from August 9 through September 5 into one entry dated August 9. However, Fuson used Ferdinand Columbus's *Historie* to supplement the original log. The ships sighted Gran Canaria Island. Contrary winds frustrated Columbus and his crew in their continuing efforts to reach land, tacking alternatively with limited success. Meanwhile, the *Pinta* remained off the coast due to continued problems with the rudder. Eventually, Pinzón anchored *Pinta* at the harbor of Las Palmas. Columbus, in a conference with Martín, promised to return with a new ship, and then he set a course for the island of Gomera and the seaport of San Sebastián.[11]

August 10, Friday[12]

The usually reliable, but slow, *Portugal Current* remained becalmed;[13] the *Santa Maria* and *Niña* made little southerly progress, revealing another situation not within the explorer's control, despite having experienced ship delays due to lack of winds or uncooperative surface currents on several occasions earlier in his career.

August 11, Saturday

Again, the wind blew only a little, and progress remained limited. Tantalizingly ahead, a short distance on the horizon, Gomera's shoreline came into view, enticing the Genoese mariner and his crew, so close and yet so far away. Columbus paced the deck, wrote little in the diary, and hoped for the wind to stir.

August 12, Sunday

Fuson, using Ferdinand's account of the first voyage, noted that Columbus happily made Gomera this day. Immediately, Columbus gave orders for a few crew members to row ashore in the skiff boat and inquire as to the availability of a ship; he needed another seaworthy craft, preferably one with a shallow draft, able to explore inner harbors. Time became a factor, with Columbus understanding the need to not dally in the Canaries and favoring a quick replenishment of water and supplies before heading into the *Ocean Sea.*

The Lady Doña Beatriz Ines Peraza

August 13, Monday

The news proved negative today, as the shore party returned without securing any hope for a new ship. The men, while ashore, did hear about Doña Beatriz Ines Peraza. Peraza, formerly married to the governor of the island, continued to live on Gomera and frequently visited other islands of the Canaries. At that moment, she was, ironically, in Las Palmas on Gran Canaria, sailing there on a 40-ton ship that might replace the ailing *Pinta.* Her return to San Sebastián was due at any time. Columbus had no alternative but to wait.

August 14, Tuesday

Hoping that Pinzón would soon complete rudder repairs on *Pinta*, Columbus remained anchored.

August 15, Wednesday

While anchored at San Sebastián, Columbus received word that a ship was leaving that day for Las Palmas. Acting quickly, Columbus selected a man from the crew to board the ship and deliver a note to Pinzón. The note expressed Columbus's failure to secure a replacement and urged the *Pinta*'s captain to complete repairs.

August 16–23

Columbus simply remained idle and waited for Doña Beatriz Ines Peraza to return, but she did not. To his disappointment, Pinzón also did not arrive. So, for an entire week, Columbus remained on the *Santa Maria*, helpless. If he

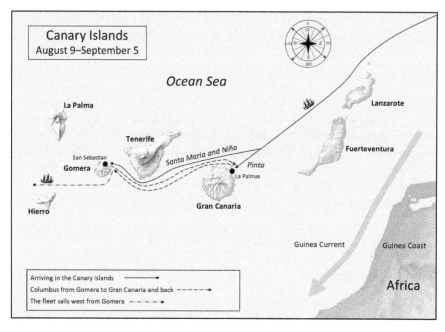

FIGURE 3.2   The Canary Islands: August 9 to September 5

sailed toward Pinzón, he might pass unaware of either Peraza's ship or *Pinta*, thereby compounding the situation.

Columbus knew the Canary Islands well as he sailed this region several times as a young merchant representative. Frustration grew as Columbus was forced to wait for Martin Pinzón to complete rudder repairs on *Niña*.

August 24, Friday

Columbus could wait no longer. With his mind made up, he ordered the captain of the *Niña* to weigh anchor and follow the *Santa Maria* back to Gran Canaria. As the ships neared the island of Tenerife, "They saw a great eruption of flames from the Peak of Tenerife [Mount Teide][14]; which is a lofty mountain." Ferdinand Columbus wrote of this geologic event, stating that his father, fearing the anxiety of the men in seeing huge flames stretch out to the sky, calmed the crew by recounting how volcanoes were a natural phenomenon occurring in places such as Italy (Mt. Etna).

August 25–30

Columbus reached Las Palmas late in August and hurried onboard the *Pinta*. Pinzón, for lack of a good reason, had not completed the rudder repairs, as if the Spanish mariner did not desire to expedite a construction remedy, alerting Columbus once again of possible duplicity. Immediately, he ordered men from the *Santa Maria* to help to find a permanent rudder solution. After days of feverish work, the crew succeeded in replacing *Pinta*'s rudder. At the same time, Columbus ordered *Niña*'s captain, Vicente Yáñez Pinzón, to alter its *latine* ["lateen" triangular] sail, transforming it into a square-rigged unit, increasing *Niña*'s sailing ability for angling into the wind (tacking).

August 31 to September 1

As the new month began, crewmen completed rudder repairs, and the fleet set sail for San Sebastián, Gomera. Often, writing on the rudder incident glossed over the affair as a minor setback, without realizing Columbus was determined to attempt the transatlantic crossing with two shallow-draft ships, *Niña* and *Pinta*, knowing full well the *Santa Maria*'s limitations while operating along unknown coastlines, harbors, and rivers. A question begs answering: Without *Pinta*, might Columbus have canceled the voyage or at least delayed the attempt? This scenario may have crossed his may during the duration of *Pinta*'s incapacitation.

September 2–5

Columbus arrived back in San Sebastián on Gomera and set about finalizing preparations for the transatlantic crossing. Everyone worked to take on as much food and water as possible, including well-salted meat and water casks filled to capacity.[15] He did meet Doña Beatriz Ines Peraza, and in her company, he was introduced to "many honourable Spanish gentlemen." These visitors, some of the first settlers on the westernmost Canary Island of Hierro, spoke stories declaring "that every year they saw land to the west of the Canaries; and others, natives of Gomera, affirmed the same on oath." This is an interesting passage, as there is no land within visible horizon limits west of El Hierro. It is even more interesting to ask why they would want to declare this observation in a formal manner—did Columbus or Doña Beatriz ask them to do so? Columbus must have known that such stories could not be true. He himself had sailed west of Hierro on his return trip from Guinea. It is a well-known fact that a person can only see approximately 3 miles or 5 kilometers to the ocean horizon while standing at sea level. However, El Hierro contains a mountain range with a top elevation of 1,500 meters.[16] At that height, a person might see 80 miles. More practical is Montaña Tenaca, a hill near the western coast of El Hierro, standing 625 meters (2,050 feet); from Tenaca, the limit reached 89 kilometers or 55 miles. This short, distant zone west of El Hierro is an area not probed by Columbus, so he may have paid some interest to this information, on the contrary; it would be of little help on this voyage.

During this conversation with these people on Gomera, Columbus relayed to them that while living in Portugal, he recalled a mariner soliciting a ship from King João II to seek land to the west. Columbus also noted hearing similar western land stories while visiting the Azores. The stories may have supplied some entertainment for Columbus, but he was preoccupied with stocking up on wood, water, meat, rope, and other supplies needed for the long voyage ahead. Evenings carried conversation late into the wee hours of the night with discussions between the captains and pilots of all three ships, reviewing the several maps Columbus planned to reference each day of the crossing. No doubt the three captains, with insistence by Columbus, ran through a variety of possible concerns, options dealing with separation due to violent storms, and daily course headings, confirming Columbus's wish that neither the *Pinta* nor the *Niña* should venture too far ahead of the flagship, the *Santa Maria*. In Kettell's and Fuson's translation of Las Casas's abridgment of the journal, a reader senses that Columbus did not doubt his plans; he only revealed the emotions of determination and urgency that he should lead the way. Yet, reading the Admiral's own words at this point in the journal may have revealed subtleties within his psychological state of mind. Did he realize, for example, that the next morning he would set out on the most transformative voyage in history? How could he know? Logic suggests, along with his previous statements to the Portuguese and Spanish committees who grilled him on the reliability of his sailing distances and destinations, that Columbus, indeed, understood the political and economic ramifications now on the line. One wonders what he thought about on the evening of September 5 as he laid down to sleep, isolated in his small confining cabin, a Genoese merchant representative surrounded by a Spanish crew that he did not yet know, a crew that reluctantly agreed to participate and had many doubts about the voyage.

As historian Felipe Fernández-Armesto has noted in his book, *1492: The Year the World Began*, the pre-1492 Spanish conquest of the Canary Islands became "a vital part of the context of Columbus."[17] The Italian explorer, in his short time on Gomera, most likely experienced a sense of how Spanish authorities controlled the European settlers, mostly Spanish and Indigenous peoples, the Guanche. Notwithstanding Columbus's lack of recording these experiences in his logbook, Fernández-Armesto provided a description of how the Guanche people successfully resisted Spanish attempts at establishing a permanent colony. Finally, a contingent of Spanish soldiers defeated the last uprising in 1488–1489. The immediate, on-site determination to enslave any native fighters was softened by Isabella and Ferdinand through the recommendations of an appointed special committee, although native lands were not restored to their original owners. Thus, we see a snapshot preview of what happens when a Spanish exploratory enterprise encounters a "primitive" or "savage" rudimentary culture.[18]

Notes

1 Kettell, *First Voyage of Columbus*, 10. Kettell's translation is mirrored almost exactly by Lardicci, *A Synoptic Edition*, 37.

2 Delaney related how the Spanish monarchs, after defeating the Moors at Granada, desired to rid their newly united nation of Jewish faith-holders. To this end, on March 30, 1492, an official decree went out declaring that all persons practicing Judaism make the choice, convert to Christianity or leave Spain. A time span of 4 months belied the limit of toleration; after that, all Jews would be forcibly removed. *Columbus and the Quest for Jerusalem*, 66, 70.

3 Fuson, *The Log of Christopher Columbus*, 51–53, and Dunn & Kelley interpret the passage as "great favors and ennobled me," 19.

4 Samuel Morison reported that the title *Almirante* derived from a tradition in Moorish kingdoms, meaning "Sea Lord." By 1492, an already existing Admiral of Castile, held by Don Alfonso Enríquez, exercised access and control over waters in and around Spain and the Canary Islands. This control included settling fishing or other commercial disputes, resolving conflict over seaport access, and dealing with piracy. For Columbus, this title became prized over that of Viceroy and Governor. *Admiral of the Ocean Sea*, 365.

5 In fact, it is the earliest detailed and comprehensive extant sailing log in the history of any civilization.

6 Dunn & Kelley, *The Diario*, 21. While this may sound as if Columbus is soliciting sympathy for the task of extensive journal writing, he knew that officials in the Spanish court would later question all his claims, and he wanted direct observational evidence to secure his rights.

7 Columbus used Italian (Roman) miles, adding 4 miles to an Italian league. All subsequent voyage maps will display leagues sailed into modern nautical miles, with three nautical miles equaling 1 league, as suggested by Robert Fuson.

8 Kettell, *Personal Narrative*, 12. Columbus, according to the journal entry that day, while in Palos preparing for the voyage, became aware that Rascón and Quíntero held a negative opinion of the voyage. Evidence does not disclose the foundation for their feelings. The duo may have had a personal dislike of Columbus (being a foreigner), or they knew of and disapproved of Columbus's plan to sail far out into the *Ocean Sea*. Fuson, in his account of this entry, believed Rascón held a partial legal interest in the *Pinta*. If this is true, Rascón had a financial reason for his objection.

9 Davidson, *Columbus: Then and Now*, 213. Reading the passage carefully, Davidson believed Columbus only blamed Gascon and Quintero for conspiring to delay the voyage and not the rest of *Pinta's* crew. Of course, Columbus could not know, at this point, of any mutinous designs as he resided on the *Santa Maria*, depriving him of daily and direct communication with the situation.

10 Cohen, *Christopher Columbus*, 39. Lardicci's translation substitutes "intelligent" with "great resourcefulness." *A Synoptic Edition, Historia*, LC 3, 179.

11 The fledging seaport did become completely secure from indigenous insurgency until 1489, affording Columbus a unique opportunity to see the recently enacted administrative system operating at the time. Fernández-Armesto, *1492*, 275. Fernández-Armesto credits the Canary Islands, correctly, as a stage on which the concept of colonial exploration, settlement, and exploitation would model future territorial enterprises.

12 The last August date recorded in the *Diario* was August 9; it begins again with the entry for September 6. The events between the two dates were discussed in Ferdinand's *Historie* and are referenced here from Fuson and Keen.

13 The Portugal Current is broad, diffusing its potential for a more rapid force; also impacting is the Portugal Coastal Countercurrent, particularly strong in the summer months. Bischof, et al. "The Portugal Current System."

14 Kettell, *Personal Narrative*, 13.

15 Taviani, Columbus: *The Great Adventure*, 89.

16 For example, Malpaso Peak reaches to 1,501 meters or, 4,925 feet.
17 Fernández-Armesto, *1492*, 274.
18 Fernández-Armesto sees the Canary Islands as a model from which Columbus and the Spanish Crown viewed extra-territorial expansion when encountering what they believed to be inferior or "infidel" cultures. Fernández-Armesto, *1492*, 274–78.

PART II

The Mid-Transatlantic Crossing

Part II details the multi-week voyage as the tiny fleet, stocked full of water and supplies, sets out on a westerly course, initially with crew support and high hopes of finding an early landfall. Readers learn of how Columbus kept two distance calculations, with the author purposing a theory previously expounded by other scholars, satisfying the needs of his Spanish crew with his previous logging methodology used when sailing on Genoese and Portuguese ships. An interesting episode looks at the first recorded scientific confrontation with the physical geographic phenomenon known as magnetic variation and how Columbus explained the events to his crew. As Columbus approaches the Atlantic frontier at 30 degrees west longitude, which he determined by known hours sailed and distance covered, mystery and confusion abound as the tiny fleet enters previously unknown waters, eventually initiating crew discomfort, then nervous small group discussions, finally demanding concessions from Columbus. Maps help give the reader a visual reference to each stage of the transatlantic crossing, noting course diversions, usually concluded by Columbus with Martín Pinzón of the *Pinta*, hoping to sight one of many expected islands lying off the coast of Asia.

Suspense builds daily, with Columbus attempting to reveal an ever-lessening of his pre-voyage confidence in course and distance. Events inch toward a mid-October showdown as sightings of birds and flora increase, only to reveal the western horizon of a seemingly endless ocean. Then it happens. On the evening of October 11, 1492, first Columbus claimed to see a light (fire), and then a crew member saw an actual landmass. Columbus drifted near the island and waited for the first light of day to move in closer, with excitement running high, and expectations running even higher. Columbus knew this would be a turning point in his career, but did he contemplate its full ramifications?

DOI: 10.4324/9781003464143-6

4

INTO THE *OCEAN SEA*

Canary Islands and Beyond, September 6–19

> To this end I decided to write down everything I might do and see and experience on this voyage, from day to day, and very carefully.
> —Christopher Columbus, *Diario*, 1492

The Voyage West Begins and the Deception of Recorded Mileage

September 6, 1492

The voyage began with little to no wind on September 6. For the most part, the three ships drifted approximately seven miles, an inauspicious start to a transoceanic attempt.[1] Columbus did not account for drift in calculating the distance he covered, only noting that he attempted to sail with little results due to a lack of wind. Interestingly, he reported his final position as somewhere between Gomera and Tenerife. This is possible, as he probably steered SE to gain distance from Gomera's eastern coastline. For at least part of the day, Columbus worried about a report of Portuguese ships waiting in ambush near the island of Hierro. This concern leads to an interesting dilemma. Columbus could ignore the report and sail directly west as soon as the winds picked up, or he could move southwest until the fleet cleared the southern coast of Hierro, then change direction to the west. It did not occur to Columbus to present this conundrum in the log entry. However, he may have diverted to the south and simply chose not to record this action. Why? Because he understood well his instruction not to move into known Portuguese waters, Columbus now resided near that point—the southernmost coast of Hierro.

Since we do not have Columbus's original log, only Las Casas's abstracted copy, researchers must question the content. Also, by all accounts, Columbus

DOI: 10.4324/9781003464143-7

did not want a report in his logbook, in any way, of a mention that his ships approached or crossed into Portuguese waters, threatening Spanish rights of sovereignty over any islands and mainlands discovered. There remains today an uncertainty about the directions and distances noted in the journal and recorded by Las Casas, suggesting a historical mistrust by all reading and interpreting his findings, beginning with this day's entry.[2]

September 7, 1492

Frustration must have set in early this morning, as Columbus found himself in the same situation as the previous day. His log recorded that the wind did not blow until early the following morning, as September Trade Winds in and around the Canary Islands weaken beginning in late summer and early autumn.[3] A conservative calculation of seasonal wind flow and current drift places the fleet approximately 8 additional miles further to the southwest as they prepare for stronger winds. The log does not indicate a sailing direction for this day, and this fact disrupts the sequencing of the distance sailed to an ultimate location on this day. There is a remote possibility that Columbus attempted to steer SW, providing him with the option to reset a course due west between Gomera and Hierro or continue southwest below Hierro. In selecting the latter, the Trade Winds are historically stronger.[4] If Columbus did select the latter, the latitudinal difference for his Caribbean destination would extend 30–40 miles south. That destination would be a point between the islands of Rum Cay and Samana Cay, as opposed to Watlings Island (San Salvador).[5]

September 8, 1492

The day started once again with only a slight wind. Luckily, later in the afternoon, the winds came up, and Columbus ordered a course heading due west. Maintaining that course proved difficult in a surprisingly heavy sea.[6] Overall, westerly progress moved along at a minimal pace, with Columbus noting 9 leagues (30 nautical miles) sailed. With little headway made in the first three days, Columbus must have hoped for strong winds to rise, as the voyage from Palos now stood at over 30 days.

September 9, 1492

Beginning the morning of the 9th, Las Casas's version of Columbus's actions refers to a curious decision by Columbus to record two daily distances sailed, one of which would be the true mileage and the other reduced by some arbitrary amount. The rationale for this is explained with these words: "that the crew might not be dismayed if the voyage should prove long." Many scholars have simply accepted this comment as further proof of Columbus's deceitful and self-serving nature. However, at least one scholar has attempted to explain another theory, a theory more in line with nautical tradition. James Kelley explained, "The admiral seems never to have intended to keep the truth from the crew, but rather to relate progress in units they could most readily understand."[7] In this account, Kelley revealed how the captains of the *Niña* and *Pinta*, (the Pinzón brothers) used the standard geometric mile (4,060 feet) instead of Columbus's Roman mile (4,860 feet).[8] Thus, Columbus kept the higher mileage figures to himself (geometric miles) while providing the lower calculation (Roman miles, 4,800 feet per mile) to his crew on the *Santa Maria*.[9] In his mind, this action was not duplicitous but rather a practical reality, as his tried-and-true method for measuring distance sailed. However, later, the captains and pilots of the other two ships disagreed with Columbus on the miles-to-date sailed.

This was the first day the fleet made good progress, sailing about 30 leagues. Frustratingly, Columbus soon learned that he could not immediately depend on the *Santa Maria*'s pilot(s) to steer a true westerly course. For some reason, the ships steered to the northeast, with *Niña* and *Pinta* following dutifully. Columbus needed to correct the heading several times that day. This issue of needed course correction may have to do with the nervousness of *Santa Maria*'s pilot, Sancho Ruiz, or a pronounced variation in magnetic readings of the ship's compass. As will be shown later, problems with magnetic variation become pronounced when compass readings vary from pole star (Polaris) sightings.[10]

September 10, 1492

This day, the logbook reported the fleet's best sailing mileage so far: 60 leagues or 180 nautical miles. Again, Las Casas, paraphrasing, noted that Columbus remained committed to reporting a lesser mileage to "the men." Why would Columbus repeat his concern? Recall that Columbus would be giving a copy of the log to the Spanish monarchs, and they would see this comment. The language used here raises Columbus's concern about the crew being "dismayed" on the 9th and "that the men might not be terrified if they should be long upon the voyage." This makes no sense; the crew knew they would be sailing some distance into the Atlantic. The voyage had just started, and the ships were still within the known waters of the eastern Atlantic. In addition, almost the entire crew brought considerable previous sailing experience to this voyage, and they certainly possessed the ability to gauge wind speed and ship progress throughout each day. The difference in mileage for this day revealed a 20% reduction for the crew. However, as you will see, Columbus is not consistent in his calculations, or Las Casas incorrectly transcribed the figures, reducing the mileage by as little as 6% on September 17.

September 11, 1492

Continuing his course west, Columbus reported seeing a "fragment of the mast of a vessel." From its size and shape, Columbus determined the ship's design as a 120-ton vessel. The ship's position that day put it on a longitude line with the Azores to the north and the Cape Verde Islands to the south, each approximately 700 miles distant. In essence, Columbus's trip laid a midway route between the two known island groups. Although this area of the Atlantic remained in known waters, ships did travel to this longitudinal zone; the mast might easily have drifted from either island group mentioned above. The mast proved too heavy when crew members tried to recover the piece. Columbus wrote that he covered 20 leagues, yet "reckoned" (for the crew) 16 leagues.

September 12, 1492

The account given for this day simply noted a western course covering 33 leagues but "reckoned less." At this point, the latitude and longitude of the ship's location approximated nearly the same value, around 28 degrees. Columbus must have counted this as a good sailing day, achieving 100 nautical miles with no concerns.

September 13, 1492

Making the same distance on this day as the last, Las Casas wrote that the currents ran contrary to their course. This seems odd, as retrograde currents rarely occur at this point in the Trade Wind system. On this day, Columbus noted that the compass heading varied slightly to the northwest from the position of the north star when they checked it at sunset. The next morning, 12 hours later, the needle varied the same amount but in the NE direction (Fuson). Kettell translated it differently, saying the variation was "about as much" in the same (NW) direction. Morison's account agrees with Fuson's writings, reasoning that Polaris appeared to rotate, due to the Earth's rotation, 180 degrees between sunset and sunrise the next day. Dunn & Kelley reasoned that, at this location in their voyage, magnetic variation did not play a major role, just the apparent distance from true north to Polaris, approximately 3.5 degrees. Columbus left this notation short, not wanting to raise a concern with his men.[11]

September 14, 1492

The winds slackened this day, as Columbus noted only 20 leagues (60 miles) sailed. Alert sailors made visual contact with several birds, including a *grajao*[12] and a "tropical bird, or water-wagtail." The log reported that these birds are never seen far from land; Columbus even ventured to limit their habitats to existing within 25 leagues from any land. Where he obtained that specific figure is unknown, possibly from a discussion with excited crew members. The mention of birds and other signs became a regular notation in the Columbus log, and it is certain that every sighting was promoted as an indication of land nearby.

September 15, 1492

The sea remained calm, and the wind strongly flowed this day, with the three ships covering 27 leagues (81 miles). At sunset, a blazing light immediately attracted the attention of Columbus and the crew. They saw "a remarkable bolt of fire fall into the sea." The flaming meteor assuredly frightened the crew, as Columbus reported that it hit the ocean about 4 or 5 leagues from their position. Despite the relative sophistication of most sailors of the 15th century, astronomical events such as a meteor striking the ocean in their near vicinity certainly raised concerns, if not fears, of impending doom. As you will see, another worrisome event added to their anxiety. That anxiety was understood when considering they had now sailed almost 700 miles west of the Canary Islands. Additionally, they had just reached 30 degrees west longitude or the 330 degrees global longitude point.[13] Most of the crew never previously sailed this far west; they were approaching the Atlantic frontier line—unknown waters, the *Ignotum Oceanun*, lie ahead.

Spanish cartographers, and Genoese as well, set the 0 degrees longitude line through the Canary Islands. Longitudinal degrees were set out in an easterly direction, extending 360 degrees back to the Canary Islands. In this manner, Columbus planned to head west using the reliable Trade Winds at a latitude of 28 degrees north, with an early destination to reach the 330–340 degrees global longitude, which equaled Columbus's and Spain's limit of western ocean penetration; these were known or familiar waters.

September 16, 1492

Aggressively, the winds blew consistently and strongly, enabling the little ships to make 39 leagues (117 miles) with "very pleasant weather." The described shipboard environment appeared, according to Las Casas's understanding, "most delightful, wanting nothing but the melody of the nightingales." Columbus, from time to time, did in his journal compare his voyage and land experiences to those of Spain, and he does so on this day. The September weather at his current location seemed like "Andalusia in April" (southern Spain). With the beautiful weather, sailors spotted large green stretches of surface weeds. Columbus knew of this phenomenon appearing in other eastern Atlantic regions, and he declared it a sign that land was near. Fuson, in his translation, referenced the weed sightings as the fleet entered the Sargasso Sea,[14] a vast area of floating weeds. Columbus, elated to see the phenomenon, as did his crew, realized the unexpected patch of weeds did not necessarily

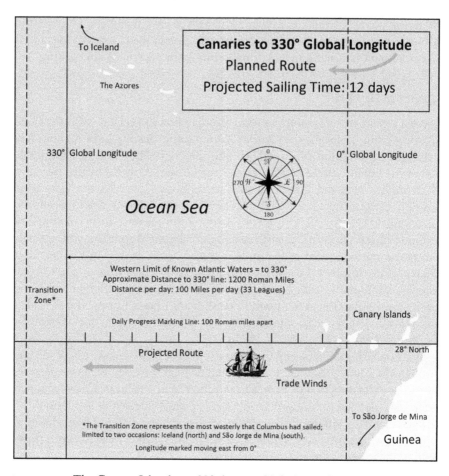

FIGURE 4.1 The Canary Islands: to 330 degrees Global Longitude

indicate nearness to the Asian continent; he stated, "the continent we shall find further ahead." On the contrary, Columbus and his crew believed the seaweeds drifted from some nearby island or reef, offering a tantalizing opportunity to search for that island, anchor in a pristine harbor, feel the firm, soft granules of beach sand as they relaxed, gather food, and water, knowing that Columbus may have been right; they were getting close.

The Difficulty Measuring Latitude at Sea and Magnetic Variation

September 17, 1492

The current proved strong, as the wind blew aggressively and reliably all day. Las Casas indicated that Columbus mentioned that the floating weeds appeared in large patches with short interruptions of clear seas. Most of the crew thought this meant a land sighting might occur at any time. Interestingly, the crew found the seawater in this ocean region less salty than in locations easterly, and the sea breezes softer. Columbus recounted how dolphins appeared; one of *Niña*'s crew cast a harpoon and killed a dolphin. Las Casas quoted Columbus this day, noting, "The admiral says here that these indications came from the west: 'Where I hope in that high God, in Whose hands are all victories, that very presently He will give us land.'"[15] Columbus also noted he personally saw a *water-wagtail*, a bird noted for remaining close to land.

One section of the entry reveals a difference of opinion in later translations. Kettell's 1827 account reads, "The pilots took the sun's amplitude [the sun's position from true west or east] and found that the needles varied to the N.W. a whole point [11.25 degrees] of the compass; the seamen were terrified and dismayed without saying why."[16] Fuson translated the account differently, referring to a reading on Polaris (North Star), not the Sun. He also downplays Kettell's declaration that the crew was "terrified" by substituting "caused some apprehension." Lardicci used the phrase "and the sailors were afraid and worried."[17] Cecil Jane used the neutral phrases "took the north" and "mark the north again at dawn."[18] He does not mention if it was the sun or the North Star. Dunn & Kelley translated, "The pilots took the north, marking it, and found that the compasses northwested a full point [i.e., 11.25 degrees]; and the sailors were fearful and depressed and did not say why."[19]

Why Kettell translated the method as utilizing the sun's amplitude, a method that may require the use of a quadrant or astrolabe for direct observation is unknown. He may have referenced the scientific fact that locations north of the Tropic of Cancer (23.5 degrees north latitude) always throw a shadow true north as the sun achieves its highest position in the sky; that shadow can be accurately measured.

There is another explanation for Kettell's version. European countries used the Julian calendar in 1492, while today we use the adjusted Gregorian version. Columbus and most mariners knew that the vernal and autumnal equinoxes marked the point where the sun rises due east and sets due west. Under the current Gregorian calendar, the autumnal equinox always falls between September 21 and 24. For Columbus, that day was September 17. This is the exact day he selected to measure the sun's amplitude. It is this author's theory that Kettell's use of the term amplitude fits the astronomical definition: the angular distance of a celestial object from the true east or west point of the horizon at rising or setting. On the morning of the 17th, that distance was 0 degrees. Thus, using a quadrant, Columbus and his pilots turned the instrument on its side and level. Next, they waited until the sun rose, fully exposed on the horizon. A pilot sighted along one edge of the 90 degrees side of the quadrant to the center of the sun, while another man held a compass just above the quadrant. Thus, the distance between magnetic north and true north may be determined.

The above explanation is noteworthy, as Kettell's early account is different from all subsequent versions. This leads one to believe that he was in error when thinking Columbus used the sun as a measuring object. However, the other translation versions refer to the term *pilots*, but it only takes one person to use a compass, sight the North Star, and record the difference. Fuson does admit that Columbus could have used the autumnal equinox as a general celestial guide in combination with plain dead reckoning for navigation. Up until September 17, an amplitude reading would register a little to the north of west, then after the equinox, increasingly south of west.

Kettell moved to next explain that Columbus ordered another amplitude check the next morning.

> The Admiral discovered the cause, and ordered them to take the amplitude again the next morning [September 18], when they found that the needles were true; the cause was, that the *star*, moved from its place, while the needles remained stationary.[20]

It appears that Kettell was in error when using the term *Sun* for the first reading, or that Columbus decided to use the North Star at dawn on the 18th as a check on the previous measurement.

Samuel Morison, in his excellent analysis of the Columbus log, does not mention amplitude. He believed that Columbus and his pilots used Polaris as their true north point on the 17th. Morison equated the wide difference between true north and magnetic north to the described distance of Polaris to true north (3.25 degrees) and the effect of magnetic variation.[21] Columbus's fleet, according to Morison, passed from east variation to west variation on the 14th. This zone of magnetic reversal confused Columbus as they attempted to read their compasses. By the 17th, the ships had reached a point where they were at 2 degrees magnetic variation west.[22] One can add 2 degrees to 3.25 degrees, and you arrive at half a compass point, 5.25 degrees west of true north. Morison dismissed the missing one-half point by stating the pilots could easily have made a mistake.

All translations report that the next morning (dawn of the 18th) the reading was "true." Columbus told his crew that the explanation was simple, Polaris had moved. Morison gave credit for Columbus knowing this astronomical fact, even though Columbus was not sure why it moved. Polaris had, in the 12 hours from the first reading, appeared to rotate 180 degrees and resided now on the other side of true north. Thus, the apparent distance had erased the perceived distance discrepancy; the compass and Polaris "were true."[23]

We do not know the exact magnetic variation amplitudes or isogonic patterns for 1492. Several attempts have been made during the late 19th century, but they are based on limited data points. However, the National Center for Environmental Information, part of NOAA, did compile and map east and

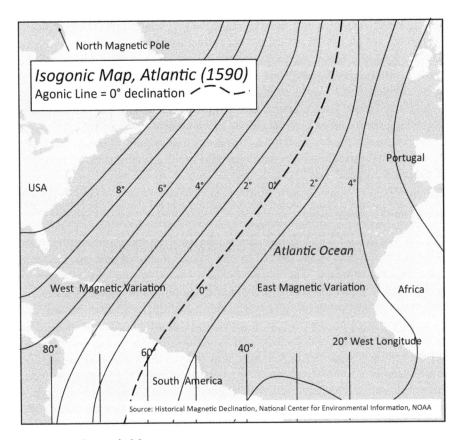

FIGURE 4.2   Isogonic Map

west magnetic patterns for dates as early as 1590, when multiple data points provided sufficient data to imply a global pattern.

Entering Unknown Waters (*Sea of Darkness*)

September 18, 1492

Already suspicious that some crew members might sabotage the voyage, Columbus listened carefully when Martín Alonso Pinzón in the *Pinta* pulled alongside the *Santa Maria* to inform the admiral he sensed land nearby. When asked to explain this impulse, Pinzón described "a great number of birds go toward the west" and sought permission to sail ahead. Taking a few minutes to consider his captain's request, Columbus pondered his current position and situation. His fleet passed the 330 degrees global longitude (30 degreeswest longitude) line days before; now, he was penetrating Region 3, an area completely unknown, a sea of darkness, and not sailed by any Iberian mariner.

Letting Pinzón cruise in advance and make the first landfall might prove disadvantageous for his preferred desires. The only possible land in this zone, at this westerly location, according to Columbus's pre-voyage calculations, would be small miscellaneous islands. Then again, it just might be Antillia, purported to be of sufficient size to lay an official claim and resupply.

As Pinzón raced ahead, a large, dark cloud appeared in the north. Columbus interpreted this to mean that the clouds gathered around a nearby island. Yet, when Pinzón returned later that day, he reported no island. This day, the Trade Wind current carried the ships smoothly and rapidly, accumulating 55 leagues of progress—a good day.

September 19, Wednesday

The day started out with a pelican appearing near the ships and another later in the afternoon. Las Casas seemed to imply it was a second bird, not the same one from that morning. This is significant as most pelican species, as mentioned by Las Casas in this entry, fly near land, rarely exceeding 20 leagues.[24] Columbus today appeared more interested in sighting land than on any day since departure. John Boyd Thacher translated Columbus's nervousness: "The Admiral did not wish to delay, beating [changing course] about in order to find out if there was land, but he was sure that toward the north and toward the south there were some islands, as in fact there were, and he was going between them."[25] Dunn and Kelley, and Lardicci remarked that Columbus now made it clear that his "purpose was to continue forward as far as the Indies, and the weather was good."[26]

Checking his onboard maps, Columbus pondered the nearness of the islands. Which islands could they be? The fact that Las Casas wrote, "as in fact there were," indicates that Columbus believed many of the medieval mappae mundi and portolan charts depicting wayward groups of islands throughout this region of the *Ocean Sea*. In the end, logic prevailed when Columbus declared to his crew that the island might be Antillia but could not be Cipangu, and Cipangu remained Columbus's first choice for landing, if he stopped at all. He had believed as much in prior analyses of maps and globes, such as Fra Mauro's map.[27] His reasoning for this is clear: He wanted to "discover" something big, something important, not trivial islands such as the Canary Islands, Porto Santo, or Madeira. Later, once contact with a "civilized" island or mainland was secured, he could find and claim smaller, less important geographic places.

Now, Las Casas shifts from third-person narration to the written words of Columbus, stating, "And the weather is good, so that, God being pleased, all will be seen on the way back."[28] Las Casas then explained how the pilots reported their sailing distances. *Niña*'s pilot found himself 440 [1,320 nautical miles] leagues from the Canaries; the *Pinta* 420 leagues [1,260 nautical miles];

and the pilot of the *Santa Maria*, exactly 400 [1,200 nautical miles].[29] Thacher claimed that Columbus persuaded the other pilots that his figure indicated the correct distance sailed, preferring the lower number to allay crew fears. It is noteworthy that frustration must have reared up daily as hopeful signs of land during daylight hours dissipated by nightfall. Las Casas in *Historia* sensed crew uneasiness, writing, "That they were going through another world whence they would never return."[30]

This description fits nicely with this author's description of Region 3 noted earlier in this book, where, for the first time, no one onboard any of the three ships had sailed this far west. In effect, they had now reached the 15th-century Atlantic frontier, where anything might happen. To add to the crew's dilemma, the daily prevailing winds and currents pushed the ships inexorably west; the question arose: Can we successfully find a heading to take us home? By the next morning, another 25 leagues receded behind them; deeper and deeper, they probed the *Ocean Sea*.

Notes

1 He left around 12:00 p.m., so he drifted for 18 hours that day. Studies of surface current speed in and around the Canary Islands for September measure a low of 10 cm per second to a high of 30. This is equal to just over nine nautical miles of travel over a 24-hour period. Gyory, "The Canary Current," Ocean Surface Currents.

2 This author conducted a geographic computer-measured analysis of this possibility using the same sailing distances and corrections for drift and magnetic variation. However, no evidence has surfaced suggesting that Columbus did, in fact, conduct a flanking move south to avoid Portuguese contact. It is interesting to consider one scenario in which the Portuguese captain positioned his ship at a point some 20 nautical miles west of the southern coast of Gomera. At this strategic point, centered latitudinally between Hierro and Gomera, the Portuguese would have over a 50 percent chance of sighting and engaging Columbus's small fleet. Concerning Las Casas and mileage written in the journal, scholars point to his lack of understanding of everything and anything nautical, including the difference between a measurement on the high seas—the difference between miles and leagues being one example.

3 Azorin-Molina, "Wind speed variability over the Canary Islands," Abstract and Conclusion #1.

4 Morison, *Admiral of the Ocean Sea*, 198.

5 There is no direct evidence to conclude Columbus continued SW on the following day, as all accepted translations specifically cite that on September 8, he "steered their course W (West)." However, Columbus may have done this to flank any Portuguese ships waiting for him in the waters between Hierro and Gomera. Also, as noted earlier, by proceeding southwest to a lower latitude, he would have picked up stronger Trade Winds. Watlings is sometimes spelled Watling.

6 Heavy or rough seas in the eastern Atlantic are more common in the late autumn and winter months.

7 Kelley, "The Navigation of Columbus," 127–9.

8 The more feet per mile, the results in fewer miles covered.

9 The Geometric mile results in more miles, while the larger Roman mile equates to fewer total miles covered. Kelley's theory here does help account for the subsequent

issues historians have encountered when reconciling Columbus's given interisland Caribbean sailing distances.

10 There are a variety of reasons why the fleet may have been off course at the start of their westward journey. Chief among these is a problem with the *Santa Maria*'s compass. Pilots usually followed the *loxodromes*, or rhumb lines, drawn on an existing sea chart. Often the effects of known currents are built into the rhumb lines, but in this case, the *Santa Maria*'s may not have had such as sea chart or understood the impact of currents west of the Canary Islands. However, the entry implies that Columbus did, in fact, have this information. See Fuson, *The Log of Christopher Columbus*, "Navigation," 42–44.

11 Dunn & Kelley, *The Diario*, 31. A similar situation arose on September 17.

12 This bird was probably a red-billed chough, a member of the crow family. The *grajao's* distribution included southern Spain, Western North Africa, and the Canary Islands.

13 This location is as noted on Ptolemy's map of the world. Measurement originated in the Canary Islands and proceeded eastward around the globe, with most versions of Ptolemy's maps restricting locations from 0 degrees to 180 degrees. This author extrapolated from 180 degrees to 360 degrees.

14 Columbus did not yet realize how extensive the sea of weeds was. Today, it is approximately in the same location as it was in the 15th century. The massive spread of seaweed is hundreds of miles wide, with a northern limit near 35° north Latitude and a western extension to about 70 degrees west longitude.

15 Jane, *The Journal of Christopher Columbus*, 11

16 Kettell, *First Voyage of Columbus*, 17.

17 Lardicci, A Synoptic Edition, DB 9, section 5, 41.

18 Jane, *The Journal of Christopher Columbus*, 11.

19 Dunn & Kelley, *The Diario*, 33. The translators explain that sailors sighted Polaris (North Star) and compared it to their compass reading.

20 Kettell, *Personal Narrative*, 19.

21 Magnetic variation, the difference between the true north and the magnetic north pole, fluctuates through time. It is measured using lines of equal variation, termed *isogonic*. No one is certain as to the isogonic variations in 1492, as the National Oceanographic and Atmospheric Association (NOAA) has only estimated back to the year 1590. This author contacted scientists at NOAA and relayed Columbus's journal information concerning his accounts on September 13 and 17 to see if they could build a global magnetic variation construct. However, at the time of this writing, no map exists. Personal communication, July 7–10, 2021.

22 Morison never explains how he knew the magnetic variation in 1492. As noted in the above footnote, NOAA scientists today suggested to this author that it is impossible to determine magnetic variation that far back without knowing the exact location of magnetic north at that time or substantial global variation readings; even then, isogonic lines distribute unevenly, compounding formulations of distribution. However, backtracking from San Salvador Island and using mileages and course directions stated in the journal, one can estimate magnetic variation implied from the 1590 NOAA model.

23 Of course, Polaris's observed movement resulted from the Earth's rotation; Polaris does move, but its distance is so remote that observed changes in Polaris's position from Earth are difficult to measure, taking months or years and using parallax measurements at 6-month intervals. See Taviani, *Columbus: The Great Adventure*, for a more in-depth discussion of this incident, 93.

24 For the most part, this is true. Pelicans gather along the coastal regions of every continent and usually range locally for breeding and feeding purposes. However, when necessary, pelicans have been known to fly hundreds of kilometers from tagged locations—usually along coastlines.

25 Thacher, *Christopher Columbus: His Life, His Work*, 522. Dunn & Kelley translate this section exactly as Kettell.

26 Dunn & Kelley, *The Diario*, 37. Las Casas goes on to add that Columbus "on the way back all would be seen," indicating that Columbus remained committed to finding the Asian coast as his top priority. Lardicci, *A Synoptic Edition*, DB 11, section 6, 42.

27 Caraci believes that Juan Gil's notion that Columbus may have used "one or more nautical charts… derived from or analogous to Fra Mauro's globe." Caraci suggests that "A new more careful reading of the legends of that globe in relation to the statements made by Columbus at that time of the first voyage could be useful." Personal communication, July 17, 2023.

28 Ibid.

29 Fuson, *The Log of* Columbus, 64. Dunn & Kelley, interestingly, do not state this section as a quote from Columbus, preferring "and the pilot of the ship in which the Admiral sailed," assuming these to be paraphrased from Las Casas. These reported distances support the idea that Columbus used a standard mile different from that of the Spanish pilots on the *Niña* and *Pinta*. The percentage change between the Spanish Geometric Mile (4,060 miles) and Columbus's Roman Mile (4,860) is approximately 19 percent, representing a five percent change from *Pinta*'s figure and a ten percent change from *Niña*. This might be explained by considering the accumulated errors of daily nautical readings from different ships and/or understanding Las Casas's transcribed numerical errors.

30 Lardicci, *A Synoptic Edition, Historia*, LC 11, 183.

5

SEARCHING FOR THE INDIES

September 20 to October 11

> I am having serious trouble with the crew, despite the signs of land that we have and those given to us by Almighty God.
> —Christopher Columbus, *Diario*, September 23, 1492

Looking for an Island, any Island

September 20, Thursday

Columbus needed to respond to his anxious crew, and he did. For the first time since leaving Gomera, he ordered a course change. The direction chosen, WNW, however, revealed constantly changing winds, making the new tack difficult; the ships eked out only 8 leagues. Visits by interested pelicans (possibly terns) briefly freshened hopes of land as sailors caught, surprisingly, one bird. Another pelican flew over from the northwest, reviving the idea that the bird flew from its home island in search of food. A few sailors, no doubt, hoped their captain would now order a slight direction change to trace the bird's path back to its source; Columbus did not. Later, a new patch of dark green seaweed appeared dense and almost ominous due to its thickness and color, and progress slowed. Rumors quickly spread, reminiscing about old stories about how Saint Amador sailed unaware into an area of the frozen sea, unable to dislodge his ship.[1] Columbus ordered the pilot to steer clear of the thickest accumulations, while nervous crew members leaned their heads over the ships' sides, searching for clearings ahead.

September 21, Friday

Making only 13 leagues, Columbus decided not to report additional crew anxiety but focused on the environmental aspects of his current geographic

DOI: 10.4324/9781003464143-8

setting, noting, "The sea was very smooth, like a river, and the air the best in the world."[2] With an additional whale sighting account, a reader might assume that Columbus and crew now appeared relaxed, as if enjoying some sort of pleasure cruise. The crew may have thought otherwise. With the course now set in an NNW direction, Martín Pinzón and Columbus hoped an island bump might suddenly appear on the horizon. No disconcerting statements referencing crew fears made it into this day's description despite sliding farther into Region 3. Instead, the account described vast amounts of seaweed stretching out far to the horizon, thick and green, only interrupted momentarily by a breaching whale, always a welcome sight as Columbus believed whales never strayed far from a seashore. At 42 degrees west longitude or 318 degrees global longitude, the fleets were drifting, not sailing, slowly deeper into unknown waters.

September 22, Saturday

No one sighted land today. The wind, not quite settled in one direction, allowed Columbus to bear a new heading WNW. Understanding the character of the wind, the pilots guided the ships efficiently, fully covering 30 leagues. Columbus noted, "This contrary wind was very necessary for me, because my people were much excited at the thought that in these seas no wind ever blew in the direction of Spain."[3] On one hand, this might appear as good news to the crew, but Columbus realized that "contrary winds" also left open a scenario with nervous crew members demanding a return to Spain. Later in the day, the ships entered a seaweed-free zone, only to reenter another large patch in the evening.

September 23, Sunday

Columbus, somewhat undecided and under pressure to find land, allowed frequent course changes. Early in the day, he ordered a NW run, and then asked the pilot to steer more to the north. Not happy with the results of these command decisions, the Genoese explorer, for a brief time, tried a direct westerly course. The result only allowed 22 more leagues of sailing progress. They saw a dove and a booby, which is reported to live near freshwater rivers. Masses of seaweed stood before them like a gigantic three-dimensional carpet, complete with tiny crabs. The lonely, cautious ships moved steadily through the morass of surface weeds, Columbus and crew, prayerfully thankful, internally hoping for continued progress.

Later in the day, grumbling stirred among the crew. Where was the land? Hints of dissatisfaction permeated the isolated small-group crew conversations. The wind direction varied first from the west, then from the southwest. Yet the surface remained calm, a strange situation. Word spread from crew members, suggesting their time was running out for any return to their homeland.

More ominously, that afternoon, the "sea rose very much," as if out of no action of the wind. Yes, no wind accompanied this strange event. Thankfully, toward nightfall, as if from a silent Columbus prayer, Columbus believed God answered his request; a strong wind erupted, but the wind came from the direction they steered. Progress then slowed. Columbus, astonished at such a perceived divine event, wrote, "Thus the high sea was very necessary to me, such as had not appeared but in the time of the Jews when they went out of Egypt and murmured against Moses, who delivered them out of captivity."[4] Now at 45 degrees west longitude (315 degrees global longitude), he needed to make an important decision. He prayed; it was Sunday.

A Nervous Crew Puts Pressure on Columbus

September 24, Monday

The decision predictably pointed west. Columbus ordered the fleet to head due west once again. There would be no altering course to search for islands; if they appeared, then he would halt; otherwise, on to the Indies. Columbus saw God's hand in this decision, hoping that a strong, reliable easterly wind would push them toward their goal. But no; instead, weak, contrary winds prevailed. Las Casas's journal entry is brief this day, but Ferdinand Columbus in *Historie* described a growing crew distrust of Columbus and his decisions. The voyage appeared at a critical point. Most resentments recast the idea that the fleet had already sailed too far and still no islands or mainlands appeared. Certain men saw any further attempt west as the flagrant obsession of a foreigner, only desirous of personal fame and fortune.[5] All three ships leaked, and provisions ran low. Rumors circulated in favor of presenting an ultimatum to the Italian, out-of-touch dreamer—turn back or be pitched unceremoniously overboard. The ships dragged along, claiming only 14 leagues.[6]

September 25, Tuesday

Pressure mounted for Columbus to do something. Slight winds continued, and little distance was covered. By early afternoon, Columbus signaled for Martín Pinzón to bring *Pinta* alongside. Pinzón then came onboard the *Santa Maria*. Retiring to the admiral's small cabin, the pair of mariners reviewed a map Columbus had sent to Pinzón three days prior. The map must have depicted many small islands in this vicinity, as noted by Las Casas in his copying of the Barcelona journal. After some discussion, Columbus convinced Pinzón to follow the agreed-upon course, due west.

The reader should be aware that years later, the Spanish crown in 1513 attempted legal action to halt further honoring of the *Santa Fe Capitulations* on the grounds that it was Martín Pinzón who, at this point in the voyage, urged Columbus to continue and that it was Pinzón who guided the ships en route; without such action, no discovery would have followed.[7]

Pinzón went back to his ship. As sunset began, Pinzón again maneuvered close to the *Santa Maria*, shouted that land was seen, and demanded the agreed-upon prize money.[8] Immediately, crew members on all three ships repeated *Gloria in excelsis* (Glory to God in the highest). Everyone, including Columbus, followed with their eyes, the pointing arms extending outward from Pinzón, straining in a SW direction, seeking a lump of land sitting on the surface of the *Ocean Sea*. Some crew members believed they saw something; others did not.

Columbus then ordered the small fleet to change their heading toward the sighted land. Darkness came, and the lump of land faded. Notwithstanding, the fleet continued the SW heading all night. Volunteers on each ship abandoned scheduled sleep time to linger at their ship's bow, hoping to see the land fires of some unknown civilization. The ships had sailed 4.5 leagues W and then 17 leagues SW.

September 26, Wednesday

The fleet's crew greeted dawn with anticipation not seen since leaving Palos, Spain. Columbus held course for a short time, but soon the reality of yesterday's sighting appeared; the land sighted by *Pinta*'s crew "was nothing but clouds." Disappointed yet determined, Columbus abandoned any further search in a SW direction and resumed sailing to the west. No word was mentioned as to how the crew reacted as the ships returned to a seemingly endless course west. The wind, once again, reliably held from behind, pushing the little ships ahead. This was a perfect sailing day with the sea "like a river, the air soft and mild." Columbus recorded 31 leagues but "reckoned" only 24 leagues for the logbook.

September 27, Thursday

Another day and perfect sailing weather calmed the fears of the crew. With 24 leagues of ocean crossed today, the pilots held to what they thought was a magnetic compass heading west. Unknown to them, the ships' compasses drifted approximately 3 degrees NW due to magnetic variation.[9] This estimate is the value given by Samuel Morison but is rarely noted in other books about the first voyage. As reported earlier, this author queried NOAA scientists on this matter, providing journal details in hopes of verifying Morison's calculations, but nothing conclusive derived from that inquiry. No matter the accuracy of Morison's calculation, some value of magnetic variation occurred as they continued a straight-line course due west. In effect, the ship's course shifted slightly to the SW. They were now heading in a W-by-S direction.

September 28, Friday

Columbus may not have known his exact position at this time, but his small fleet had arrived at 50 degrees west longitude (310 degrees global longitude). With his unbeknownst southern drift, he was back in the 28 degrees north latitude zone, very close to the latitude when he began his voyage. The wind calmed, drifting seaweed thinned out, and some of the crew caught dories (narrow-bodied small fish) as the fleet glided along, making only 14 leagues.

At this point, Columbus had sailed 1,783 nautical miles from the Canary Islands, and his fleet was deep into the *Sea of Darkness*. He originally estimated approximately 3,000 miles from Spain to reach Asia; it would be an additional 1,320 nautical miles to his first landfall—close to his pre-voyage calculation.

September 29, Saturday

The wind picked up a bit, and the admiral's fleet made 24 leagues. Seaweed appeared, again, in a full circle around them, yet did not seem to impede progress. A *rabihorcado* (Frigatebird), seen regularly in the Cape Verde Islands, flew nearby, and Columbus recalled how the red puff-bellied, long-beaked bird intimated pelicans to regurgitate food, whereupon the frigatebird devoured the contents. As with pelicans, the crew believed this bird did not stray far from land. Las Casas, in his description, appeared quite pleased with the ocean conditions and the crew's contentment. Longitude-wise, the ships entered the 52 degrees west longitude zone (308 degrees global longitude). They attempted to steer due west all day.

September 30, Sunday

Approaching 53 degrees west longitude, Columbus looked concerned about the lack of strong breezes. The fleet only covered 14 leagues of distance. Today, various species of birds flew about the fleet, indicating, as Columbus noted, "that they are not straying about having lost themselves."[10] For the admiral, this meant that land must be close at hand.

Las Casas made an interesting mention of a star observation made by Columbus that evening and the following dawn. The two stars of the Ursa Minor (Little Dipper) constellation that form the far side of the ladle, Beta (Kochab) and Gamma (Pherkad), were referred to as *the Guards*. Shining bright, Kochab is a 2.06 magnitude star, with Gamma Pherkad not far behind at 3.0 magnitude. The other stars in the Little Dipper fade at magnitude 4.2 or dimmer; thus, ancient and medieval astronomers called the two brighter stars, the *guards* of the north star (Polaris). From Earth, Kochab and Pherkad appear to rotate close to Polaris. Like the long and distant hands of a clock, the nighttime rotation tells time.

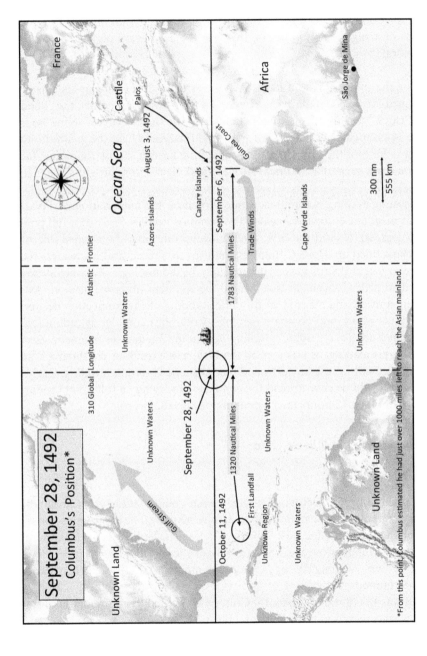

FIGURE 5.1 September 28, 1492

The entry translation from Kettell reads,

The constellation called *Las Guardias*, which at evening appeared in a west-erly direction, was seen in the NE. the next morning, making no more pro-gress in a night of nine hours; this was the case every night, as says the Admiral.[11]

This is quite impossible and most likely an error by Las Casas in his original abridgment of the journal. In the evening on the 29th in September, the "hands of the clock" at sunset, the *guards* pointed west; this is correct. Nine hours later, a 24-hour clock equals 135 degrees, and this would have the *guards* point-ing to the SE, not the NE. Columbus must have known this astronomical fact and would not suggest a comment such as "making no more progress in a night of nine hours."

This same evening, Columbus wanted to check the culmination of Polaris with his magnetic compasses again. The compass needles deviated a full point [10–11 degrees], toward the NW. The following morning, the compass needle and Polaris lined up. Here, Columbus confirms to himself and his readers that the answer is that Polaris moves; interestingly, he did not logically conclude that it was the Earth's movement that created the apparent observed motion. As if to assure himself and his crew of his understanding of the connection between celestial navigation and compass readings, Columbus confidently announced, "the needles are always right."[12] Sailing now in the 3.5 degrees magnetic varia-tion zone, his reading, as was true on the 17th, was a result of combining Pola-ris' displacement from true north and the magnetic variation, totaling nearly 8 degrees. It would be easy to read the compass as varying "a full point" toward the NW and then 12 hours later estimating the needles as true.[13]

October Arrives but Still No Land

October 1, Monday

The journal entry for October 1 needs special consideration. All translations point to Columbus again attempting to deceive his crew. The entry states that the fleet continued sailing due west, covering 25 leagues. Unknown to the admiral, he was transitioning from the 3.5 degrees magnetic variation to 4 degrees. So, in reality, he was heading W by S. For the moment, variation accumulation remained limited.

As it was the first of the month, Columbus decided to compute the overall distance since clearing the island of Hierro. The *Santa Maria*'s pilot, Pedro Alonso Niño, added his daily mileages, and they came to 578 leagues (1,734 nautical miles). Las Casas reported that Columbus told his crew they had sailed 584 leagues, hiding the truth of the real number, 707 leagues (2,121 nau-tical miles).[14]

It stretches logic to think that Columbus continued to deceive his men, thinking that a 129-league difference made that much of a difference. The fact also needs challenging that Niño, an accomplished navigator in his own right, calculated a different figure than his superior.[15] As already argued in a previous section, the difference is more likely the result of reporting the Geometric Mile (Portuguese) standard to his crew, which Spanish mariners used, while retaining the more familiar Roman Mile standard for himself.[16] It is interesting to note that no crew objections arose in the last few days, despite their admiral's determination to continue westward. If the crew, on September 24, reached high anxiety about the distance sailed, why are they quiet now? Or did Columbus simply refuse objections to this day?

October 2, Tuesday

Again, much the same occurred this day with no crew objections as the ships churned out 39 leagues. Ocean currents powerfully drove each ship along a silent, smooth surface. Las Casas reported that Columbus praised God for the mass of seaweed now running in an east-to-west line. This indicated a strong, unrelenting subsurface current pushing the ships where Columbus wanted them to go. Today, someone on board the *Santa Maria* caught a fish. Another crew member pointed to a seagull; were they getting close?

October 3, Wednesday

The wind grew again today. Everything pointed to a fast push to the Indies. An incredible 47 leagues (141 nautical miles) were recorded in the logbook. Sharp-eyed crew members spotted sandpipers sitting on thick seaweed, and the seaweed itself looked to have blossoms or fruit projecting upward. On the negative side, no birds flew near the fleet this day, and Columbus worried. He noted the possible scenario where the fleet may have "left the islands behind them, which were depicted on the charts."[17]

Columbus also briefly talked with the crew about not wanting to "beat about" any longer looking for islands, preferring to reach straight and fast for the "Indies." In concluding his comments to his men, he warned that a delay "would not be wise." One wonders exactly what this comment was meant to explain. Were they running low on fresh water and provisions? Did Columbus fear a mutiny? Did he mean not wise for his men, himself, or both?

October 4, Thursday

In an unreal display of sailing efficiency, the fleet zoomed along, making 63 leagues (189 nautical miles). It would seem that Columbus, in recording his greatest daily distance, did not disclose happiness or even satisfaction with this feat. Such distance progress pushed the fleet into the 5.5 degree magnetic variation zone, increasing the schism between the direction they thought they were sailing; their true direction now edged ever to the south.

A large flock of sandpipers and two pelicans arrived and landed among the rigging. One of the ship's boys threw a rock and hit one.[18] Later, more birds of a different variety appeared overhead. Again, there is no account of crew dissatisfaction.

October 5, Friday

Friday proved to be another great day for sailing, with the ships making 57 leagues. Columbus noted it was perfect sailing weather—strong, steady wind, and few whitecaps—just a smooth surface. Las Casas felt the admiral's words described the day best. "To God," he says, "be many thanks given, the air being pleasant and temperate, with no weed, many sandpipers, and flying fish[19] coming on the deck in numbers."

By the end of the day, Columbus's fleet entered the 6 degree magnetic variation area, again tricking the pilots into a more southerly course than believed.

October 6, Saturday

This day, the wind slackened a bit. The fleet made 40 leagues, still a solid day's sailing. Las Casas entered a contradictory statement today in which he claimed Martín Pinzón pulled *Pinta* alongside the *Santa Maria* and came onboard for a discussion with the admiral. According to the Kettell, Jane, and Miller translations, Pinzón wanted to steer W by SW, desiring to find Cipangu or some nearby island. Columbus demurred, explaining that Pinzón did not want to steer straight for the mainland (Cathay). The admiral countered by arguing that they should continue due west and pick up Cipangu or other islands on the voyage home. Columbus understood the geographic reality that the true location of Cipangu was unknown, or any other island in this part of the *Ocean Sea*. Once before, they diverted their course without achieving anything, so why do it again? He explained to Pinzón and his crew that if they stayed on a due west course, they must strike the Asian mainland.

Fuson, in his translation, recognized how Columbus sensed the decision to remain on a strict due west course added to the crew's anxiety.

October 7, Sunday

Weak winds lessened even more as the day dragged on. Their daytime progress only reached 23 leagues. Columbus's due west course ran slightly more south than he knew, for the fleet reached the 7 degree magnetic variation zone. Their western longitude extended to 69 degrees, while their north latitude mark lowered to 27 degrees. Columbus did not record a bearing check on Polaris for this day; if he had, he might have noticed the lower latitude, a latitude designated as Portuguese waters.

Vicente Jáñez Pinzón, Martín's brother, as captain of the *Niña*, sailed out ahead of the fleet. Its sleek body and sharply cut sail proved a fast caravel. Vicente believed he could spot land and report to Columbus; in doing so, the admiral would be obliged to recognize the sighting and the promised award. A little later in the day, Columbus heard a cannon shot from *Niña*, the signal for sighting land. Vicente lowered his sails and waited for *Pinta* and the *Santa Maria* to arrive. By now, the evening offered a clear horizon, but no land appeared in the distance. Birds flew over, coming from the north and heading southwest. Some of the crew believed this to be a sign of birds flying south for the coming winter or that land must exist to the southwest.

Columbus considered the latter possibility, as he knew that Portuguese discoveries often came about by following the flight direction of birds. He then ordered a course change for the first time in days. He would now follow the birds; the pilots steered WSW. This new course change occurred just before sunset. With some breeze, the fleet made another 5 leagues at night, for a daily total of 28 leagues.

October 8, Monday

The new direction, WSW, provided some hope to the crew of sighting land. While the breeze relented and the fleet only made 12 leagues, the sea, once again, flattened like a tabletop, smooth and slow-running. Columbus likened the movement to a Spanish river near Seville. Las Casas again copied some of Columbus's words: "Thanks be to God," says the admiral, "the air is very soft like the [sic] April at Seville; and it is a pleasure to be here, so balmy are the breezes." Seaweed abounded, as did the flocks of birds; one of them seemed to follow their course.

The day before, October 7, Vicente Pinzón, captain of the *Niña*, fired a cannon shot, signaling a land sighting. Also, that day, large flocks of birds flew overhead, winging their way south. Columbus, thinking land was close, ordered the fleet to sail in a southwest direction.

October 9, Tuesday

The fleet continued on a SW course, in reality, a SW by S heading. Considering the 7.5 degree magnetic variation, the weather remained beautiful, but the breeze slowed. Anxious to try anything that might allow for an island or mainland sighting, Columbus, after sailing 5 leagues, abruptly changed to a W by N course for 4 leagues. The fleet, as sunset approached, had sailed 11 leagues. Birds appeared in great numbers, surely a sign of land nearby. The last few days, Columbus limited his entries; he must have been nervous, spending endless

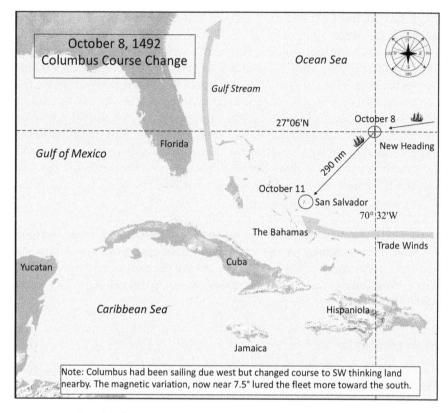

FIGURE 5.2   October 8, 1492: Course Change

hours on deck, searching for land. The fleet now sat at 71 degrees west longitude (289 degrees global longitude), further west than any other European ship in history.[20] Land should have appeared by now; something was wrong.

October 10, Wednesday

Returning to a WSW course, they achieved an impressive 59 leagues. The ships now arrived in the 8 degrees magnetic variation zone and resided, by the end of the day, at 73 degrees 25 minutes west longitude and 24 degrees 38 minutes north latitude. Columbus still did not record doing a celestial reading on Polaris. If the ship remained in calm waters, he would have noticed that their location now was well below the 28 degrees north latitude line. This is a critical moment in the voyage, as his instructions included strong language from the Spanish monarchs to avoid Portuguese-claimed waters. The prior treaty of Alcáçovas (1479) between Spain and Portugal prominently declared that all waters of the *Ocean Sea* below the Canary Islands, thus far uncharted, belonged exclusively to Portugal. The southern tip of Hierro was the southernmost point of the Canary Island group. Hierro's southern peninsula sat at 27 degrees 38 minutes north latitude. Columbus was sailing in Portuguese waters. Or was he; the intent of the treaty referenced eastern Atlantic locations and made no note of future expeditions to the west?

Finding land had now become a top priority. The crews of all three ships complained that the voyage looked hopeless. Many expressed fears and wanted to turn the ships around. Columbus attempted to speak with his crew, "giving them good hopes of the advantages they might gain from it." Further complaining drew a serious and firm response from the admiral; Las Casas explained, "however much they complain, he had to go to the Indies, and that he would go on until he found them, with the help of our Lord."[21]

October 11, Thursday

Steering WSW, Columbus noticed the ocean becoming "heavier," winds blowing billowing from behind, waves reaching the highest since leaving the Canaries. The crew at first felt uneasy, holding to their assigned positions and ready for orders. As the day wore on, numerous sightings of floating objects became routine; one sailor saw a cane and a log. Another crew member spotted an interesting object. He leaned over the railing of the *Santa Maria* and, with a long pole, retrieved a wooden stick; it was straight. On closer examination, cut markings on the side of the stick reminded another sailor of a lance he had made using an iron tool. More objects appeared. A small piece of a stalk plant floated by. Quickly thinking, someone on the ship grabbed a long hook, snatching the object. Upon seeing it, Columbus immediately thought of similar plants "which grow on land."[22] Quite out of the ordinary, a flat, wide wooden board drifted close to the *Santa Maria*. They did not stop to pick it up, but the artifact appeared human-made. Meanwhile, on the fast-moving *Niña*, a blossom-rich branch touched the side of the ship. Upon inspection, the plant carried a load of Roseberries.[23] News spread from one ship to another, and "these signs encouraged them, and they all grew cheerful."[24] Up to this point, the fleet covered 27 leagues and did not realize the magnetic pull of 8 degree variation from their compass needle.

On the spur of a moment, just after sunset, he ordered a course change; they would head again due west. Darkness descended without cloud cover, and Columbus ordered everyone to keep a sharp lookout for land—the crew was already searching, searching for a firelight or a dark bump sitting atop the western horizon.

Columbus felt invigorated too. Anticipating a sign of land, he stood on the quarterdeck searching for the sea ahead. Around 10:00 p.m., he announced to the crew that he spotted a dim, distant light. Quickly, Columbus yelled out to Pero Gutierrez to come over and look. Gutierrez verified the sighting. Now, Columbus asked Rodrigo Sánchez of Segovia, the fleet's comptroller, to search for the light, but to no avail. Then it appeared to Columbus again, but no one saw this second glittering light. Certain he saw a firelight, he led the crew in chanting the *Salve Regina*,[25] after which everyone continued to study the horizon. In the mounting tension of anticipation, Columbus spread the word, offering a "silken jacket" to the first person to signal land on the *Santa Maria*.

Midnight came, and no one relented their search. Now, without permission, Martín Pinzón in *Pinta* surged ahead as if to announce a sighting. Two hours later, after cruising another 22.5 leagues since their course change, Juan Rodríguez Bermejo de Triana, on *Pinta*, saw a black outline stretching north to south a few miles ahead. Shouting to his captain below. Rodrigo cheered gleefully, anticipating the ten thousand maravedis reward.[26] Captain Pinzón, in *Pinta*, blasted a cannon signal and waited for *Niña* and the slow-moving flagship to pull close.

Columbus immediately judged the distance to land at 2 leagues (6 miles). Thinking about safety first, he gave orders for all ships to take down sails and to "lay to" until daylight; aware of island reefs in the Eastern Atlantic, Columbus cautiously waited, his tiny fleet corking up and down, drifting SW with the current, too far from shore to lower the anchor. His ships sat near 74 degrees west longitude (286 degrees global longitude) and 23 degrees north latitude.[27]

Was he frightened, jubilant, or a combination of both? Did he know that in a few hours, he would act out one of the most seminal moments in world history? The journal tells us nothing of his emotions during the 3 hours he and his crew anxiously waited for dawn to appear.

Notes

1 Keen, *The Life of the Admiral Christopher* Columbus, 51
2 Here, Dunn & Kelley mirror the translation by Kettell and Fuson. Dunn & Kelley, *The Diario*, 39; Fuson, *The Log of Christopher Columbus*, 66.
3 Markham, *The Journal of Columbus*, 27. The changing wind direction that day surprised Columbus and the crew. His understanding of the North Atlantic gyre left unanswered the mid-ocean variability of currents and winds. He fully believed that they would need to reach the far western portion of the *Ocean Sea* to uncover favorable returning winds.
4 Ibid., 28. Thus begin the many occasions on which Columbus believed divine intervention helped save, or at least point to, a helpful solution.
5 The 1515 testimony of Juan Portuguese, a former servant of Columbus, revealed that Martín Pinzón and Columbus discussed turning back, but both agreed to continue the voyage. Wadsworth, *Columbus and His First Voyage*, 112–13. However, the witness's memory may have failed him, as he incorrectly noted that the voyage lasted 6 months before discovering land; in reality, the voyage extended just over 1 month.
6 See Keen, *The Life of the Admiral*, 52–53 for an extended discussion by Ferdinand Columbus of how "the men grew ever more restless and fearful." He goes on to admit that crew members whispered in small groups, not wanting to die "in the attempt" to keep going. Provisions ran short, all three ships reported leaks in their hulls, and, after all, their leader was a foreigner, hinting at mutiny.

7 The legal action continued for years, with both sides, the Columbus family and the Pinzón family, bringing evidence, often sailors from the first voyage or family members of the crew, giving their accounts. The collectively archived documents from the proceedings are known as *Pleitos de Colón* and reside at the Archives of the Indies in Seville, Spain. For more information and the testimonies of Francisco Garcia Vallejos, Garcia Fernandez, and Juan Dominguez, see Morison, *Journals and Other Documents*, 188–91.

8 Columbus had agreed, as an incentive to encourage all three crews, to pay a reward for the first confirmed sighting of land.

9 See the pull-out extended map following page 226 in Morison's book, showing the proposed magnetic variation, circa 1492. Apparently, Morison used Columbus compass reading to estimate specific variations of magnetic declination, then, without explanation, laid out additional and increasing isogonic lines at regular intervals.

10 Kettell, *Personal Narrative*, 26.

11 Ibid., 27.

12 N. H. de Vaudrey Heathcote noted that northern European seafarers and scholars knew about magnetic variation before 1492, but surprisingly, Mediterranean mariners did not, 102.

13 Dunn & Kelly conclude that neither magnetic variation nor the apparent movement of Polaris can account for the dramatic compass change, explaining that the compass must have been moved near a "keg of nails or some other large ferrous mass." 49. This explanation suggests incompetence on the part of the crew taking the reading, and with Columbus present, a scenario highly unlikely given the experience these sailors and when taking vital compass readings.

14 Miller, *The Journal of Columbus's First Voyage*, 12.

15 Pedro Niño also sailed with Columbus on voyages 2 and 3. Later, King Ferdinand and Queen Isabella bestowed the high honor of *Chief Pilot of the Ocean Sea* on Niño.

16 If the crew had demanded a western limit, in leagues, at this point, one might see why Columbus offered distinctly different calculations.

17 This is an important entry as it suggests Columbus carried multiple charts and maps, and these tools he checked religiously at this point in the voyage. Miller, *The Journal of Columbus's First Voyage*, 13.

18 Yes, it is true. It is difficult today to believe that Spanish parents allowed young boys, some of them as young as 12, to participate in a transatlantic voyage of discovery. However, as we know, Columbus himself went to sea at the age of 14. Also, many of the crew members did not know the full extent of Columbus's plans; rumors abounded. On the *Santa Maria*, Pedro de Terreros reported; and on the *Niña*, Juan Arraes served.

19 Flying fish (family *Exocoetidae*) range from 7 to 18 inches in length; they can propel their bodies up through and out of the sea at speeds over 30 miles an hour. The many subspecies of flying fish are seen in the temperate latitudes of the Atlantic and Pacific Oceans.

20 Viking exploration and settlement on Newfoundland placed their furthest contact point west at 59 degrees or 301 degrees global longitude. Of course, there remains the possibility of other yet-to-be-discovered Viking settlements in Canada.

21 Miller, *The Journal of Columbus's First Voyage*, 13.

22 This is possibly referring to a sugar cane stalk that Columbus routinely saw on the islands of Madeira and Porto Santo when he was younger.

23 This is most likely a red raspberry or strawberry plant that was native to both South and Central America.

24 Kettell, *Personal Narrative*, 31.

25 The *Salve Regina* is a prayer (hymn) sung to the Virgin Mary. Sailors in the 15th century chanted the prayer repeatedly as a sincere request for thanks and/or divine intervention in times of stress or peril.

26 Spaniards used the *maravedi* as a monetary counting unit. Ten thousand *maravedis* in 1492 was a considerable amount of value in gold or silver coins. It should be noted that many historians state clearly that Columbus cheated Juan Rodríguez Bermejo out of the reward, which sounds a bit petty considering the riches that Columbus planned to acquire once land was sighted.

27 See Appendix I for a short history of the many Columbus landfall theories, including a discussion of the effects of winds, currents, magnetic variation, and leeway drift.

PART III
The Columbus Landfall and Search for the Mainland

October 12, 1492, realized the first recognized social contact between Europeans and Indigenous peoples of the Caribbean region for thousands of years; it certainly ranks as a top-level, some would say the top-level, global event of the first order. Columbus attempting to understand the physical and social environment he stumbled upon, explored with a keen eye, first on Guanahani Island, quickly followed by short voyages to other Bahamian islands, then on to the larger islands of Cuba and Hispaniola (Haiti and the Dominican Republic). Columbus strived to maintain cordial relations, acquiring guides to help him navigate the many island destinations; Las Casas's transcription leads readers to believe Columbus kidnapped these Lucayan guides and interpreters, something to which Columbus himself admitted later in a letter to the Spanish monarchs. However, the forced taking of Indigenous peoples from San Salvador, Cuba, and Hispaniola has an interesting climax shortly after the destruction of Columbus's flagship, the *Santa Maria*, as examples of an increased level of trust showcase a preponderance of evidence suggesting at least some curious natives made the decision to travel with Columbus to Spain. The reader will take a deep look at the written evidence that asserts the kidnapping charge, using various recognized translations, the well-regarded *Real Academic Española Diccionario*,[1] and the 1611 *Tesoro de la lengua castellana o Española*. In this manner, readers can evaluate the juxtaposition of evidence for and against the kidnapping charge.

During these first days of exploration in the Bahamas, the reader will learn about Lucayan culture, including an observed social structure. At the highest sat the village *cacique*, or chief. Below the cacique, two other social groups comprised the rest of the population: the *nitaínos* and *naborías*. The *nitaínos*,

DOI: 10.4324/9781003464143-9

or nobles, *behiques* (shamans), and clanlords. Columbus recorded the physical environment, including plants used by the Lucayans for food and shelter, and noticed how eager the Indigenous peoples sought to serve him and his crew, helping form the opinion that they would willingly desire to become Spanish vassals (subjects).

Note

1 The following validation of the dictionary comes from the University of Wisconsin-Madison: "The Diccionario de la lengua española (a.k.a. DRAE or *Diccionario de la Real Academia Española*) is the standard dictionary of Spanish (a.k.a. Castilian) edited and produced by the Royal Spanish Academy (RAE is the acronym in Spanish). Its first edition dates from 1780, and its latest one is the 22nd ed., published in 2001. This online version is comprised of the 22nd edition plus some of the work done for the 23rd edition, which will be published in 2014. DRAE is considered the most authoritative dictionary for the Spanish language. It includes commonly used words in any of the Spanish-speaking countries. It also includes numerous archaic and unusual words with the aim of understanding ancient Spanish literature." Library, Databases. For a history of the *diccionario*, see Edward Davis Terry. "Spanish Lexicography and the Real Academia Española: A Sketch," *Hispania*, Vol. 57, No. 4 (Dec. 1974), pp. 958–964.

6

THE FIRST ENCOUNTER

October 12–14

> I presented them [Indios] with a variety of things, in order to secure their affection, and that they may become Christians, and enter into the services of their Highnesses and the Castilian nation.
>
> —Christopher Columbus's Letter to Luis de Santangel, 1493

The Day the World Changed

October 12, Friday[1]

Among historians and geographers that support Morison's claim that Watlings Island is San Salvador, there is universal support that Christopher Columbus and crew waded ashore on the leeward or west side of the island, where Long Bay's beaches run for miles.[2] However, this author disagrees with Morison on the anchorage and beach landing sites. Appendices I and II discuss these differences with accompanying maps based on reef location and depth.

Wherever he landed, Columbus's footprints on San Salvador canceled the geographic isolation of the Western Hemisphere that began thousands of years ago. In dramatic flair, the flamboyant mariner ordered the skiff boats on all three ships to be lowered. Then Columbus, Martín Pinzón, and Vicente Pinzón led an excited group of chosen crew members toward shore. Italian scholar Paolo Taviani describes the physical scene as Europeans eagerly rowed toward land.

> Within the coral reef, the water is warm and transparent, with a range of colors running from deep blue to a changeable green like that of spring leaves. From the shoreline, thick clumps of mangroves advance into the sea; their roots seek, deep below the salt and sandy surface, the indispensable sustenance of fresh water.[3]

DOI: 10.4324/9781003464143-10

Traditional renditions of what follows next appear, which I have compiled from reading numerous accounts. From the *Santa Maria*, Columbus surged ahead, accompanied by Rodrigo Sánchez of Segovia, royal representative of King Ferdinand and Queen Isabella, and Rodrigo de Escobedo (the official fleet notary). As they observed the quickly approaching sandy beach, Columbus and company saw images of people emerging, then disappearing, from a not-to-distant sub-tropical forest of small trees. The naked natives, a few of them, apparently all males and quite young, peered from just behind the three-lined frontier, only steps from the bleach-white sandy beach, glancing first at Columbus's skiff and then at the small boats leaving the *Niña* and *Pinta*. One might imagine that not one native spoke, staring momentarily at each other, perplexed and confused. The crystal-clear water glistened below the skiff, and Columbus noted brightly colored, striped fish darting in all directions, fleeing the oncoming craft. Glancing toward the shore once again, the people vanished.[4]

One must consider if Columbus understood the importance and consequences of what he was about to do. He had already run through in his mind the geo-political protocols he would follow, depending on the situation encountered. These options included discovering new lands unoccupied by people, discovering new lands occupied by "civilized" peoples (e.g., Cipangu or Cathay), and discovering new lands occupied by "savage" peoples—three scenarios and three different protocols. Which one would it be?

So much ran through his mind. One might describe the scene as follows: First and foremost, he needed to consider the safety of his men and ships. He could see that this island was small and not the endgame of the expedition. As his thoughts processed the visual scene, Columbus and company saw, appearing now from several directions, dark-skinned people (Lucayans)[5] gathered a few hundred yards from the water, at the edge of the tree line. They wore no clothes—nothing. No one in the skiff spoke; everyone simply looked ahead, in awe. From the glistening, crystalline beach, some 70 feet deep, to the lush, light green groundcover growing close to the sand and the darker green foliage of the nearby forest of small to medium-height trees, the physical scene expanded before their eyes. What was Columbus thinking? What were the Lucayans thinking? The above-fictionalized description has become part of the Columbus legend, highlighted by such writers as Washington Irving described this scene: "Columbus made signal for the ships to cast anchor, and the boats to be manned and armed. He entered his own boat richly attired in scarlet and bearing the royal standard." Irving describes the Indigenous peoples at first sighting writing, "the inhabitants were seen issuing from the woods, and running from all parts to the shore, where they stood gazing at the ships."[6]

There is no precise way to determine where Columbus and his crew first spotted land on the night of October 11, 1492. However, my computer analysis puts the landfall sighting near the southeast corner of San Salvador, some 6 nautical miles distant.

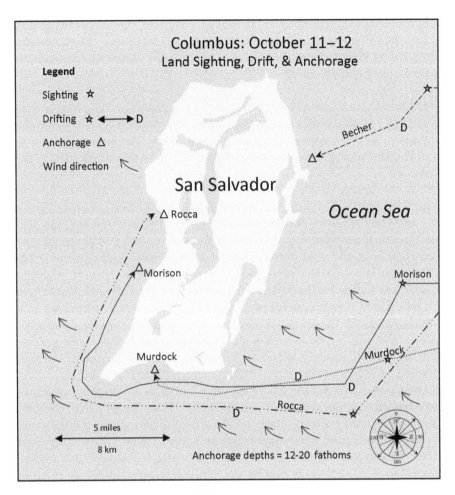

FIGURE 6.1   Columbus: October 11–12

Continuing an imagined scene at the first landing, we might see Columbus insisting on being first, easily jumping enthusiastically into the increasingly shallow water. He wanted to be first, no matter what might happen next. This was his day; he waited many years for this moment. The dark-skinned people continued to gather a short distance away. No one counted, but there seemed to be at least a dozen, all men. They did not speak. Columbus looked in their direction, checking for any aggressive behavior, and then turned to Martín and Vincente to step forward with him to a level spot on the beach. Columbus hesitated for only a few seconds. He knew what to do but wanted to glory in the moment. Motioning for men to display the royal standards, Columbus according to Las Casas's account, declared a claim to the island and noted later, "before all others took possession of that island for the King and Queen his sovereigns, making the requisite declarations."[7] These were the words of Las Casas, not Columbus. Thacher, in his translation, references a 1689 document compiled by Vicente Joseph Miguel that suggests the exact prayer Columbus spoke on the beach; it reads,

> O Lord, Eternal and Almighty God, by Thy sacred word Thou hast created the heavens, the earth, and the sea; blessed and glorified be Thy name, and praised be Thy Majesty, who hath deigned to use Thy humble servant to make Thy sacred name known and proclaimed in this other part of the world.[8]

Onlooking Lucayan observers knew not what these strangers were doing, yet they remained steadfast at their position near the tree line, noticing the light color of the newcomers' skin, hair jutting from their faces, and coverings over their chest, legs, and arms; some of them had their heads covered as well.[9] Ida Altman recently wrote that the natives "Accustomed to the arrival of migrants, raiders, and traders on their shores, the people who lived on the islands might not have found the appearance of Columbus's three ships as surprising as is often assumed."[10] The Lucayans stared in astonishment at the many brightly colored and adorned banners now being waved about by Spaniards making their way out of the surf. Columbus dropped to his knees; the rest of the crew followed, all this occurring without a sound from the strangers.

Giving sincere thanks to God for leading them to land, Columbus appropriately named his new discovery San Salvador (Holy Savior). At this time, Columbus did not know the exact size of the island, having only sailed around the southern coastline. At 63 square miles and only 6.5 miles wide at its greatest extent, San Salvador is small. From north to south, the island runs 12 miles, covered with alkaline lakes dotting the entire area. A wide variety of trees, brushes, and grasses existed, as described by Columbus in subsequent log entries. Fruit trees abounded on the island, and one study suggested that the vegetation may have been transported as Indigenous peoples migrated from Cuba or Hispaniola.[11]

As for the "dark-skinned" people he was about to meet, the Lucayan people struggled to work the sea and land, fishing from shore and dugout canoes along preferred shallow reef locations, and planting and harvesting maize, squashes, and fruits.[12] Jeffrey Blick estimated the island's population based on archaeological evidence at two major sites and several smaller locations, between 500 and 1,000 persons. This aggregate population spread out in small extended families of 12–100, concentrating in 2–4 major villages and over a dozen smaller locations. Two of these sites, Blick excavated, uncovering data on native use and consumption of natural food sources, land, and sea, which allowed him to conclude that the native population remained stable for hundreds of years due to limited resources.[13]

Columbus's first description of the Lucayans is positive and foreboding, declaring in the same sentence,

> As I saw that they were very friendly to us, perceived that they could be much more easily converted to our holy faith by gentle means than by force, I presented them with some red caps, and strings of beads to wear upon the neck, and many other trifles of small value, wherewith they were much delighted, and became wonderfully attached to us.[14]

First impressions tell the reader about the intent of the writer. Columbus's first announcement was not about seeking gold or personal financial gain; it was all about faith conversion. Desiring to start on the right foot, he returned their perceived friendliness by handing out gifts—gifts worthless to Spanish civilization but treasured by the Lucayans, ushering in hours of cross-cultural economic exchange. Spaniards came to the beach, and Lucayans rowed out in canoes to the ships. Glass beads and hawk's bells passed from European hands to anxious villagers, while crew members gladly accepted squawking parrots, balls of cotton thread, and stone-sharpened wood javelins. Las Casas noted, "Trade was carried on with the utmost good will." Interestingly, during the rest of the afternoon, only one girl appeared on the beach; surprisingly, all the natives looked young, under 30.[15]

Columbus spent much of this day's journal entry describing the physical appearance of his new friends, seeing them similar to Canary Islanders, neither white nor black, possessing attractive shapes and faces, faces painted a variety of colors—mostly black, other times red or white.[16] The Spaniards quickly noticed the Lucayans displayed no weapons, except for their crude spears. One or more curious Lucayans attempted to grab Columbus's sword as he drew it from the scabbard, cutting "themselves through ignorance."

Soon, in an attempt to communicate, Columbus's interpreter, Luis de Torres, knowledgeable in Hebrew, Chaldaic, and Arabic, failed to understand anything the Lucayans spoke. Gesturing with their arms and hands, Torres and Columbus asked why so many of the men's naked bodies contained scars. Two or three Lucayans pointed in different directions, motioned in a striking pose, and pointed to their scars. From this, Columbus theorized that neighboring islanders raided San Salvador regularly, searching for captives. In truth, he was right, with widespread pre-Columbian slaving practices common throughout the Bahamas and, indeed, the entire Caribbean region.[17]

Toward the end of this first day's log on shore, Columbus expressed hope for the future of the Lucayan people, calling them "ingenious," eventually becoming "good servants." Here is another critical statement of the admiral's intentions. He did not use the term *slaves*. The term *servant* in 15th-century Spanish, Portuguese, and Genoese social-economic environments referred to a citizen devoted politically, economically, and socially (religiously) to their ruler.[18]

In Columbus's case, throughout the journal and in the majority of subsequent letters and memoranda, he pledged servitude to King Ferdinand and Queen Isabella of Spain. Politically, servants of Spain remained loyal to the monarchs and no other foreign entity. Economically, it meant you paid taxes to support the monarchs, willingly or reluctantly giving a portion of your earnings on a regular basis. Socially, Spanish servants learned the language, participated in sanctioned community events, and maintained their Catholic Christian faith— official expectations that asked all Spaniards to abide by these traditions of culture and life.[19]

What is missing from this understanding is the assumption that a *servant* of Spain maintained a certain condition of freedom: freedom of movement, freedom of livelihood, freedom of marriage, and freedom to raise a family. Spaniards did have the right to relocate anywhere within their nation or live in outlying areas, such as the Spanish-held Canary Islands or extra-Spanish economic ghettos in other European countries. Spanish *servants* included farmers, tinkers, mariners, merchants, and a host of other occupations. Apprenticeship opportunities became commonplace in major urban centers such as Seville. No rigid social class restrictions existed preventing a lowly farmer, or in the case of Columbus, a trading representative, from courting and proposing to a member of a higher social level; the opposite arrangement also existed as a free choice. This was Spanish society in 1492; Columbus wanted to provide this *servant* opportunity to the Lucayan people, not slavery; the idea of a servant class was not new to Caribbean societies.[20]

Slavery would only become an option under specific social-political conditions. Kathleen Deagan adroitly summarized those circumstances.

> Although the conquered populations were obligated to contribute labor as a token of their submission to Spain; nevertheless, they were theoretically granted the privileges of Castilian subjects as long as they adopted Christianity and accepted the sovereignty of Spain. The status and privileges of their chiefs [caciques] were formally recognized. However, those new subjects who continued resistance (and the conquistadors defined the concept of resistance in very broad terms) were considered appropriate candidates for enslavement and despoliation.[21]

Servitude to the Spanish monarchs, in Columbus's mind, meant a better life, protection from enemies, economic opportunity, and, most importantly, conversion to Christianity, thus offering eternal life; it was the life that he and his men were experiencing and would now offer, in his mind, to these people. The Lucayans would come to understand and appreciate, ironically, only one of the above benefits noted: protection from slave raiders. They already participated in a simplistic intra-island economy that regularly extended geographically to nearby islands. As for Christianity, they knew not, although to please the strangers, these islanders later mimicked Spaniards, making the sign of the cross and calling out words from the *Ave Maria*.[22] They did understand the concept of honoring and obeying their village leaders, called *caciques*.

It is generally agreed today that the Lucayan and Taíno peoples lived in a political system built on hierarchical and "nonegalitarian chiefdom, each headed by an absolute paramount leader," called a *cacique*. Some researchers, such as Deagan & Cruxent, believed a cacique's position relied on a matrilineal connection, holding power for their lifetime. On occasion, women also held the power of a cacique, demanding village compliance with set rituals, and providing necessary community labor, working in the fields, and joining armed groups to defend their village from incursions by Carib raiders or neighboring Taíno caciques.[23] Living in large homes, usually located in the center of a village, caciques could have many wives, and they wore colorful adornments and garments.

William Keegan and Morgan D. Maclachlan agree that a matrilineal tradition dominated in Lucayan society unequivocally stating, "The Taíno [Lucayan] people represent a major, theoretically significant instance of matrilineal social organization."[24] The authors agreed that the tracing of the female line helped establish a rank social line where the possibility existed of a woman inheriting the role of cacique or another village noble, and this system encouraged local political stability. Interestingly, it is suggested that an avunculocal situation occurred where the newlywed couple moved to live in the husband's village; they lived in the hut of his mother's brother. When outside threats arrived and men remained absent for extended periods, women assumed more of the village responsibilities of food supply, especially horticulture, which strengthened women's role as wives and sisters. The authors cite evidence that ongoing pre-Columbian warfare drained the male gene pool, encouraging remarriage and a subsequent trend toward polygyny.[25]

Below the caciques, two other social groups comprised the rest of the population: the *nitaínos* and *naborías*. The *nitaínos*, or nobles, included the cacique, "*behiques* (shamans), and clanlords."[26] According to Keegan, the *nitaínos* usually held loyalty to a hierarchy of lineage from the small village clanlords up through and to the regional cacique; the area covered by this political structure was called a *cicicazgo*. An example of this arrangement is the regional chief, Behecchio, cacique of the Xaragua province in western Hispaniola.[27] Lucayans living on the smaller islands of the Bahamas exhibited a limited geographic version of the Cuban and Hispaniola models of political leadership, with village clanlords playing a major role in the political structure. Little is known about the *naboría* class of villagers, except that Spanish observers believed that it did contain some "personal slaves" derived from being taken as prisoners during a raid on another village, in which that person remained in service for a designated length of time. Allison Bigelow, in her chapter "Seasons of Gold," uses the term *naborías* to mean servant.[28]

It might be difficult for us today to understand 15th-century allegiance to monarchical servitude, but to Columbus and his crew, social-political expectations for citizens included servitude, and yes, the royal court demanded everyone, native or foreign-born, to acquiesce. Spanish servitude did come with national protection, and personal freedom of movement was somewhat assured, depending on the financial ability of the individual. Pre-contact Lucayan servitude on the smaller islands, such as San Salvador, involved obeying rules and traditions laid down by their village cacique. When called upon, they joined other villagers in defending against inter-island raiders, usually Caribs.[29] Daily survival tasks dominated their lifestyle: growing maize (referred to as *panizo* grass) and agave, hunting small game and birds, and fishing coastal beaches.[30] Local islanders worked shells and nearby mounds of limestone to fashion a variety of hand tools, such as scrapers and abraders, to prepare their food. Often, small village sites contained a central area where food was prepared and stored; here, archaeologists have found a treasure trove of remains. People cooked in other locations, nearer individual huts.[31] Hunting for sea turtles or trading for them with neighboring peoples remained high on the list of favorite food items. The Lucayans employed various-shaped weirs made from tree branches. Seeds found in the Bahamas may have been obtained on the islands of Cuba and Hispaniola. Berman and Pearsall believed that the quantity of debris seeds discovered at sites in San Salvador led to the conclusion that Lucayans constructed and maintained "home gardens."[32]

The Lucayan lifestyle before Columbus proved challenging. The Bahamian islands, being small, lacked sufficient resources to sustain increasingly larger populations, hence the desire to initiate and sustain inter-island trade. Archaeologist Irving Rouse believed that the interisland Caribbean contact, especially trade and war, at the time of first contact was "widespread," with some islands highlighting that trade with specialized products.[33] In the case of the Lucayan people, trade proved the motivating factor in prompting the interisland movement. In other areas of the Caribbean, particularly Guadeloupe Island in the Lesser Antilles, warfare by Carib raiding parties thrived during the time of European contact.[34]

As already noted, Columbus rarely saw Indigenous peoples older than 30 years old. Yet, this was their world, relatively safe except for the occasional Carib raiding expeditions or destructive Caribbean hurricanes.[35] It was their world, a small world, where close family ties made life and honored traditions sacred, something to cherish and keep without interference—the Lucayans called their island *Guanahani*.

Archaeologists trace the Lucayans (Palmetto people) on Guanahani (San Salvador) arriving on the island from northeastern Cuba and northwestern Haiti migration, beginning around AD 800 and lasting until 1200. It is believed that prior inhabitants, Ostionoid villagers, may have arrived only a short time prior, around AD 600.[36] Rouse, in his review of Caribbean migration, carefully separates population movement, or repeopling, from colonization and immigration.

In the prior case, the Ostionoid population movement "almost completely eliminated the Casimiroids [previous inhabitants of the Caribbean]."[37] This infers that the newcomers arrived in force and with aggressive intentions, conquering territory previously occupied—most of the villages, or all of them. Colonization, according to Rouse, implies a smaller migration with the "invaders" claiming a limited geographic area, leaving the remainder of the island under previous control. Immigration for Rouse sees a small number of newcomers eventually being absorbed into the local culture. For Guanahani, archaeologically, a Palmetto population movement exerted full control by 1492.

Interestingly, Charles Mann, in his widely read book, *1491*, believed "for the most part the initial Indian-European encounter was less of an intellectual shock to the Indians than to Europeans."[38] This belief, framed around the argument that the Europeans, particularly Columbus, expected to find far more advanced societies, clothed, and possessing the technology and lifestyle familiar to Spanish culture. The Indians, with a highly advanced philosophical mythology in place, "were not surprised that such strange people *existed* [emphasis by Mann]." Traditional myths envisioned supernatural beings, a common feature of many, if not all, of the pre-contact Indigenous societies of the Americas.[39]

Taíno creation myths represented a major focus of their religious and artistic expression. One Spanish monk, Ramón Pané, came over with Columbus to Hispaniola during the explorer's second voyage in 1493. Living with the Indigenous peoples, he studied and wrote about Taíno spirituality and their creation myths. From two caves, one called Cacibayagua and the other Amayauba, the original population emerged, only to be separated, men and women, on separate islands. Another myth describes how all the fish in the surrounding sea came from a magical gourd.[40]

Interestingly, Las Casas switched from his paraphrasing of the day's events to Columbus's quoted description of events when the discussion focused on the interaction between the Europeans and the Lucayans. Columbus wrote, "I intend at my return to carry home six of them to your Highnesses, that they may learn our language."[41] Depending on which translation you read, the statement may indicate an invitation to some of the Lucayans to be his guests on a return trip, or Columbus is planning to take them by force—initiating New World slavery.[42] Las Casas claimed, "These are the words of the Admiral," and they may be true, or Columbus's meaning was lost in translation, or the natives agreed to go—let us investigate further when the issue comes up again on October 14.

The Lucayan Islanders Barter with the Europeans

October 13, Saturday

At daybreak, word spread throughout Guanahani villages of the strange visitors, and canoes packed with anxious Indios fought to position their craft

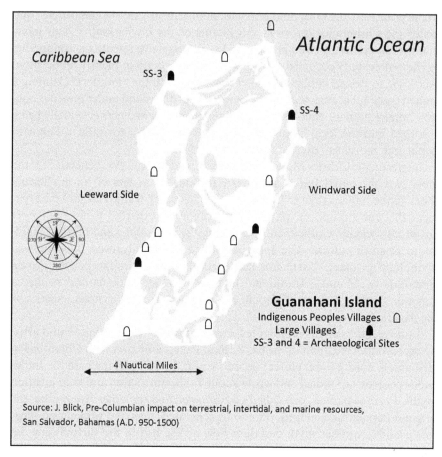

Caribbean Sea

Atlantic Ocean

SS-3

SS-4

Leeward Side

Windward Side

Guanahani Island
Indigenous Peoples Villages
Large Villages
SS-3 and 4 = Archaeological Sites

4 Nautical Miles

Source: J. Blick, Pre-Columbian impact on terrestrial, intertidal, and marine resources, San Salvador, Bahamas (A.D. 950-1500)

FIGURE 6.2 Guanahani Island

alongside all three Spanish vessels. [43] Those present included many of the same natives as the day before, but also Lucayans with homes along the east coast of the island or Pidgeon Creek, who arrived after paddling several miles around the island in a *canoa* (canoe) or walking overland on well-worn island paths. Columbus and crew marveled at the size of the larger canoes; quickly counting, the explorer totaled 40 people in one or more dugout vessels.[44] With the ongoing and brisk bartering exchange, the Lucayans became more comfortable with their new guests, with some natives freely reaching up to grab the hand of a Spanish sailor and others shimmying up thick, rough ropes tossed over the ship's sides. Once onboard, sailors came face-to-face with the Lucayans, Columbus among them. A few natives sported small pieces of gold "hanging from the nose." Columbus and Torres anxiously questioned these nose-pierced natives using gestures, pointing to the gold, and then making a wide sweep of the ocean. Puzzled islanders soon caught on, returning the gestures by pointing their arms in a southward direction, others pointing to the southwest. From these crude kinesthetic exchanges, Columbus conjured up a mental picture of an Asian potentate reveling in boatloads of gold only a short distance away.

When Columbus set foot on a beach in San Salvador, known by the Indigenous inhabitants as Guanahani, numerous villages dotted the perimeter of the small island. Most of these villages were quite small, housing an immediate extended family of 15–25 individuals. At least four large villages existed, two of which we believe Columbus saw on the leeward (western) side of Guanahani.

Excited, Columbus tried to communicate verbally but failed. Feeling the language frustration, he continued with attempts for more information through hand and arm gestures. He wanted volunteers to guide him to the gold. "I endeavored to make them go there, and afterward saw that they were not inclined for the journey."[45] Robert Fuson, in his translation, reported the passage slightly differently: "I have tried to find some natives who will take me to this great king, but none seem inclined to make the journey."[46] If we believe this statement is a true representation of Columbus's feelings, then he did not want to take, by force, any Indigenous peoples without their consent. All translations clearly reveal that Columbus detained no Lucayans that day.

This is a significant statement, opening the possibility that later he did convince seven Lucayans to serve as guides and interpreters, although it equally connotes Columbus's frustration and final determination to forcibly detain them. The interpretation of this event lays the foundation for challenging all subsequent accusations by Las Casas, implying a forced kidnapping. On this subject, Stanford scholar Carol Delaney, as we shall see in later incidents, notes that on other occasions, several Taino did request or agree to travel to the home of the newcomers, Spain. The logbook noted that at least some of the Lucayans believed these newcomers to be "gods from heaven," worthy of worship; as is true with many cultures, the unknown creates curiosity and fear.[47] Despite the openness with which the Spaniards traded and interacted with them, the Lucayans did not know them. This uncertainty obviously played into their initial hesitation about wanting to remain onboard the ships.[48] Taviani explains this uncertainty as an example of cultural misunderstanding. Without mutual language communication and knowledge of each other's value system, one could only assume behavioral expectations, as the true nature of that culture is not known or appreciated.[49]

Columbus, looking for ways to communicate to the Spanish monarchs a sense for the geography of this new island, indicated that San Salvador was "fairly large and very flat." San Salvador is 63 square miles in area; saying it was "fairly large" might seem a stretch when one realizes his previous experiences with islands included Gomera (142 sq. miles), Madeira (309 sq. miles), possibly he thought about Porto Santo, a mere 16 square miles.

The trading and socializing continued throughout this second day of landfall. Columbus was disappointed as night approached; his men reported that all the received trade items appeared worth little. With darkness, the natives returned to the canoes and, hence, to their villages. Men from the *Niña* and *Pinta* also reported seeing little gold. Columbus, undeterred, in his cabin late in the evening, as he wrote of the day's events, vowed to "make [for] the island of Cipangu." Surely gold awaited discovery.[50]

Exploring Guanahani

October 14, Sunday

Today, exploration began in earnest, with Columbus ordering each ship captain to *layover* the skiff boats and assign a handful of men as rowers, leaving the remaining crew behind. With little to no observable large reef structures to his immediate north, the three skiff boats, at first headed NW, with boat crews rowing in rhythm while a bow observer checked for possible underwater rocks. At between 600 and 800 feet from shore, this first leg of their journey proved relaxing, and depth checks revealed safe passage in 10–15 feet of water. After one mile, the coastline turned northeast, exposing new dangers. Intermittent reefs appeared ahead, he continued. Natives appeared on a nearby beach, at first less than a dozen, then more came "down to the shore," pointing and gesturing.

While Bonefish Bay appeared large and tranquil, Columbus noticed only a narrow break in the reef; he was determined to proceed NW for 0.5 mile, where a wide opening in the reef appeared. The three skiff boats slowly proceeded toward the shore, where Lucayans from the south, who had been following Columbus's route from the beach, met up with other, more numerous islanders coming from a large village to the north.

As Columbus drew near the shore, the Lucayans shouted and waved with their arms, making upward gestures. Columbus assumed that this meant the Indios believed the Spaniards came from heaven. Unprompted and desiring to get close to the gods, "some brought us water and other victuals; others, seeing that I was not disposed to land, plunged into the sea and swam out to us."[51] The athletic Lucayans swam around the boats, again gesturing and, in their own way, asking if the Spaniards indeed came from the sky.

In an attempt to determine the size of Guanahani, Columbus used a small skiff boat and skirted the shoreline and extensive reef islands. Rounding the north end of the island, he entered what is called Graham's Harbor. Briefly encountering native villagers, he estimated that he could build a suitable fort to guard the prospective future harbor.

One older native finally made the swim and attempted to pull himself up onto Columbus's skiff. Once inside, he sat and stared at the explorers and said nothing. Other, more extroverted Lucayans, men and women, three or four now inside the boats, called back to others still standing on the beach;

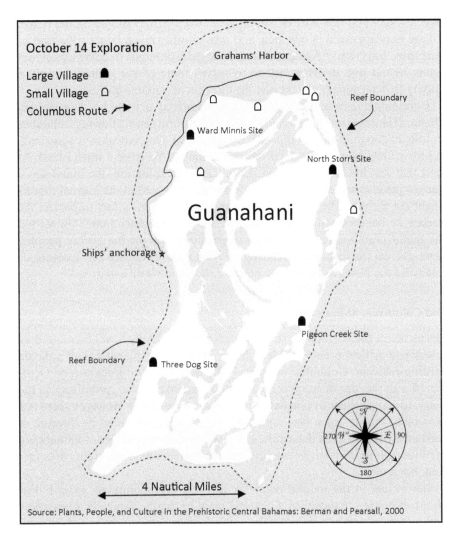

FIGURE 6.3   October 14 Exploration

Columbus imagined they were saying, "Come and see the men who have come from heaven."[52] After a short while, Columbus allowed the boats to draw more closely to shore, within 300–400 feet of the beach. From here, dozens of Lucayans gestured for Columbus to come to shore, the natives desiring to see the strangers up close. Yet dangerous rocks still lingered below the surface.

Nervous about approaching the shore at this point, Columbus gave orders to row northeast, following the coastline, maneuvering safely between the beach and outside a long, extended reef. Within 200 yards, the stark sandy-white seafloor appeared uninterrupted by rocks. This clear seabed area widened as they rowed north inviting a landing. Large numbers of Lucayans from

Bonefish Bay and new natives coming from the north, clustered on the beach. Village huts appeared in one area, and then another much larger collection of huts came into view.[53] Again, the natives urged Columbus to come ashore, yet again; he did not, desiring instead to survey more of the western coastline, hoping to determine its extent and the location of suitable harbors.

Continuing to row, the Spaniards now entered a wide bay-like lagoon, Grahams Harbor, today. The coastline turned abruptly east, allowing Columbus to fully understand the north-south dimension of San Salvador; it was small, approximately 14 miles. In the distance, Columbus observed a small island. At least that was his first impression. Upon closer examination, the island was a narrow peninsula averaging 170 feet in width. He noted in the journal that he might cut through the narrowest part and build a fort—a fort to protect the harbor he believed could hold, "all the ships of Christendom." On second thought, Columbus, reflecting on his interactions with the Indigenous peoples, demurred on the fort idea, declaring, "I do not, however, see the necessity of fortifying the place, as the people here are simple in warlike matters."[54]

Did Columbus Kidnap Lucayans?

Let us take a break from the story to explore more deeply how historians may investigate critical events and search for alternative explanations or validate existing evidence. Columbus most likely did detain several Lucayans on October 14 with the idea of using them as guides and interpreters, promising, in the diary, to return them to Guanahani at some future date.[55] However, there is a possibility that it was a language misunderstanding, as noted by Taviani, at least on the day of their departure. Is it possible that the charges of kidnapping are founded on derivative evidence and therefore assume the status of a factoid, not a fact?[56]

It was late in the journal entry for this day that Columbus again talked about bringing a handful of Lucayans back to Spain. Typically, researchers and writers desiring to describe this critical event defer to the initial Spanish transcription by Martín Fernández de Navarrete in 1825.[57] It was Navarrete who discovered the Las Casas manuscript in 1790. Understanding its value and utility, he labored for years translating the lengthy document. What followed was a cascade of scholars with translations into English: Kettell (1827), Thomas (1882), Markham (1893), Thacher (1903), Lyon (1986), Dunn & Kelley (1991), Fuson (1992), and Francesca Lardicci (1999). All these translations are based on Navarrete's transcription, except for Eugene Lyon, Oliver Dunn & James E. Kelley, and Francesca Lardicci. Dunn & Kelley deserve special attention as their work began with a precise computer-assisted effort to transcribe the original Las Casas manuscript.[58] Fuson believed their transcription and translation efforts to be a "singularly important contribution to the inventory of Columbus materials."[59] Francesca Lardicci, an Italian scholar of high caliber, received the honor of producing a translation of the log book of Columbus, now considered to be the scholarly standard of reference for the 1492 voyage.

In Dunn & Kelley's work, the original Spanish words of Las Casas appear alongside the English translation.[60] This allows a reader or researcher to review and analyze the text to either accept or challenge the translation. Of course, this assumes they correctly interpreted the original words, abbreviations, and other symbols. These factors may also be challenged. Let us look at Columbus's quoted words as written down by Las Casas. First, we will see Navarrete's base translation used by Samuel Kettell. It reads,

> I do not, however, see the necessity of fortifying the place, as the people here are simple in war-like matters, as your Highnesses will see by those seven which I have ordered to be taken and carried to Spain in order to learn our language and return unless your Highnesses should choose to have them all transported to Castile or held captive in the island. *I* could conquer the whole of them with fifty men and govern them as I pleased.[61]

A more modern translation by Fuson sets out a different tone.

> I do not think this is necessary [to build a fort], however, for these people are very unskilled in arms. Your Highnesses will see this for yourselves when I bring to you the seven that I have taken. After they learn our language, I shall return them, unless Your Highnesses orders that the entire population be taken to Castile or held captive here. With 50 men, *you* could subject everyone and make them do what you wished.[62]

Immediately, the reader is drawn to Kettell's translation phrase, "I have ordered to be taken and carried to Spain," suggesting Columbus participated in a forced abduction of Indigenous peoples. Fuson rejects the phrasing and prefers, "I bring to you…" leaving the door open to voluntary participation. Dunn & Kelley agree with Fuson's translation, stating, "The seven I did take to bring and learn our language." Also, notice how Kettell's understanding is that Columbus wanted to act directly against the Lucayans, stating, "I could conquer the whole of them with 50 men and govern them as I pleased." Dunn & Kelley, in their computer translation, refocus Columbus's intent as an alternative action that he would not take but that King Ferdinand and Queen Isabella might consider the idea, using the phrase, "because, with 50 men, all of them [Lucayans] could be held in subjection and can be made to do whatever *one* might wish."[63] Thacher, in his translation, supports the idea that Columbus understood he could not enslave anyone, only to suggest that if the monarchs desired, they could control the entire island.[64] It is clear from the *Capitulations of Santa Fe*, the critical agreement between Columbus and the Spanish monarchs, that enslavement of Indigenous peoples was not mentioned, indicating it was not expected, but would it be desired or allowed? As such, Columbus did not comprehend how Ferdinand and Isabella would want him, as Viceroy and Governor, to interact with local populations.[65] Yet he knew from personal observation during the final phases of the *Reconquista* that hundreds, if not thousands, of captured Moorish prisoners of war became enslaved, selling them in local, regional, and trans-Mediterranean markets. The intention here from Columbus is a question to the Spanish monarchs. He also saw Portuguese captains participate in securing slaves from local tribes during his visits to the Guinea (West African) coast.

Let us probe deeper into the actual writing of Las Casas, analyzing the original text and markings via Dunn & Kelley. They transcribed the key section of these sentences in Castilian Spanish as "de siete q[ue] yo hize tomar p[ar]a l[e]? llevar y deprender nra fabla y bolvellos." Two key Castilian verb forms here need pressing. First, *yo hize* (I have) in old Castilian dialect usage translates from the base verb form *hacer* to an action taken at a definite time in the past, mixing together what modern Spanish separates. Thus, Las Casas combined *hice*, the preterite for *yo hacer*, and *hizo*, the preterite for *él*, *ella*, or *Usted*, to write the term *hize*.

Now comes the interesting and most challenging part: Determining the understanding of the use of *tomar* (to take or receive) and realizing how dramatically a sentence's meaning can change. In old Castilian, as well as Spanish today, the verb form *tomar* has more than five distinct meanings. There are many basic levels of concept understanding and usage for this key verb.[66]

Interpreting the above usage functions by levels of concept, only one level of usage for the verb *tomar* noted in the *Real Academia Española* dictionary indicates the taking of an object or people forcibly or seizing something without permission.[67] It is suggested that Las Casas interpreted Columbus's Barcelona copy of the journal as the explorer intended, indicating a non-violent intention; otherwise, Las Casas would have interjected the key phrase *por fuerza* (to force). If this understanding is correct, then the concept phrase may read, "Your Highnesses will see this for yourselves when I bring to you the seven that I have taken with me." Fuson noted this distinction and recorded the sentence as such. Another usage indicated in the dictionary is even more forgiving, simply indicating that "Your Highnesses will see this for yourselves when I bring to you the seven that I have with me." In both scenarios, there is no evidence to indicate forcible abduction.

Let us refer to the 1611 Spanish dictionary, one of the oldest available to scholars. *Tomar* is referenced with several applicable usage samples. The first notation has nothing to do with *taking* but rather with *receiving*, relating to the term *vale recibir* (something worth receiving).[68] *Llevar* is referenced in the 1611 dictionary as *es mudar alguna cosa de un lugar a otro*, meaning (is to move something from one place to another). Now, let us revisit the October 14 entry, as noted by Dunn & Kelley, where Columbus talks about bringing some Indigenous peoples with him. The key phrase is, "de siete q[que] yo hise tomar p[ar] a l[e?] llevar y…" Dunn & Kelley's translation is "seven that I caused to be taken in order to carry them away to you and…" Substituting the concept of "something worth receiving," we can conjecture that Columbus was trying to convey that he received visitors (Indios) and was bringing them to Spain, teaching them the language, and returning them. The concept of forced removal is not necessarily implied; in fact, just the opposite is implied, suggesting that some of the Indios requested to travel with the "gods" on the "ships from the sky."[69]

The above analysis is arrived at more completely when considering the actions of Columbus up until this time, implementing and maintaining positive social interactions on the first two days of contact. Back-and-forth bartering, friendly exchanges of communication gestures, freely given gifts, and Columbus's thoroughly positive statements about the Lucayan people support the acceptance of either of the first two usages of concept understanding. In addition, he could have taken captives the day before, when he first wanted to do so, but he demurred. However, any conclusions at this point are premature.

The phrase "the seven I have taken with me," as suggested above, reads completely non-accusatory and is further supported, even by Kettell and other scholars using Navarrete's translation, later when Columbus describes his return to the ship *Santa Maria* and sets sail in search of larger islands. He wrote,

> I returned to the ship and setting sail, discovered such a number of islands that I knew not which first to visit; the natives whom I *had taken* on board, informed me by signs that there were so many of them that they could not be numbered; they repeated the names of more than a hundred.[70]

Again, this passage indicates that natives are onboard the *Santa Maria*, and they are attempting to communicate with the admiral. One logical assumption that can be arrived at in reading this account is that the Lucayans were in awe of the newcomers and agreed to come on board; they had already spent countless hours on the ships trading. A suggestion can be put forward that they initially misunderstood, all seven of them, that Columbus wanted them to go with the Spaniards; later, this changed as Columbus explored areas farther away from San Salvador. Thacher, at this point in his translation, makes Columbus's intentions clear: "The natives were not to be sold into slavery. They were not to be left in Spain. They were to be taken to the Sovereigns for their further disposition."[71] Thacher then suggests that language training for the seven Lucayans would help ensure future economic relations between Spain and the islands. Hinting that the seven may have volunteered to go, Thacher added,

"We shall see shortly that the Indians were not unwilling captives." This sentiment is echoed by Columbus scholar John Stewart Collis, while referencing Columbus's activities of October 25, said, "Some natives had volunteered to function as guides."[72] This concept is echoed by Carol Delaney, when she noted, "It is also possible that some of them wanted to go, because that became a common request."[73] Actually, as we shall see, at least two of them had second thoughts as Columbus moved farther away from San Salvador.

However, Las Casas, writing years later about this incident in his magisterial compilation of Spanish conquest and misdeeds, noted, "How far the admiral was from grasping the letter or spirit of divine and natural law, and from what, according to this law, he and the monarchs were obligated to do with regard to these peoples." This is an important statement about the schism of moral understanding between the secular and religious worlds of 15th-century Spanish Christianity. Continuing, Las Casas declared, "He [Columbus] was extremely far away from the goal that God and his church had in mind for his voyage." Having no doubt this event was a conscious act of kidnapping, Las Casas went on, "It indeed seems that he detained them against their will... It seems that this ought not to have been done against their will."[74]

Columbus, well aware of slavery in Genoa, Portugal, and Spain, also witnessed the evil institution being practiced in the Portuguese Atlantic colonies, and along the coast of West Africa, Frances Karttunen remarked, that the Portuguese captains maintained a "practice of carrying men off the Guinea coast in West Africa to learn the Portuguese language."[75] Karttunen, when referring to Columbus's first voyage, remarked that the explorer "succeeded in bringing back to Spain a small group of indigenes for exhibition at court" and later served with Columbus as native interpreters.

Columbus experienced Portuguese slavery, not by owning any slaves, but his place of residence for years occurred in Lisbon and on the Portuguese colony islands of Madeira and Porto Santo. He could see the impact of slavery every day, understanding that the West African slave trade produced large numbers of slaves for Lisbon, the seat of Portuguese power, having approximately a ten percent black population, most reduced to abject slavery, some manumitted. Numerous groups of slave work gangs worked continuously along Lisbon's large dock area, the same docks Columbus frequented.[76] Large-scale use of black slaves by Portugal ensued during the 1480s when ship captains focused on the Bight of Benin region, naming the useable seaport there as *Rios dos Escravos* (Slave Rivers), trading brass and cloth for captured slaves.[77] Selected slaves received training in the Portuguese language so as to interpret the Portuguese work instructions for the above-mentioned newly arrived slave work gangs and domestic servants.

The above discussion, admittedly, proved interesting in my research, even inviting further investigation. I had always assumed that the Lucayans had indeed been taken by force, with no exceptions. If one challenges Las Casas's transcription and translation, historians can turn to another primary source for comparison, and there is another source, a primary source, one that has settled the matter: Columbus's letter to King Ferdinand and Queen Isabella. The letter, one of several versions, was in Spain soon after Columbus's return. The following is a portion of that letter discussing the taking of Lucayans.

> And as soon as I arrived in the Indies, in the first island which I found, I took by force some of them, in order that they may learn and give me information of that which there is in those parts, and so it was that they soon understood us, and we them, either by speech or signs, and they have been very serviceable. I still take them with me, and they are always assured that I come from Heaven, for all the intercourse which they have had with me; and they were the first to announce this wherever I went.[78]

This letter appears to end the investigation, from the person in question, clearly labeling Columbus as a kidnapper, despite his assumption that they remained in awe of him; the only caveat being that Columbus's original letter is lost.[79]

Although another primary source, this one from Gonzalo Fernández de Oviedo, in writing *Historia general de las Indias*, mentions two incidents concerning Columbus and Indigenous guides, the first event describes how "Several Indians volunteered to board the ships and guide them," referencing an episode as Columbus sailed from Cuba to Hispaniola.[80] Later, in his writing, Oviedo admitted "Columbus arrived at Palos with the Indians he had taken from these islands, except for the one who died at sea."[81]

Ferdinand Columbus's writing, *The Life of the Admiral Christopher Columbus*, does describe his father, on October 14, taking "seven Indians" to serve as interpreters.[82] In summary, the overriding evidence strongly suggests that Columbus did detain and continue to hold the Indigenous persons; this would happen again on the island of Cuba. However, with the sinking of the *Santa Maria* later in the voyage, as we shall see, the situation with Columbus's captive guides changed dramatically.

With his native guides and interpreters on board, Columbus ordered his tiny fleet to lift anchors from San Salvador later in the day. Columbus sailed in a southwest direction, locating a large island approximately 15 miles on the horizon. As he did so, he believed all the islands in this area to be nearly flat, "exceedingly fertile and populous." One must question how Columbus knew this after only visiting San Salvador. Interestingly, to finish off his daily journal entry, he said, "The inhabitants [are] at war with one another, although a simple race, and with delicate bodies." The idea of interisland warfare is a concept that Columbus used later to rationalize his military intervention on subsequent voyages.

The Bahamas consists of an extensive array of islands running southeast to northwest. Columbus happened on one of the smaller islands, San Salvador, as

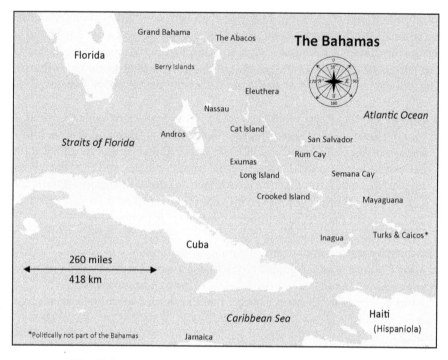

FIGURE 6.4 The Bahamas

he named it. Located in the central region of the Bahamas, San Salvador sits in a strategically important location, offering local Indigenous people living at the time of European contact canoe access to other Bahamian islands for trade and ceremonial exchange.

Notes

1 This date is on the Julian calendar, which remained in effect during Columbus's travels.
2 See Appendix II for a detailed study and map of Columbus's beach landing site.
3 Taviani, *Columbus*, 99. In addition to mangroves and palm trees, a wide variety of bushes cling vicariously to rocky outcrops interspersed between the sandy beaches.
4 For one such account, see John Stewart Collis's *Christopher Columbus*, 80. Also see John Dyson, *For Gold, God, and Glory*, 161.
5 The name *Lucayan* is a Spanish-derived term meaning "people of the small islands." See Keegan, "Lucayan Settlement Patterns."
6 Irving, Christopher Columbus, 149. Irving, using the descriptions noted in the *Diario*, embellished the landing event, particularly when writing about the subsequent interactions between the Europeans and the Indigenous peoples; see Irving, 149–54. For a complete authoritative account of the landings, see Dunn & Kelley, *The Diario*, 63–69.
7 Kettell, *Personal Narrative*, 34–35. Dunn & Kelley's translation reads, "And he said that they should be witnesses that, in the presence of all, he would take, as in fact he

did take, possession of the said island for the King and for Queen his lords, making the declarations that were required," 65.

8 Thacher, *Christopher Columbus*, 532.

9 Ferdinand Columbus, in his father's biography, described how the Lucayans of San Salvador wore their hair "with hanging thick and very dark, short hair, cut above the ears, although a few had let it grow to shoulder-length and had bound it around their heads with a thick cord, almost like a braid." Lardicci, *A Synoptic Edition, Historie*, FH 28, section 8, 148.

10 Altman, *Life and Society in the Early Spanish Caribbean*, 1. Altman reminds readers that we only have Columbus's version of these first encounter impressions.

11 Berman & Pearsall, "Plants, People, and Culture in the Prehistoric Central Bahamas," 222. Three fruit tree varieties were identified, including hog plum, pigeon plum, and coco plum, 233.

12 Blick, "Pre-Columbian Impact," 175. Blick describes an already overworked physical environment before Columbus arrived, putting pressure on the Lucayans to maintain population levels. He concluded that "relatively small human populations, with limited technology, can have significant impacts on island ecosystems." 181.

13 For more information on Blick's findings, see Appendix II. The largest concentration of Lucayans in San Salvador resided along the western and northern shores of Pidgeon Creek, an area not visited by Columbus.

14 Kettell, *Personal Narrative*, 35. Columbus later claims to have given *asi paño como otras cosas muchas* (cloth and many other things) on every island, but cloth is not specifically named on most occasions, as are glass beads. Rosenbach, *The Spanish Letter of Columbus*, 3. Fuson and Dunn & Kelley's translations are quite similar concerning the actions of Columbus and his crew and the reaction by the Lucayans.

15 Fuson, *The Log of Christopher Columbus*, 76. Lardicci made the point that Columbus may have anticipated encountering an "unsophisticated population" with the idea of trading items of little value to the Spanish for higher-valued products, such as gold. *A Synoptic Edition*, DB 28, note 3, 630.

16 Later, on Cuba and Hispaniola, Spaniards provided additional descriptions of Taíno appearance; this included shaving their heads in various sections and having "tufts of tangled hair in such shapes that it cannot be described." Face and body piercing also remained a common attribute of both men and women, including bone and gold plugs on the ears, nose, or mouth. See Deagan & Cruxent, "Reluctant Hosts," 29–30.

17 Columbus learned more about interisland slaving conditions during visits to Cuba and Hispaniola (Haiti). On this day, he noted these raiders might have come from mainland Asia, hoping he was close to Cathay and the riches of the Indies. This topic is of critical importance in analyzing Columbus's later experience when facing hostile Carib forces, and we will address this issue later in this work. See Martinell, Gifre (1989): 21–57 for an investigation of the mechanics and success of gesturing between the Indios and the Europeans—as taken from Lardicci, *A Synoptic Edition*, DB 28, note 3, 630.

18 Columbus wrote on the first day that he believed, "They should be good and intelligent servants, for I see that they say very quickly everything that is said to them; and I believe that they would become Christians very easily, for it seemed to me that they had no religion." Dunn & Kelley, *The Diario*, 67–68. Once Columbus brought Christianity into the social equation, he eliminated slavery.

19 The reader might know that at the same time Columbus began his journey, Ferdinand and Isabella passed a law forcing Jewish citizens to convert to Catholic Christianity or face expulsion. A few Jews converted; most left Spain, voluntarily or forced. Columbus believed from his early observations that the Lucayans apparently "have no religion," thinking this condition made Christian conversion easy. Years later,

after Columbus's death, Spain adopted a *requerimiento* (requirement) legally establishing religious hegemony [Roman Catholic] over indigenous peoples of the circum-Caribbean region. Altman, *Life and Society in the Early Spanish* Caribbean, 2.

20 Las Casas later denoted several groups of islanders, one of which he called *Ciboney* people, "who were kept as servants by the other Cuban Indians." Keegan, *The Caribbean Before Columbus*, 12. For a deeper understanding of Columbus's views on Indigenous peoples based on Spain's court advisors, see Claudia Alvares, "New World Slavery: Redefining the Human," 133–35.

21 Deagan, "Colonial Origins and Colonial Transformations in Spanish America," 4. Deagan sees religious conversion as a "goal equal to that of economic exploitation."

22 Hail Mary prayer in the Catholic faith.

23 Deagan & Cruxent, "Reluctant Hosts," 32

24 Keegan & Maclachlan, The Evolution of Avunculocal Chiefdoms," 613.

25 Ibid. In this manner, a tradition developed where a man with several wives created social and military alliances with the extended families of each wife. 620. For more on this subject, see M. Ember, "The Conditions that May Favor Avunculocal Residence," 203–09.

26 Keegan, *Taíno Indian Myths and Practice*, 116.

27 Ibid. Caonabó and Guacanagarí are two additional examples of regional caciques on Hispaniola at the time of European contact.

28 Bigelow, Seasons of Gold," 79.

29 Until recently, researchers thought that Carib raiders came from as far away as Puerto Rico and the Lesser Antilles. However, new evidence reveals their presence also on Hispaniola and Cuba. Taviani claimed that Caonabó, the Indigenous cacique responsible for later killing all Spaniards left on Hispaniola, was not Taíno but Carib. Ferdinand Columbus alluded to this in his *Historie*, declaring "that King Caonabó mentioned above was the greatest and most famous Indian of the island, and that because he was not a native of it (Hispaniola) but of the Caribbees [Caribs]." *Historie*, 173.

30 See Berman & Pearsall for an analysis of the flora of San Salvador. "Plants, People, and Culture in the Prehistoric Central Bahamas: A View from the Three Dog Site, and Early Lucayan Settlement on San Salvador Island, Bahamas."

31 Ibid., 223–24. Archaeologists have found glass beads, made from a variety of materials, scattered throughout the Three Dog site.

32 Ibid., 232. For more on the arboriculture of the Bahamas, see Berman, 232–3.

33 Rouse, *The Taíno*, 17. He points to the island of Gonâve, on the western coast of Haiti, where islanders focused on making and trading highly desirable wooden bowls. Also, see Anderson-Córdova, *Surviving Spanish Conquest*, Appendix I, 169.

34 Ibid. See "Historical Evidence for Interisland Contact in the Contact Period," 123–4. She summarizes by stating that there is strong evidence to suggest that interisland contact was both widespread and ongoing.

35 Studies have shown that San Salvador Island has historically received a higher frequency of storms and hurricanes than other Bahamian Islands. See Park, "Comparing Two Long-term Hurricane Frequency and Intensity Records from San Salvador Island, Bahamas," 892.

36 Rouse, *The Taínos*, 99–101. Evidence for these dates is determined from pottery analysis, then synthesizing data from all over the Greater Antilles (Cuba, Haiti, Puerto Rico, Jamaica).

37 Ibid., 72–73.

38 Mann, *1491*, 156.

39 The idea of supernatural beings rang strong in pre-contact Taíno beliefs; see Guitar & Estevez, "Taíno," 120–***4. See their quote from Las Casas when the Spanish priest asked them, "Who is this cemí [Zemi] that you call upon?" 1021.

40 Guitar & Estevez, "*Taínos*," 1020.
41 Kettell, *Personal Narrative*, 37. Dunn & Kelley's translation reads, "I will take six of them from here to Your Highnesses in order that they may learn to speak." 69.
42 In reality, slavery in the pre-Columbian Americas existed everywhere. Historian Christina Snyder wrote, "Captivity and its most exploitive form—slavery—was Indigenous to North America, it was widespread, and it took many forms." *Slavery in Indian Country*, 4. Columbus found that larger villages contained slaves, most often captured prisoners from raids, raids usually resulting in payback for prior aggressive hostilities. Slaves existed on at least three of the large Caribbean islands, Hispaniola, Cuba, and Jamaica, displaying a three-level system of social hierarchy consisting of "hereditary chiefs and deities, warriors, slaves." Dugard, *The Last Voyage of Columbus*, 214. This does not, in any way, excuse Columbus or his men from any subsequent actions.
43 The term *Indios*, coined by Columbus, thinking he was in the Indies, is respectfully used interchangeably with Indigenous peoples and Indians in describing the native peoples of the Caribbean in general terms. More specifically, the archaeological terms Lucayans, Taíno, and Caribs are used to describe inhabitants of specific geographic regions of the Caribbean.
44 Caraci believes the term came from Columbus's use of the term *almadia*, "a term the Portuguese had taken from the Arabic to indicate the boats they had encountered along the western coasts of Africa, which is dug into the trunk of a tree." Personal communication, July 17, 2022.
45 Jane, *The Journal of Christopher Columbus*, 26.
46 Fuson, *The Log of Christopher Columbus*, 78.
47 Dunn & Kelley, *The Diario*, 75. The reference here is to October 14, when Columbus used the skiff boat to get close to the western shore of Guanahani, and natives followed along on the beach, calling out to fellow islanders, "Come see the men who came from the heavens." How Columbus knew, after only a short time on Guanahani and not knowing the language, what the Lucayans were shouting, is difficult to believe. Yet other evidence comes from various interactions between Cuba and Hispaniola. It is as if Columbus wanted to believe that he could understand the Indios from the beginning, despite admitting later that he could not understand them. James Axtell makes it clear that early explorers and settlers understood the importance of language understanding when he wrote, "The key to the continent was information—reliable, unambiguous, and digestible—and the quickest and best source of it was the Indians." "Babel of Tongues," 15.
48 One may well understand this point of view, likening it to an alien visitation today. How would a typical Earth citizen react? In most instances, the Indigenous peoples fled by sitting on the Spanish ships; then, in a short time, their hesitation faded, and they came forward, often eagerly canoeing or swimming out to the ships, remaining for hours, sometimes going, and coming again during the day.
49 Taviani, *Columbus*, 102. The foundation of this cultural misunderstanding, for Columbus, resided in his strong religious belief that it was his duty, his calling, to convert the Indigenous islanders to Christianity, believing, at first, they had no religion. For the Lucayans, it is difficult to know their thoughts on first contact, although they may have processed, in their own way, the physical and technological differences, with the Spaniards possessing unique physical attributes (white skin and facial hair) and little understood weapons (guns, metal swords).
50 Taviani believed that Columbus, at this point, felt vindicated in thinking that San Salvador lies close to Cipangu. The maps the explorer had consulted, and the maps he now carried with him, revealed dozens, if not hundreds, of small islands lying near the fabled island. See *Columbus*, 105.
51 Kettell, *Personal Narrative*, 39.

52 As noted previously, it seems incredible that Columbus could, in any way, know much of the Arawak language. Francesca Lardicci, in her superlative translation, *A Synoptic Edition*, noted that Las Casas wrote, "All these are the admiral's exact words, recounting what I recount here," concerning an entire section of text that is the third-person narrative. These kinds of errors on the part of Las Casas support critics who claim one must be cautious when reading direct quotes credited to Columbus. Passage taken from Lardicci, *A Synoptic Edition*, LC 30, section 6, 202. Lardicci's concern is noted on page 654, commentary LC 30. Las Casas uses another direct quote in his *Diario* but references it in a third-person reference in his *Historia de las Indias*, in almost the exact same word use and sequence. See Lardicci, commentary, LC 85, 659. Later, in LC 90, section 37, Las Casas reverses himself and uses the first-person in *Historia de las Indias*, the first of only two such instances, and then reports the event in a third-person narrative in the *Diario*. Lardicci, LC 90 commentary, 659.

53 This was most likely the site Blick excavated, SS-3, or the Ward Minnis Site studied by Berman and Pearsall.

54 Kettell, *Personal Narrative*, 40.

55 Bradford noted that on this day, he "committed the first great sin in this new Eden." *Christopher Columbus*, 121.

56 A factoid may be fictitious or unsubstantiated. Its ongoing use in the written record is thus relayed from one author to another, becoming, in time, a fact.

57 For a list of transcriptions post-Navarrette, see Fuson, *The Log of Christopher Columbus*, 8–10.

58 Lyon's effort was not computer-generated. For more details on the methodology used by Dunn & Kelley, see their main publication, *The Diario of Christopher Columbus's First Voyage to America, 1492–1493*, published in 1991.

59 Fuson, *The Log of Christopher* Columbus, 10. One reason Fuson and indeed subsequent Columbus scholars praise the Dunn & Kelley effort is due to their inclusion, side-by-side, of Las Casas Spanish exact word use and the adjacent English translation.

60 Dunn & Kelley used the Carlos Sanz facsimile reproduction of the original Las Casas manuscript. La Casas's verbatim notes become an original record—ideas written or spoken by the actual person at that time.

61 Kettell, *Personal Narrative*, 40.

62 Fuson, *The Log of Christopher* Columbus, 79–80.

63 Dunn & Kelley, The Diario, 75. The authors' translation clearly states that Columbus is bringing the Lucayans to the Spanish monarchs, and they, not him, would decide subsequent actions. Of course, transporting them from the island with permission is kidnapping and unjustified.

64 Thacher, *Christopher Columbus*, 538.

65 One reason for Columbus's statement centers on the idea that he expected to find more "advanced" societies, demonstrating equal or greater technology and military equality—such as he believed existed in Cipangu and Cathay.

66 The usage of "to take with force" can be investigated with the *Real Academia Española* (Tricentennial Edition), 2020. In old Castilian and modern Spanish, the term "to take by force" would be "para tomar por la fuerza." Yet, when looking at *tomar*, many usage applications are apparent. Each usage changes the intent of the meaning, *to take*. The most common usage means "to take with you" such as "I will take my book to school," meaning the transport of an item. Another usage translates dramatically into "to have," for example, "I have to eat" or "I have with me seven natives." None of these usage applications imply *take by force*.

67 The *Real Academia Española* is a recognized source for scholars needing an understanding of Spanish language usage, historical and contemporary, specializing in linguistic regularization, dating back to its first edition in 1780.

68 Covarrubias Orozco, Sebastián de, *Tesoro de la lengua castellana, o Española*, See definitions for tomar (page 379) and llevar (page 191). The 1611 Spanish words were then translated into the *Diccionario de la lengua castellana* resulting in the expressions noted above.

69 For those wishing to see the original translation of this day and all other entries of Navarette's work, see Viajes de Cristóbal Colón, 29–30. Two of the three top translation results from the *Real Academia Española* for *tomar* describe an action of receiving, not taking; one example is stated as "Receive something and take care of it" and the other is "Receive or accept in any way." The one result using the interpretation "to take" is shown with the following example: "Take, even if it is not by hand," indicating not by force.

70 Kettell, *Personal Narrative*, 41.

71 Thacher, Christopher Columbus, 533. Delaney supports this supposition, as we shall see later.

72 Collis, *Christopher Columbus*, 88.

73 Delaney, *Columbus and the Quest for Jerusalem*, note 11, 268. She also agrees with this author that enslaving (kidnapping) Indigenous peoples at this point in the voyage would appear to be something Columbus would want to avoid, at least until he understood the dynamics of the regional geopolitical situation.

74 All three quotes from Las Casas, *Historia de las Indias*, in Lardicci, *A Synoptic Edition*, LC 30, sections 13–17, 202–03. One should the conceptual hesitation by using the phrase "It indeed seems…" The use of the term "seems" indicates appearance or likelihood, yet dissuades a firm commitment of fact.

75 Karttunen, "Snatched from the Shore," 218. Karttunen began the article by highlighting the November 12, 1492, quote from the logbook where Columbus ordered men to go ashore in Cuba and bring back "seven head of women, small and large, and three boys." 216.

76 Vogt, "The Lisbon Slave House and African Trade, 1486–1521," 1. For more on the Portuguese slave trade in the eastern Atlantic, see Ivana Elbl, "The Volume of the Early Atlantic Slave Trade, 1450–1521" (1973): 31–75. For a more recent study, see Newson, Linda A., "African and Luso-Africans in the Portuguese Slave Trade on the Upper Guinea Coast in the Early Seventeenth Century" (2012): 1–24.

77 Vogt, "The Lisbon Slave House and African Trade," 2–3. The 1480s coincided with a dramatic call for domestic slaves in Lisbon.

78 Jane, "First Voyage of Columbus," 10. Columbus's letter may have been written during his return voyage, with a postscript added in Lisbon. That original letter, probably in Spanish, is lost. Three versions appeared shortly after his arrival in Spain. Cecil Jane believed that Columbus wrote only to the Spanish monarchs and that other versions of the letter were authorized by them for further distribution. "The Letter of Columbus," 50. For a more recent and excellent account of the first letter, see Delaney, The Quest for Jerusalem, 122–3.

79 No original manuscripts of the letter exist today. There are numerous printed copies published shortly after Columbus's arrival and later. For more on the letters of Columbus, see Zamora, *Reading Columbus*, 10–14.

80 Carrillo, *Oviedo on Columbus*, 51. See section 3.7.2. There is no mention of this episode in Columbus's logbook.

81 Ibid., 52. See section 3.7.12. This incident is not mentioned by Columbus's son in his father's biography.

82 Keen, *The Life of the Admiral Christopher Columbus*, 64.

7

A SEA OF ISLANDS

October 15–27

> They [Indios] let us go anywhere we desired and gave us anything we asked.
> —Christopher Columbus, *Diario*, October 16, 1492

Rum Cay and a Lucayan "Escapes"

October 15, Monday

Columbus had his discovery; he made it happen. He was excited to explore its potential and understand its breadth, its fullness, and its ability to fulfill his destiny. To this end, he sailed late in the day on the 14th in SW direction, making at least 15 nautical miles before deciding to "stand off" and wait until daylight to approach what appeared to be the largest of several islands. From this strategic location, the curious explorer could, in the cool morning, make for one of at least three islands: Rum Cay to the south, Concepción Island (SW), and probably the southeastern tip of Cat Island.[1] He chose to visit Rum Cay, thinking the island was larger than the other two and optimistically calculating land dimensions to determine habitation. In short order, the ships arrived off the southern shore by late in the afternoon. He estimated Rum Cay's eastern shore, the side that Columbus noted "runs north and south a distance of five leagues;" the correct distance is about 2 leagues (6 miles); the same type of error is seen with Columbus specifically noting he sailed the east to west coastline 10 leagues (30 miles).[2] As he neared the western peninsula of Rum Cay, on the lee side, an excited Columbus anchored, where the reef disappeared and deep water prevailed. He also based his decision on the information the San Salvador guides provided, the guides claiming that certain chiefs on the island possessed "large golden bracelets on the legs and arms" in a village nearby.[3]

DOI: 10.4324/9781003464143-11

Columbus sat idle as the sun set, pondering the advice given by the "*Indios* amid gesturing and murmuring, preferring to go ashore in the morning."[4] He must have sensed that some of them now regretted their decision to help the "men from heaven." Around midnight on the 14th, one native on the *Niña* daringly leaped into the sea, swam to a nearby canoe, and made it to shore. Notice that this action did not occur on the *Santa Maria* but on the ship that Vincente Pinzón commanded. It is not clear if Columbus and Pinzón restrained their Guanahani captives; none of the primary sources mention the topic. Later, during the 15th, when Columbus explored Rum Cay, another Indio on the *Niña* leaped overboard as natives paddled a large canoe alongside the ship. Getting into the canoe, the paddlers quickly headed for shore. Spaniards on *Niña* attempted to chase down the Indian canoe, but to no avail. Lardicci describes what happened next: "Some of the men [Spaniards] from my company went ashore after them, but they all ran away like chickens."[5]

This is an interesting episode and one worth investigating. Both escapes occurred on Vincente Pinzón's *Niña*, with no other reported attempts from the other vessels. We do not know how many Lucayans were on Martín Pinzón's *Pinta* at that time, although later, there were at least two; that would leave three with Columbus on the *Santa Maria*. With the Lucayans being detained forcibly by Columbus and Pinzón and made to serve as guides and interpreters, one can imagine taking the opportunity to escape, as Rum Cay was close to their home island, and it might be their last chance to return. No other attempted escape events from the other five Lucayans occurred on the voyage, as reported in the journal. All five remaining natives were baptized in Spain with Columbus and the Spanish monarchs standing in as godparents, confirming to the gathered witnesses the Lucayans' profession of faith.[6]

Carol Delaney explained the fate of the five Lucayans.

> One of the Indians, a relative of the cacique (chief) Guacanagarí, was named Don Fernando, after the King, another Don Juan, after the Infante, and the one who was close to Columbus was named Don Diego Colón—the name of both his brother and his son. Don Juan chose to remain at court [in Spain]; the others chose to return home on Columbus's next voyage. Apparently, only two of them survived the journey; one was Columbus's "godson," Don Diego, who became his able interpreter and accompanied him on many of his travels.[7]

It should be noted here that religious actions against slavery by Papal decrees occurred as early as the 10th century, but the 1435 Papal Bull (official declaration) condemned the enslavement of Indigenous peoples specifically on the Canary Islands, requiring enforcement by Spanish and Portuguese officials. The edict cogently mentioned that "baptized residents... or those who are freely seeking Baptism" and a promise that new Christians cannot be enslaved or their property confiscated.[8] The Spanish monarchs well understood this religious directive, which they encountered often when deciding the fate of captured Muslims during the *Reconquista*.[9] Hence, Ferdinand and Isabella transferred the Canary Islands situation to the newly reported islands of the New World, founding the proposition that all converted Indians shall be free.[10]

Returning to forced slavery, one needs to ask the question: Why would you want a forced slave to serve as a guide and interpreter? How would one know if the information given as a guide was correct? Or, even more interesting is the use of a kidnapped individual to act as an interpreter. This does not make sense unless the interpreter has been trained and is currently a trusted source, as was the case with the Portuguese involvement on the West African coast. By the mid-15th century, Portuguese merchants, working out of Lisbon, developed an "effective method for obtaining and training interpreters." Here is a description of how the system worked:

> Each of our ships had negro interpreters on board, brought from Portugal, who had been sold by the lords of Senegal to the first Portuguese to discover this land of the blacks [Blacks]. These slaves had been made Christians in Portugal and knew Spanish [sic] well; we had them from their owners on the understanding that for the hire and pay of each, we will give one slave to be chosen from all our captives. Each interpreter, also, who secured four slaves for his master was to be given his freedom.[11]

One is hard-pressed to accept the example above for the Columbus situation; guide maybe, but interpreter, no.[12] However, Columbus's case is different. In the Portuguese situation, they used captured Africans who had already received training in the new language, Portuguese, and were given an incentive to participate—capture four slaves, and you receive your freedom. In Columbus's episode, his Indio guides and interpreters knew no Spanish; their only incentive, according to Columbus, included their being returned at some later date. We also do not know the situation with the African interpreters as they interacted ashore. But, with Columbus, he sent his interpreters ashore with only one or two, or in some cases, completely unaccompanied, to contact local tribes—a perfect opportunity to flee or ask for help from local peoples encountered. Although, outside the scope of this book that focuses on the first voyage, one can find examples where Columbus completely trusted his Lucayan guides to go to village caciques and report messages, interestingly, the Lucayans always returned to their ships—why would they do this if they had been kidnapped? (Figure 7.1).[13]

From San Salvador, Columbus viewed several distant islands. He decided to head southwest based on information derived from his recently captured Indigenous guides arriving for a short stay on a small island he called Santa Maria de la Concepción. Finding no gold, he continued his southerly trek to reach another island he named Isabella, after his royal supporter, the queen of Castile.

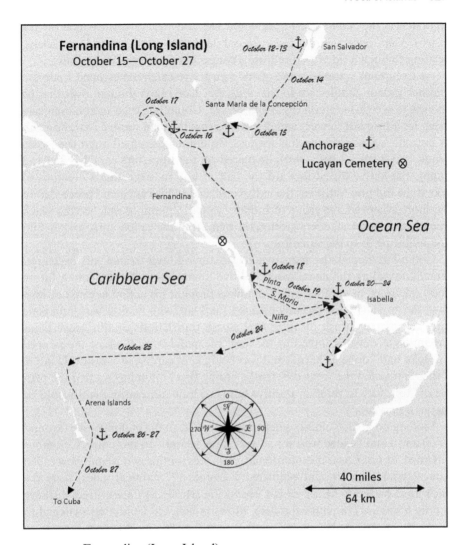

FIGURE 7.1   Fernandina (Long Island)

The Search for Gold Begins

October 16, Tuesday

At dawn, Columbus once again waded ashore to proclaim possession, naming this island *Isla de Santa María de la Concepción*. The lush island impressed Columbus. He soon gathered information on the naked people and sent shore parties searching through trees and bushes for gold; none was found. After securing sufficient water supplies and trading a few items with the local people, Columbus, after only a few hours, returned to his ship, disappointed. As he approached the *Santa Maria*, he could see and hear a disturbance on the nearby *Niña*; once again, a Lucayan onboard that vessel jumped overboard, desiring to hitch a ride to shore from a canoe resting alongside the ship.

As Columbus watched some of his men try to catch the escaped Lucayan, another Indian paddled up to the *Niña*, but Columbus shouted over that he wanted to see this man on the *Santa Maria*. Columbus tried to communicate using his native interpreters and discovered that the man wanted to trade a ball of cotton. Acknowledging this request, Columbus presented a red cap, some beads, and a hawk's bell, which he placed on the Lucayan's ears. Excited and happy, the native thrust forward the ball of cotton, expecting Columbus to take it; he did not. Satisfied, the native returned to his canoe and proceeded to the shore, where a large group of Indians waited. Columbus watched the beach intently as several islanders greeted the man from the canoe, surrounding him and inquiring as to the situation.

Columbus hoped the man would explain his well-treated gift exchange, thereby revealing the newcomers' positive intentions and anticipating future good relations. In another way, Columbus thought his action negated or lessened the impact of the recently escaped Lucayan, who by now was long gone into the interior brush of Rum Cay. Some translations of this scene paint Columbus as devious, intending to "fool" the natives into thinking the escaped Lucayan had "done us harm" and was being kept captive as a result. Dunn & Kelley translated the scene differently, noting that Columbus wanted the people of Rum Cay to think in positive terms so that subsequent visits would be met in friendship.[14]

Finding no gold, Columbus departed Rum Cay in the mid-morning (around 10:00 a.m.) and headed west for a "very large island." In this entry, Columbus recorded, or Las Casas misinterpreted, distances for this new island, now called Long Island. The account estimated 9 leagues (27 nautical miles) from the anchorage on Santa Maria de la Concepción (Rum Cay); the correct distance is only 6 leagues (18 nautical miles). Morison believed Columbus switched to *land leagues* once he began cruising between the islands. However, there is no evidence for this assertion, and no previous known account of a *land league* being used by Spanish or Portuguese explorers in the Eastern Atlantic exists.[15]

A continuing confidence in his remaining Lucayan guides prevailed as Columbus sailed to this new island, believing their stories involving natives wearing golden earrings and nose ornaments. While watching the San Salvador guides gesture their communication, lookouts spotted a lone small canoe. Columbus ordered a course correction to intercept the vessel. The lone occupant waved enthusiastically and began paddling toward the *Santa Maria*. Once safely grappled alongside the larger ship, the Lucayan, without prompting, climbed the rope ladder and jumped on deck. Columbus immediately greeted the visitor, and with his interpreters nearby, the admiral learned that the man had come from San Salvador to Santa Maria de la Concepción and was now heading toward Fernandina.[16] One of the Lucayan interpreters questioned why he wanted to come on board. As this continued, Columbus noticed the man carried a fist-sized lump of bread, a water calabash, some red soil, and, interestingly, dried leaves, causing Columbus to recall the natives telling him it held a high value in Lucayan society.[17] Ferdinand Columbus, in writing his *Historie*, added that the Lucayan possessed a small wooden bowl that contained green glass beads and two *blancas*, a sure sign the man had originated on San Salvador.[18] This is the first evidence of interisland communication between Lucayans.[19]

For the rest of the short trip to the new island, Columbus served Spanish bread, honey, and water to his guests. Recalling this event as he wrote out the daily report, Columbus mentioned how much he wanted to please the Indigenous peoples so that future Spanish contact would permit a profitable trading experience. After all, the key economic goal of his voyage centered on him establishing a working relationship with the peoples of the "islands and mainlands" he discovered.

Later that evening, the Lucayan visitor, still on board, now happily departed and paddled toward a nearby village. The next morning, Columbus followed and laid off near the coast without anchoring. As with the other islands, the admiral, noting the extensive reefs running the length of the island, remained off the coast, well away from the beach.[20] Once on land, the admiral named the island *Fernandina* (for King Ferdinand). Reacting to natives on the beach who showed familiarity with the gold samples he showed them, Columbus predicted he would find their source. The possibility of finding riches is the unquenchable lure of action; the inaction of opportunity guarantees failure. Columbus favored action.

Soon, the Lucayans who had paddled from San Salvador spread "favorable accounts of us," and local natives piled into canoes, briskly paddling seaward to see the men from heaven. Again, as played out on San Salvador and Santa Maria de la Concepción, islanders maneuvered their canoes alongside each of the three Spanish ships in hopes of climbing aboard to trade. For his part, Columbus spread the word to give generously and to make sure that "each man" received something; items gifted to these Lucayans included "strings of ten or a dozen glass beads, plates of brass... thongs of leather, all of which they estimated highly."[21] During the exchange, Spanish sailors offered islanders a taste of molasses; apparently, the treat was well received.

Later that day, groups of Spaniards debarked and searched for fresh water. The scouting party did not need to search, as eager Lucayans led them to a local freshwater source, a highly valued resource in a region where freshwater rivers and streams do not exist.[22] Columbus, impressed to see the Lucayans helping to carry the water back to the ships and observing how eagerly they sought to "serve" the Spanish visitors, wrote, "The natives... and seemed to take great pleasure in serving us."

Leaving the north end of Long Island (Fernandina), Columbus wanted to follow up on a Lucayan story told by some excited natives who had come onboard about a gold mine purportedly on Fernandina or on another nearby island. Initially, he hoped to sail southeast with the idea of circumnavigating the island, thinking that the story correlated well with some of the tales gestured by natives from San Salvador. Always trying to analyze the environment and people encountered, Columbus wrote,

> These people [on Long Island] are similar to those of the islands just mentioned and have the same language and customs; with the exception that they appear somewhat more civilized, showing themselves more subtle in their dealings with us, bartering their cotton and other articles with more profit than the others had experienced.[23]

Columbus and crew noticed how cotton fibers were strung together to form a type of cloth, mostly small and used by young women, "hiding their secret parts." The variance in precipitation and soil thinness localized the successful growing of the crop. In addition to cotton, Columbus imagined natives sowing and reaping corn. The explorer spoke of a curious plant that grew unique individual branches, none repeating the same shape, texture, color, or leaf structure.[24]

With a delight in personal observation of physical features, Columbus also recorded reports from his crew. From their ships and the seashore, the crew talked of brightly colored fish and whales. From the land, a report came from a ship's boy of seeing a large snake; others saw parrots and lizards of different sizes and shapes. What they did not see were the usual domesticated animals, including sheep and goats. Later, the explorers would encounter dogs that did not bark. From the journal entry for this day, a reader senses the wonder of seeing so much new and interesting flora and fauna—an environment unlike Italy, Portugal, or Spain (Figure 7.2).[25]

On the island he named Fernandina, after Ferdinand, king of Aragon and co-ruler of Castile, Columbus enjoyed a brisk exchange with local Indios, as he now called the native people of the islands, insisting his men give every visitor that paddled out to the ships glass beads and "thongs of leather."

A Lucayan Village and Cemetery

October 17, Wednesday

A quick meeting with the few Lucayans on the *Santa Maria* convinced Columbus to head SSE, following Fernandina's coastline and avoiding the reefs where necessary. For the first time, Columbus admits that "all the Indians" agreed that an island called Samoet lay to the south, where bountiful amounts of gold

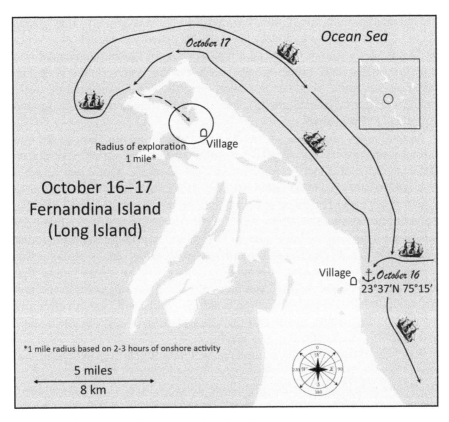

October 17

Ocean Sea

Radius of exploration
1 mile*   Village

October 16–17
Fernandina Island
(Long Island)

Village   *October 16*
23°37′N 75°15′

*1 mile radius based on 2-3 hours of onshore activity

5 miles

8 km

FIGURE 7.2   Fernandina Island: October 16–17

existed. Just before they set sail, Martín Pinzón on *Pinta* reported that the three remaining natives onboard his ship informed him that a short sail to the NNW would allow them to round the north end of Fernandina, Columbus's previous goal. The wind seemed to agree, blowing hard from the southeast. The fleet set sail for the NNW and, within a short time, approached the head of the island. Columbus immediately noticed what appeared to be an excellent harbor containing an opening through the reefs. At first, he thought it was a river; however, a shore party moved inland in search of fresh water and found no river existed.[26]

While the shore party attempted to find water, Columbus marveled at the environment. When among the dense tree growth, he could not help noticing the different varieties of trees and shades of green that highlighted different plants, something he never, or rarely, encountered in all his travels in the Old World. As he walked, Columbus came upon a small village. The Lucayans hesitated at first, then appeared friendly, immediately desiring gifts from the Spaniards and trading whatever tool, food, or weapon they possessed. On this trip,

Columbus allowed a few of the ship's boys to come along, and they traded pieces of broken dishes and glass for shell-sharpened tree-branch spears. For the first time, Columbus described a typical Lucayan home: tent-shaped reed structures with a small funnel-shaped hole at the top to vent smoke. As in San Salvador and Santa Maria de la Concepción, the village consisted of 12–15 huts. Averaging 4–6 inhabitants per hut, one can estimate the village population at 50–90 Lucayans.[27]

As small dogs ran among them, the Spaniards found out through the San Salvador interpreters that married women in this village wore a type of cotton garment, either a short skirt or two-legged covering. One crew member reported later that he attempted to barter with one native who had a gold-piece pinned to his nose. The sailor swore he could make out small letters carved in the gold but hesitated, thinking the no-trading policy was still in effect from Columbus. This imagined coin excited Columbus, confirming in his mind that riches lie nearby. As historian Fernandez-Armesto observed, "Columbus was hoping to find such prospects opening in reality before his eyes, as proof that he was close to the prosperous economies of Asia."[28] At this point in the voyage, Columbus remained focused on making contact with Asian rulers and securing trading rights, leading to the establishment of a profitable trading post; colonization remained a non-sequitur.

Water casks full, Columbus continued sailing until he rounded the island, where the San Salvador Indians successfully gestured that no gold existed on the leeward side of Fernandina. Columbus understood; he turned around and began heading for the windward shore and a course SE. After some hours, heavy rain fell on the fleet, accompanied by thick clouds, preventing the fleet from attempting to find an overnight anchorage. Finally, nearly reaching the southern tip of Fernandina, Columbus halted for daybreak.

October 18, Thursday

With extensive reefs guarding the windward side of Fernandina, Columbus cautiously remained between 3 and 5 nautical miles from the shore. While he did not know it, several Lucayan villages dotted the coast. Recent archaeological work revealed the first recorded finding of an Indigenous cemetery in this area. Researchers representing the Antiquities, Monuments, and Museum Corporation (AMMC) reported their findings in 2016, stating that a local resident came upon the site just north of Clarence Town on Long Island. Skeletons of two individuals, one male and the other a female, resided alongside each other, both buried face-down. Michael Pateman, a representative from AMMC, was quoted as saying, "This is the first time we have ever excavated multiple Lucayan burials on a beach dune… Previously, all burials found in the Bahamas have either been in caves or discovered in blue holes."[29]

In mentioning caves, Columbus proved silent, yet they pervaded the pre-Columbian era, with researcher Robert Carr and others listing, as of 2012, 15 caves on Long Island, 13 on San Salvador, 9 on Rum Cay, and 5 on Crooked Island. Of these sites, at least one petroglyph and/or pictograph site was recorded on each island.

Realizing the island of Fernandina appeared long and narrow, without a large Indio population or a rich chief (cacique), and therefore little to no gold, Columbus was determined to stay aboard ship at the southernmost point. Anxious to find Samoet, the island San Salvadorian natives claimed contained gold, the Genoese explorer considered his options; he needed to act, but where to go?

Isabella (Crooked Island) and the Search for *Samoet*

October 19, Friday

In the morning, Columbus called a meeting of the ships' captains, informing Martín and Vicente Pinzón to head on slightly different headings: *Niña* to the SSE, *Pinta* to the ESE, while Columbus's flagship would sail SE. Not trusting the directions given by the Lucayans onboard, Columbus calculated different course headings, hoping it might increase their opportunity to sight land. Later, as we shall see, Columbus would regret allowing Martín Pinzón to sail independently. After a brief 3 hours of cruising in quiet waters, land appeared to the east. The *Santa Maria* changed course toward land, followed by the other two ships.

Arriving off the coast of this new island, forward lookouts reported the usual concentration of reefs, making a close anchoring unpredictable. The land today carries the name Crooked Island; Columbus, finding the need to honor his patron queen, gave it the name Isabella. Without anchoring, the fleet moved to explore the leeward-curving coast south. Taking advantage of a reliable north wind, they moved SE, then SW. After 12 miles, an opening in the island's landmass appeared. Columbus wanted to enter this lagoon, but depth readings found the sea bottom extremely shallow.[30] Not wanting to waste time anchoring and sending in the skiff boats, Columbus decided to sail on, changing direction to the SW. Soon the coast bore due south and abruptly ended after 12 more miles. Taking depth readings for a possible anchorage, the crew reported deep water—very deep water.[31] No reef structures impeded a close approach, so Columbus maneuvered the fleet into a 30-foot-deep location, only 600 feet from the beach. Content for the moment, orders went out to secure the anchorage, deciding to postpone a landing until the next day.

From the ship, Columbus observed the nearby coast, admiring the dense tree coverage and small hills. Optimistically, he believed these small hills held fresh, running creeks. This comment does not match the current topography of Long Cay or Crooked Island. The highest point on Long Cay is a short ridge, about 1 mile in length, culminating no higher than 52 feet in elevation, while on Crooked Island, the windward hills extend about 12 miles, with a high point only reaching 100 feet. In terms of vegetation, Columbus exaggerated the apparent economic possibilities, stating, "I believe that there are many herbs and many trees that are worth much in Europe for dyes and for medicines."[32]

Conjecturing from the poop deck of the *Santa Maria*, Columbus could not see any shoreline Indio villages, yet he believed this peninsula was part of Samoet, the island named by Guanahani Indians as rich with gold. He continued to make plans for an inland expedition to search for the island's cacique. On further thought, he wrote, "I don't give much faith to what they [Guanahani interpreters] say, as well because I do not understand them."[33] One can read a growing concern, even desperation, to find "gold or spices in quantity."

October 20, Saturday

In the morning, instead of going ashore, and upon further attempted communication with his interpreters, Columbus decided to retrace his course NE and NW and return to the northern tip of Isabella. The Indios onboard continued to gesture, pointing north and saying "Samoet." Knowing not what else to do, he ordered the fleet to sail in that direction. The wind pounded down from the north, slowing the fleet's progress to a crawl. With a slight turn of the wind after sunset, the fleet captains ordered each ship to tack, and they made some distance.[34] Then, hours later, Columbus, not trusting the rugged coastline reefs, ordered the fleet to "lay to" (take down sails) without anchoring. The Pinzón brothers thought the fleet should move toward shore and attempt anchoring; they did, but Columbus thought it unsafe for the deeper draft of the *Santa Maria*, to remain some distance out to sea.[35]

October 21, Sunday

In the morning, Columbus changed his mind and moved in slowly to the already anchored caravels, sitting securely at the far northern tip of Crooked Island, not far from where the fleet had come together two days earlier. Going ashore, Columbus found one lone abandoned hut; apparently, its occupants fled only moments earlier, leaving all or most of their possessions intact. Giving strict orders that no one should confiscate anything, Columbus walked inland, again praising the lush vegetation, declaring its environment as similar to that of Andalusia, the second time he noted this in his journal. Providing extra detail on the sweet sounds of Indigenous birds, the exploring team saw large numbers of multicolored, squawking parrots flying about and perched on tree branches.

Thinking again about possible future trade items, Columbus inspected several fruit specimens, all of which appeared unknown to him and his search party. Sample specimens were carefully bagged and later stored on the *Santa Maria*.[36] This action, along with many other incidents on these first islands of discovery, points to the fact that Columbus did not exclusively seek gold on his voyage; spices, fruits, seedlings of strange and unique plants, and parrots also stimulated his interest. On this island, aloes abounded. Columbus recognized the thick, fleshy leaves, and considering their potential sale, he asked the men to gather a quantity of the succulent plant.[37]

He walked on through dense foliage, encountering a large snake; it looked unusual in color and markings, and a Spaniard followed it into the adjacent lagoon, killing it. Columbus had it skinned as a trophy specimen and later presented this unexpected prize to the Spanish monarchs on his return.

Reaching a point about 2 miles inland, the exploration party came upon a village of several huts. Surprising the Lucayans at first, Columbus halted his approach only to see the villagers racing away, carrying some of their possessions. Inspecting some of the huts revealed the same type of food items and stone tools found on other islands. Once again, Columbus made it clear that nothing was to be touched; instead, the men, as a group, stood near the huts non-aggressively in hopes the native inhabitants might return; they did. Moving cautiously, a few of the Lucayans appeared from behind the thick trees and bravely approached the motionless visitors. One brave soul walked right up to Columbus and just stood there, gazing at the Genoese sailor. Columbus broke the silence, handing the Indio the usual gifts of tiny bells and shiny glass beads. Pleased, the native grinned.[38]

A brief, friendly exchange continued with other Lucayans who now joined their leader, their cacique. Columbus asked the cacique to help him locate the water. At this point, it is not clear if Columbus had any of his interpreters with him during this encounter. However, later events proved that they were indeed there, translating Columbus's appeal for help. It does not appear that any force or threat preceded this verbal exchange, for the landing party returned to the fleet and found the island Indios not far behind, lugging containers of fresh water. In return for their efforts, Columbus presented each of the water carriers with a string of glass beads. Happy, the Lucayans spoke to the interpreters, who then relayed the message that the islanders would come back tomorrow.

Columbus, back in his small cabin, planned a general search of the island in the morning, hoping to find the great cacique that the Guanahani Indios spoke of—the chief with gold bracelets. Apparently, Columbus's communication skills improved with his interpreters, writing in the journal that he believed them when they gestured, then described a much larger island called (*Cibao*) Cuba, where large ships gathered to trade, ships mastered and crewed by skilled mariners.[39] Yet, beyond Cuba, a much larger land existed that the interpreters called *Bosio* or *Bohio* (Hispaniola).[40] The dream of riches appeared strong in

Columbus's mind that night as he wrote about obtaining gold and spices, but where should he go first? Another thought arrived. These large islands might or might not be the fabled island of Cipangu, but he resolved to not dally; the search for Cathay, the exotic city of *Quinsay* or *Guinsay* (Hangzhou), and the *Gran Can* (Grand Khan) focused his attention. He apparently recalled his instructions in the signed agreement: Find and deliver King Ferdinand and Queen Isabella's letter of introduction, request a reply, and return that reply to the Spanish monarchs. Lardicci recorded this recollection as "I will decide what I am to do. But at any rate, I have decided to go to the mainland and to the city of Quisay [Quinsay]."[41] This was the prime directive of the entire expedition—not to find meager amounts of gold and spices but to set up a trade relationship, beginning with political recognition, followed by commercial agreements, eventually leading to a series of strategically located trading posts on the Asian coast. This was his immediate and long-term goal, at least for today (Figure 7.3).

Isabella Island proved interesting to Columbus, and he led an exploratory search party ashore in hopes of finding gold and other valuable commodities. Thanks to the quick action of two of his Lucayan guides, the local Indios, who had initially run from the village, reappeared and eventually engaged in a friendly commercial barter.

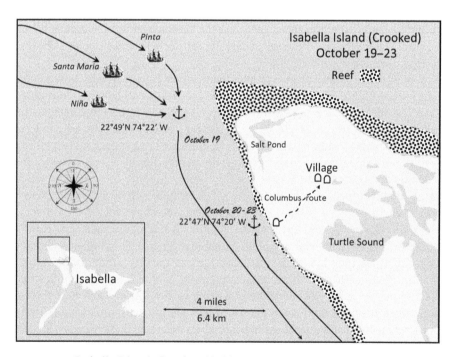

FIGURE 7.3   Isabella Island: October 19–23

October 22, Monday

Remaining at anchorage off the north tip of Isabella Island (Crooked Island), standing next to his shipmaster, Juan de la Cosa,[42] and wondering about the distance and location of the fabled Cipangu, Columbus refocused his thoughts as several canoes filled with Lucayan visitors approached the *Santa Maria*. There was no keeping the curious Indios away. As the vessels came closer, Columbus hoped one of the canoes might carry "the king or other person" mentioned by the San Salvador interpreters, but that did not happen. Smiling and waving, shouting, and gesturing, naked and painted, these islanders jockeyed for the best positions alongside the three-masted, square-rigged *não*.[43] Helpful Spanish crew members uncoiled two narrow rope ladders, one for each side. Watching the scene, Columbus knew which Indios had been to the ship the day before, the natives nimbly jumping up, reaching out, and grabbing the rope. Other first-time visitors remained in their canoes, sitting and holding back, watching intently, curious. In addition to the usual skeins of cotton, Lucayan traders brought well-honed, sharp-tipped darts. Spreading out on deck, each group of three or four moved to Spanish crew members standing in equal numbers. Soon, recalcitrant natives, still sitting in their canoes, slowly climbed the rope ladders. The same scenario played out on the *Niña* and *Pinta*.

Prepared to barter, crew members held out "bits of glass, broken crockery, and pieces of earthenware." Making his rounds of the brisk ship-born marketplace, Columbus observed small pieces of gold "fastened in their noses." Quick-minded Spaniards spotted these samples and offered shining new hawk's bells and glass beads no bigger than a pebble. The Guanahani interpreters, after speaking directly to this group of Indios, turned to Columbus and intimated with gestures and some words that these people now believed the Spaniards to be gods. Columbus did not try to dispel this belief.

Later in the day, Columbus went ashore in search of fresh water. Luckily, a small lagoon not far from the anchorage contained a low-saline water composition, and a shore party filled their casks. Martín Pinzón, moving off on his own, explored the dark green lagoon and came across a *seven-palms-long* (1.2-foot) snake, displaying skin features similar to the one they killed the day before. Columbus noticed the abundant aloe plants clustered for easy harvesting all around the lagoon; the crew picked "as much of the aloe as they could find."[44]

October 23, Tuesday

Frustration grew in Columbus today. Yesterday, the afternoon rain made exploring the inland difficult, so he returned to the ships, hoping a rich cacique and his entourage would present themselves; none did. Not wanting to dally any longer at this location, he made plans to sail south to *Cibao* (Cuba), basing this thought on the continued enthusiastic gestures and selected key verbal phrases from his Indio interpreters. Now the wind did not cooperate. All throughout the day, the air stagnated with no wind. The rain came, warm to the touch, something he had never experienced in Europe. As he began to realize that large quantities of gold did not exist on any of the present islands, Columbus switched his economic interest to spices. Admitting his limited knowledge of flora, especially useful commercially viable plants, he conjured up new thoughts of discovering an island rich in spices. Finding aloewood, he demanded the crew to collect quantities of the material and secure it on the *Santa Maria*. Columbus decided any profitable island would do; he no longer needed to find Cipangu, stating, "One should go where there is a lot of commerce."[45] This sudden change in his thinking reveals his bitterness and his desire to succeed; it is interesting that he would share such frustration in a journal that he knew the Spanish monarchs and others in Court would be reading. This might indicate that Columbus planned on using the logbook as a source for an edited official report. On the issue of spices, he believed they held some promise for reward, but he would need to find large quantities of them.

The Lucayan interpreters remained unmentioned in the log during this time. As noted above, Columbus believed that, following their advice to sail south to Cibao, riches might be obtained. Surely, Cuba was a far destination for the five remaining Guanahani natives; from the southern tip of Guanahani to Puerto Sama on the northern Cuban coast, it was 186 nautical miles, paddling on a course due south through the passage between Long and Crooked Islands, then heading in a southwest direction.[46]

Where Is Cibao (Cuba)?

October 24, Wednesday

What a difference a day makes in the mind of Columbus, or in the transcription of Las Casas, as this morning the explorer was sure that Cibao was the exotic Asian kingdom of Cipangu, and as he mentions its many noteworthy obtainable products, gold, once again, is first on the list. Yesterday it was spices, today it is gold; it did not seem to matter; he resolved to get there. No longer doubting his interpreters, Columbus confidently declared, "For I believe that it is so, as all the Indios of these islands, as well as those I brought with me in the ships, told me by signs."[47] Admitting he could not understand their spoken language, Columbus may have aligned the Indian gestures to earlier experiences making and studying "spheres" (globes) and several mappae mundi (world maps).[48] It all made sense now; this Cibao had to be Cipangu; it was big and it was in the right location; his geographic planning seemed on target.[49]

Determined, anxious, and exuberant, Columbus, before sunrise this day, appeared on deck and ordered the fleet to up anchor and proceed on a course

WSW. Expectations plummeted with dawn; the sun came up and the wind went down—to nothing, becalmed again. No doubt praying for divine intervention, a hopeful Columbus noticed a breeze rise up in the early afternoon. Immediately, he ordered full sails employed on all ships: "mainsail with two bonnets, the foresail, spritsail, mizzen, main topsail, and the boat's [skiff] sail on the poop [back deck]."[50] The race was on. Columbus had had enough of these small islands; he wanted Cibao; he wanted to see a rich cacique; and he wanted riches, something—anything substantial.

Cruising well until sunset, a top-mast lookout reported a land sighting to the NW. Consulting a hastily drawn chart of islands he had no doubt sketched from first arriving in San Salvador, Columbus believed the land to be the southern tip of Fernandina, lying at a distance of 7 leagues. Then the wind suddenly increased. With a guarded intuition, he ordered the fleet to halt. Not knowing the remaining distance to Cibao or the situation of reefs expected when approaching that island, he smartly played it safe. He wrote,

> Because all these islands lie in very deep water so that no bottom can be found beyond two Lombard shots' distance, and then [from this distance to the shore] it is all patchy, one part being rocky and another sandy, and hence it is impossible to anchor safely.[51]

His description accurately recounts his experiences inspecting the coastlines of San Salvador, Santa Maria de la Concepción, Fernandina, and Isabella islands.[52] Happy to have made the right decision, yet somewhat chagrined, he added, "that night we went less than two leagues." One can sense the annoyance of weather conditions and physical environmental realities beginning to build in his personality as he laid down to sleep that night, he could not put up sails, he could not anchor, and he could not proceed to Cibao.

October 25, Thursday

At this point in the log, Las Casas switches from the first-person narrative to the third person. Heading in a WSW direction for several hours, Columbus ordered a due west course, arriving at a point where land appeared around three in the afternoon. Lookouts on the caravels counted seven islands, but from the taller lookout post on the *Santa Maria*, sharp-eyed men reported eight islands, all positioned in a north-to-south orientation, apparently small and low-lying, smaller than previous islands visited.[53]

This is the end of the day's log entry, but one may assume, as Morison does, that Columbus approached the islands, now known as the Ragged Islands, saw they were quite small, turned south, and followed the island chain, surveying the situation, resolute to find something other than another tiny rock outcropping.

The varying reef concentrations of these islands suggest that Columbus moved slowly this day, occupying his time searching for possible anchorages, attempting to communicate with his Indio interpreters, counseling La Cosa on possible navigational hazards, and, when necessary, pulling alongside the caravels for a quick exchange of information. This probably explains why the journal entry was brief—either that or Las Casas decided the nautical information held no importance.

October 26, Friday

The entry for today ran shorter than the previous day. There is little doubt that Las Casas decided not to include more information, as Columbus sailed 5 leagues, anchored in a shoal of respectful depth, and simply sat there. Dunn and Kelley, in their translation, note how the Indio interpreters gestured to Columbus that Cibao resided about a day and a half from their present location. Changing the subject, Las Casas reminds the reader what Columbus thought about dugout canoes cut from one tree, hollowed out, and paddled but not sailed. This information is redundant, having been described twice previously; why would Columbus repeat this fact again? The short entry ends with Las Casas describing how the Indio guides provided "signs" that Cibao contained much land and held quantities of gold and pearls—Columbus, thus confirming that Cibao must be Cipangu. Dunn & Kelley admit that Las Casas, at this point in the original manuscript, canceled *por se* (by itself), changing it to *por las senas* (of the signs). This change may seem minor, but immediately following this, Dunn & Kelley cite more cancellations and question the Spanish terms he uses.[54] It is sections such as the above that call on academics to question Las Casas's method of text abstraction.

October 27, Saturday

Continuing in the third person, Las Casas describes how Columbus named the line of islands *Las Islas de Arena* (islands of sand, today Ragged Islands) due to the shallow shelf that continued as the fleet sailed south for 6 leagues. Winds increased, allowing the fleet to make eight miles an hour as they slightly changed course to SSW until one o'clock in the afternoon, continuing to gain 28 additional miles as the sun went down. At sunset, land appeared, and heavy rain commenced. Excited to get close to what appeared to be a large island, the largest yet visited, Columbus held his emotions in check, shortened all sails, *luffed up* (turned into the wind), and drifted in a zigzag pattern. He was somewhere between 15 and 20 miles off the north coast of Cibao (Cuba).[55]

Amazingly, Las Casas recorded nothing more for this day from the original Columbus log; one may have expected more expressions of anticipation. Columbus expected the next day to land somewhere on the island of Cipangu, the island he read about, the island known for its riches, especially gold, golden roofs, golden plates and goblets, silk-thread shirts—all the items mentioned by Marco Polo in his famous book, *Travels*. Columbus had studied Polo's legends intensely, most likely taking notes, discussed its passages with fellow mariners, with each royal commission, Portuguese and Spanish, assigned the task to review Columbus's *Enterprise to the Indies*, and shared highlights with King João of Portugal and with King Ferdinand and Queen Isabella of Spain.

Yet, on the night before he was to achieve a key destination, Cipangu, he wrote nothing else. Consider Columbus's extensive comments on October 11 as he *reefed* the sails off the coast of San Salvador, biding his time till daybreak. Nevertheless, Las Casas's entry ends without mention of Columbus's expectations or premonitions. There was heavy rain, and the crew "spent the night on watch," according to Las Casas, but surely when Columbus did retire, he would have recorded some excitement for the coming day, some hint of how he felt having arrived at this moment. Recall how Las Casas, in the original Barcelona copy, combined the October 11 and 12 entries. For this entry in November, he switched from his third-person narrative to Columbus's first-person description of the landing and the Indios. Why isn't the October 27 entry similar? Morison has Columbus ordering the tiny fleet to follow a zigzag maneuver to maintain their approximate position until dawn.

Notes

1 William F. Keegan, archaeologist of the Caribbean, believes that Columbus may have left from the Long Bay site on the northern tip of San Salvador, "then before mid-crossing he could have seen many islands—Conception Island and Long Island to the west and Rum Cay to the south—creating an unbroken south and western horizon of islands." Personal communication, June 30, 2022.
2 Morison has suggested that Las Casas or the scribe who copied the original Barcelona copy misused leagues for miles.
3 Thacher, *The Journal of Christopher Columbus*, 539. For more information on the Lucayan village sites on Rum Cay, see Sears and Sullivan, "Bahamas Prehistory." This is the first of many action events where Columbus made directional decisions based on his Indio interpreters. Believing them at first, he soon came to question their accuracy.
4 This was the first reference name given to the inhabitants of Guanahani, Columbus believed he found outlying islands of the Indies; he used the term for all Indigenous peoples except for the Caribs.
5 Lardicci, *A Synoptic Edition*, DB 31, section 16, 51.
6 Also present and sanctioning the baptisms were King Ferdinand and Queen Isabella, and the young Infante (second son), Don Juan.
7 Delaney, *Columbus and The Quest for Jerusalem*, 120. It is a pity that more information on these Lucayans and their post-voyage experience was not recorded. The reference to the native given the name Don Fernando is probably to one of the Indians that came on board later at Guanahani.
8 Papal Encyclicals Online, Sicut Dudum, "Against the Enslaving of Black Natives from the Canary Islands," Pope Eugene IV.

9 The papal decree did not apply to instances of non-Christian war prisoners, as in the case of Muslim forces. Later, during subsequent voyages, Columbus honored the papal directive, but many Spanish colonists in the New World ignored it. Columbus did not attempt to enslave any Indigenous peoples except the Caribs, war-like natives living in the interior of Hispaniola. This would occur during the second voyage after discovering the massacre of his men at La Navidad. Even then, he did not take military action immediately; finally, additional Spanish deaths occurred inland, and Columbus, under pressure, led a force against the Caribs. Defeating them in battle, Columbus ordered the taking of several hundred prisoners. It should be noted that the friendly *cacique*, Guacanagarí, pleaded with Columbus to act; the *cacique* and hundreds of his warriors, allied with Columbus, joined in the battle.

10 This philosophy does not consider situations where captured war prisoners or persons committing "unnatural" acts such as sodomy and cannibalism occurred; in those cases, slavery, remained a viable option, offering an opportunity to readjust unacceptable 15th-century Spanish social behavior.

11 Fayer, "African Interpreters in the Atlantic Slave Trade," 281. The original source is from J. A. Crone., translated and ed. *The Voyages of Cadamosto (1461)*, New York: Negro University Press.

12 Frances Karttunen would most likely disagree with this point on general terms; however, actions committed by the Portuguese may or may not reflect the actions of Columbus during the scenarios noted during his first voyage.

13 See Appendix III for more on the issue of Columbus and slavery.

14 See Dunn & Kelley, *The Diaro*, 82–83. Lardicci agrees; see page 51, DB 31, sections 15–25. The account is what Columbus believed the *Indio* on board the *Santa Maria* thought about the escaped man.

15 Columbus, that same day, recorded the land extension of Long Island at 28 leagues (84 miles), drastically long; the correct distance is 18 leagues (56 miles). These figures are too far off for Columbus to have miscalculated, especially when considering he sailed the entire length of the island. More likely are errors by Las Casas or a scribe who penned the Barcelona copy.

16 Columbus visually verified the interpreter's gestures when he spotted glass beads and a couple of Spanish coins that he had given as gifts on San Salvador.

17 They were tobacco leaves, and Columbus would encounter natives smoking the substance in Cuba.

18 Lardicci, *A Synoptic Edition, Historie*, FH 31, section 38, 150. A *blanca* was a copper coin of little value.

19 Keegan tied the trade organization well developed at the time of European contact, with specialized craft production as one of the key trade items beginning around AD 1000. This interisland trading network included Cuba, Hispaniola, and the Bahamas. *Taíno Indian Myth*, 118. Scott M. Fitzpatrick, in "Seafaring Capabilities in the Pre-Columbian Caribbean," believed that "frequent interaction was taking place prehistorically in the region." 101. He noted the preference by Indigenous peoples to set up "exchange networks and settlement 'lifelines.'"

20 He referenced anchoring two *lombarda* (small cannon shot) distant, about 600 yards, from shore. However, modern depth readings would put the depth at 22 feet, too close for Columbus to risk anchoring. From this point, depth readings increase to several hundred feet, too deep to anchor, but allowing him to "free anchor" drift in position.

21 The reader should not be too impressed with Columbus's generosity, as the value of these items in Spain was quite low. Yet, one can imagine a Lucayan excited about a brass plate, as they did not have access to glass, leather, or metals. Kettell, *Personal Narrative*, 46.

22 There are no rivers or streams on these islands that run continually; islanders rely on rain-gathered supplies.

23 Kettell, *Personal Narrative*, 47.
24 This observation has puzzled botanists for years, as no known plant displays this quality.
25 Much of this visual excitement for the flora and fauna helped convince Columbus and his men they were somewhere near Cathay. Taviani noted that the sight of parrots, palm trees, spices, and gold—all mentioned in Marco Polo's writings, which later helped Columbus make the geographic connection. *Columbus*, 105.
26 There are no sizeable rivers anywhere in the Bahamas. Seasonal small creeks only flow immediately after rainstorms. The reference to a river simply infers an opening of the coastline by a water body, usually the entrance to a bay.
27 Once the Lucayans felt the newcomers posed no threat, they eagerly traded. Berman and Gnivecki describe this desire to trade as an ongoing phenomenon for years after Columbus, noting how Spanish ships used the Bahamian islands as stopover points to attain water and food, with Lucayans swimming or canoeing to the closely moored ships. They also note that Amerigo Vespucci may have set up several campsites on these islands to scrape his ships' hulls. 36.
28 Fernandez-Armesto, *1492*, 195. The idea being that Columbus landed close to the Asian mainland; geographically, he was almost there, where "civilized lands and profitable trade" awaited. Yet, as each new island proved economically disappointing, Fernandez-Armesto believed Columbus supplanted economic goals for spiritual conversion, as such, redirecting the goals outlined in the *Santa Fe Capitulations*.
29 *The Tribune*, November 16, 2016. A blue hole is a deep, naturally occurring cavern or sinkhole displaying a characteristic deep blue hue. For more information on how the Lucayan people use caves throughout the Bahamas, see Robert S. Carr, et al., *A Global Perspective on the Ritual Use of Caves*.
30 This reef-free zone separates Crooked Island to the north from Fortune Island, also known as Long Cay.
31 This location, now named Windsor Point at the tip of Long Cay, realizes a dramatic seafloor depth change of over 1,000 feet in just under 0.25 mile.
32 Markham, *The Journal of Christopher Columbus*, 52. It is probable Columbus took this opportunity not to comment directly on Long Cay's economic potential, but rather all the islands visited to date.
33 Ibid., 53. Columbus's back and forth, on whether he trusts the San Salvador interpreters' reveals his fear of missing key islands where he can find a rich cacique willing to trade gold for Spanish goods. Also, his statement that he did not understand the Guanahani interpreters buttresses this author's argument that Columbus did not kidnap his seven Indios, the crude language exchange initiating misinterpretations on the part of Columbus and the natives.
34 Tack is a nautical term used to describe the action of sailing into the wind. If the wind is coming into the ship from the starboard side (right side as you face the front), then you are on a starboard tack, with your sails set at an angle on the port or left-facing front of the ship. If the wind comes across the stern or end of the ship, then you are said to be *jibing*.
35 Fuson, *The Log of Christopher Columbus*, 89. Fuson translated Columbus's decision as "I did not dare approach the coast in the dark."
36 Columbus desired to bring home profitable trading commodities such as fruits and spices, or cotton, should the collected gold amounts prove insufficient. Lardicci, *A Synoptic Edition*, DB 36, section 9, 56–57.
37 The journal quotes the amount brought back to Spain as ten quintals, or 100 base units, such as 100 pounds or kilograms.
38 Lardicci translated this to mean "very contented and happy." *A Synoptic Edition*, DB 36, section 18, 57.

39 Columbus, in a letter, later attempted to describe the meaning of *Cibao*, translated to mean, "In the language of these Indian people, it means mountains, very large, and the hills are so green." Translation by the author.

40 The term *Bohio* refers to large constructed multifamily houses usually built with stout wooden support poles thatched with palm branches and straw. The geographical reference here is to the large island of Haiti (Hispaniola), where these structures were common and larger than those in Cuba.

41 Lardicci, *A Synoptic Edition*, DB 36, section 22, 57. The intent here is that Columbus wanted to find a major gold mine and the "very large ships and many seaports" on Cipangu, which the Lucayans called *Colba*, yet he believed Cathay lay close and he should not dally any longer.

42 La Cosa, from Santoña, Spain, owned the *Santa Maria* and on this voyage served as Master; his responsibilities included carrying out Columbus's commands, seeing that all crew completed daily routines, and coordinating course headings and corrections with the ship pilot, Ruíz Sancho da Gama. See Fuson, *The Log of Christopher Columbus*, for full roster listings of all three ships.

43 Also known as a *carrack*, it sported three or four masts and was large enough to combine service as an ocean-going vessel and a coastal cruiser, square-rigged on the front mast (foremast) and main mast, often with a lateen-rigged (triangular sail) on the shorter mizzenmast (at the rear of the ship). See Fuson, Chapter 3, "The Ships and their Navigation," *The Log of Christopher Columbus*, 37–42.

44 Markham, *The Journal of Columbus*, 56.

45 Lardicci, A Synoptic Edition, DB38, all, 58. Much of his frustration derives from not being able to recognize many of the new plants, seemingly concerned about the plants' commercial applications.

46 This route assumes leaving the southwest coast of Guanahani, close to where it is expected that Columbus landed; this was an area that has undergone considerable archaeological investigations, uncovering a major village at the Three Dog Site. See Mary Jane Berman and Deborah M. Pearsall, Plants, People, and Culture in the Prehistoric Central Bahamas, 219–239. Also see William F. Keegan and Steven W. Mitchell, "The Archaeology of Christophers' Voyage Through the Bahamas, 1492," 102–08.

47 Ibid., 57.

48 Markham suggests the globe was the one built by Martin Behaim. While Behaim's globe appeared in 1492, it is often theorized that Columbus was privy to early renditions of the base-map sections used for the globe's production. Caraci rejects this notion, believing that the only map Columbus may have seen is the Fra Mauro map (globe) while in Portugal.

49 This entire section appears frightfully ambiguous, suggesting either innocent misinterpretations by Las Casas in his translation and transcription of this passage or purposeful misalignment of original textual intent.

50 Ibid., 58. Bonnets were extra sailcloth attached to the mainsail on either side.

51 Jane, *The Journal of Christopher Columbus*, 43.

52 Ideally, the fleet should be anchored at depths of 25–100 feet.

53 Columbus stated his position at the sighting location as 5 leagues distant, which would put them about 15 miles from the shorelines of these islands.

54 Dunn & Kelley, *The Diario of Christopher Columbus's First Voyage to America*, 115. Lardicci inserted the changed account, reading, "Partió de alli para cuba, porque, por las senas que los indios le dabvan," meaning "He left there for Cuba, because of the signs that the Indians gave him." See Lardicci, *A Synoptic Edition*, DB 40, 8–9, 334 for original Spanish; for English translation see page 59.

55 This author places his position on the night of October 27 at 21°13'N 76°01'W.

PART IV

Cuba and Hispaniola

Finally, Columbus reached a major island, Cuba, which the Indigenous peoples called *Cibao*, raising expectations that gold could be found on the ground and existed concentrated abundantly just below the ground, easy pickings for gold-hungry Spaniards. The people the Europeans met were somewhat different in customs and language from the Lucayans; these new tribes called themselves *Taíno*, meaning "good people." As the fleet cruised along the Cuban coast, Martín Pinzón decided to strike out on his own, pulling little *Pinta* off in an easterly direction. Columbus watched aghast, believing it to be insubordination, a type of mutiny. Every harbor and every inland river revealed the lack of the riches needed to impress the Spanish monarchs. His Lucayan guides told him of a much larger island, not too distant, where a great chief (*cacique*) reigned over a fabulous kingdom. Columbus, of course, thinking of this in his European mindset, imagined it to be *Cipangu* (Japan).

A new day and a new island continued to bring frustration and unrest as the remaining two ships scooted from west to east on the northern coastline of Hispaniola. Then it happened; something bad was bound to occur, and it finally came about on Christmas day. Columbus's flagship, the *Santa Maria*, ran aground on shallow reefs with the ship's boys attending to the helm. Seawater poured in; the vessel foundered but remained stuck on the coral with no chance of repair. Reluctantly, Columbus ordered the ship abandoned and all her supplies taken to the nearby shoreline. The next day, a local cacique named *Guacanagarí* offered help. Soon, dozens of native volunteers worked alongside the Spanish crew to retrieve the rest of the food and supplies. At this point, the reader will learn how Columbus and Guacanagarí willingly built a trusting relationship, a bright hope for a future commercial and political arrangement.

DOI: 10.4324/9781003464143-12

With the *Santa Maria* a hopeless wreck, Columbus makes a dramatic decision: He will leave a number of Spanish volunteers on Hispaniola; many have offered to stay, and 38 or 39 are selected. The chosen men came together as Columbus reviewed with them the expectation of good behavior with the Indigenous peoples and to assist Guacanagarí, should Carib raiders attack. With the rest of his men on the tiny *Niña*, Columbus headed out and met up with Pinzón. Together, the two ships cruised east with the determination to sail back to Spain, guided by Columbus.

8

CIBAO (CUBA)

October 28 to December 5

> I have never seen anything so beautiful. The country around the river is full of trees, beautiful and green and different from ours [Spain], each with flowers and its own kind of fruit.
>
> —Christopher Columbus, *Diario*, October 28, 1492

Columbus Believes *Cibao* is Cipangu (Japan)

October 28, Sunday

Columbus surely rose from his sleep in a high state of anticipation; everything depended on Cibao proving to be what his Indio guides claimed it would be. Orders went out for the Pinzón brothers to set sail and follow an SSW heading toward the land sighting. Geographers and students of Columbus debate the area Columbus first approached in Cuba, with some scholars thinking it was Puerto del Padre, Bay of Gibara, and Bay of Bariay (Playa Blanca), with a few proposing Nipe Bay. To reach Nipe Bay, the fleet needed to sail due south; therefore, one may consider this location a remote possibility. Puerto del Padre does not have a major river, although a tidal estuary connects Playa La Boca at the shoreline to the inland bay of Puerto del Padre. This "river" is only 1,000 feet wide and requires elimination, as Columbus wrote the river "is quite wide enough to beat about." This leaves the Bay of Bariay and the Bay of Gibara as the two remaining candidates. Morison favors Bariay with a mouth opening of one-half mile and a river extension into the lower bay running for one mile; two small streams come together, forming the Bariay River as it flows into the Bay of Bariay. Gibara is the opposite; the opening into this bay is not quite one mile wide, with the large Gibara River flowing into the bay from the interior.

DOI: 10.4324/9781003464143-13

Both bays are of sufficient depth and width to match Columbus's description. These locations are separated along the coast by only 7 miles and are within the sailing parameters of the SSW heading noted in the logbook, Gibara being west of Bariay.

Dunn & Kelley provide a clue as they translate the term for the river's depth as *Braças*, not as a *fathom*, as many translators do, but as a reference to a Roman measurement *aune*, equal to 2.7 feet. In the journal, Las Casas noted the river's mouth measured a depth of 12 braças, making the total depth 32 feet. This interpretation sounds correct, Columbus often preferred depths between 30 and 50 feet to anchor. Ironically, this does not help in the final analysis, as both the Bay of Bariay and the Bay of Gibara measure to this depth.[1] However, the Bay of Bariay extends inland, only widening slightly after a mile and appearing as a large-mouth river. Morison also came to this conclusion and named Bariay as the first Cuban area to be explored. The Cuban government has recognized this site as Columbus's first Cuban landfall and has declared the entrance to the Bay of Bariay a *Monumento Nacional Park*, marking the entrance of the bay with a plaque.

Searching for a Taíno King (*Cacique*)

Columbus noted, "There are a great number of palm trees of a different kind from those in Guinea [west Africa] and from ours [Spain], of a middling height, the trunks without that covering, and the leaves very large, with which they thatch their houses."[2] Excited and anxious to see Cipangu, Columbus led an exploratory party of men ashore. Two huts sat not far from the beach. Approaching Spaniards saw no inhabitants, but they did encounter a "dog that never barks" and fishing items.[3] Returning to the skiff boats, Columbus continued upriver, describing the flora and fauna; the distant rising mountains pleased him, for he knew fresh water would now be available. Always comparing New World geography to Europe, Columbus could see in the distance to the southwest the high ridges of the Sierra de Micaro, with peaks between 3,000 and 4,000 feet. He correctly noted that these mountains of Cibao matched, in height and extent, the mountains he recalled seeing in Sicily.

Interestingly, his reliable, or is it unreliable, guides, the Guanahani captives, indicated that Cibao contained ten great rivers and that the land was so large that paddling a canoe would take longer than 20 days to circle around.[4] This giving of detailed facts is one of the first indications that the Indio guides began to trust Columbus; they supplied Columbus with specific geographic information, allowing the explorer to suspect that he, indeed, had finally arrived in Cipangu.[5]

Two canoes suddenly appeared, but just as quickly disappeared when the paddlers saw a skiff boat with Spanish men taking depth soundings. Continuing his communication with the Guanahani Indians, Columbus learned that gold mines existed, and pearls abounded all up and down the coastline. Columbus believed the pearl story, as he linked recently seen "mussel-shells" to their proclivity in the sea environment. It was during this exchange that one or more Indio guides made a reference to a great king (cacique) who sent ships from his kingdom, completing a voyage ten days from the west. Enthralled, Columbus immediately linked this great cacique to the Gran Can (Great Khan of Cathay). After all, his research using available mappae mundi and written sources put the coast of Asia between 10 and 15 days west of Cipangu. The geography of exploration was coming together—maybe not exactly, as he thought, but near enough. Cibao was Cipangu; the other small islands filled in nicely with the regional ocean setting envisioned and portrayed on many maps of the time. Frustration gave way, and Columbus felt buoyant and confident, but still anxious. He thanked God again, deciding to name the "river" *San Salvador*; it was Sunday (Figure 8.1).

When Columbus reached Cuba, he was excited to see wide bays such as Bariay, affording future opportunities for setting up trading posts in safe harbors. He saw Indio villages abounding on the inland shores of these bays, with rivers reaching into the interior.

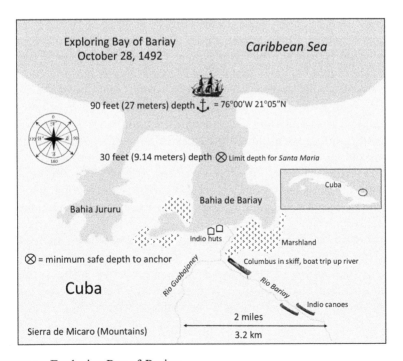

FIGURE 8.1 Exploring Bay of Bariay

October 29, Monday

Las Casas once again referred to the Guanahani guides in such a way to indicate Columbus trusted their advice to sail NW in search of a great cacique, reading into the gesturing that this "king" lived in a "city," with the interpretation that this meant more than the simple thatched huts so far encountered. Lifting anchors, the fleet paralleled the coast, but the directions and distance given by Las Casas have been debated. At one point, the translation reads, "then east ten leagues." This makes no sense. Historians believe Las Casas did not fully understand the difference between leagues and miles as Columbus used them once he arrived on Guanahani Island. Some historians and geographers, such as Morison, believe that Columbus switched to a "land league" when noting interisland distances. However, reading the entry with a geographic lens, one can see that the fleet most likely sailed as far north as Puerto Manatí by evening.[6] Morison placed Columbus at Playa La Boca (Puerto Padre), basing that on the entry's mention that "He [Columbus] saw another river much larger than the other,"[7] but the critical part comes next: that this was told to him by the Indio guides; he did not see it himself. Thus, Columbus saw a river, and the Lucayans indicated this was a large river.

Columbus did see from his ship a cluster of huts; he ordered the fleet to anchor, naming the river the Rio de Mares (River of the Seas), today the Bay of Manatí.[8] In quick order, he sent words for two skiffs to approach the shore. Calling over to one of his Lucayan guides, Columbus told him to accompany the Spaniards. Here is another significant mention of the improving relations between the Guanahani and Santa Maria de Concepcion Indios and Columbus, at least from his standpoint; Las Casas wrote, "and one of the Indians he had brought with him, for now, they understood a little, and show themselves content with Christians."[9] Apparently, Columbus went ashore in one of the skiffs and, as usual, found the local Taíno peoples gone.[10] Inspecting the surrounding huts, Columbus thought the level of improvement on the structures suggested a slightly more advanced society, admiring the use of large leaf palm branches set out in a pleasing architectural design that hinted at structural strength. He did not know it, but these people were Taíno, not Lucayan, still linked by cultural and language customs. Taíno peoples inhabited most of Cuba except the eastern interior, which possibly included Carib tribes (Figure 8.2).[11]

Despite the extensive marshlands encompassing much of the Bay of Manatí, Columbus realized that the wide "river" extending inland offered protection from storms and the possibility of a deep interior harbor. As already noted above, he named the bay's extension to the ocean the Rio de Mares (River of the Seas).

With the usual respect for personal belongings, Columbus gave strict orders that nothing be taken, an action rarely adhered to by subsequent Spanish and

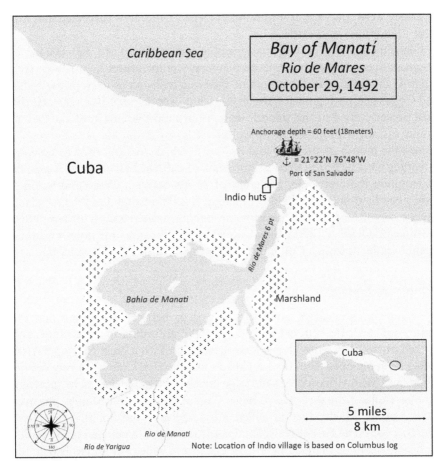

FIGURE 8.2 *Bay of Manatí*

English explorers. On its face value, this gesture supports the theory that Columbus was not interested in conquest or enslaving anyone, at least on this voyage. This would change during his second voyage after discovering the massacre of the men he left behind and the constant pressure he received from Taíno caciques to intercede in the intertribal warfare between Taíno and Caribs. For now, he wanted to contact the great chiefs or caciques and initiate trade agreements that would benefit both participants.

Some Spaniards found several intricately carved masks, and Columbus wondered if they related to any religious beliefs or were just art ornamentation. Wild dogs ran about but never barked, and some huts contained birds that appeared to be pets—as they sat "tame" in their houses, Las Casas reported that Columbus marveled at the number of fishing implements, fruit trees, and birds of every description. A few men reported seeing several skulls that looked as if they were cow's heads. From this evidence, Columbus suspected that this large island must have cattle.

Glancing inland, Columbus assumed the nearby mountains, 500–600 feet in height, influenced the cooler, more temperate temperatures he was now feeling.[12] At the same time, the mouth of the river, really an estuary, proved salty, and Columbus, noting fresh water in every hut, wondered of its source. He did surmise correctly that the smooth seawater around the mouth of the "river" would sustain a profitable pearl culture. Excited about its possibilities, he named the mouth of the river and its "port" *San Salvador*, a nod to God for providing what he hoped to be a future port-of-call, the first one, a port capable of handling the first major exchange of goods between Cibao and Spain— remember, he thinks the island is Cipangu. It is interesting that the first island he "discovered," he named *San Salvador*, hoping, as he stood on the beach that morning on October 12, the island would serve as a launching point for transatlantic trade; in reality, Columbus never again returned to *San Salvador*.

October 30, Tuesday

Constant communication now began to occur between Columbus and the Indios onboard. He believed that, sailing NW, according to the gestures and spoken words, they would reach lands associated with a great cacique.[13] After seeing so many open estuaries on Cibao's north coast, Columbus believed his guides and forthwith ordered sails to be hoisted. After 15 leagues, he spotted a cape covered in palm trees that stretched 3 miles; then a river opening appeared. At this point, Martín Pinzón pulled *Pinta* up close and boarded the *Santa Maria*; a conversation between captains ensued with Pinzón stating the Indios on his ship claimed that inland, a short distance, a wide river flowed NW to the great city of *Cuba*. A great cacique lived there and ruled a "great continent" that extended north. The *Pinta*'s Indios gestured that this cacique was at war with the Gran Can, whom the Indios called *Cami* and who lived in a land called *Fava*; this is what Pinzón told Columbus.[14]

On the spot, Columbus decided to go in search of the city of *Cuba*. He requested that one sailor who had previously been to Guinea volunteer to take a copy of the letter of introduction that King Ferdinand and Queen Isabella had given him, along with a couple of the Guanahani Indios, who now wished to show the way and then return to their island. Here again, we read how Columbus planned on returning the Guanahani guides. Interestingly, there is no further mention in the logbook if and when the two Indios did in fact leave the fleet for home. However, as we shall see later, after the wreck of the *Santa Maria*, Columbus could not take all the Indios to Spain on the *Niña*. What is known is that several, probably five, remained.[15] The log notes no further action for this day. Columbus's location at this point was near Cayo Guajaba (21°49'N 77°25'W) (Figure 8.3).

FIGURE 8.3   Cayo Guajaba

Columbus's desire to search north for Cathay was halted at Cayo Guajaba as he sensed an approaching storm and he sought shelter. Had he continued north, Columbus would have discovered Cuba's inland "river," the Bahía (Bay) of Jigüey, used as a trading route by Indigenous tribes, extending northward for many miles.

October 31, Wednesday

A strong wind forced the fleet to "beat up and down" the coast, hoping to find a safe harbor. Coming upon another narrow "river," lookouts spotted shoals at the entrance, and despite encouragement from the Guanahani Indios, who thought it easy to paddle a canoe in shallow waters, Columbus balked. They had actually tacked SW to the *Bay of Nuevitas*, some 25 miles below Cayo Guajaba. After further tacking, Columbus sensed an approaching storm, and the fleet made for Rio de Mares and safety.

A Lucayan Initiates Friendly Relations with Cuban Taínos

November 1, Thursday

In a repeat of the events of the 29th, Columbus sent the skiffs to the beach, finding the people gone, so the boats started to return. A Taíno man appeared, standing near his hut. The man looked nervous, so Columbus ordered the skiffs back to the ships. After eating his noon meal, Columbus had an idea. On deck, he could still see one or more Taíno milling about near the beach, looking and pointing at the Spanish fleet. At this moment, Columbus called to one of his Guanahani guides, gesturing and speaking in a few words that the Indios now understood. The Lucayan guide appeared to know what to do. From a skiff, he called out, at shouting distance, "They must not be afraid because the Spaniards were good people and did no harm to anyone; neither were they from the Great Khan, but rather they had given of their possessions in many islands where they had been."[16] It is absurd to think Columbus or Las Casas, as this is written as a third-person narrative, could understand the Arawakan language to any degree that would allow for such a refined understanding of this communication.

Jumping from the skiff, the Lucayan swam briskly to the shore. Was this an escape attempt? No, apparently two Taíno villagers met him at the beach and escorted him to a hut, where they asked many questions. The Lucayan, probably the one who later took the Christian name Diego, recounted his experiences traveling to several islands from Guanahani with the Spaniards. This was another perfect opportunity for the Lucayan to disappear into the interior; Cuba was large, and the Spaniards would never be able to find him. Once safe, the Indio could make his way back to Guanahani; however, he did not go. Why not? One can only assume he felt secure and desirous of pleasing the Spaniards. One wonders at this point if Columbus had somehow communicated to his guides that they would eventually be returned. This is additional evidence that the remaining Lucayans desired to carry on as guides and interpreters; more evidence will appear later in the voyage.

Word spread through the village and slowly a group gathered, boarded their canoes, and paddled out to the fleet. Since this was Cibao and not wanting to offend any nearby great cacique, Columbus spread the word to not accept gifts but only give gifts. Through the Lucayan interpreters, Columbus showed samples of gold to the Taíno traders, seeking to know if they had any and if they would be willing to trade. The Taíno nodded, calling Columbus's specimens *nucay*. Gifts flowed, mostly glass beads, from the Spanish to their newfound friends, and within a short time, Columbus allowed some of the crew to go ashore. No gold appeared all day, but Columbus saw one Taíno with a silver piece "fastened to his nose."

Taíno messengers ran inland to inform other tribes of the arrival of the Spaniards. One Taíno villager told a Lucayan guide that merchants were coming from the interior to buy items from the new arrivals; they would provide information on the great caciques who ruled inland. These caciques lived only four days from the coast, reportedly sending messengers throughout the land about the arrival of gods with gifts.

Las Casas writes how the Taíno, like their Lucayan counterparts, mimicked Spanish prayers and Christian gestures, making the sign of the cross and voicing the *Salve* and *Ave Maria* "with their hands raised to heaven."[17] According to the description of these events and the note that Las Casas added about the Lucayan and Taíno natives, there was no language barrier between these Arawakan-speaking Indigenous peoples despite the 200 miles that separate Guanahani Island from the northern coast of Cuba; this counters other evidence that will be presented in the December 22 entry.

A mention in the entry for this day talked about "a great war" between the Taíno tribes of the coast and the Great Khan, called *Cavilla* by the Taíno, who rules a province called *Bafan* within the interior. This information is quite specific and must have come through the Lucayan interpreters. Recent archaeological evidence suggests that Caribs did live in the Greater Antilles of the Caribbean at the time of European contact. Carib tribes migrated from the northern coast of South America and possibly through the Lesser Antilles, making their presence known on Hispaniola (Haiti), Jamaica, and the southern islands of the Bahamas.[18] This probably occurred just before or after AD 1000. While the study noted in the previous sentence did not investigate a Carib presence in Cuba, the researchers noted that additional investigations needed to occur. To this end, there remains the possibility that Carib villages existed in areas of eastern Cuba, especially within the modern provinces of Guantanamo and Holguin, regions within a short canoe traverse to Hispaniola.[19] The geographic proximity of the extreme western portion of Hispaniola to the extreme eastern tip of Cuba, which is a short 55 miles, provides geographic evidence that Carib to Taíno contact certainly remained a distinct possibility, if not a probability (Figure 8.4).[20]

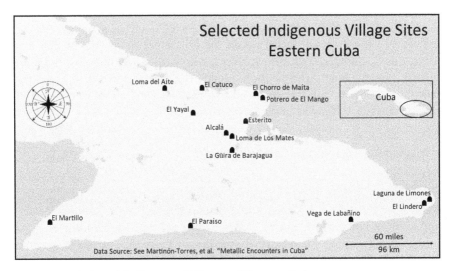

FIGURE 8.4   Selected Indigenous Villages of Eastern Cuba

Cuba was well populated at the time Columbus visited in late 1492. In addition to the main Taíno tribe that dominated the north-coastal and interior regions of the large island, the Guanahatabey tribes struggled in the far north-western area, while Caribs raided villages along the southern coast.

Carefully, Columbus moved the fleet deeper into the Rio de Mares (Bay of Manatí), and scout skiffs out front took depth readings as the ships approached: First, the *Niña*, then the *Pinta*, entered with their shallow 6-foot keels, and finally the *Santa Maria*, sporting a 12-foot keel. The mouth of the "river" quickly opens to a bay-like width of three-quarters of a mile. The mini bay has a west bank channel about a quarter of a mile wide and continues with a reasonable ship depth of 40 feet, making Columbus and his ships' pilots confident. The west side, one-half mile wide, flattens to shallow depths, lowering from 11 feet to 1 foot.

About one-half mile upstream, the "river" narrows to one-half mile in width. Another one-half mile upstream the Rio de Mares slightly widens, with the deeper channel switching to the east side. Columbus and his captains carefully maneuvered the *Niña*, *Pinta*, and *Santa Maria* upstream, following the deep 40-foot channel, reaching what is today Puerto Manatí; or Columbus remained near the west bank, most likely within one-half mile of the mouth, protected from Caribbean winds and waves by the Punta Jesus peninsula that juts out to the northeast. Interestingly, the Rio de Mares continues upstream 2.5 miles before the "river" opens to the Bay of Manatí proper.[21]

Buoyed by recent events in Cibao and believing a few days before that the land would be Cipangu, he now changed his mind and suggested Cibao as the Asian mainland. Thacher blamed this as an error on the part of Las Casas's transcription. Yet, Las Casas comes out of the third-person narrative and quotes, "I am... before *Zayto* and *Guinsay* [cities in Cathay], 100 leagues a little more or a little less." If the quote is correct, then Columbus imagined that he had reached the shores of eastern Asia. In an attempt to provide further evidence, Las Casas noted that the explorer felt how the sea "comes in a different manner... to the north-west he found that it was becoming cold."[22] From the maps he either had with him or he had studied earlier, Columbus considered that the cities of Cathay lie in the northern latitudes.

Is This Cipangu (Japan) or Cathay (China)?

November 2, Friday

Wanting verification of his theory that he had reached Asia, Columbus gathered a shore party consisting of Rodrigo de Jerez and Luis de Torres, who possessed a speaking knowledge of Hebrew, Chaldean, and some Arabic. Additionally, he selected two Indios to accompany the Spaniards: a Guanahani

Lucayan (probably the same one whom he had sent to the beach the day before) and a local Taíno who volunteered to serve as a guide to the interior. Packing strings of beads to trade for food and several specimens of spices, the exploring party listened as Columbus gave them two goals: to search for spices like those given to them and to seek out and deliver a message. Thacher translated the message as follows:

> How they [Spanish monarchs] sent the Admiral that he might give to the King [cacique] on their part their letters and a present, and in order to learn of his state and gain friendship with him that he might favour them in whatever they might need, etc.: and that they might learn of certain provinces and harbours and rivers of which the Admiral had information and how far distant they were from there, etc.[23]
>
> The intent on Columbus's part was to complete his prime directive, establish contact with an Asian ruler of wealth, and initiate a friendly relationship, leading to future trading contracts and, most likely, trading posts. This has nothing to do with conquest, slavery, or even cultural domination. He is focused on promoting the commercial aspects of a new geopolitical relationship.
>
> While no further narrative explaining the exploration shore party is known, one can conjecture they went in canoes down the estuary "river" into the *Bay of Manatí* proper, selecting the largest stream flowing into the bay, the *Yarigua River*, which runs upstream to the south, then southwest into the interior.[24] They disappeared for several days.
>
> That night, Columbus again recorded a huge error in reading the latitude of the pole star, Polaris, estimating 42 degrees using a crude quadrant. Either that or Las Casas transposed the numbers, as his true latitude that night was 21 degrees—the missing three degrees is within the expected range of error given the instrument used and Columbus's inexperience in using it; there is another possibility: he may have recognized a familiar cartographic landmark from a map he carried and decided to go with a figure that supported his preconceived notions of Cathay's eastern terminus.[25]

November 3, Saturday

With the skiff boats launched in the morning, Columbus ventured upstream, accompanied by a few other crew members. He found the mouth of the *Yarigua River*, which pours into the *Bay of Manatí* after traveling 2 leagues (6 miles).[26] Here, he found fresh water. A few hundred yards ahead, Columbus spotted a low hill, probably Loma Dumañuecos, standing 423 feet (129 meters). From here, forests of mangrove trees 50–70 feet high and palms equally as tall stretched as far as he could see, which prevented his ability to see meadows or villages. No doubt, as he stood on top of the hill, he searched in a southwestern direction, in the direction the *Yarigua River* flowed, and hoped his embassy of Spanish and Indio ambassadors had successfully reached a great inland cacique. In short order, Columbus returned downstream to his ships, where dozens of canoes surrounded his fleet, and a brisk exchange of goods revealed a new Indio exchange item, a hammock.[27]

November 4, Sunday

After another day of waiting for his embassy to return, Columbus spent the morning ashore, attempting to hunt birds seen the day before. Upon returning to the ships, Martín Pinzón held out two sticks of cinnamon, stating that one of his crew[28] had seen a Taíno with a handful of the spice. Impressed and anxious to find a profitable trade item, Columbus also learned that another crew member from the *Pinta* claimed to have seen cinnamon trees a short distance inland. Hiking later to that location, Columbus found nothing. Frustrated first by false stories told by his Lucayan guides and now by one of his own men, Columbus attempted to ask the local Taíno where cinnamon grew; they pointed southeast. When shown pieces of gold and silver, one old local resident told the Lucayan guides that many caciques in *Bohio* wore the metals on their necks, arms, and legs; as a bonus, the senior Indios claimed that large ships constantly visited the ports, eager to trade. One can imagine Columbus's eyes widening as the story went on.

And the story did go on; farther away from *Bohio*, an island existed with cyclops-type men, frightening with their dog-like snouts, who raided nearby islands for cannibalistic rituals, cutting the throats of victims, cutting off genitals, and drinking their blood. Gruesome indeed, yet similar stories pervaded communication exchanges on some of the islands Columbus visited. At first, he would dismiss such claims; later, he believed them to be partially true, attributing these actions to the Carib peoples.[29]

Recovering from this exchange, Columbus recounted in the day's entry his belief that Cibao possessed great agricultural potential, suggesting the Indios' *mames* (cassava/manioc) grew bountifully and that cotton grew everywhere. The *manioc* plant, also called *yuca*, is a woody shrub that can be bitter or sweet in a natural state. It is transformed by mixing the crushed plant with water into a thick paste. From here, the dough can be dried and formed into a cake layer, becoming a staple bread fit for human consumption. Additionally, Indigenous farmers of the Greater Antilles cultivated arrowroot and sweet potatoes. Las Casas and Oviedo both mention the growing of manioc on Hispaniola.[30] The early Spanish settlers adapted to the taste and use of the plant, particularly those persons living near the inland valleys of the northern coast of Hispaniola, where the plant thrived along large rivers, such as *Río Taque del Norte* Río Taque del Norte, and the adjacent floodplains.[31]

On the larger islands of Cuba, Puerto Rico, Jamaica, and Hispaniola, Indigenous farmers used a slash-and-burn technique similar to that found in numerous other areas of the world, especially in the equatorial regions. Smaller villagers needed to utilize all their members for the arduous job of clearing the fields, forming dirt mounts with pointed sticks, and cultivating the young plants. With abundant rainfall amounts and consistent help, new tubers grew quickly. Over time, Spanish overlords counted on the crops to feed themselves and their Indigenous labor force.[32] In supplementing the manioc mainstay, Indigenous peoples of the Caribbean looked to the sea; an abundance of shellfish and fish provided needed protein.[33] Rouse noted the bounty of wild fruits, vegetables, and guava berries growing in large patches, especially in the many mangrove swamps and along the shorelines. On a more limited basis, manatees and turtles could be found, considered high-value products by the Taíno.[34] Guitar and Estevez highlighted the spectacular success that Taíno farmers maintained in the northern valleys of Hispaniola's inland region, mentioning how these Indigenous peoples achieved a "truly sedentary style of agriculture," affording time to develop other areas of their culture.[35]

November 5, Monday

Early in the morning, Columbus and the Pinzón brothers decided it was time to "careen" the ships, one at a time, to scrape and check the lower panels of the ships' hulls. Where the Puerto de Manatí is today, the channel depth of the "river" decreases gradually from 40 feet to a 5–6-foot shallow shelf, allowing the ships to be river-anchored and adequately buoyed for subsequent refloating. Meanwhile, the boatswain of the *Niña*, probably Bartolomé García from Palos, pleaded with Columbus for the reward for having discovered mastic on land. Columbus then sent two men, Rodrigo Sánchez and Maestre Diego, to see if the product was indeed mastic. The trio brought back specimens of the sticky gum and tree bark. Columbus had seen mastic years before on his trading expedition to the island of Chios in the eastern Mediterranean.[36] Appropriately impressed, he promised García to present the material to the Spanish monarchs. This is another important component of evidence highlighting Columbus's desire to seek out products other than gold. He wrote that harvesting the product at the right time of year would supply high yields, predicting those yields to reach a thousand quintals a year.[37]

Commenting on his anchorage, Columbus confirmed his belief that the Rio de Mares was "one of the best in the world," noting that a rocky point protects the entrance to the "river." He believed later Spanish explorers might build a fort at the top of a small hill; it would offer a perfect location to defend the entrance. This northwest-pointing mini-peninsula, juts out three-quarters of a mile, ending in a massive rock outcrop that reaches a height of 62 feet (19 meters), a perfect fortress location.

The Ambassadors Describe a Large Taíno Village and Tobacco

November 6, Tuesday

Today, the exploratory party of ambasssadors returned, all of them, as the Indian guides did not run away. A long debrief ensued, with Torres explaining how the party followed the river and continued inland for 12 leagues (36 miles), finally arriving at a large Indio village containing 50 houses and holding a thousand Indians.[38] Each house rose higher and enclosed greater areas than the smaller houses of the coastal peoples, with Torres describing the design as like a tent.[39] As with earlier initial cultural encounters, the two Spaniards admitted they received royal treatment, with the villagers believing them to be from heaven, showing reverence by kissing their hands and feet, and making "signs of wonder."[40] Lardicci translated this section as another instance of the Indios "being astonished and believing that they had come from the sky."[41]

In short order, the guests were escorted to the house of the cacique, who gestured, everyone then sat down in a circle inside a roomy structure. Standing behind the Spaniards, the Lucayan interpreter explained the "good deeds" done in all the islands visited and on Cibao.[42] Meeting over, the cacique motioned for several women to enter, who then seated themselves and began to kiss the hands and feet of the two explorers, curious to determine if they were flesh or not. The cacique fed and housed them and asked them to stay several days, but the Spaniards knew that Columbus desired to know what products might be traded or obtained. When shown cinnamon, pepper, and other spices, the cacique and some of his elders gestured toward the southeast, indicating none of the items grew in or around the village.

The Spaniards and the Indio interpreter spent the night, and the next morning, when Torres and Jerez asked the Indio interpreter to tell the cacique that they must return to their ships, word spread around the village that the "gods" were returning to their heaven. Dozens, then hundreds of villagers gathered around the cacique's hut, desiring to accompany the ambassadors. It is not clear if the wording "were eager to bear them company, thinking they were returning to heaven" indicated they wanted to go on the ships and return to Spain or only go with them to the Bay of Manatí. Instead of a mass escort, the cacique allowed one of the "principal men" and his son, or the son of another villager, to join the Spaniards for the return trip.

Next comes another critical event in the Columbus and Indigenous people's relationship. Returning to the ship, the Taínos met Columbus and, upon questioning, described with gestures and speech to the interpreter that more islands, one of them quite large, lie to the southeast; this last part referenced the large island of Bohio (Haiti). In fact, the elder appeared knowledgeable on regional geography, and Columbus, at first, thought he might "carry him home to Spain."[43] When it became dark, Columbus sensed the Taínos becoming nervous; upon questioning by the interpreter, it was learned that the villagers desired to return home. With the *Santa Maria* beached for hull-scraping and not wanting to "oppose" the elder, Columbus let him go. Dunn & Kelley use the term "not willing to anger him."[44] Kettell, and Dunn & Kelley disagree on the action. Kettell stated next, "and so let him return, requesting him to come back the next morning, but they saw him no more." Dunn & Kelley translate this to note that the words mean that the Taíno elder promised Columbus he would come back, but he did not. Cecil Jane uses the phrase,

> I suppose that he was afraid—and in the darkness of the night he was anxious to go ashore... not wishing to offend him, he [Columbus] let him go; the Indian said he would return at dawn, but he never came back.[45]

The ambassadors recounted to Columbus their seeing many Taíno holding "fire-brands" which they smoke. Las Casas, in his *Historia*, describes the event in detail.

> The two Spaniards met upon their journey, great numbers of people of both sexes; the men always with a firebrand in the hands and certain herbs for smoking: these are dry, and fixed in a leaf also dry, after the manner of those paper tubes which the boys in Spain use...having lighted one end they draw the smoke by sucking at the other end, this causes a drowsiness and sort of intoxication, and according to their accounts relieves them from the sensation of fatigue. The tubes they call by the name of *tabaccos*.[46]

The Spanish ambassadors informed Columbus that no large and important villages appeared on their journey except for the one they visited, causing Columbus to consider sailing to an alternative location. Although the mention of much cotton being grown caused Columbus to write that it would provide a reliable crop for the trading post, he realized that it was not currently cultivated by the Indigenous peoples but grew boundless among the trees and bushes. Turning to religious matters, Las Casas quotes Columbus: "I hope in our Lord that your Highnesses will devote yourselves with much diligence to this subject and bring into the church so many multitudes."[47] In prayer-like fashion, Columbus hoped the Spanish monarchs desired to spread the faith, the Catholic faith, throughout all the lands he discovered—ending this section of the entry with Amen.

Moving on to maritime matters, Columbus felt jubilant; with the *Santa Maria* recently scrubbed clean of barnacles on her underside, the ship looked to be in top shape. His immediate plans called for a route southeast, again following the suggestions of his Lucayan guides, believing them to be correct now that he received verification from several Cuban Taíno, anxious and ready to search for new islands, gold, spices, anything that might be profitable. Nowhere does he anticipate or indicate a goal of subjugation or conquest. All dressed up and ready to go, but the winds did not cooperate, he remained bound to the Bay of Manatí.

November 7, Wednesday through November 11, Sunday

Day after day, the winds proved contrary, and he remained anchored at Rio de Mares. The crew continued work on caulking the ships. Meanwhile, Columbus noticed trees that appeared similar to the mastic trees on the island of Chios in the eastern Mediterranean Sea. He ordered a sample of the resin tapped so that he could show it the Spanish monarchs, another attempt to find a marketable product.

The Geography of Linking Religious and Commercial Goals

November 12, Monday

Finally, the wind shifted from the SE, and Columbus signaled *Niña* and *Pinta* for action. During the last few days of inaction, the Lucayan guides enhanced their stories of gold, boldly claiming that to the east, an island called *Babeque* (Great Inagua) possessed so much gold that laborers brought the precious metal from interior regions to selected processing sites at the coast. Here, trained metalworkers heated the gold, pounding it into bars. This sounded too good to be true. Now the gold would not only be gathered, brought to the coast for easy access, and transformed into commercial products regulated by size and weight; this had to be too good to be true. Las Casas's writing of this confirms Columbus's main goal of finding products that he could buy or find and collect himself. However, as you may have noticed, the specificity of communicated information begs the assumption that hand gestures alone could fashion such an intricate description, affording another point of questioning Las Casas's transcription: Did he add detail to an otherwise simple, direct account or did Columbus add this feature, hoping to reveal the region's future productivity?

Sailing from the mouth of the Rio de Mares, the fleet moved east by south, finding another "river" after 8 leagues (Bahia de Malagueta). The mouth of this river looked dangerously narrow, so Columbus continued an additional 4 leagues, where he spotted "another river, which seemed to be of great volume."[48] Naming it the Rio de Sol (River of the Sun), today it is the Bay of Puerto Padre. Columbus entered the wide opening, realizing the channel had decreased quickly to 1,000 feet; he ordered the fleet to halt. Las Casas noted that Columbus decided not to proceed upstream as no major city was in sight, only small villages, and, most importantly, the wind favored an easterly course, getting him closer to *Babeque* and the gold.

In a long section of this entry that highlights his experiences at Rio de Mares, Las Casas quotes Columbus concerning his friendly feelings about the Taíno and their willingness to convert to Christianity, or at least, their outward gestures of making the sign of the cross and repeating simple prayers. Columbus ties this religious goal next to the commercial possibilities, as if to persuade the Spanish monarchs that physical discovery and intercultural contact can have multiple benefits. He mentioned mastic, cotton, and aloe; he had already named these products in previous entries. Here he brings it all together, almost like a sales pitch, which he no doubt gave many times in his younger life as a trading representative for various Italian merchants. Interestingly, Columbus believed he was close to Cathay and predicted that harvested Cuban tobacco would find its way to the markets of the Great Khan, adding another profitable commercial product to the growing list of commodities.

In discussing his commercial interests, Columbus sees the days when Spanish commercial hegemony would rule the entire region, within rural areas but especially in their towns, buttressed by "the extremely large amount of gold in these lands."[49] Of course, an example of this untapped wealth might need to be shown at this point in the voyage, and Columbus enthusiastically indulges his thoughts, writing, "The inhabitants dug it from the earth, and wore it in massay [large] bracelets at their necks, legs, and arms."[50] If gold was not enough, Columbus sweetened the vision by adding "pearls and precious stones, and an infinite amount of spices."[51] He does mention some detail about tapping trees that reminded him of the mastic forests on the island of Chios; he promised to bring samples of the small amount he, as of yet, collected; he also promoted the growing of cotton, producing large amounts of the product to sell to the Indigenous peoples and for trade with Cathay. Columbus continued to add viable agricultural products to the list of possible profitable trade items; this time it was aloewood, although he noted that it might not grow in great quantities.[52]

Continuing the first-person narrative, Las Casas now describes one of the crucial events suggestive of the kidnapping charge against Columbus. Here are the descriptions as translated by Kettell, Thacher, and Lardicci.

> Yesterday, a canoe came to the ship with six young men, five of them came on board, whom I ordered to be detained, and have them with me; I then sent ashore to one of the houses and took seven women and three children: this I did that the Indians might tolerate their captivity better with their company…
>
> *Kettle, 84–85*

> Yesterday there came to the side of the ship a canoe with six youths upon it and five of them entered the ship. These I ordered kept and I am bringing them with me. And afterwards I sent to a house which is west of the river, and they brought seven women, small and large, and three children. I did this that the men might conduct themselves better in Spain by having women from their country than they would without them…
>
> *Thacher, 564*

The original Spanish is shown below; the quote below is a sample from the November 12 log entry.

Así que ayer vino abordo de la nao una almadia con seis mancebos, y los cinco entraron en la nao; estos mandé detener é los traigo. Y después envié á una casa, que es de la parte del río del Poniente, y trajeron siete cabezas de mujeres entre chicas é grandes y tres niños. Esto hice porque mejor se los hombres en España habiendo mujeres de su tierra que sin ellas...[53]

Lardicci translating Las Casas's *Historias de las Indias* on this incident wrote:

...so it happened with the Admiral, who, wanting to perfect his plan, sent a boat with some sailors to a building that was beside the river to the west, and they seized and brought back seven women, both young girls and grown women, along with three children...

Lardicci, 223

It is true that Columbus wanted, as he said, people from Cibao to complement those taken from the smaller islands. He noted their cultural differences from the Guanahani Indios and thought it wise to have some Cuban natives go to Spain, learn the language, and return to their lives, either to help as interpreters for later commercial exchanges or simply inform their people about their experiences, helping to induce continued good relations.[54] In the November 12 entry, the same one that talks about detaining Indios, Las Casas, in third-person narrative, wrote,

He said the Sunday before, November 11, it had appeared to him that it would be well to take some persons from those dwelling[s] by that river in order to take them to the Sovereigns that they might learn our language so as to know what there is in the country, and that in returning they may speak the language of the Christians and take our customs and the things of the Faith.[55]

Therefore, if we accept that Columbus may have been desiring to continue his benign policy of friendly relations, why would he now want to flagrantly kidnap five young Taíno men and quickly thereafter send a boatload of sailors ashore to capture women and children? Fuson's translation and others relate how Columbus felt the women and children might have a positive effect on the behavior of the males once in Spain.[56] Surely, these actions would have left a negative impression on the villagers and the entire region as word spread to other areas. The whole point of contact was to develop a good working relationship for subsequent commercial contacts. There was no logic in kidnapping these Indios and jeopardizing future relationships, or was there? At this time in the voyage, Columbus did not entertain island-wide colonization; only commercial contact, control over a limited geographic area, and building trading posts; those were the terms of his agreement with the Spanish monarchs. Besides, he genuinely believed that Cuba was part of the Asian mainland and thus subject to political and military authority from the Great Khan or someone like him. Kidnapping subjects of a foreign ruler is the worst action one can take while attempting to initiate a positive cultural and political encounter. Columbus already had six or seven Lucayans; why would he need more individuals to show proof of his discoveries? For a deeper investigation of Columbus's attitude and actions toward the Indigenous peoples, see Appendix III.[57]

Is it possible that Columbus realized that the slight but noticeable language differences between the Lucayans and the Taíno posed problems for future trade interactions? If so, then why not bring back a few people from each region, train them in the fundamentals of the Spanish language, and bring them back to their respective homes, setting them up as interpreters for future trade negotiations and agreements?

Notice that Columbus also wanted to have the Indios learn the Catholic faith. To accomplish this, the Indigenous interpreters might, with newly acquired language skills, verbal understanding, and reading proficiency in Spanish, convert to Christianity and help convert their fellow islanders. Columbus thought this feat might readily be accomplished because "I have seen and I recognize," says the admiral, "that these people have no religion, nor are they idolatrous."[58] In this statement, he expands the geographic impact of this social engineering by declaring that in a short period of time, Christian conversion would extend throughout the Lucayan Islands and Cuba.

Las Casas, writing in his *Historia*, furious over Columbus's overt act of kidnapping, chastised the explorer, calling this action "nefarious," indeed, a sin, noting how serious it was to deprive anyone of their freedom, an action condemned by God and worthy of divine retribution. Las Casas saw this as an act against "natural law" and all the basic tenets of proper Christian behavior.[59]

Columbus finishes this daily entry discussing the recent cold weather, an observation tied to a decision to curtail sailing further north. Instead, he sails east by south, at least 18 leagues to a cape he named Cabo de Cuba, Cabo Lucrecia today (Figure 8.5).

With a dramatic change of heart, Columbus quickly reversed the fleet's direction and now headed south, thinking the many deep bays offered more opportunities for finding gold and other products of value.

November 13, Tuesday

In the early morning hours before sunrise, Columbus "beat up and down" to get a better look at what appeared to be two mountain ranges separated by a

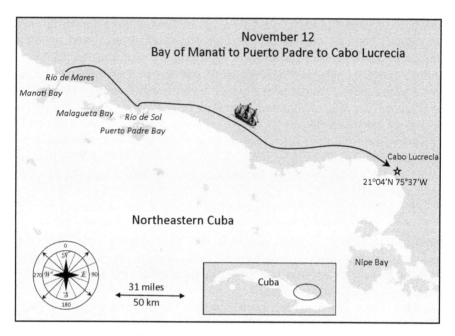

FIGURE 8.5 November 12: *Bay of Manatí* to Puerto Padre

wide gap. From their vantage point offshore and looking SW, the explorer thought these mountains represented the extreme geographic extent of Cuba to the east and the western terminus of *Bohio*, the latter representing the location of vast amounts of gold.

With dawn breaking clear and bright, Columbus steered the fleet toward the land, passing a "point" that looked to be 2 leagues in length (Playa Larga to Playa Punta de Mulas). Now, a wide gulf opened, and the fleet moved SSE cautiously toward the coast. Here at a location just west of Guajaca Uno, Columbus viewed a cape 5 leagues distant to the east (Cayo Moa Grande). The fleet halted, and a tense discussion between Columbus and his Indio interpreters ensued. The two mountain ranges, the Sierra de Micaro and Sierra de Manguey, stand tall about 25 miles apart, with peaks rising to over 4,000 feet for the former and 3,800 feet for the latter, framing in a wide lowland divided by the Rio Sagua, teasing the explorer that higher elevations might be sources of gold mines. Columbus pondered landing but changed his mind when the Indios reminded him that even more gold existed in quantities on the island of *Babeque*, somewhere to the east.

Decision made, Columbus ordered the fleet to move in an easterly direction, sailing 56 miles. From this point, lookouts claimed they could see the coast of *Bohio* in the leeward direction, some 80 miles in the distance, with the coastline running ESE and WNW.[60]

November 14, Wednesday

Not sighting land and nervous about continuing eastward, Columbus "stood off and on" until daylight, judging it not safe to proceed. The wind blew light, and it came directly at them. His native guides gestured that it would take three days of canoeing to reach *Babeque*. Playing it safe, Columbus ordered a course change once the wind shifted, heading east by south, then south until reaching land. Immediately, lookouts reported harbors, small islands, and inlets. Nervous about reef structures, Columbus ordered the fleet to sail NW by W in search of a good harbor. He saw many coastal openings, but none looked promising. He continued for 64 miles, where they saw a wide opening that appeared to be deep with a river—today the Bay of Sagua de Tanamo. Using the skiff boats, Columbus entered the "river," which reached a depth of 70 feet. Following the "river" inland, he watched a wide bay open before his eyes, a small island directly in front of them, and a much larger island in the background. Veering to the west, crew members recorded depths greater than 100 feet, allowing the skiffs to easily maneuver between the small and large islands.[61] Las Casas wrote that the crew could not count all the islands; today there are ten larger and a few smaller islands, most covered in palm trees. From the bay, Columbus could see the crest of the Sierra de Micaro Mountains swinging wide in a semi-circle only 10 miles in the distance, an impressive sight. It was impressive enough for Columbus to comment on their beauty and size to the Spanish monarchs that no higher mountains so close to the coast existed anywhere else.

Now, Las Casas interprets Columbus's next comments as a possible reference to the explorer's early study of mappae mundi, showing countless islands sitting off the east coast of Asia.[62] Excited about the geographic connection, Columbus imagined riches, precious stones, and spices and named the bay La Mar de Nuestra Senora (The Sea of Our Lady) and the entrance "river" Puerto del Principe (Port of the Prince).

November 15, Thursday

The next day, using the skiff boats again, Columbus and his crew discovered aloe plants and mastic trees. Taking soundings as they cruised among the bay islands, crew members consistently found depths exceeding 90 feet with no subsurface rocks.

November 16, Friday

As on most previous islands, Columbus ordered men to prepare a cross to be placed near the entrance of the river or bay he explored, a way of claiming the land for the Spanish monarchs. From the description given by Las Casas,

Columbus selected Punta Gitana as the site for a quickly made cross of branches, about one-half mile from the entrance to the bay. This promontory, at a location where the "river" narrowed, offered a high point to build a future fortress, controlling sea traffic coming and going. Just offshore, the depths sank considerably, forcing large ships to steer close to the promontory. The concept of fortress building is akin to the commercial goal of establishing a trading post, where, at the beginning of the relationship, trade is conducted within the safety of a walled enclosure, another indication that Columbus continued to see a trading post as the first step in his limited colonization plan. Las Casas saw this comment in his copy of the logbook and expanded on the idea in his *Historia*, writing, "It seemed to him that a fortress could be built there at little expense, if at any time in that sea of islands there should turn out to be some great commercial activity."[63]

When Columbus returned to the *Santa Maria*, just outside the bay, he found his Indios "fishing" for "very large snails." Impressed with their diving ability, he requested they bring up "nacaras" (oysters) in the hope of securing some pearls; none were found. From the description here, the Indios, all of them, had another opportunity to escape if they desired, but none did. While this was occurring, some crew members brought back a small cat-like animal, called "taso" by the Spaniards; others caught a new pig-like large fish, covered in a hard shell. Everyone seemed impressed by this creature, and Columbus ordered it salted for presentation to Ferdinand and Isabella.

November 17, Saturday

Excited about the possibility of exploring the bay island, Columbus ordered the skiff boat offloaded. While maneuvering to the southeast, he and the skiff crew encountered "very fertile" landscapes. Depth readings surprisingly revealed an average of 30–50 feet to the bay bottom.[64] He found a small beach, uncommon for its location, deep within the protected bay and nearby a river of "sweet water."[65] Possibly exaggerating, Las Casas noted that the exploration party found large nuts, oversized rats, and very large crabs.

After cruising around for much of the day, Columbus returned to his ship only to discover that two of the Cuban Indios had "fled," having been on the *Niña*. No other information appeared in this entry to describe the scenario of how this happened. Much like the other early instance of escape by the Guanahani Indios, it appears that the captives were not locked below deck, bound, gagged, or subjected to any other method of imprisonment. The original Spanish text reads: "En este dia de los seys mancebos que tomo en el rio de Mares, y mando que fuesen en la caravela Niña, se huyeron los dos mayoresde edad."[66] Again, the verb for tomar (*tomo*) is used without any additional indication that they were restrained, only that they had been taken from the Rio de Mares. If they were truly captives, then why were they allowed to go fishing the day before? The other key verb here is *huyeron*. This term translates as "to run away" or "to flee." This incident is reminiscent of the earlier episode where two Guanahani natives jumped ship. The Indios most certainly felt homesick and desired to return to their homes before the fleet moved further away. This is especially true, as we will see as the fleet nears Bohio and the possibility of encountering Caribs.[67] It is interesting to note that at this point, the only Indigenous peoples to escape jumped from the *Niña*, commanded by Vicente Pinzón. Columbus now carried 18 Indigenous captives, 8 men, 7 women, and 3 children, among all three ships.

November 18, Sunday

Columbus and crew devoted the day to erecting a large permanent cross they had constructed at the northeast entrance to *Tanamo Bay* on the clear hilltop measuring just over 170 feet, affording a dramatic view of the ocean and southward into the bay. He also noticed impressive changes in tides within the confines of the bay, more than any other site he previously visited on this voyage (Figure 8.6).

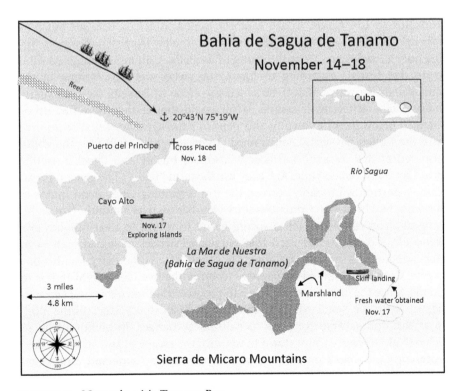

FIGURE 8.6   November 14: *Tanamo Bay*

The dramatic vertical landscape attracted Columbus to the opening of yet another Cuban bay, *Tanamo Bay*. As he entered the wide opening between the land, he saw the largest bay yet, shallow, yet wide, dotted with islands stretching eastward.

November 19, Monday

Possibly in hopes of finding the island of *Babeque* (Great Inagua), Columbus set sail after a morning of no wind in an NNE direction, making 21 miles by sunset. According to Las Casas's account of this day, the fleet saw, off to the east, *Babeque* as it came into sight at a distance of 60 miles; this is impossible and must be a translation error on the part of Las Casas.[68] As evidence, Columbus continued sailing NE, not east toward the island sighting, and raises the question of why he would do this if his goal were to reach the island, reaching out 72 miles from his starting point.

November 20, Tuesday

This is an interesting entry today. Columbus became apparently confused, according to Las Casas, as the explorer hoped to get to *Babeque* but now believed the island lay to the ESE, but the wind blew from that direction. Sitting only a few leagues from the island of Isabella, Columbus pondered what to do. He feared, according to Las Casas, who was now writing in the third-person narrative, that if he sailed too close to Isabella the Guanahani Indios might "effect their escape." How could they if they were tied up or confined below deck? Evidently, this confirms the hypothesis that at no time were the Indios physically constrained. Interestingly, Kettell uses the above term "effect their escape," Lardicci, Markham, Fuson, and Thacher use the term "get away," while Dunn & Kelley use the term "flee."[69] The general thrust of the assertion is probably correct; the five remaining Guanahani Indios at this point had been with Columbus since October 14, over a month. No doubt, some of them, as before, felt a strong desire to return to their families and island life. Columbus admitted that language barriers remained high, with each side not clearly understanding the other. Yet, as the entry for this day asserts, Columbus wanted desperately to bring the five Guanahani Indios to Castile. Since the Guanahani Indios had progressed in learning basic communication with the Spaniards, they could show Spanish officials and the monarchs that Indios were receptive to cultural exchanges. In addition, the 12 *Cibao* (Cuban) natives, now down to ten with the escape of two Indios, would represent Columbus's initial contact with the Asian "mainland," an island frontier of the Great Khan.

Columbus, also desiring to move on to contact the large island of *Bohio*, reversed course and steered back to Puerto del Principe, not quite reaching his destination.

Martín Pinzón Abandons Columbus

November 21, Wednesday

Contrary wind and seas made progress difficult this morning, making only 24 miles. With a wind change, the fleet headed S by E, making another 12 miles. From his point, a frustrated Columbus brought out the quadrant to check his latitude, finding it to equal 42 degrees, the same he measured for Rio de Mares. Las Casas now interjected comments suggesting, "if this was the fact, he [Columbus] must have been in as high a latitude as Florida; in this case, what is the situation of the islands he has been mentioning?"[70] Kettell noted a Spanish source indicating that Spanish quadrants of the 15th century often contained scales that showed "double altitude" measurements. It was expected that the reader of the quadrant would divide that number by two, thus getting a correct latitude reading of 21 degrees north. Obviously, Las Casas was unaware of that maritime fact; either that or Columbus wanted to, as before, not disclose the true latitude for fear of Portuguese retribution.

Las Casas now connects Columbus's thoughts on latitude, heat, and gold: The hotter the geographic environment, the greater are the deposits of gold; no evidence for this reasoning is supplied.

Meanwhile, in a puzzling move that appeared to be disobedience, Martín Pinzón changed direction and sailed off to the east, purportedly to discover *Babeque*. The entry credits one of the Indios onboard the *Pinta* for stimulating Pinzón's gold lust, with Pinzón not bothering to confer with Columbus but acting unilaterally.[71] Columbus may have been shocked, yet Las Casas only provides this quote from the admiral: "He [Pinzón] has done and said many other things to me."[72] This provocative statement says a lot. Columbus, a foreigner in command of the fleet, faced mutiny on the outgoing transatlantic voyage, then praise once the land was reached. The crew held loyal as island after island appeared to confirm Columbus's geographic knowledge of the Indies and Cathay. Now, with Columbus sailing north, then turning around and attempting to sail back to a place where the fleet had already spent considerable days without finding gold, Pinzón had reached his limit; he, Pinzón, would find the gold. The incentive came from one or more of the interpreters on the *Pinta* who said, "that there was an island called *Hayani* where there was much gold, and they directed him [Pinzón] to where it was."[73]

The interesting question to ask then is: Did Martín Pinzón commit a treasonous act, or can this be understood more correctly as an opportunity to act independently for the benefit of the overall voyage? From a Columbus standpoint, one can see his disappointment, especially knowing that Pinzón did not bother to inform the fleet commander of his intentions. One of the *Pinta*'s crew, Francisco Garcia Vallejo, recalled,

> One night Martín Alonso [Pinzón] took his leave and departed from the admiral and he went to an island that is Babueca and after he discovered it, he went two hundred leagues to the southwest from there and he discovered the island of Española…and there Martín Alonso told [Columbus] how he had discovered the island…and the gold and he brought nine hundred pesos of gold and gave them to the admiral.[74]

Ferdinand Columbus made it clear in his father's biography that Pinzón's breach of commitment was an egregious act of insubordination, writing that the Spaniard "was moved by greed to separate from the Admiral by the excuse of contrary wind or any other excuse."[75] Lawrence Bergreen, in his *Columbus: The Four Voyages*, cites the importance of Pinzón to the expedition, hinting that the Spaniard felt empowered to set out on his own to honor the goal of the voyage and find gold. In a way, Bergreen suggested Pinzón and Columbus shared equal responsibility, preserving unilateral options as acceptable.[76]

Historian Samuel Morison, having an extensive sailing background, understood Pinzón's flight writing,

> Pinta was a smarter *sailer* than Santa Maria, especially in the conditions of light wind and heavy head swell that prevailed on November 21; and very likely Pinzón was exasperated at continually having to shorten sail in order not to outdistance the flagship.[77]

Las Casas, in describing this incident in his *Historia*, expounded on Pinzón's decision with the caustic comment, "But Martín Alonso did not care about anything except going away."[78]

November 22, Thursday

Confusion abounded today as Columbus, fighting the changing wind patterns, sailed SE, still upset with Martín Pinzón's actions the day before. As the *Santa Maria* and *Niña* approached the north shore of Cuba, Columbus took in sail and hoped that the *Pinta* would return.

November 23, Friday

Still sailing slowly south, Columbus continued looking for the north coast of Cuba. The Indios on board, probably the ones from *Cibao* (Cuba), gestured and told the Guanahani Indios about vast gold deposits on *Bohio*; on *Bohio*, natives with one eye in the forehead lived along with cannibals. Showing fear, not of the Spaniards but of the cannibals, the onboard Indios ceased talking. Columbus now believed the story, as he had heard it several times before that these Caribs, holding weapons greater than the Lucayans or the Taíno, came to islands regularly to kidnap and harvest humans. The logic employed here by Las Casas for Columbus connects the fact that all kidnapped Lucayans and Taíno taken away by the Caribs never returned, according to the Indio interpreters.[79]

November 24, Saturday

Navigating all night, Columbus's two ships sighted the north coast of Cuba at a location known today as Cayo Moa; he had sailed by this point earlier on November 14 as he journeyed west to Rio de Las Mares. Fearing dangerous reefs extending for miles, Columbus sent the skiff ahead to an opening between islands. Finding a "fine sandy bottom" reaching depths of 30 or more feet, Columbus carefully and slowly entered the harbor, only three-quarters of a mile wide. He noticed a flat island 2 miles long and 0.5 mile wide to their starboard side as they entered the "sea." Mountains could be seen inland just a few miles away; it was another dramatic meeting of land and water. With the skiff boats, they discovered a freshwater river, probably the Rio Moa; palm trees abounded.

November 25, Sunday

Up early this morning, even before daylight, Columbus and a few men rowed SE for 4 miles to a cape that jutted out into the bay. Nearby, the exploration party discovered a "fine stream running down a mountain with loud murmurs," probably the Rio Cayo Guam. At the stream's entrance, Columbus believed he saw "certain stones which shone with spots of a golden hue," thinking they resembled the recent gold finds at the Tagus River in Spain.[80] Meanwhile, one of the ship's boys shouted with joy at seeing pine trees at the summit of nearby mountains. Again, Las Casas paints Columbus dreaming about how the apparently straight, tall timber might some day supply the planks for Spanish ships. Later, some men chopped and shaped a few timber specimens for a mizzenmast and yard arm for *Niña*. The rest of this entry has Las Casas recounting Columbus's awe and excitement about the commercial possibilities of the many raw materials in the bay (Figure 8.7).

Frustrated for not finding gold nuggets laying about on previous islands he visited, Columbus perked up when he noticed gold-like stones in the Rio Cayo Guam. Noticing rising hills and mountains in the nearby distance, he believed he had finally found a major source of gold deposits.

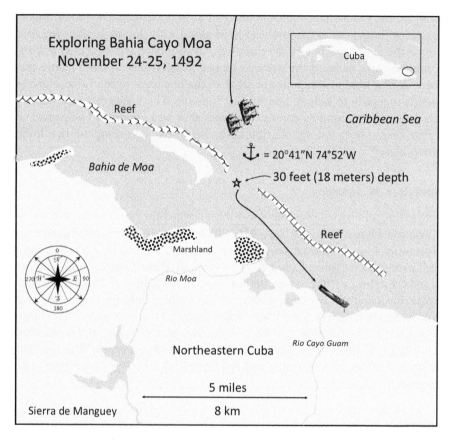

FIGURE 8.7   November 24–25: Exploring *Cayo Moa Bay*

November 26, Monday

At sunrise, Columbus ordered the ships to depart, heading SW sailing 40 miles to Cabo del Pico (Punta Guarico). From here, the coast turned SE by S, and the crew spotted another cape (Punta Plata), which Columbus named Cabo de Campana, tacking for the rest of the day due to light winds. As before, the mountains framed the entire coastline, with Las Casas describing the scene in detail as "the whole most enchantingly covered with tall and flourishing trees."[81] Columbus noted three fine harbors, Bahia de Canete, Bahia Yamaniguey, and the Rio Jiguani, as he cruised close to the coastline, but no villages appeared, although smoldering campfires indicated people did live in the region. Looking to the southeast, Columbus thought he saw a separation of the land by a water divide and a large landmass to the SE, believing the land to be *Bohio*.

At this point, Las Casas derives from his reading of the journal that Columbus believed the local Indios, afraid of the Caribs on *Bohio*, only built their villages away from the coastline, explaining why no signs of human structures were encountered. Going further, Las Casas claimed the Indios were "struck speechless with terror, thinking they should be devoured." This is probably a true observation; the Indios continued to talk about natives with "faces of dogs, with only one eye," although Las Casas added that Columbus at first did not believe this, preferring instead to attribute the Caribs to peoples of the "Great Can."[82]

November 27, Tuesday

This morning, Columbus found the *Santa Maria* and the *Niña* drifting 15–20 miles SE from Cabo de Campana, but seeing a wide opening in the land, he turned and steered NW, where he found a large bay *Baracoa Bay* As he approached the bay, an impressive, square-shaped "hill" appeared (Monte del Yunque) at first, looking like the top of a separate island. He also noted a large river flowing into the bay; in fact, he recorded seeing seven rivers of varying width, the last of which was about 20 miles SE of Cabo de Campana. At the site of the last river (Rio Toa), the crew spotted a large village. At the same time, the Indigenous peoples in that village spotted the strange ships. Instantly, the villagers poured onto the beach shouting; they were armed with spears, and a few carried several of these weapons. Columbus, at first, thought it a good idea to lower the sails, and then he ordered the skiff boats to approach the shore. The sailors rowed cautiously, armed with their own weapons and gifts. As the Spanish boats came close, the throng of excited warriors retreated quickly into the nearby trees, watching and waiting. Three of the Spaniards then hopped from one of the skiffs and waded slowly onto the beach; later, it was learned that the three sailors selected to go ashore had learned some rudimentary words and phrases from the Guanahani and Taíno interpreters.[83] Walking ashore with orders to make contact, the shore party moved toward the village. This is when the villagers *en masse* faded further into the trees and away from their homes. Entering the village, the Spaniards found no one and then returned to their ships.

Columbus, disappointed once again that Indios would not parley, set sail to points east, sighting a fine cape (Punta de Miel) after covering 2 miles. Continuing 0.5 league, scouts reported a "very remarkable harbor (Bahia de Baracoa)," beautiful landscapes, some smoke, and a possible indication of a village, so he decided to investigate. Wanting to lead the first skiff ashore, Columbus helped to take depth soundings as the crew rowed toward shore and entered what looked like a harbor entrance. Finding 30–60 feet of depth, he was pleased.

No villagers dared step forward, so the Spaniards explored up a river for a short distance and returned to their ships. On board, Columbus immediately sat down in his tight cabin to record his feelings about this place and his adventures in Cuba.

> How great the benefit that is to be derived from this country...such lands there must be an infinite number of things that would be profitable...I will make my followers [crew] learn the language. For I have perceived that there is only one language up to this point. After they understand the advantages, I shall labor to make all these people Christians.[84]

The above quote succinctly summarizes Columbus's two great intentions for the first voyage: to discover places where desirable commercial products may be traded from the inhabitants and at some point in the future, to Christianize the population.

In the same passage, Columbus declared that not one of his crew had been lost or even became ill up to this point in the voyage. This is a remarkable achievement when considering this was a dangerous discovery expedition across the *Ocean Sea* to unknown destinations, places, climates, and encounters with previously unknown Indigenous populations.

Returning to the beach area, Columbus scanned the entire breadth of the crescent-shaped bay; he liked what he saw. Immediately, he knew this would be a perfect site for a trading post. Las Casas translated, "He says that was a suitable place to build a town, or city or fortress, because of the good harbor, good water, good land, good surroundings and abundance of wood."[85] Some of the crew went ashore, exploring inland, where they discovered several villages but no people; they had fled (Figure 8.8).

At this point in his journey, Columbus appeared less depressed concerning the lack of gold, readjusting his thinking toward looking for other profitable commodities and toward Christianizing the Indios. Upon reaching the *Bay of Baracoa*, he reiterated his primary intention of setting up a trading post.

November 28–29, Thursday

Rain fell heavily, and Columbus decided to stay in port. He allowed additional crews to search inland for Indio villages. One group moved to the northwest and found a village with no people, as usual. However, looking inside the huts, all interior furniture and belongings had also been removed, except for a "cake of wax" found in one hut. They did find an "old man" and asked him to come back to the ships; he agreed. Upon conversation with onboard Cuban interpreters, Columbus first dressed the Indio, gave him small gifts, and asked about the local people and customs. After the Cuban native left, the crew that brought him told Columbus about finding "a man's head hanging from a beam in a small, covered basket." Columbus believed these to be the "heads of the principal men" of the village, and he did not then connect this event with possible Carib involvement (Figure 8.9).[86]

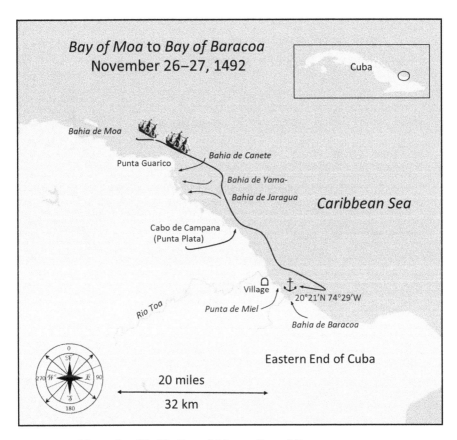

Bay of Moa to Bay of Baracoa
November 26–27, 1492

Cuba

Bahia de Moa

Punta Guarico

Bahia de Canete

Bahia de Yama-

Bahia de Jaragua

Caribbean Sea

Cabo de Campana
(Punta Plata)

Village

20°21′N 74°29′W

Rio Toa

Punta de Miel

Bahia de Baracoa

Eastern End of Cuba

0

270   90

180

20 miles

32 km

FIGURE 8.8   November 26–27: *Bay of Moa* to *Bay of Baracoa*

However good his intentions were at this point in the voyage, Columbus still had difficulty making positive contact with many of the Indigenous people in the villages he encountered. Fear of the unknown visitors may have had something to do with Columbus finding only empty villages.

November 30, Friday

When the rain stopped, the wind changed and came from the east, forcing the fleet to remain once again idle. Another day, another shore party; this time Columbus sent eight armed men and two of his trusted Indio guides ashore to explore the area and try once again to make contact. They were hoping that the "old man" they met with yesterday would report positive comments to his fellow villagers about the newcomers. After much searching, the shore party did come across an open field where four Indios busied themselves working the planted crops and digging. Looking up, one of the Cuban Indios spotted the white men; all four of them took off with a head start that did not allow the Spaniards or the Indio interpreters to catch up and attempt communication. Onward the

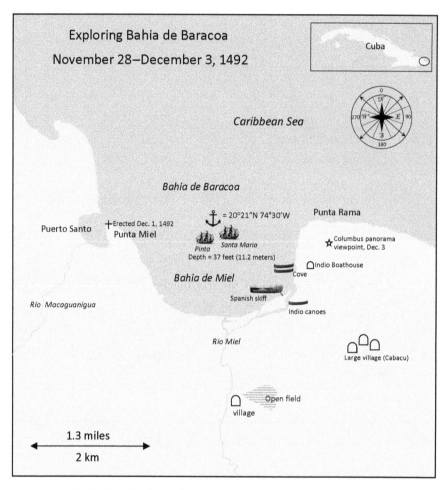

FIGURE 8.9 Exploring the *Bay of Baracoa*

shore party traveled for most of the day; every village, small and large, contained no people and few large artifacts—everything had been carried away. Apparently, the "old man" did not convince the local populations of Spanish goodwill and intentions. On the way back to the ships, following the river, the shore party inspected a very large canoe, the largest yet seen, measuring 95 spans (arm lengths) in length. The men estimated it could carry over 100 people.[87]

December 1, Saturday

With the wind still refusing to turn, Columbus decided to set up a large, rough, wood-hewn cross at the entrance to the port at Baracoa.[88] Wanting to impress the Spanish monarchs with the prospect of having Puerto Santo (Baracoa) serve as one of the key ports of call, Columbus described specific information on how to proceed into the harbor, nearby reefs, offshore rocks, and sea depths.

December 2, Sunday

Another day of contrary winds forced Columbus to postpone sailing further along the Cuban coast. Some of the ships' boys joined other crew members in exploring the rivers flowing into the bay. One boy brought back rocks to show Columbus, insisting that gold particles resided on the surface. Columbus and the crew looked impressed; several specimens were taken below for presentation in Spain. Las Casas next wrote, "The Admiral says that there are great rivers at the distance of a lombard shot."[89]

December 3, Monday

More wind coming strong from the east continued to prevent a departure in that direction. Noticing a prominent headland 2 miles to the southeast (Punta Rama), Columbus decided to investigate the area. Ship lookouts quickly spotted another river (Rio Miel), which flowed into the large crescent-shaped bay, Las Casas, claiming that Columbus believed all the ships (large and small) in Spain might fit easily. The Rio Miel today is not as deep as reported by the journal and has been influenced by the continued growth of the nearby city of Baracoa. In fact, unless the physiography of the river delta has evolved dramatically in 500 years, Las Casas must have misunderstood this entry; more likely, the river that could fit all the ships of Spain is probably a reference to the bay between Baracoa and the headland, Punta Rama. Coming out of the river, the crew rowed along the rocky shore due north for a short distance, where they discovered a cove cut back into the rock. Along the beach on either side, five very large canoes sat idle. Impressed, the curious men inspected each canoe, finding it to be "a pleasure to look at them." Trees hid the canoes from the rising terrain behind them, but a single walking path led upward. The path led to a "very well-built boathouse, so thatched that neither sun nor rain could do any harm."[90] Columbus appeared quite excited about another canoe he found at the boathouse, for it contained no less than 17 benches and showed "goodly work."

From here, the exploratory party climbed the steep hill, negotiating a narrow, switch-backing path further. Arriving at the hillcrest, the view proved spectacular. Descending toward the southeast, he came upon a level area (today the town of Cabauc) where a large village existed. The Spaniards appeared unexpectedly from the trees and surprised the local Indio people, who quickly began to flee. Two Guanahani interpreters with Columbus attempted to shout a reassurance; at first, it did not work, but some of the local Taínos stopped and returned. Columbus approached, and "he dispatched his Indian guides [interpreters] to reassure them," and the Indio interpreters ran forward, presenting hawk's bells, brass rings, and strings of green and yellow glass beads; the recipients rejoiced.[91] After a short while in which the Spaniards saw no gold or items of value, they left and returned to their boats at the cove.

Columbus sent a couple of men back up the hill to search for a beehive he thought he had seen earlier. Meanwhile, a group of local Indios approached; one brave native "advanced to the rear near the stern of the boat and made a long speech." As the speech went along, the Indios with this man raised their arms upward, shouting single words and some phrases; Columbus could not tell the meaning of the speech or the reaction of the other Indios. When Columbus looked at one of his interpreters, he was shocked to see the Guanahani Indio turning pale, as if frightened, then trembling.[92] Fearing a possible attack, Columbus took a sturdy crossbow from one of his men and held it up for the Indios to view. Las Casas wrote that the local Taíno quickly understood this to be a weapon of great power. Handing the crossbow back to one of his men, Columbus drew his sword, waving it for them to see; he rarely did this on the first voyage. The local Taíno understood this, turned, and left the scene, but not the one Taíno who still stood by the canoe, though he was now trembling.

Columbus now believed it was a good time to leave the cove, as the Taíno had become nervous about strangers near their large canoes. The Spaniards, back in their skiff boat, rowed up the Rio Miel 1.5 miles to where a large gathering of Taínos stood, painted in colors of red and black; some sported feathers jutting from their hair; others wore simple multi-feather plumes, and all were armed with spears. Believing friendliness, the best approach, as they were outnumbered considerably, Columbus, unafraid, approached the plumed Taíno, made peaceful gestures, and began offering more gift trinkets, the usual assortment plus a few brass rings. Apparently, the Taíno stood down and began interacting with the small group of explorers. The ship's boy got into the act, trading some tortoiseshell pieces in exchange for spears; all the ships' boys preferred to trade for spears when possible.

Invited into one house, Columbus was duly impressed.

> I saw a beautiful house not very large and having two doors, as they are all built so, and I entered it and saw a wonderful arrangement like chambers constructed in a certain manner which I do not know how to describe, with shells and other things fastened to the ceiling. And I thought it was a temple, and I called them and asked by signs if they prayed in it, and they said no, and one of them went up overhead and gave me all they had there, and I took some of it.[93]

December 4, Tuesday

Finally, the wind cooperated, and Columbus set sail with the *Santa Maria* and *Niña*, cruising slowly along the coast. They came upon another "river" (Ensenada de Mata), which appeared to be narrow yet deep.[94] Three miles from this river, the crew spotted another river (Rio Yumuri); Columbus lowered sail and ordered some men to investigate the opening.[95] The skiff crew estimated the width of the river at about 100 paces (300 feet), which is quite accurate. They reported fresh water almost to the mouth of the river; noticing a "great volume of water" flowing into the ocean, Columbus surmised the river "probably had many towns on its banks." The part of his entry today is quite interesting, as Las Casas wrote, "Beyond Cabo Lindo there is a great bay, which would be open for navigation to ENE and SE and SSW."[96] The Cuban coastline at Cabo Lindo (Punta del Fraile today) immediately turns SE, opening a clear view of the open sea east. He should have noted that this was probably the eastern extent of Cuba, but he made no mention of this fact (Figure 8.10).

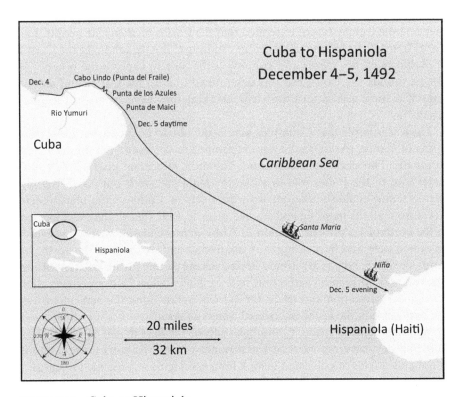

FIGURE 8.10 Cuba to Hispaniola

Columbus soon discovered that the Cuban coastline at this point turned rapidly to the SW and appeared to end; he was nearing the extreme eastern terminus of Cuba. The Guanahani guides claimed a great ruler reigned on a large island to the southeast and Columbus was determined to find that island.

December 5, Wednesday

The two ships beat back and forth for most of the previous night; at sunrise, Columbus saw a cape (Punta de los Azules) 2.5 miles from Cabo Lindo. Now the coastline dropped south, then southwest, indicating that they had indeed discovered the extreme eastern end of Cuba. Continuing, they saw a prominent cape (Punta del Maici); the admiral was tempted to stop but thought otherwise. Las Casas next claims that when Columbus and his crew "looked to the SE, he saw land, which was a large island, according to the information from the Indians, well-peopled, and called by them *Bohio. Bohio* is a reference to Haiti, which stood 52 miles from Punta del Maici.[97]

Next, Columbus, in communicating with his Indio guides, once again sensed their fear and hesitation about going any further away from their home islands. The Guanahani Indios had now become the most trusted of his guides, and they and the Cuban Taínos reiterated that the Caribs of *Bohio* ate people. Las Casas translated a section in this entry claiming Columbus thought the Caribs of Bohio must be "clever and cunning to be able to capture the others." It almost sounds like Columbus was determined to meet the Caribs and see for himself if these accusations were true, thinking they were agents of the great Khan.[98]

Las Casas wrote that Columbus assumed Cuba to be the easternmost peninsula of Cathay (Asia), yet he was determined to sail away from this new land to the SE. This does not make sense. The most important goal of the entire Enterprise to the Indies was to strike the mainland, seek out Asian trading partners, and establish relations with the rulers of Cathay. Columbus understood from all the maps he had studied prior to 1492 that Cathay was located to the north of his present location. If Cuba were the mainland, logic suggests he should steer west back along the Cuban coast and seek land to the north. At Punta de Maici, he was at latitude 20 degrees north, already in violation of the Spanish and Portuguese agreement to leave lands below 28 degrees north for Portuguese navigation and trade. Or did Columbus think the agreement was not applicable in the newly discovered waters of Asia?

With his decision made, Columbus ordered the fleet to sail SE. The ships sailed all day, covering most of the distance needed. At sunset, the admiral commanded *Niña* to sail ahead to look for a good harbor. Vincente Pinzón and his crew did find the *Bahie du Mole* on the southern side of Cape Mole Saint-Nicolas. They lowered sail and set out lanterns for Columbus to follow.

The ever-cautious admiral hesitated and waited for the following sunrise to join *Niña*.

December 6, Thursday

About 4 leagues (12 miles) from the Cape Mole Saint-Nicolas, Columbus viewed the cape where *Niña* lay anchored; he named the location Cabo del Estrella and the port Puerto de San Nicolas (*Baie Du Mole*). He estimated the entrance to be 1.5 leagues wide (about 4 miles); this is another mistranslated figure as the opening is only 1.75 miles wide. As the *Santa Maria* entered this wide bay, Columbus noted a "fine beach" and a low-lying area apparently containing fruit trees. Conjecturing further the explorer imagined nutmeg and other spice plants intermingled among the cluster of trees.[99] He also spotted a river 3 miles into the harbor on the southern shore, *Riviere La Gorge*.

Amazed by the deep soundings his crew recorded while proceeding into the bay, Columbus found depths ranging from 15 to 40 fathoms (90–360 feet).[100] As they probed deeper into what must have delighted Columbus as a prospective trading port, he noted the "clean bottom" with no large reefs or underwater rocks. He even exaggerated the possibility of anchoring "a thousand carracks" in the eastern portion of the bay; one location that he termed "a creek," actually the narrow northeast extension of the bay, appeared to run deep and "clean" to the shore, writing, "Where the ship may be laid alongside the grass, it is up to eight fathoms."[101]

Exuberant over the bay's future maritime host possibilities, Columbus now provided a running description of the land and the air, discussing the size of the trees and the "very fine air." The valley he saw straddling *Riviere La Gorge* appeared beautiful, well-watered, and available for cultivation; again, he imagined large Indio villages somewhere inland on this low-lying plain. There was some truth to his conjecture, as the crew spotted many large canoes, as seen in Cuba.

During the cruise around *Du Mole Bay*, Columbus's Indio guides stood close to him, another sign that they were not incarcerated below decks. The admiral could tell by their behavior that they remained nervous, almost scared, being in these waters of *Bohio*. At this point, the Indios, according to Las Casas's translation, became "mistrustful of him [Columbus] for not taking his route that way [toward Cuba and Guanahani]. Going further, Las Casas wrote, "For this reason, he [Columbus] declares that he puts no trust in any of their representations [gestures], nor they in his."[102] Postulating, Las Casas believed the admiral would not be able to use his Taíno guides, insinuating that their only purpose now was to be held as captives and displayed as such to the Spanish monarchs. Frustrated, Columbus decided not to delay any longer in this harbor, wishing to move on to the east.

From the Indigenous perspective, one can readily understand their hesitancy, growing distrust, and outright fear. Bergreen, in his book at this point, expressed the thought that "The more familiar they became with him and his men, the more they gravitated toward the explorer."[103] Hawk's bells and colored glass pieces initially supplied their interest, but was it Columbus's positive connection directly with the Indios on the *Santa Maria* that prevailed? In this current situation, we can understand the natural concern of the Lucayans, and we can sympathize with their desire not to go any closer to the Carib territory, preferring a quick return to their home. Logically, Columbus, who in short order would find that his Lucayans no longer effectively able to communicate with the people of Hispaniola, especially those living further east, should have returned the five Lucayans to Guanahani. This is evidence that he intended to keep them, at this point, against their will, for presentation to the Spanish royal court; however, this condition will change in a few short weeks.[104]

This section of the entry is highly suspected of Las Casas's transcription accuracy. First, *Du Mole Bay*, far and away, contained the best prospects for developing a large-scale harbor, trading post, and commercial outpost; Columbus himself said this earlier in the entry. Why would he not want to investigate the inland regions, at least for a few days, and make friendly contact on this

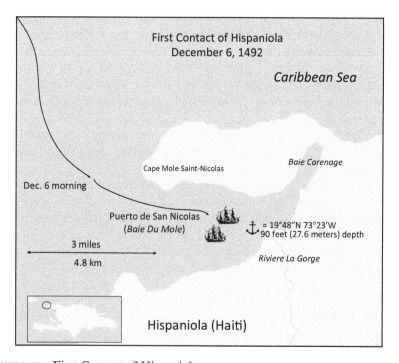

FIGURE 8.11 First Contact of Hispaniola

new and promising island? Las Casas remarked, "He [Columbus] trusted in our Lord that the Indians he brought with him would learn his [Spanish] language, and he theirs, and afterwards he would come back and speak with these people."[105] In this translation, Columbus is focused on bringing the Cuban and Guanahani Indios back to Spain to learn the Spanish language, and then on the next voyage, Columbus would bring the Indios back to their homeland. However, Markham's translation reads, "He [Columbus] trusted in our Lord that the Indians he brought with him would understand the language of the people of this island [Haiti]."[106] Dunn & Kelley agree with the first account given by Lardicci (pages 83–84), as do Fuson (page 129) and Thacher (page 583), while Kettell aligns with Markham.[107] It would appear that Kettell and Markham's translation is incorrect based on the majority of translations supporting the idea that Columbus did not trust his guides at this point, instead desiring only to bring them back to Spain and not use them in future contacts with the Indios of Haiti. However, this scenario is false, as later events will show (Figure 8.11).[108]

Delighted that the first harbor he encountered in Hispaniola proved more than accommodating for ships, with the ability to serve as an excellent trading post location with easy access to Cuba and islands already visited, Columbus had good reason to believe that this large island may indeed be the fabled Cipangu of Marco Polo's writings.

Notes

1 Modern depth-sounding charts note that the mouth of the Bay of Bariay has undergone extensive dredging.
2 Markham, *The Journal of Christopher Columbus*, 59. Visitors to the Bay of Bariay Monument Park can still see groves of these palm trees; Columbus saw them clearly from his anchorage.
3 Columbus ordered his men not to touch anything, as he "wanted only to observe what kinds of things those people used for their nourishment and service." Lardicci, *A Synoptic Edition, Historie*, FH 41, section 10, 152–53.
4 Most atlases refer to five major rivers in Cuba: Cauto (213 miles long), Toa (81), Guama (51), Yumuri (34), and the Almendares (28). However, if the Guanahani natives referenced rivers on the north Cuban coast, closest to their homeland, there are at least ten smaller rivers spilling into the many bays present.
5 This information may have come from any of the Guanahani natives who had canoed on multiple occasions to Cuba. Their descriptions of the geography appeared accurate to Columbus, with a few exceptions.
6 The journal references sailing until the evening hour of vespers, which is 6:00 p.m., a traditional Catholic time for evening prayer. Running an average of 8 miles per hour, Columbus made approximately 55 miles from his anchorage at Bariay. This author used the 3 miles per league as Columbus had used for the transatlantic crossing, interpreting the "and then another point, ten leagues to the east" as a reference to Punta Cobarrubia, which is 10 miles east of Manatí.
7 Markham, *The Journal of Christopher Columbus*, 61.

8 This location is contrary to Samuel Morison and Robert Fuson's determination of the Bay of Gibara. Both authors believe that Las Casas or a scribe misunderstood the maritime references and used leagues instead of miles. However, this author has run the mileages using the rate of 3 miles for 1 league, discovering the log statements from Dunn & Kelley's translations better match up the geographical locations noted.

9 Ibid. This viewpoint is myopic, looking only at it from Columbus's point of view, although it is true that there would be no further escape attempts by his guides. However, this account in a way suggests that the Guanahani persons on board were not forcibly kidnapped but rather taken by assumed agreement by both parties with a significant amount of misunderstanding due to the lack of effective verbal communication, or they simply were adjusting to their enforced detainment on the Spanish ships. It is interesting to note that Columbus made no mention of the sex of his Guanahani guides; presumably, they were all male. Later this will be shown as Columbus brings on board females to accompany his captives. See Lardicci, *A Synoptic Edition*, DB 43–44, sections 8–10, 60–61.

10 For purposes of this study, the term *Taíno* (Men of the Good) will refer to those Indigenous peoples living in Cuba and Haiti, except for elements of the Carib tribe that inhabited eastern geographic locations on both major islands. In Columbus's contact with these peoples, he believed that the Taíno lived mostly on the northern coastal areas, while the more warlike Caribs ruled inland kingdoms and eastern portions of Hispaniola.

11 The Lucayan peoples, a branch of the main Taíno migration north, occupied the Bahamas, living in smaller village units due to the limited physical size of the islands. Language differences apparently remained minor, as Columbus's Guanahani interpreters had no trouble communicating with people living on other islands of the Bahamas. It should be noted that archaic tribes of people, the Guanahatabeys, inhabited the far northwestern portion of Cuba at the time of contact but had no contact with Columbus during this voyage.

12 A ridge of high hills, which Las Casas transcribed as "lofty," arc in a crescent shape; These "mountains" stretch from the SW to the SE, with the Bay of Manatí in the middle.

13 It should be noted that the term *cacique* usually refers to a male ruler of a designated geographical region. On the smaller islands, it could mean recognition of the entire island, while on Cuba or Hispaniola (Haiti), natural water or topography defined ruling limits. A woman married to a ruler carried the title *cacica* in Puerto Rico. See Olga Jimenez de Wagenheim, *Puerto Rico: An Interpretative History from Pre-Columbian Times to 1900*. Markus Wiener Publishers, (1998).

14 The mention of the Gran Can by the Indios is interesting. Obviously, Pinzon repeated the name so often to his Indio guides that the Indios connected the name to some other cacique on Cibao, possibly a reference to a suspected Carib presence in the eastern portions of Cuba. Recent archaeological evidence has confirmed the Carib presence in Hispaniola, and this author suggests that contact with Eastern Cuba may have occurred on an ever-increasing scale at the time of Columbus's landing.

15 Delaney believes that all five who sailed with Columbus to Spain were baptized; one remained in the Spanish court; the rest sailed home on the return voyage in late 1493; however, one or more may have died (probably smallpox) on the return voyage. One or more returned to their home island, and at least one volunteered to stay with Columbus, continuing his service as an interpreter. See p. 120. Peter Martyr wrote that Columbus brought back ten Indios, with one staying in Barcelona at the royal court; the others returned with three dying on the voyage home, one being dropped off on Hispaniola, and the other two jumping off the ship near the shore and escaping. Eatough, *Selections from Peter Martyr, Decades* 1.2.11, 54.

16 Thacher, *The Journal of Christopher Columbus*, 555. Lardicci and Dunn & Kelley translate Las Casas's paraphrase similarly.

17 Ibid., 556.

18 Ross, et al. "Faces Divulge the Origins of Caribbean Prehistoric Inhabitants." The researchers admitted that more research needs to be done to discover the full deployment of Carib settlements in the Greater Antilles. Alonso de Ojeda, a former participant in Columbus's second voyage to Hispaniola, sailed under Spanish authority, not Columbus's, along the South American coast, where he encountered numerous Carib tribes, fighting tense battles constantly and verifying their presence in large numbers. See Dugard, 74–75.

19 See Rocca, "Mapping the Proposed Caribbean Zoonotic (Swine Influenza) Epidemic of 1493," *Terra Incognitae*, Spring 2024. Interisland canoe routes are proposed and mapped based on Columbus's reporting of personal observations and in communication with Lucayan and Taíno interpreters.

20 A third group of Indigenous peoples, the Guanahatabeys, existed in small numbers in the western portion of Cuba, an area not visited by Columbus on his first voyage. The Guanahatabeys, most likely the original peoples of the Caribbean, migrated from mainland areas to the islands 4,000 years before European contact. Later Taíno and Carib invasions pushed these primitive peoples ever westward, where they struggled for survival in small, isolated villages. Scholars believe they may have been enslaved by Taíno and Carib caciques and finally made extinct, or nearly so, by the time of Spanish contact. See Fernandez, "The Forgotten Innocents." On the possibility of ongoing raids by Caribs into Cuba, recall the Guanahani natives complaining about Carib raids on their island, more than 300 miles from the northern coast of Hispaniola.

21 Columbus is not clear how far up into the river channel he anchored; however, both locations provided easy access to beach shorelines. Morison's suggestion that the *Bay of Gibara* is most likely incorrect as the sea floor depths drop immediately after entering the mouth of the bay, reducing from 32 feet depth to 20 feet in the span of only 700 feet, offering little or no protection from the winds and high seas. The full-length "river" of the *Bay of Manatí* to its mouth, where it enters the Caribbean Sea is 3.5 miles long, explaining why Columbus thought it a major river.

22 Ibid., 557.

23 Ibid., Lardicci's translation is identical.

24 Morison believed the Bay of Gibara to be the mouth of the Rio de Mares, yet the main river coming into that bay is the Rio Yabazón, which splits into a west and east fork, both of which run a distance of between 13 and 15 miles. They both end near interior mountain ridges of between 800 and 900 feet, more than the journal's notation of a small hill.

25 Fuson claimed that the error involved recording the arctangent instead of the tangent latitudinal reading. He noted that 21 degrees is the arctangent of 42, yet other sources cite 88 as the arctangent. A more likely answer centers on the assumption that Columbus did not want to report any latitude locations below 28 degrees for fear that Portuguese legal sovereignty may be in question. The 42-degree latitude, for Columbus, estimated from a version of the 1489 Martellus map, envisioned his location near the NW to SE coastline of the extreme Asian peninsula jutting out into the *Ocean Sea*—providing cartographic proof he was indeed closing in on the province of Cathay.

26 This matches closely to the current river geography of this area.

27 Dunn & Kelley, *The Diario*, 131.

28 Ibid., Dunn & Kelley suggest it was Juan Arias de Tavira, one of the few Portuguese crew members.

29 See logbook entries for November 23, December 17, and January 2. See also Wadsworth, "The Letters of Columbus Announcing his Discoveries," 93.

30 Anderson-Córdova, "Subsistence and Technology," 18–19. The author noted how some tribes planted manioc in large fields, consisting of raised dirt mounds. See also Rouse, *The Taíno*, 18.

31 Ibid. Interestingly, the author noted the possibility of irrigation in the more arid regions of western Hispaniola. 19.

32 Ibid., 18–19. The author cites noted geographer Carl Sauer, *The Early Spanish Main*, 52. For more on the slash-and-burn technique, see Guitar & Estevez, 1015. The authors described the *konukos* as fields consisting of two-foot-high planting mounds. They also noted that other crops besides manioc were planted on these mounds. Interestingly, once planted, maturing manioc required little cultivation in terms of constant attention, weeding, and watering.

33 Keegan noted that fish remained a food staple, with Taino culture believing fish were the first creatures created by the gods. Various techniques, including spearfishing and basket traps, provided efficient tools to capture individual fish, while elaborate reed corrals came into use for shallow areas where fish congregated. *Taíno Indian Myth*, 130. The author also believed that villagers roasted fish over fire, at times using a smoking technique to preserve the product.

34 Rouse, *The Taíno*, 4.

35 Guitar & Estevez, "Taínos," 1015.

36 Chios remained under Genoese control from 1346 until 1566, and a substantial defense undertaking from Genoa in which Columbus may have been involved became a common occurrence as the Ottoman threat lingered nearby. See Lardicci, *A Synoptic Edition*, DB 51, note 14, 635.

37 As he wrote this, Las Casas added aloe to the list of valuable products that might be harvested in Cuba. Later, in this day's entry, Las Casas wrote that an Indio told Columbus that mastic helped people suffering from stomach pain.

38 Using several mapping sources, including Google Earth, USGS National Advanced Viewer, and ArcGIS software, this author measured the distance along the *Yarigua River* from where it pours into the *Bay of Manati*, leading to a location northwest of the city of Las Tunas today.

39 Dunn & Kelley translated this to mean tents similar in shape to those the Moorish military used. *The Dario*, 137.

40 Kettell, *Personal Narrative*, 77.

41 Lardicci, *A Synoptic Edition*, 65, DB50, section 6.

42 Kettell translated how two Indio interpreters accompanied the two Spaniards; this appears to be an error, as Dunn & Kelley, Lardicci, and Thacher noted it was one person.

43 Not take, but "carry him" is used in most translations.

44 Dunn & Kelley, *Dario*, 139.

45 Jane, *The Journal of Christopher Columbus*, 56.

46 Kettell, *Personal Narrative*, 79.

47 Ibid.

48 Jane, *The Journal of Christopher Columbus*, 57.

49 Ibid., 67.

50 Thacher, *Personal Narrative*, 83.

51 Ibid., 83. The image here begs the reader to imagine a vast reservoir of possible profitable commodities and a meek population eager to trade for trifles, an economic opportunity one cannot ignore.

52 Aloewood, or agarwood as it is known today, is a wood resin, usually dark in color and fragrant to the smell, used historically and today as incense and some types of perfumes, often used during meditation.

53 Las Casas, *Relación del primer viage de D. Cristóbal Colón para el Descubrimiento de las Indias*, 62. See also Navarrete, *Viajes de Colón*, 64 for the original Spanish wording.

54 This would be akin to the African experiences when Portuguese explorers brought them to the Iberian Peninsula and returned them later. Many of those who returned to their homeland simply melded back into their societies and were never heard from again, as Columbus noted.

55 Thacher, *The Journal*, 263.

56 Ferdinand Columbus, in his retelling of the first voyage, writes that the Spaniards took twelve Indios "captive" with the sole purpose of having these people "give information about their country" to officials in Spain. This is from Benjamin Keen's translation of Ferdinand's *The Life of the Admiral Christopher Columbus*. See page 71. Additionally, Ferdinand writes that the husband of one of the women asked to join his wife, and Columbus agreed.

57 The Indigenous peoples Columbus acquired from this location may have all been released on Hispaniola after the wreck of the *Santa Maria*, as written accounts from Spain speak of only seven to ten natives appearing before the Spanish court; Columbus was adamant that no one, Spanish or native, died during the first voyage.

58 Lardicci, *A Synoptic Edition*, DB 51, section 11, 67.

59 Ibid., 223–24.

60 Columbus thought this was a separate island from Cuba. From his location that day, he could view the northern coast of eastern Cuba.

61 The small island is Cayo Juanillo, and the large one is Cayo Alto, the latter reaching over 150 feet in height.

62 Kettell assumes that Columbus, or Las Casas, is referring to the Martin Behaim 1491 map of the world and later a globe. However, there is no evidence that Columbus ever saw this map, yet it remains a possibility, and there existed many other pre-1492 mappae mundi that located numerous islands off the Asian coast, such as the 1489 map by Henricus Martellus.

63 Lardicci, *A Synoptic Edition*, LC 55, section 6, 227. At this location, Columbus had his men search for pearls, but the oysters brought up to inspect revealed no pearls inside; however, this shows how he continued to try to match a commercial product to a specific future trading post site. Columbus's plan for trading posts or *factorias* followed the already established pattern set out by the Portuguese along the west coast of Africa from "Madeira to Mina de Guinea." Caraci, Personal Communication, July 22, 2023.

64 Las Casas errored here in the direction, as most of the islands in the bay lie to the southeast. The only islands in the southwest section are Cayo Alto and Cayo Limon. Depth readings are current for the year 2021 and may have been different for Columbus.

65 There are numerous small rivers and creeks in the southeast section of *Tanamo Bay*, but Columbus probably is referring to Rio Cojetal.

66 Lardicci, *A Synoptic Edition*, LC 56, section 7, 534. The first line translation for the key verb *huyeron* in the Real Academia Española is: "walk away quickly, by being afraid or other reason."

67 A middle position on this episode may conclude that miscommunication, as in the case of the Guanahani Indios, ran both directions, with Columbus thinking he was inviting them to go with him and the Cuban natives thinking it was only an invitation to board the ship—a highly sought opportunity. However, Ferdinand Columbus, writing in his father's biography, referred to the taking of the Cubans; "[Columbus] ordered some of the people of that Island [Cuba] made captives; for he intended to take some persons from each island…so the Christians seized twelve persons, men, women, and children." Keen, *The Life of the Admiral*, 71.

68 The highest point on Great Inagua is East Hill at 132 feet (40 meters). At that height, the best distance an observer might see land from a ship would be 14 miles.

69 Lardicci also uses the term "get away" in the translation of Las Casas's *Historia*, LC 57, section 6, 228.

70 Kettell, *Personal Narrative*, 94. Florida was not discovered until 1513 by Ponce de Leon, so Las Casas is freely interjecting into the narrative at this point. Las Casas, continuing his comparison to Florida, wrote that Columbus would have been "cold" in the waters off Florida; this is incorrect.

71 Las Casas, in the *Diario*, wrote that it was one Indian, while Ferdinand Columbus uses the plural "Indians" when referring to the discussion Pinzón used as a motivating factor in sailing off on his own. See Lardicci, DB 58, sections 6–7, 72; and *Historie* in Lardicci, FH 58, sections 2–5, 156.

72 Thacher, *The Journal of the First Voyage*, 569. Columbus's comment noted in the logbook by Las Casas is repeated verbatim in the *Historia*, as translated by Lardicci, *Historia*, LC 58, sections 8–9, 229.

73 Wadsworth, *Columbus and His First Voyage*, 102. This statement came from Manuel de Valdovinos, a witness during the subsequent lawsuits filed by the Columbus family against the Spanish crown, in court on September 19, 1515.

74 Wadsworth, *Columbus and His First Voyage*, 107–08. This testimony was given on October 16, 1515. Vallejo was a citizen of the town of Moguer, near Palos.

75 Keen, *The Life of the Admiral*, 74. Ferdinand noted how Pinzón moved away slowly until, by nightfall, he had disappeared into the eastern horizon.

76 Bergreen, Columbus: The Four Voyages, 32–33.

77 Morison, *Admiral of the Ocean Sea*, 270.

78 Lardicci, *A Synoptic Edition*, Historia, LC 58, section 13, 229.

79 Eatough, *Selections on Peter Martyr, Decades* 1.1.8, 46. Martyr provides shocking details on how the Caribs "caused constant distress to their (Taíno) islands," including the castration of young boys to make them "fatter and more tender for the table."

80 Kettell, Personal Narrative, 100.

81 Ibid.

82 Ibid., 103–104.

83 Lardicci, *A Synoptic Edition*, Historia, LC 63, section 13, 231. Lardicci translates Las Casas's *Historia*, relating how two or three of the Spaniards had previously spent time with the Guanahani Lucayans, learning a few words while trying to carry on rudimentary conversations.

84 Markham, *The Journal of Christopher Columbus*, 90. Lardicci noted how Las Casas explained, using the first-person direct quote of Columbus, on this same day, November 27, that the explorer bitterly commented that he, nor any of the crew, could not understand the language of the Indigenous peoples encountered, and they could not understand him.

85 Lardicci, *A Synoptic Edition*, 78, DB 64, section 9.

86 Kettell, Personal Narrative, 111. Indigenous weavers constructed baskets from local palms and the agave plant for multiple daily uses including exchanges of trade items and tribute. Oviedo and Las Casas encountered baskets and wrote about them, with Oviedo writing that the Carib baskets appeared superior to those of the Taíno. See Berman & Hutcheson, "Impressions of a Lost Technology," 417–418.

87 Lardicci, *A Synoptic Edition*, Historia, LC 66, section 5, 235. Las Casa in *Historia* recounted that the canoe could hold 150 people; this, indeed, would be a very large canoe. Additionally, the Spanish friar believed the islanders constructed these large canoes from the many red cedar trees that proliferated the large islands of Cuba and Hispaniola, 235.

88 The cross today is kept at the parish church of Our Lady of the Assumption in Baracoa. In 2011, the National Cuban Commission of Monuments declared the Cross of Parra a national monument, commemorating Columbus's 1492 visit. Baracoa is celebrated as the oldest continuously occupied city in Cuba.

89 Markham, *The Journal of Christopher Columbus*, 94. The plural form may be the problem in this translation, as there is only one river flowing into the bay at Baracoa, measuring outward 1,000 yards, the farthest possible distance of a ship-carried Lombard canon. Also, Lardicci translates the gold in the river episode as "some sailors" discovering the stones, not a boy. Lardicci, A Synoptic Edition, *Historia*, LC 67, section 13, 235

90 Ibid.

91 Bergreen, *Columbus: The Four Voyages*, 39. There is a strong possibility that it was only one Indigenous interpreter, not several, that was "dispatched," as noted by Las Casas in *Historia*. See Lardicci, *A Synoptic Edition*, 235–36. The message here is clear: Columbus believed in the loyalty of his interpreters by this point in the voyage, even allowing them, ironically, to act as the newcomers, handing out trinkets to other Indigenous peoples.

92 Las Casas in the Diario has us believe that the Guanahani interpreter understood enough of the old man's speech to react in fear, yet in Las Casas's *Historia*, he claimed neither Columbus nor anyone else in their party understood anything the Taíno man said. See Lardicci, *A Synoptic Edition*, *Historia*, LC 68, section 16, 236.

93 Thacher, *The Journal of the First Voyage*, 579.

94 Columbus's eye for estimating the depth of bays and rivers from a distance was remarkable. *Ensenada de Mata* is approximately 1,000 feet wide but reaches 30 feet deep inland for about .5 miles.

95 The distance from Bahia de Mata to Rio Yumuri is a little over five miles, not three miles.

96 Markham, *The Journal of Christopher Columbus*, 97.

97 The peninsula of Mole Saint-Nicolas would have been the nearest point of contact coming from Punta del Maici to the SE. The highest point on Mole Saint-Nicolas is 287 feet high; someone standing in a crows-nest on the *Santa Maria* would just see the tip of this peak at 23 miles, so it is impossible that Columbus saw any portion of Haiti from Cuba.

98 Las Casas in *Historia* made two important points on human communication at this point in the voyage. First, Columbus still felt that he did not understand his Lucayan interpreters enough to have confidence in their attempts to learn about the geography and people of Hispaniola. Second, he clearly distinguished that Indigenous peoples on Cuba and Hispaniola could understand each other with few exceptions, while Lucayans had difficulty with the classic Taíno language, at least those encountered so far on the northern coasts of Cuba and Hispaniola. Lardicci, *A Synoptic Edition*, *Historia*, section 5, 237.

99 Dunn & Kelley, *The Diario*, 205.

100 Current depth readings range from a high of 1,200 feet as you enter the bay to a low of 32 feet in Baie Carenage (Carenage Bay).

101 Lardicci, *A Synoptic Edition*, DB 71, section 24, 83. The author, using data from Navionics software, found only one location where that depth runs close to the shore, and that is on the southern shore as a ship first enters the bay, the "creek," known today as Carenage Bay, which Columbus claimed ran 11 fathoms (66 feet) throughout. Today, the bay averages 40 feet in depth.

102 Kettell, *Personal Narrative*, 123.

103 Bergreen, *Columbus: The Four Voyages*, 41. Bergreen believed that Columbus communicated a sense of high purpose to the Indios, in such a manner that they now wanted to serve the newcomers from heaven.

104 Lardicci, in interpreting the Las Casas version of this incident in *Historia*, extends Lucayan thinking to the point where they no longer believe Columbus will return them to Guanahani; this indicates, or at least suggests, that Columbus had, either originally or sometime since the abduction, attempted to communicate to them

that they would be returned to their home island sometime in the future. See Lardicci, *A Synoptic Edition, Historia*, LC 71, section 30, 240.
105 Lardicci, *A Synoptic Edition, Historia*, DB 71, section 32, 83–84.
106 Markham, *The Journal of Christopher Columbus*, 102.
107 See Lardicci, 83–84, Fuson, 129, and Thacher, 583. The reader can well relate to the Lucayan and Taíno mistrust increasing at this time, as it was probably their first visit to the big island of Hispaniola (Haiti). As the days move along, followed by peaceful encounters, this mistrust disappears.
108 Much of the time, translators do not take a holistic approach to language translation, and this is particularly true of historical language development. The case in point centers around key verb forms that most readily convey an accurate overall description of the current situation. This is particularly true when alternative synonyms more precisely fit an ongoing course of behavior.

9

HISPANIOLA

December 7–25

> Because the inhabitants of all these islands live in great fear of the people [Caribs] of Caniba.
>
> —Christopher Columbus, *Diario*, December 11, 1492

Exploring Bohio

December 7, Friday

Columbus had noticed the day before a prominent cape standing some 20 miles to the northeast of this new island; he named this location Cabo de Cinquín (Pointe Jean-Rabel). This morning, he made for the cape, and a sailor accurately measured the depth from "a Lombard shot distance to shore" at 20 fathoms (120 feet). Just before arriving at the cape, Columbus noticed a gap in the transverse ridgeline of low mountains paralleling the coastline, cut through by a river (*Rivière de Jean Rabel*), covered in barley plants, again suggesting large Indio settlements. And, again, despite the positive signs, he did not investigate.

From the cape, he did see a large island 15 miles to the northeast, which he would designate as the Isla de Tortuga (Turtle Island).[1] Deciding to continue cruising along the northern coastline of *Bohio*, the two-ship fleet arrived at a "harbour, both broad, and of such a depth that no bottom was obtained at the entrance, and the water was fifteen fathoms deep a few feet from the shore; it extended about a mile into the land."[2] Today, this bay is known as *Baie de Moustiques* (*Mosquito Bay*).

At one in the afternoon, Columbus, noting the coming of rain, opted to remain at this bay, naming the place Puerto de la Concepcion. Landing, a large group of men, including Columbus, went ashore to explore, hoping, on the

DOI: 10.4324/9781003464143-14

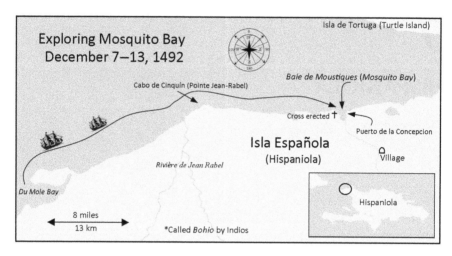

FIGURE 9.1 Exploring *Mosquito Bay*

way in, to catch fish. In one moment, a skatefish, similar to what the men had seen in Spanish waters, leaped into one of the two skiff boats. Ashore, the land looked much like they had seen in Cuba; a myrtle tree, which thrives in Spain, was seen. At one point, five local Indios fled when Columbus came upon them; nothing new here (Figure 9.1).

Moving eastward along the northern coast of Hispaniola, Columbus came upon another broad bay, offering more choices for a future trading post.

December 8, Saturday

Strong winds kept the Spanish fleet bottled up in *Mosquito Bay*. Once again, Las Casas translated incorrectly the intended distances of Columbus.[3] The former noted a distance of 36 miles between the bay and the island of Tortuga; the actual distance is just over 9 miles. Nothing else of note is recorded in the entry today; curiously, Columbus did not send a shore party to explore the immediate environs. The triangle-shaped valley that spreads inland for 2 miles is mostly flat and easy to traverse.

December 9, Sunday

The rain came down today, discouraging inland exploration. Columbus estimated that Bohio was, as the Indio guides had gestured, a very large island, roughly calculating the circumference at 200 leagues (600 miles). This was not a bad guess for only seeing a small portion of the coastline; the actual perimeter of Haiti and the Dominican Republic is just over 1,200 miles. He believed that due to the sheer size of *Bohio*, great villages must exist, yet he noted how, as with all other locations visited, the local people fled, making signal fires before leaving, as if to warn everyone in the vicinity. Columbus thought this fire-signal system helped these peoples prepare for Carib raiding events.

In estimating the width and length of *Mosquito Bay*, Columbus divulged his method of measurement for a league. He calculated 1,000 paces (the length of a step, or 3.9 feet today) as the width, accurately gauging this distance; this measurement is approximately three-quarters of one mile. Las Casas interpreted this as one-quarter of a league (3 miles to a league).[4]

Columbus, noting the beautiful landscape of the Riviere Moustiq (Moustiq River) and its' accompanying divergent topography, dramatic high hills sloping down to the sea, and a level gently rising plain framed by two freshwater rivers, declared this location to be "some of the most beautiful plains in the world, almost like the lands of Castile, only better."[5] Thrilled to see a European-like geography, Columbus bestowed the name *Isla Española* (Hispaniola) on the entire island of *Bohio*.

December 10, Monday

Strong northeast winds prevented the fleet from continuing to explore by ship in an easterly direction, so Columbus finally sent a group of men ashore to examine the immediate area. The six men were given a mission to probe inland "two or three leagues" with the hope of finding Indios and opening a friendly conversation; no mention was made of sending any of the Cuban or Guana-hani interpreters. Disappointingly, the group found no houses or people. They did see traces of human occupation, and interestingly, they came across a "wide road," indicating an advanced transportation need. They also saw many mastic trees but did not harvest any samples as it was not the right time for collecting, "as it does not coagulate."[6]

December 11, Tuesday

The wind remained contrary, coming in strong from the east and southeast. Columbus gazed out at nearby Tortuga Island and conjectured it to be quite large. The original scribe, or Las Casas, made another mistake in stating the distance from Mosquito Bay to Tortuga Island as 10 leagues; it is about 10 miles. Las Casas next provides advanced geography information that Columbus could not have known as he stood aboard the *Santa Maria* in Mosquito Bay, stating that the coast of Hispaniola "trends to the south."[7]

Columbus wanted to cruise between Hispaniola and Tortuga to learn more about the big island; several Cuban guides informed the admiral that sailing east would bring them to the island of *Babeque* (Inagua Island); this statement counters what they had told Columbus while in Cuba. Inagua is due north of Mosquito Bay, not to the east; the guides were confused, and by pointing to the east, they were in effect leading the Spaniards away from Cuba. Why would the guides do this if they were held against their will?

Communication improved to the point where Columbus was recording and believing his Indio guides that *Bohio* was larger than *Cibao* (Cuba). However, the guides insisted that *Bohio* was not an island but part of a large land area behind Hispaniola, running inland without end—a continent. Pressed for more information, the Cuban guides called this mainland region *Caritaba*. A portion of *Caritaba*, known as *Caniba*, was, as the story continued, peopled by warlike tribes (Caribs) that raided the islands, making anyone captured, prisoners, prisoners that never returned, eventually eaten by their captors. The above description by the interpreters, in referencing *Caritaba* lying behind (inland) from coastal *Bohio*, describes a physiographic transition of Hispaniola (Haiti/Dominican Republic) from lowland areas near the ocean to the interior mountainous region.

Still writing in the third person, Las Casas understood that Columbus was gaining confidence in his guides in that they were now giving him accurate geographical information without misunderstanding. Mentally reinvigorated, Columbus sent a shore party to explore. They discovered more mastic trees and aloe plants.[8] Fishing from the ships and the shore, crew members caught salmon, dories, skates, and shrimp. One can sense the upbeat change in journal writing; he was getting close—close to something important. Cuba might not be a mainland peninsula; possibly the land "behind *Cibao*" opened a gateway to the lands of the Great Khan.

December 12, Wednesday

Today began, as before, with dominating eastern winds, preventing a voyage in that direction. Instead, Columbus organized a shore party to erect a cross, a large cross at the entrance to Mosquito Bay. Finding a level elevated area with a commanding view of the bay's entrance, the crew proceeded to set the cross into the ground as "an indication in the words of the Admiral, 'that your Highnesses possess the country, and principally for a token of Jesus Christ our Lord, and the honor of Christianity.'"[9] The site was chosen for its dramatic rise, only 400 feet from the beach.

With the cross standing tall and sturdy, the three crew members walked down the south side of the bluff to seek out an Indio village. As they entered the low-lying plain, they heard voices. Following the sound they eventually encountered a large crowd of villagers. Immediately, the Indios ran inland. What takes place next may be controversial. Las Casas, slipping back into the third person, describes the three Spaniards as having been given orders by Columbus to "take some of the natives if possible."[10] The idea was that Columbus wanted to show the Indios "some good offices and dissipate their fear." This quote is from Kettell, but Markham quotes Columbus, not Las Casas, in the first person, writing, "I had ordered that some should be caught, that they might be treated well, and made to lose their fear." Fuson believes Columbus wrote the following in the first person: "They were carrying out my orders, to take some of the Indians in order to show them honor and cause them to lose their fear of us." Markham agrees with Fuson and adds, "…and see if they had profitable things, as it appeared it could not be otherwise on account of the beauty of the country."[11]

Interestingly, Lardicci translates Las Casas's *Historia* for this event using the third-person narrative, writing, "because the admiral had commanded them to capture some natives in order to show them honor and reassure them and to learn if there was anything of value in these lands." Lardicci also used the term "capture" for the base word *tomar* in her translation of the December 12 logbook entry. Dunn & Kelley point to the fact that Las Casas at this very moment, as if to make clear that Columbus intended to make captive some of the natives, translate the passage as, "because he says, 'I had ordered them to catch some [people] in order to treat them courteously and make them lose their fear, which would be something profitable since it seems that the land cannot be otherwise.'"[12]

The original Spanish text used by all the above translators uses the base word *tomar* in describing the action taken by Columbus; this can mean with or without one's permission. However, the intent here appears more focused as an act to temporarily bring the villagers to the ships to initiate friendly relations. It certainly can be argued that this is nothing less than a temporary kidnapping orchestrated by Columbus. Dunn & Kelley, and Lardicci emphasize that Las Casas reverts to the first-person quote, having Columbus narrate the orders he gave to take a few natives.[13]

A more likely explanation is that a frustrated Columbus was tired of not being able to contact the Indigenous tribes and believing that bringing them to the ships and showing friendly gestures, providing gifts and clothing, having his Indio interpreters converse with them, and sending them back to their village, would initiate a reciprocal, cordial response.

Eventually, the Spanish shore party found a local woman "who could go no further." Escorted back to the *Santa Maria*, Columbus described the female as a "very young and very beautiful girl." Apparently unafraid of the newcomers and the Spanish ship, the woman began exchanging information with the Cuban and Guanahani Indios "because they all had the same language."[14] Impressed, Columbus ordered clothing for the woman, and it was suggested she put them on without pressure. This was followed by the presentation of gifts to her, including the usual beads, hawks' bells, and brass rings. In short order, she was escorted back to the beach; in the skiff were a couple of sailors, and they became alarmed as the woman began gesturing, that is, pointing to the ship. At least three Cuban or Guanahani guides must have been in the skiff, also for she demanded, speaking, to go back to the *Santa Maria*.[15] Upon further questioning, the woman wanted to return to the big ship and remain with the Cuban women and the Spanish. This is an interesting turn of events and helps point to the possibility that other "captive" Indios with the Spanish may have desired to stay with the Spanish "gods."

However, she was eventually convinced to help the Spanish by showing them the path to her village. The translation speaks of them following a road, not a path, indicating usage by a large population. The entry concludes with Columbus recalling the small piece of gold attached to the girl's nose, a hopeful sign.

The Taíno of Hispaniola

December 13, Thursday

This entry begins by naming "the three men" but not referencing if they are the Spanish or Indios that went ashore with the girl. The number "three" had only been used in the previous entry to describe the Indio guides. Most probably, it referenced the Spanish men accompanying the girl, but it is interesting that Las Casas or Columbus did not mention the Indios returning. The men arrived back at the *Santa Maria* well past midnight without reaching the village. In debriefing with Columbus, it was learned that the girl went ahead to her village unescorted, telling the Spaniards that many villagers would come to the ships soon. Again, this would have been a perfect opportunity at night, for the three Indio guides to flee and seek safety in the girl's village— they did not.

Columbus, impatient, selected nine Spaniards and one Indio guide to go quickly to the village, now having an idea of its location. The Indio selected, probably a Cuban, went along acting as an interpreter, understandingly having a closer language-dialect connection to the Taíno of Hispaniola. After walking inland some 12 miles to the southeast, they came upon a large, open valley. The native village appeared quite impressive and spread out. Upon nearing the huts, the villagers picked up what they could and fled. Getting closer, the Spaniards counted over 1,000 huts, with Columbus later estimating the population at 3,000 inhabitants, the largest gathering of Indios to date. The Indio guide with them ran ahead, attempting to chase down those fleeing. As he ran, he shouted words to assure them that the Spanish meant them no harm; again, this was a perfect opportunity for the Cuban or Guanahani guide to run free from the Spanish—he did not.

When the villagers believed the newcomers were not from *Cariba* and they would not be captured and eaten, 2,000 of them slowly came back to the village. In awe at the Spanish dress, facial beards, and body armor, the villagers at first remained at a discreet distance, waiting to see what would happen next. Eventually, brave villagers walked up to the Spaniards and put their hands gently on the top of their guests' heads as a sign of respect and friendship. It took a while for the crowds of Indios to stop trembling, but soon food was brought from the huts and offered to the white men. Yams delighted the Spaniards, and Columbus went into a detailed description, saying yams,

> are roots like large radishes, which they sow and cultivate in all their lands, and is their staple food. They make bread of it and roast it. The yam has the smell of a chestnut, and anyone would think he was eating chestnuts.[16]

Bread and fish were also presented. The lone Cuban or Guanahani guide now conversed with the villagers, telling them that the leader of the "white gods," Columbus, would like parrots. Soon, parrots of varying colors and sizes were brought out of the huts and given as presents.

This event highlights the jubilation of celebrations that Taíno villagers enjoyed on a regular basis before European intervention. Called *arietos*, these dedicated events centered on first plantings, harvests, the arrival of important guests, such as Columbus, and honoring the solstices. On a social level, marriages and family births allowed families to celebrate these additions to local clans through simple, sometimes elaborate dances and songs. Victory in defeating competitive clans or successfully repulsing an outside invasion called for a village-wide celebration, recalling through verbal legends the exploits of ancestral heroes. Fasting before *arietos* by only taking a juice made from herbs and "cleansing their bodies in the river using the same herbs" ensured a proper state of appreciation and respect for the subsequent celebration.[17]

When the Spaniards indicated they needed to return to their ships, village leaders objected, wanting their guests to stay the night. As this exchange continued, a separate large group of villagers arrived. As the throng neared the Spaniards, it was clear to see the young girl who had returned the night before among the group. Sitting atop the shoulders of her husband and other natives, the girl, still clothed, appeared. Apparently, the husband and other family members wanted to thank the Spanish for honoring her yesterday on the *Santa Maria* and for the gifts given. There were no hard feelings about detaining her.

Returning to their ships, the nine Spaniards gave Columbus and Vincente Pinzón a glowing report of their experience. On the geography aspect, Columbus learned that the land "in Castille [sic] could not be compared with it." Las Casas wrote that Columbus now believed this new land to be the best environment yet seen in his travels: cultivated soil with water sources nearby, trees green and full of fruit, plants tall and covered with flowers, roads broad and well maintained, a climate like April in Spain, nightingales singing; it had to be the "most pleasant place in the world."[18] In fact, the land rang alive at night with birds, crickets, and frogs sounding the music of life, and there were fish— fish such as in Spain. Aloe, mastic, and cotton abounded. Everything was here, everything except gold. Ending his long description of Hispaniola on a pensive note, Columbus declared, "Gold was not found, and it is not wonderful that it should not have been found in so short a time." This message was clear; he was not to be blamed for not finding substantial amounts of gold; he needed more time.

The men also claimed to have seen villagers with skin "whiter than the others" seen up to that time. Two girls had skin "as white as any that could be seen in Spain."[19]

The entry ends with Columbus attempting to compute his latitude. The logbook reads a measurement of 34 degrees, which is incorrect; his current location was just short of 20 degrees north latitude.[20]

December 14, Friday

Finally, a land breeze sprung up that morning, and the two-ship fleet left Puerto de la Concepcion expecting to sail due east. However, the wind died, then later returned blowing toward the NNE. In this situation, Columbus set a course for the island of Tortuga. Arriving near the coast, he sighted a prominent point, naming it Punta Perna (Pointe de la Valee) after sailing 12 miles.[21] With no apparent bays or "rivers" to explore, Columbus turned east and followed the southern coastline of Tortuga, arriving at Punta Lansada (Pointe des Oiseaux) in a short time.[22] The waving coastline contained short beaches with quickly rising land formations, uninviting for an anchorage and beach landing. Taking note of the irregular topography, Columbus decided that the island contained "very high country" but was not mountainous, postulating that the area must be beautiful, well populated, and boast productive cultivated fields.[23]

Later that afternoon, the wind turned, coming from the east. Columbus, again frustrated, made the decision to turn back and return to Puerto de la Concepcion, despite his ardent desire to seek the island of *Babeque*. Maneuvering the ships in a changing wind, Columbus and Vincente Pinzón were only able to arrive at a point 6 miles east of the entrance to the Puerto de la Concepcion (Port-de-Paix) (Figure 9.2).

Known as Tortuga Island today, this large island proved to possess a difficult southern coastline for anchoring, few harbors, and rugged coastal outcroppings, making approaches often impossible. Columbus instead cruised eastward, eventually returning to the north coast of Hispaniola.

December 15, Saturday

The tiny fleet attempted another run at Tortuga but had to "stand off" when a strong easterly wind defeated any progress along the coast. They turned back to Hispaniola, steering toward a river they had seen from a distance the day

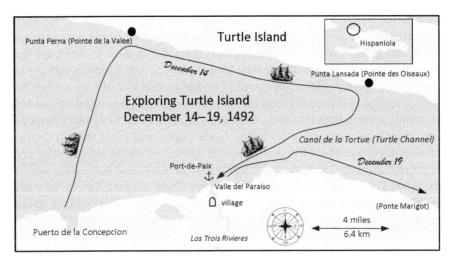

FIGURE 9.2   Turtle Island

before. Arriving and anchoring a short distance from the river (Los Trois Rivieres), Columbus and some men rowed to find the opening, and when they did, the admiral was disappointed, finding the entrance to have only one fathom (6 feet) of depth and 800 feet wide. Hoping to row upstream and visit a village his men had spotted days before, the small crew found it difficult to row against a strong current. Eventually using a rope tied to the front of the skiff, the men pulled the boat upstream "two lombarda-shots" (approximately 1,200 yards).[24] At this point, they saw a valley area that Columbus thought was another beautiful geographic place; this is where the river turns and flows east for a short distance. Turning back, the Spaniards found several Indios standing near the mouth of the river; immediately, the natives fled.

Back on board the *Santa Maria*, Columbus took pen to paper and recounted this trip, naming the river *Guadalquivir* since its width reminded him of that river in Spain.[25] The valley he visited briefly received the promising title Valle del Paraiso (Paradise Valley); this area extends inland between foothills to the east and west of the river, today, the town of Paulin, Haiti, is near the center of this valley. Morison, in writing his Pulitzer prize-winning biography of Columbus, visited this valley, stating he could verify the area was lined with "wooded mountains and banana groves; it is one of the loveliest of the Antilles."[26]

I Am No God

December 16, Sunday

Once again attempting to explore Tortuga, Columbus hoisted anchors at midnight but sailed for 3 hours before the wind shifted from the east; they "stood close to the wind," now halfway between Tortuga and Hispaniola. The wind grew stronger. Out of nowhere, lookouts spotted a lone canoe containing a single occupant. Immediately, Columbus ordered the pilot to intercept the Indio and offer help, wondering how long the canoe might remain upright in such a strong wind and rising swells. The Indio man did not try to flee; he eagerly agreed to come on board the *Santa Maria*, and several sailors hoisted his small canoe to the main deck. According to the record, Columbus "feasted him, presenting him with glass beads, hawk's bells, and brass rings."[27] A discussion may have ensued with the rescued Indio describing his plight to one or more Cuban and Guanahani interpreters; he may have been surprised to see other Taíno natives aboard the strangers' ships, making him more comfortable. He gave directions to a village, likely his home, some distance to the south.

Arriving at the location indicated, the Indio went ashore, unescorted, providing a positive story of how the Spanish explorers intervened to help him. Already informed of the Spanish presence at Mosquito Bay and the Spanish shore party that had moved in their direction days earlier, the caciques of the village agreed to visit the newcomers. Over 500 villagers spread out on the beach, most likely at what is today Port-de-Paux, Haiti, gazing outward toward the *Santa Maria* and *Niña*, both ships standing close to shore, only 400 feet away.[28]

After a brief hesitation, small groups of Haitian Indios came to the ships; it is not clear from the original text if they canoed or swam, but since the distance was short, they may have swum.[29] Once on the ships, sailors discovered the natives carried no items to trade except for tiny pieces of gold stuck in their noses and ears. Nonetheless, Columbus ordered that they all be well-treated.

At this point, Las Casas shifts once again to the first-person, allowing Columbus to show his hope in how Queen Isabella and King Ferdinand will want to interact with these people. Las Casas does this intentionally to preview colonial intent.

> For they are the best people in the world, and the gentlest; and above all I entertain the hope in our Lord that your Highnesses will make them all Christians, and that they will be all your subjects, for I hold them [regard them as yours].[30]

This quote has sparked critics to show Columbus's paternalistic inclination toward the Indigenous peoples on the first voyage. The key verb phrase in this quote is "I hold them." Thacher and Jane use the phrase, "I regard them as yours." Kettell reads it as an already-done deal, stating, "and that they may become your subjects, in which light, indeed I already regard them." Fuson wrote, "They will all belong to you, for I regard them as yours now." The Las Casas Spanish text reads, "tengo mucha esp[er]anca en nro se nor q[ue] vras altezas los hara todos expianos y sera todos suyos q[ue] por suyos los tengo." Dunn & Kelley, as well as Lardicci, interpret this as "I have much hope in Our Lord that Your Highnesses will make all of them Christians and that they will be your subjects, for I consider them yours [already]."[31]

There is no doubt that Columbus wanted the Indigenous peoples to eventually become subjects, as he was, of the Spanish monarchs, but two key areas need further investigation. The first is the phrase "will make all of them Christians." This phrase infers a forced conversion. One thought is that Columbus repeatedly wrote that he believed the Indios possessed no entrenched religion; along these lines, he may have still believed conversion would be much easier than the Jewish situation, with the added belief that the Taíno considered the Spanish to be "gods" themselves and, in Columbus's mind, relatively easy to bring into the Church.

Looking out from the *Santa Maria*, Columbus noticed Indios surrounding one person, giving him more room and showing respect. He immediately thought this must be the village cacique, and to honor the chief, the explorer sent a group of men and an interpreter to give a present, which was well received. On shore, the Cuban or Guanahani interpreter talked with the cacique, who appeared to be young—no more than 21 years old. Standing next to the cacique, a village elder listened intently and helped keep the conversation going by offering a few words of advice. Learning that the Spaniards were "men from heaven" searching for gold and "wished to go to the Isla de *Babeque*." The cacique nodded approval, pointing to show the direction they needed to sail to reach their goal. Additionally, he waved his arms, motioning and saying that whatever the "men from heaven" needed, his people would supply.[32]

In penning his entry, Columbus wanted to inform the Spanish monarchs of how white the inhabitants were in this village and of the good soil, soil that, according to Columbus, rose to the top of the mountains, allowing plowing with oxen, transforming the landscape "into arable lands and fields." He noted the cultivation of *ajes* (a type of potato) in large fields, sporting carrot-shaped roots, serving it as bread, "and they grate them and knead them and make bread of them." Columbus looked impressed when he came ashore to witness the Indios planting small *ajes* branches; the fields appeared well manicured, witnessing constant care and upkeep.

In the afternoon, the village cacique came to the *Santa Maria*. Columbus tried to dispel the myth that he was a god, explaining that he was a servant of the king and queen of Spain. The cacique did not understand this. Looking at the Cuban and Guanahani Taíno for help, the interpreters only repeated that the Spanish came from heaven. A meal was served with the cacique, his entourage, the Taíno interpreters, and Columbus all participating. The meal went well; afterward, the cacique returned to his village.

Reviewing the day's events, Columbus wrote another paternalistic suggestion for the Spanish monarchs that prophetically provided a future scenario that would come through, although not in Columbus's time. Las Casas became so upset at this next section that he, as usual, decided to translate a direct quote for his *Historia* from whatever copy he possessed. It read,

> They have no weapons, and they are all naked and have no aptitude for arms, and they are very cowardly, for a thousand of them will not come out to meet three of ours; and so they are for being given commands and for being made to till, to plant, and to do everything else that may be necessary; and you may build towns and teach them to go around clothed and adopt our customs.[33]

To assure his reading audience that he did not say these words, Las Casas wrote, "These are the admiral's exact words." Then he unloads on Columbus with a powerful description that reveals his prejudice toward Spanish policy in New Spain, years after the explorer's death.

> It should be noted there that the natural, simple, benevolent gentleness and humble condition of the Indians and their lack of weapons, together with their nakedness, gave the Spaniards the audacity to think of them [the Indians] as worth little and to subject them to such extremely harsh labors as those to which they did subject them. And, certainly, on this point the admiral spoke at greater length than he should have, and from that with he conceived here and produced with his own mouth must the evil treatment that he [Columbus] later inflicted upon them have derived its origin.[34]

Las Casas's statement has given rise to much misinterpretation concerning Columbus's views and deserves unpacking and analysis. However, any lengthy discussion here would break the chronological presentation of the journal reports. Refer to Appendix IV for a brief comparative explanation regarding Las Casas's comments and Columbus's initial intentions.

December 17, Monday

Still waiting for a favorable wind to exit the Port-de-Paux area, Columbus watched as local Indios visited both ships in the hope of trading and seeing the newcomers. He stood in awe as his native traders brought gifts—food from their cultivated fields, exotic spices from the interior, and gold—but such small amounts of gold. One group brought a set of arrows that Columbus understood to belong to the "people of Caniba" or the "Canibales." Looking them over, crew members told Columbus the arrows appeared deadly, long, and sharpened for maximum penetration; the sailors also reported a couple of Indios showing "two men who had lost some pieces of flesh from their bodies."

The Guanahani and/or Cuban Indios relayed information to the effect that cannibals had "eaten from the body."[35]

To return trading visits, Columbus sent men to the village with instructions to trade for gold, if available. It should be noted here and elsewhere that on the first voyage, Columbus always traded for gold, not stealing it. Nothing much appeared, except for a few pieces of thin specimens beaten into the shape of a leaf. Here Las Casas, once again, gets confused in his translation, saying that Columbus, who did not go ashore with the group of Spanish traders, saw an Indio in the village; he looked to be important, a sort of head cacique, or governor of the region. Las Casas uses the term *cacique* as a native term used in context to describe the person of highest power, garnering the most respect from fellow villagers. The cacique held a large, thin piece of gold leaf, the largest yet seen; it immediately drew the attention of the Spanish traders. Desiring to trade for the precious metal, the Spaniards held out beads and bells. The cacique retired forthwith and returned with only pieces of the gold leaf, trading each separately while eyeing the Spaniards anxiously for what would be offered. When the last piece was traded, the cacique gestured that more would be provided the next day—an excellent trading strategy when dealing with gold-hungry explorers.

Later, in the afternoon, more interaction occurred on the beach, with a small number of Spaniards exchanging items with a native retinue that included the cacique and many of the villagers. The villagers sat on the sand as one group, a sign of peace, as did the cacique. On the horizon, a canoe appeared, approached the surf, and came ashore, nearly in front of the gathered villagers. Indios piled out of the canoe and moved toward the cacique and the Spaniards. The cacique stood up and immediately gestured angrily for the uninvited guests to leave, sending a physical message by picking up nearby stones and flinging them at the other Indios.[36] Getting the message, the visiting group of Indios turned and began moving toward their canoe. At this moment, the cacique picked up another stone and placed it in the hand of one of the Spaniards, the master-of-arms (Alguacil), gesturing to the explorer to throw the stone toward the Indios; Alguacil refused, whereupon the cacique gestured that he "favored" Columbus and that there was much gold on Tortuga, more than on Isla Hispañola.[37]

Columbus did not participate in this event but later surmised that *Baneque* (*Babeque*) Island must be the source of gold, where the gold mines existed. The cacique's performance this day influenced Columbus, who now believed the "fountain head" of the gold region resided nearby. He was convinced that gold mined in *Baneque* made its way to the other islands, including Isla Hispañola (Hispaniola), Cuba, and, to some extent, the smaller islands. Through his interpreters, he learned that *Baneque* lies only a short distance, four days' journey, somewhere near 40 leagues; Columbus quickly calculated he could easily cover that distance in one day, if only the wind would change.

Columbus and a Cacique Break Bread on the *Santa Maria*

December 18, Tuesday

The cacique had promised more gold today, and Columbus waited; no one and nothing appeared. Instead, he ordered a religious celebration, for it was to be a day honoring the Annunciation of the Blessed Virgin; a full-flag regalia event ensued with dressing out of flags, banners, and Lombard shots out to the ocean. On hearing the shots, the cacique appeared on the beach with a retinue of Indios, about 200 in number. The cacique motioned to the Spaniards on the beach that he desired to visit Columbus on his ship. The men, knowing that Columbus would want to meet and greet the Indio leader, helped him into one of the skiffs and rowed him to the *Santa Maria*; other Indio advisors and observers followed in canoes.

The following event reveals an interesting side to both Columbus and the cacique. After climbing the rope ladder and jumping onto the deck, the cacique scanned for Columbus, who knew nothing of the approaching villagers. A crew member escorted the cacique to Columbus's small cabin, and upon entering, the Indio chief found the explorer eating a meal. The cacique did not hesitate; he moved quickly to the tiny table where Columbus sat, and he himself sat down in an open chair. Quite taken back by this unexpected move of the cacique, Columbus gestured toward the remaining food items, offering his hospitality. At that moment, the cacique motioned to his attendants to leave the cabin, except for two elders; doubtless, the cacique wanted to be alone with Columbus. This act done, the cacique sampled Columbus's lunch, giving samples of food and drink to his two elders. As they ate, neither spoke much, when the cacique did speak, Columbus believed he could understand a little of the talk, calling the cacique's words "judicious and intelligent."[38]

Meanwhile, the cacique's attendants sat on deck, no doubt curious as to what was happening inside the cabin; no doubt, Columbus's crew felt the same.

In describing this scene, Las Casas switches to the first-person narrative.

> All this was done with great state, and very few words, which as near as I could understand what he said, were uttered in a very sensible manner, his two attendants watching his countenance, conversing with him, and answering him with the greatest degree of veneration. The meal finished, an attendant brought me a girdle shaped like those in Castile, but of different workmanship, this he presented to me and I accepted, as well as two pieces of gold, beaten very thin, of which metal I am inclined to think they possess very little…I saw that he was pleased with the hanging [blanket] over my bed, and made him a present of it, with some fine amber beads which I wore upon my neck, and some red shoes and a flask of orange-flavored water; with these gifts he was wonderfully delighted, and both he and his counsellors appeared to feel much regret that we could not understand one another's' language.[39]

Columbus's imagination now got the best of him as he watched the cacique gesture with his arms as if to say that the villagers stood ready to give the visitors whatever they needed. Why Columbus did not have one or two Cuban or Guanahani interpreters there is unknown, but it did make him admire the cacique, his mannerisms, and his stately conduct; these were no savage, pre-civilized peoples. Wanting to show his respect for the caciques unannounced visit, Columbus displayed a new Castilian gold coin, containing the images of King Ferdinand and Queen Isabella, to the cacique. Trying to gesture that he was a servant of these monarchs, Columbus pointed to himself and the flags of Spain that stood in the corner of the cabin, especially pointing to the cross emblem. The cacique appeared impressed.

This incredible meeting ended with the cacique lowering himself into a waiting canoe while Columbus's crew fired a Lombard salute. Later, the cacique's brother came to the ship and received gifts; it was during this exchange, most likely with a Cuban or Guanahani interpreter, that Columbus learned the name for the Indio king: It was *cacique*. Another older villager also visited the *Santa Maria*, an "important retainer of the king."[40] Through the interpreters, Columbus learned of nearby islands where gold might be found; one island was made of gold! Pointing in an easterly direction, Columbus is now determined to see these lands. Momentarily, Columbus thought for a moment to take the man with him to guide the ships to the gold; he did not, although he wished he knew the language well enough to ask him to come. The elder seemed pleased with his visit, and his gifts, and Columbus imagined the old man agreeing to accompany the Spaniards, joining the other Indios already remaining with the fleet.

This is another interesting comment on how Columbus "kidnapped" Indios. Why would he bother thinking about asking the older Indio? According to Las Casas, "nevertheless, as he considered these people to belong to the sovereigns of Castile, he was unwilling to offend them."[41] So, if that is true, then why would he be willing to offend the Indios on Cuba and Guanahani that he "kidnapped?" The reasoning here is flawed, but the translation is correct: Columbus did not want to "offend" any of the tribes on this initial visit to initiate trading agreements; cordial relations are always the foundation of good business practice, and this was a business adventure. However, Las Casas translates a section that states, "He [Columbus] remarks that if this person had not been one of the principal men of the king [cacique] he should have taken and carried him along with him." This quote from Kettell is counter to Lardicci, who phrases it this way:

And he would have liked to take the old man with him, if he had not been such an important person to the king... although he believed that if he had known the language in which to ask him, the old man would have agreed to go with him.[42]

Notice the key connector from Kettell that indicates "he should have taken," meaning that Columbus would definitely "kidnap" the Indio. Lardicci's "would have liked to take," but is balanced with asking the Indio; in other words, Columbus first wanted to ask the Indio to go. Dunn & Kelley use an interesting phrase: "If he knew the language, he would beseech him to go." Beseech is a strong word, meaning to implore, plead, and appeal. A person going to this extent is clearly trying not to offend someone, yet they need their help immediately. The original Spanish word written in his abridgment of Columbus's journal is *lo ragar* from which the base word *rogāre* is derived, meaning to ask somebody strongly or to beg. Therefore, Columbus wanted to primarily ask the old man to go with him.

To fully understand Las Casas's intervention here, let us look at the original Spanish text. In Dunn & Kelley's transcription and translation, the critical section is stated this way. "que lo [llevara] detuviera y llevara consigo; o si supiera la legua que se lo rogara." Las Casas scratched out the first use of the word "llevara" and wrote "detuviera" which means *to arrest or stop someone. Llevara* means to carry or take with you and does not have a negative connotation. This is a clear attempt by Las Casas to insert a pre-disposition by Columbus to simply kidnap anyone, and the only reason he did not do it in this case is that he wanted to not offend the cacique.

December 19, Wednesday

Desiring to see more of Hispaniola, Columbus left the Port-de-Paix area and steered east, hoping to clear the channel between Tortuga and the big island. Fighting the wind and current all day, the fleet turned south, looking for an anchorage. Scouts spotted four jutting points of land, a bay with a large river[43] and another bay, equally large. At this point, Las Casas interjected that Columbus, talking about the high mountains, capes, and excellent harbors, could not see all that geography at night. Nearing the land, Columbus saw what appeared to be an island on the west side of the large bay. He named it Cabo Alto y Bajo; this is actually the point that thrusts outward from the land, Pointe Marigot. Las Casas writes about a tall mountain, Monte Caribata (Mont Haut du Cap), stretching high into the sky, some 60 miles away, using references to roads that did not yet exist, at least not for Europeans.

December 20, Thursday

With the sunrise, the fleet slowly entered the bay at Cabo de Caribata (Baie de L'Acul), at 1.33 miles wide. Columbus claimed that the water feature could hold all the ships in Christendom, a claim he had already made more than once with previous bays. The journal here claims the depth at the entrance is 7 fathoms, over 40 feet; the depth today is over 60 feet at the entrance.[44]

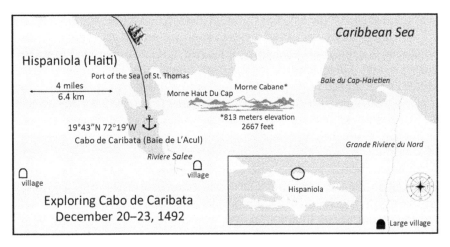

FIGURE 9.3   Exploring Cabo de Caribata

Looking southeast from the *Santa Maria*, Columbus saw a narrow valley expanding in width, from 1.5 miles wide to over 10 miles as one moves inland 5 miles; nearby mountains framed the valley in a picturesque scene. The mountains were high, averaging over 2,500 feet and running in a southeasterly direction. Columbus believed these to be the highest he had yet seen, including those on the Canary Islands.[45] Later, the crew spotted, only a league to the east, another bay, and then another bay about an additional league to the east; Columbus was overwhelmed at the possibilities for future use. As usual, smoke from inland fires indicated that the local Indios had now spotted the strange ships; a warning was out (Figure 9.3).

Another day and another "perfect" harbor, the Bay of L'Acul. The unique feature here that impressed Columbus was the bay's dramatic physical setting, framed by the tallest mountains he had yet witnessed on the islands.

December 21, Friday

Warning or not, Columbus wanted to explore this area. In praising the utility of the current place, a big, beautiful bay[46] at Cabo de Caribata, Las Casas moved to a first-person quote from Columbus.

> I have traversed the sea for 23 years, without leaving it for any time worth counting, and I saw all in the east and the west, going on the route of the north, which is England, and I have been to Guinea, but in all those parts there will not be found perfection of harbours…always found…better than another, that I with good care, saw written; and I again affirm it was well written, that this one is better than all others, and will hold all the ships of the world, secured with the oldest cables.[47]

In noting the size of the bay, Las Casas, or the original scribe, wrote 5 leagues; it is actually 5 miles. Cultivated fields spread out toward the southeast, and Columbus imagined this area to be inhabited.[48] He sent two men ashore to climb a nearby hill and search for signs of a big village. That evening, Indios paddled out, climbed the rope ladder, and gestured that they wanted to barter at night. Columbus welcomed them and bartered his usual items. Meanwhile, the two Spanish scouts returned, stating they had seen a large village. Hopeful for contact, Columbus ordered men to ready both skiff boats to go to the village location; joining them was the admiral. Nearing land, more Indios appeared on the beach, looking nervous. Columbus stopped the boats, turned to his Cuban and/or Guanahani interpreters (they were on this trip), and asked them to tell the local people to not be afraid. The interpreters did their job well, and soon hundreds of Indios appeared, women and children included. Water and cassava bread were offered to the Spaniards.

Las Casas now, once again, reverted to the first-person narrative of Columbus as he wrote about how generous and helpful the natives behaved. Columbus made a note of the "pretty women," usually hidden whenever the Spanish encountered new tribes, but not here. In fact, young women came forward and brought the water and bread noted above, along with "five or six kinds of fruits." Columbus gave an immediate order for his men not to touch or interfere with any of the Indios, especially the young women. He also made it clear: "No one should take anything from them against their will."[49]

Remaining at the beach, Columbus was surrounded by Indios, making it difficult to move inland. So, he commanded six men to go to the nearby village "to see what it was [like]." When the men reported back, they could not believe the number of items given to them—the villagers by now believed the Spaniards were from heaven. An important interjection occurs here in the reading where Las Casas wrote, "The Indians whom the Admiral had brought from the other islands also believed this, although what they *ought* to believe in respect to this matter had already been explained to them."[50]

The focus on what one *ought* to believe is critical. Columbus had explained to the Cuban and Guanahani peoples he met that he was not a god, nor were any of his men, or, for that matter, Ferdinand and Isabella. Even though Columbus explained his mortality, the Indios—all of them, in Columbus's mind, still believed them to be supernatural. From their perspective, this may explain why the kidnapped Indios remaining on the ships no longer attempted to escape; partly afraid and in awe, they now wanted to serve as a spokesperson for the Spanish gods, helping them in their adventures, with the promise they would be returned to their homelands, honored for being selected, and having gone to the Spaniards' heaven (Spain).[51]

The above is, of course, Columbus's, or more precisely, Las Casas's, interpretation, Las Casas is paraphrasing Columbus's words. This section of the logbook entry is full of remarks concerning how the Indios "honored" the

Europeans: "The Indians honored them as much as they could and knew how to, and they gave them all they had since no doubt remained in them; they believed that the Admiral and all his people had come from the heavens."[52]

From the perspective of the Taíno, the overwhelming display of friendship and offerings may well have been simply, just that, a tradition to welcome new-comers. Karen Anderson-Córdova summarizes her study of Indian responses to contact by stating that the strategies for dealing with the Spanish consisted of "flight, exchange of food and other items, and accommodation."[53] The author cites numerous examples from Columbus's voyages, particularly on December 6 and 12, noting that the Indios, through one of Columbus's native interpreters, persuaded the villagers of Spanish good intentions; the large number of villag-ers then presented food and parrots. She interprets the worldly native offerings as an understanding that the Indios regarded the newcomers as "powerful indi-viduals (or gods)," moving them to recognize that status by welcoming them, once comfortable with no danger. The idea is also presented that village caciques needed to offer more valuable goods as gifts, whereas lower-status villagers offered more "mundane gifts," including cassava bread and water.[54]

At this point, messengers from a different village appeared in canoes, led by guides. They made gestures to come first to their village before going inland to the other village. Columbus, wanting to keep both chiefs happy, agreed to go with the messengers. Yet, the people on the beach objected, wanting him to stay there; word had spread about the newcomers, and everyone wanted to see and interact with them. Columbus was able to go with the messengers of the second chief, meeting him a short distance away. Greeting the Spaniards, the cacique raised his arms to quiet his people and ordered everyone to sit. Food was already spread out on the ground and there were "a great many things to eat." Samples of the food were eaten there, while much of it was carried, by order of the cacique, to the Spanish ships. Soon, the natives brought parrots and "more eatables." Prepared to respond, Columbus gave the chief the usual-colored glass beads, bells, and brass rings.

Las Casas next interprets Columbus's future desires for a Spanish and Indio relationship. He wrote,

The Admiral gave them glass beads and brass rings and hawks' bells, not because they asked for anything but because it appeared to him that it was right, and above all [says the Admiral] because he already considers them as Christians and as belonging to the Sovereigns of Castile more than the peo-ple of Castile; and he says that nothing else is lacking save to know the language and to give them orders because all that they are ordered to do, they will do without any contradiction.[55]

Columbus gave his gifts in friendship and the hope of continued good rela-tions. Once again, however, we see Las Casas stating that Columbus considers the Indios as de facto subjects of Spain, without regard to their full understanding or engaged opinion on the matter. In this sense, Columbus unilaterally ignored their right to freedom of choice, with his own conscious belief that becoming Spanish vassals would be something eagerly sought.

When Columbus attempted to leave the feast, a great uproar commenced with people asking them to stay, and when the Spaniards returned to their skiff boats, Indios in canoes accompanied them to the ships. We also see Indios, intent on being near the Spaniards, swimming upward to 2–3 miles out from shore, attesting to their physical stamina. As Columbus climbed aboard the *Santa Maria*, his remaining crew told him another chief or cacique had come to honor the "gods." He dispatched men to this village, so the shore party must have included one or more Cuban or Guanahani interpreters, and they had no trouble finding the village. During the ensuing meeting, large pieces of gold were given as well as food. Upon returning, a considerable number of villagers accompanied the Spaniards, and when reaching a wide river, the local Indios swam it easily. However, the Spaniards hesitated and then began searching for a place they could cross easily, eventually fording the river successfully.

Writing from the *Santa Maria* later that day, Columbus found it difficult to describe the beautiful environment. He had done this so many times already with other locations; he wanted this place to be seen as superior to everything else encountered. He imagined tall mountains, a spacious harbor, an arable plain stretching far into the interior, clear rivers, and more. However, he was most impressed with the extent of the harbor, which was clearly larger and more protective from storms than anything yet observed. It being Saint Thomas's Day, Columbus named the harbor The Port of the Sea of St. Thomas, calling the location a *sea* due to its large dimensions.

December 22, Saturday

The fleet headed out early this day in search of those islands where gold abounded, as told by so many Indios during the last few days. However, the winds simply stopped forward progress, and the fleet returned to the bay. A little later, a large canoe came alongside the *Santa Maria*, to where the boat's skiff sat. Sitting closest to the visiting Indios was one of the ships' boys. In a surprise move, one of the Indios who appeared to be in charge handed a belt with a face mask embossed upon it to the boy—the mask was made of thinly beaten gold. No doubt, the boy's eyes widened, and the present was quickly moved up onto the ship for Columbus to see. Next, the Indio guests climbed the rope ladders to the deck of the *Santa Maria*.

The Cuban and Guanahani interpreters listened carefully to the older Indio who stated he was a representative of a cacique from a distant territory, communicating that his cacique wanted to see the ships and all the newcomers. This exchange of information took some time as the Cuban and Guanahani interpreters had difficulty understanding the language.[56] However, with gestures and more back-and-forth discussion, Columbus believed it was an open invitation to visit, and he was determined to do so despite the next day being Sunday, a day Columbus did not usually leave the ship. In Fuson's translation, Columbus described his intense desire to please these Indios, believing friendship would eventually lead to voluntary conversion, religiously and possibly politically. Lardicci emphasized the developing friendship by translating a reference to the Indios as "thanks to the willingness they show."[57] However, the very next phrase in the translation continues with more ominous predictions, stating, "because the Admiral already considers the Indians as their subjects."[58]

December 23, Sunday

The lack of wind once again prevented sailing from his location. Instead, he sent some of his men with the three Indio messengers who were still waiting for Columbus to come with them to their distant village. Meanwhile, Columbus made a crucial decision, a decision that speaks volumes as to whether or not his Cuban and Guanahani interpreters could be trusted to return from a mission. He asked two of them to go on their own to the nearby village they had already visited earlier. This was another clear opportunity for the two Indigenous people to disappear and eventually make their way back to their home island. Instead, the guides and interpreters went to the village, talked with the cacique, and asked him to come and speak with Columbus. They all returned to the *Santa Maria*, where the chief "brought the news that there was a great quantity of gold in that island [of Española] and that people from other parts come to buy it."[59]

An intricate conversation ensued that included intense interpretation from the Cuban and Guanahani interpreters, discussing where the gold mines were located and how the precious metal was collected. Columbus listened intently as his interpreters tried to explain it to him, but he had not yet gained enough language vocabulary to understand the full extent of the conversation. However, this meeting confirmed in his mind that copious quantities of gold existed somewhere in the interior, mountainous regions of the large island. From this point on, Columbus dismissed the idea that the gold came from other islands; Hispaniola was the place where he would complete his mission to procure gold. In a moment of prayer, he asked for divine, helpful, inspired, guidance, a sign that would tell him what to do next.

The day was full of Indio visits; over 1,000 people either stood on the beach or shouted praises, canoed around the *Santa Maria* and the *Niña*, and over 500 Indios daringly boarded the ships unannounced; everyone brought food or some small gift. Those in the canoes stood and shouted, "Take it! Take it!" Among the visitors were five more caciques or minor chiefs from nearby villages; obviously, the word was out throughout the countryside, and everyone wanted to participate. Their wives and children accompanied the chiefs, now unafraid of the newcomers. This was another day of camaraderie and celebration, with Columbus telling his crew to give out more trinkets; it is a wonder that he still had any left.

During the day, Columbus found time to pray. "May our Lord favour me by his clemency, that I may find this gold, I mean the mine of gold, which I hold to be here, many [Indios] saying that they know it." Gold would be the most impressive resource to bring back to the Spanish monarchs suffering from a cash shortage due to the recently concluded war against their Muslim enemies, the *Reconquista*. Columbus knew this all too well.[60]

When Columbus earlier that day sent six men to the visitors' village to see if the cacique had more gold than he claimed from their meeting on the *Santa Maria* the day before, Columbus spoke directly to the fleet secretary, Rodrigo de Escobedo, instructing him to go with the men and make sure they "did nothing wrong to the Indians... and the Spaniards were so immeasurably greedy that they were not satisfied with receiving the most valuable of what the inhabitants possessed."[61] Lardicci translates this passage as "The Indians were so generous and the Spaniards so greedy and immoderate, it is not enough that the Indians were giving them everything... but rather they wanted to get and take everything without giving the natives anything."[62]

Escobedo arrived at the village to a fine welcome, including dinner at the cacique's home, and was presented with large amounts of cotton balls, three geese, and some bits of gold. While this was happening, over 100 canoes visited the *Santa Maria* and the *Niña*, with Indios clamoring and shouting, hoping to trade food and receive a gift from the "gods." In an interesting side note, Las Casas wrote that the Cuban and Guanahani Indios were on deck and conversed with both the visiting Indios and the Spaniards; in one exchange, the interpreters described a spice that was put into a cup of water and served as a traditional drink.

Meanwhile, Escobedo and his group returned and reported to Columbus, speaking excitedly about a wide, well-maintained road running inland. Arriving at the village, his men found more huts than any previous location, set out in wide streets. The village sat astride the Grande Riviere du Nord, located some 5 miles from Puerto Guarico (Cap-Haitien) or 9 miles southeast of Punta Santa (Pointe Picolet).

Listening intently to his men, Columbus learned that the village contained over 2,000 inhabitants, with houses clean-swept and a large undeveloped area, like a plaza, in the middle. The cacique came out and welcomed the men; it is not certain any Cuban or Guanahani interpreters were with them, but Las Casas wrote, "This king did great honor to the people of the ship." Each household brought a gift, usually a food item or a drink. The cacique handed out cotton cloths, small and rectangular, parrots for Columbus, and some pieces of gold. The Spanish men gave the usual trinkets to the delight of all.

Indicating they needed to return to their ships, the Spaniards got up to leave, but the cacique motioned for them to stay. A back-and-forth now took place with everyone gesturing, with throngs of villagers chanting for the guests to stay. Finally, the cacique understood, and he gave orders for a number of his people to carry the gifts to the mouth of the river (Grande Riviere de Nord), where the skiff boats and canoes had remained.

Shipwreck, the *Santa Maria* Is Destroyed

December 24, Monday

Stirred to see the area described by his men, Columbus gave orders to lift the anchors and set sail before the sun came up. Sailing with him that morning were two new Indio guests. Columbus had noticed one of them yesterday; he bravely came aboard and talked freely with the Cuban and Guanahani Indios. The interpreters noticed how the local young man happily talked of gold, its abundance, and its location. This information was told to Columbus, who came over and asked the interpreters if the man would be willing to go with the Spaniards and show them where the gold mines were located; he agreed and asked if he could bring a companion. Fuson describes this event: "I [Columbus] flattered him, and asked him to go with me to show me the gold mines; he accepted the invitation, bringing with him a companion or relative."[63] In this event, we clearly see that Las Casas reported that Columbus did not kidnap the Indios.

The two new ship guests went on to describe a region where the gold was found, known as *Cibao* or *Civao*, adding that the local cacique in that region "carried banners of beaten gold. However, they added that *Cibao* was "very far off to the eastward."[64] Columbus immediately believed the Indios had mispronounced the location, thinking it was *Cipangu* (Japan), as mentioned by Marco Polo. At this point, Columbus is offered in the first-person narrative to explain to his sovereigns the difference between Cuba and Hispaniola, the latter being much superior in terms of the size of villages, and "all the people behave in a remarkably friendly manner and speak softly, not like the other Indios [on Cuba] who appear to threaten when they speak."[65] On an interesting note, the journal explained that the Indios of Hispaniola painted themselves mostly red to keep the sun from injuring them. On the societal structure of the natives, Columbus wrote that the villages are maintained clean and run effectively by a "Lord or Judge" cacique, holding absolute power, using few voice commands, and preferring to employ a set of arm and body gestures; all these commands from the cacique are "understood in a wonderful manner." Columbus is talking about the quickness of the responses from the people once a command is given, with everyone complying willingly, a learned tradition.

As is typical of his journal entries, or how Las Casas transcribed the Barcelona copy, the subject of discussion switches abruptly to explaining the geography of the Bay of Acul, where Columbus and the fleet anchored, describing the depth soundings, location of the small island, *La Amiga*, and area reefs.

December 25, Tuesday

With a Christmas eve command, Columbus ordered the fleet to head for Punta Santo (Pointe Picolet); the light wind carried them from the late afternoon into the evening, slowly east. At 11:00 p.m., knowing that he had not slept for two days and one night due to the constant coming and going of Indios and Spanish shore expeditions, the explorer decided to lie down and rest. With a calm weather system dominating the area, there appeared to be no danger. However, the sailor in charge of steering the ship asked one of several of the ship's boys to take over the helm; had Columbus been awake, he would never have allowed this to occur, but it did, and disaster was only minutes away.[66]

At that time, the *Santa Maria*, with a 12-foot draft, drifted with the current, southeast, just outside the Baie du Cap-Haitien.[67] Today, depth soundings at the entrance of the bay warn of at least 15 rock outcroppings lying only 3–6 feet from the surface; it is a veritable underwater minefield. The first rows of rocks are 6 feet underwater in some places. If the *Santa Maria* missed those, the next groupings of impediments are only 3–4 feet below the surface. The "minefield" extends over a mile, moving from northwest to southeast, as was the course of the *Santa Maria* and *Niña*, with the latter ship leading the way but to the north and out of immediate danger. The undulating seafloor before arriving at the first rock structures rises abruptly from a depth of 42–6 feet in the short distance of 600 feet; had it been daylight with a full crew at their positions taking soundings, it still would have been difficult to prevent the collision.

Interestingly, the journal described how Columbus normally would have never come this close to shore. In fact, a more normal course would have him one-third of a mile to the north, outside the entrance of the bay; there he would wait until daylight and proceed cautiously. However, the men who had visited the bay before, when visiting the cacique, "surveyed the whole coast for three leagues [9 miles]" beyond Punta Santo, finding no concerns. In fact, this more northerly course is probably the one Columbus was on at the time he went to bed. On an ironic quirk of fate, this was one of the few times Columbus had sent skiff boats ahead to survey, extensively for miles, reefs and rock outcroppings.

As noted, the fleet drifted to the southeast, and the boy pilot did not compensate for the drift. Why the pilot of the *Niña* did nothing is unknown; he probably thought the pilot on the *Santa Maria* knew what he was doing. With a 6-foot draft, the *Niña* moved ahead and tacked to the north, and so it did not strike a reef, but the *Santa Maria* did.

On the *Santa Maria*, a loud noise immediately woke Columbus. Kettell now describes what happened: "The boy at the helm, hearing the roar of the sea and feeling the current beating at the rudder, cried out."[68] Rushing to the deck, Columbus knew immediately what happened and froze in shock at seeing the boy still clutching the ship's wheel. Now, the crew appeared, including Juan de la Cosa, owner of the *Santa Maria* and Master of ship routines; it was de la Cosa's responsibility to assign the helmsman and keep the course. Columbus was furious but knew he needed to act quickly. Pointing to the skiff boat, he told de la Cosa and some men to hoist the boat, get it into the water, and be ready. Then he ordered a stern anchor to be thrown over to prevent further movement.

Juan de la Cosa and some men quickly lowered the skiff, but instead of securing the anchor, they began rowing toward the *Niña*. Columbus could not believe his eyes; it was as if his men were already abandoning the ship. The men on the *Niña*, now about 1.5 miles north and ahead of the *Santa Maria*, knew nothing about what happened as de la Cosa approached the ship. He asked permission to come aboard, and Vicente Pinzón rejected the request and began questioning de la Cosa. Las Casas wrote in the journal that Pinzón was correct in not allowing de la Cosa aboard, as there was no command given by Columbus for this to occur. Instead, Pinzón ordered his skiff boat lowered and told some men to hurry to the *Santa Maria* to secure information as to the situation and help.

Meanwhile, the crew of the *Santa Maria* was all on deck, awaiting orders from their admiral. Columbus thought fast, ordering saws to be brought out to commence cutting the masts down and thrown overboard to lighten the load on the keel, hopefully freeing the ship. However, as the minutes went by, the *Santa Maria* listed more and more; then, without warning, the ship's bottom boards cracked and opened, allowing water to rush into the bottom hold (compartment). At this point, Columbus understood his flagship was doomed. When the skiffs returned, Columbus went quickly to *Niña*, apprising Pinzón of the severe damage to the *Santa Maria* and giving orders to allow his crew to help and allow those Indios on the big ship to board the *Niña*.

Columbus stayed on *Niña* until daylight, then he went back to the *Santa Maria*; it was a total loss. He already knew this and had sent the *Niña*'s skiff boat to the shore with Diego de Arana of Cordova (Master-of-Arms), Pedro Gutierrez, representative of the royal household, and a few others, including one or more Indio interpreters, to seek help from the cacique in the large village visited by his men the previous Saturday. According to the entry, Las Casas wrote that the distance from the *Santa Maria*'s current position to the village was 1.5 leagues, or about 4.5 miles.[69]

Upon hearing the news, the village cacique wept and promised to send immediate help to Columbus. Therefore, he did, with the cacique himself leading dozens of canoes and many of his people to the shipwreck. Columbus thanked the chief and then, working side-by-side with his Spanish crew, provided instructions to the Cuban and Guanahani interpreters to pass along to the cacique's villagers. It must have been quite a sight to observe Columbus, the cacique, and the cacique's relatives—everyone frantically working alongside each other to rescue every useful item. Interestingly, had the Cuban and Guanahani Indios wanted to flee, this was the perfect opportunity as chaos ensued from dawn to dusk; the shore of Haiti loomed ahead only one mile to the southwest.

The *Santa Maria*, for the most part, remained above water level as Christmas day dawned, locked on a combination of sand and rock, allowing Spaniards and Indios time to work. As the day moved along, Spanish crew personnel sorted and guarded the rescued supplies, reassuring Columbus. Apparently, the Indios led the Spaniards to some houses near or in the cacique's village where they could store the supplies; later, armed Spaniards guarded each house. Ferdinand Columbus wrote that it was Guacanagarí who placed "armed guards" near the rescued supplies.[70] All through the hours of the ordeal, Columbus watched the cacique closely and found him to have "a remarkable presence, and with a certain self-contained manner that is a pleasure to see. They have good memories, wish to see everything, and ask the use of what they see."[71] This was Christmas day in 1492 for Columbus and crew, a day that changed everything (Figure 9.4).

Columbus went to bed early on December 24, Christmas Eve, expecting no major problems. He had no idea that a ship's boy had been given orders to take the helm. The *Santa Maria* drifted slowly into the Bay of Cap-Haitien, a bay peppered with extensive shoals and surface-exposed reefs.

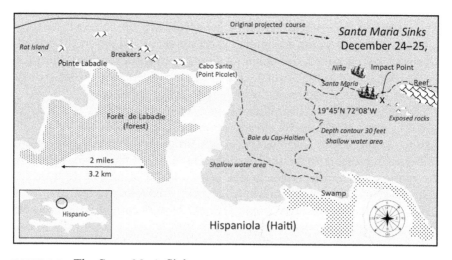

FIGURE 9.4 The *Santa Maria* Sinks

Notes

1 La Casas erroneously wrote 32 miles.
2 Kettell, *Personal Narrative*, 124–5. Modern sonar measurements record the entrance to the Bay of Mosquitos to be at 340 feet at the location of the central approach. A tongue of deep water extends into the bay for approximately one-third of a mile.
3 Markham and others believe the faulty measurement to be that of the original transcriber, not Las Casas.
4 Mosquito Bay's entrance is skewed with a western cape projecting one-third of a mile outward than the eastern entrance, allowing for considerable subjectivity in determining how Columbus estimated his measurement.
5 Fuson, *The Log of Christopher Columbus*, 131.
6 Markham, *Journal of Christopher Columbus*, 105. On the island of Chios today, the mastic collection begins around the middle of August, with a second collection in mid-September. In 1492, mastic was typically collected beginning in March.
7 The coastline change of direction was not experienced by Columbus until several days later, indicating he went back and added this information to the December 11 entry, or Las Casas did.
8 For more information on the differences in Mediterranean and Caribbean mastic, see Taviani, *Columbus*, 114.
9 Kettell, *Personal Narrative*, 129. The location of the cross is about 1,000 feet southwest of the cape entrance, on a high, flat bluff that extends inland to the west for another 1,000 feet. The bluff is approximately 350 feet in height and is the first major topographical feature seen from the middle of the bay. It is not known if the cross or a monument to it exists today.
10 Thacher, *Personal Narrative*, 129. Thacher translates this event as *take*, but for the second reference to the young woman, he uses *capture*.
11 Kettell, 129, Markham, 107 and 605, Fuson, 133.
12 Lardicci, *A Synoptic* Edition, *Historia*, LC 75, sections 6–7, 243; Dunn & Kelley, 219.
13 See Lardicci, DB 76, sections 6–8, 86; Dunn & Kelley, 219.
14 Thacher, *Christopher Columbus*, 605. This is the same language used by Las Casas in his version of the incident from the *Diario*, DB 76, section 8, 86. This statement contradicts the previous statements afforded to Columbus that the Guanahani Indios could not understand the Taíno or northern Hispaniola. Additionally, Las Casas repeats this statement in his *Historia's* version. See Lardicci, *A Synoptic Edition*, *Historia*, section 8, 243.
15 Las Casas in his *Historia* claimed that three Indios escorted the captured girl, Lardicci, *A Synoptic Edition*, *Historia*, LC 76, section 8, 243. I suggest that at least one of the three Indigenous interpreters was Cuban, as the Guanahani guides may have been having trouble understanding the Taíno local dialect. Also see Ferdinand Columbus in Lardicci, *A Synoptic Edition*, *Historie*, FH 76, all, 158.
16 Markham, *The Journal of Christopher Columbus*, 108.
17 Guitar & Estevez, "Taínos," 1023. The authors describe how villagers painted their bodies using vegetable dyes and, as a final act of ritual, thrust a stick down their throats to force stomach regurgitation.
18 Ibid., 109.
19 Ibid., 109.
20 This could be an error on the part of the original Spanish transcriber or on Las Casas. As noted earlier, Thacher believes that Columbus's quadrant was marked in half degrees, making the 34 degrees mark on the quadrant a location of 17 degrees. This could be correct, with a margin of error equal to the correct measurement of 20 degrees.

21 A straight-line course heading is only a shade over 8 miles, so the fleet may have tacked during this short trip.

22 Again, Las Casas or the original scribe made an error on the distance. The log noted the distance between the two points on Tortuga as 12 miles, but the actual distance is 9.5 miles. This, of course, may be an error on Columbus's part while estimating the onboard distance.

23 The range of high topography runs from a little over 1,100 feet in the western portions of Tortuga to just over 1,500 feet in the eastern extremities.

24 Kettell, Personal Narrative, 136. The size of the Lombard cannon used and the loading powder affect the overall projectile distance.

25 The mouth of the *Guadalquivir River* in Spain is about 1,500 feet wide today. Karen F. Anderson-Córdova summarizes Columbus's geographic descriptions, physical and human, by explaining that the Genoese believed Hispaniola was "a bountiful, beautiful land, larger than Spain, with majestic mountains...and densely populated areas, and cultivated terrain. *Surviving Spanish Conquest*, 29.

26 Morison, *Admiral of the Ocean Sea*, 285. Morison spent considerable time in 1938 and 1939 cruising the Caribbean, plotting the Columbus route.

27 Kettell, *Personal Narrative*, 137. Anderson-Córdova stated that Columbus "captured" a solidarity Indian. Lardicci disagrees, preferring to translate the events as a rescue. "He [Columbus] found a canoe with a solitary Indian in it in the middle of the gulf, at which the admiral was astonished that he could keep it afloat, the wind being so strong. The Admiral had him and his canoe brought on board the ship..." *A Synoptic Edition, Historia*, 89 DB 80, section 4–5. Dunn & Kelley agree, adding, "He treated him [the Indian] well." *The Diario*, 231.

28 The Port-de-Paux's left bank juts out slightly, stretching closer to the deep-water drop-off only 400 feet from shore.

29 Lardicci makes no mention of this except to say that the groups of Indios came out to the ships one by one at first. *A Synoptic Edition, Historia*, LC 80, sections 9–10, 246.

30 Markham, *The Journal of Christopher Columbus*, 112.

31 For these passages, see Thacher and Jane, 609; Kettell, 138; Fuson, 136; Dunn & Kelley, 230–31.

32 See Lardicci, *A Synoptic Edition, Historia*, LC 80, sections 14–15, 246–47 for comments from Las Casas concerning this incident.

33 Lardicci, *A Synoptic Edition, Historia*, LC 80, section 30, 248.

34 Ibid. Recall that Las Casas wrote these words years after Columbus's death while researching and writing his *Historia*, witnessing the full implementation of the *encomienda* system that entrapped Indigenous people to Spanish overlords in specific geographic locations on Hispaniola. Keep in mind that when Las Casas quotes Columbus, there is no way to determine to what degree he changed the intent and meaning of words.

35 Thacher, *Christopher Columbus*, 611. Up to this point, Columbus did not believe the Guanahani and Cuban Indios of the reality of viciousness shown by the Canable (Caribs). This episode would help change his opinion later in a decidedly negative fashion, but for now, he still did not believe the two Indios. In Columbus's letter to Luis de Santangel at the end of his voyage, Columbus declared that he believed cannibals existed on at least one island, writing, "inhabited by a people who eat human flesh." Delaney, *Columbus and the Quest for Jerusalem*, 121.

36 Lardicci, *A Synoptic Edition, Historia*, LC 81, section 12, 248. Lardicci specifies that the cacique threw the stones "into the water." The insinuation is that the stones were thrown in the direction of the rival uninvited Indios.

37 Ibid., by giving the stone to Alguacil, the cacique inferred friendship toward the Spaniards, an act that Columbus wanted to add to the logbook to show the success of his attempts to contract initial good relations for future commercial agreements.

38 Dunn & Kelley, *The Diario*, 243. If true, Columbus had devoted time to learning the Arawakan language.

39 Kettell, *Personal Narrative*, 145.

40 Dunn & Kelley, *The Diario*, 247.

41 Ibid., 147–8.

42 Lardicci, *A Synoptic Edition, Historia*, LC 82, section 30, 251.

43 This is the Riviere-des-Barres that flows into at El Puerto de la Granja. The town of Saint-Louis-du-Nord is located here. The second bay was located at Pointe Marigot.

44 This is true for the entire coastal area from Pointe Marigot west past Riviere des Barres.

45 This is not true; Mount Teide is 12,198 feet high.

46 Today, this large bay is named Baie de l'Acul.

47 Markham, *The Journal of Christopher Columbus*, 122. This should be 5 miles, not 5 leagues.

48 The towns of Vaudreuil and Plaine-du-Nord occupy part of this valley.

49 Thacher, *Christopher Columbus*, 617.

50 Ibid.

51 Lardicci, *A Synoptic Edition, Historia*, LC, section, LC 86, section 2, 253. Lardicci phrases this section from the *Historia* as "...they [Europeans] were not anything but other men." It is interesting that Columbus would write this admission of mortality knowing the benefits of continuing, even promoting, deification.

52 Dunn & Kelley, *The Diario*, 257.

53 Anderson-Córdova, "Cultural Transformations." 55.

54 Ibid., 56. The author also uses the December 23 logbook entry to highlight how Guacanagari, a powerful cacique, presented valuable gifts to Columbus while the rest of the crew received cotton cloths.

55 Ibid., 618. Lardicci translated, "because it seemed to him that it was right to do so." *A Synoptic Edition*, DB 86, section 10, 97.

56 This is one of the key points in the voyage that reveals language variations between the Lucayan and Taíno dialects; both are derived from the Arawakan tradition, yet local differences appeared significant.

57 Lardicci, *A Synoptic Edition*, DB 87, section 12, 98. The Dunn & Kelley phrase is slightly different: "are destined to be Christians because of the desire that they seem to have." *The Diario*, 265.

58 Dunn & Kelley, *The Diario*, 265. More emphatically, Lardicci carries the point, in other words: "He [Columbus] made them the monarch's people already, and so that they would serve him [with] love." Lardicci, *A Synoptic Edition*, DB 87, section 12, 98.

59 Markham, *The Journal of Christopher Columbus*, 128–9.

60 See Columbus's letter to the Spanish sovereigns, Wadsworth, *Columbus and His First Voyages*, 92. The money obtained, according to Columbus, should be used to rebuild the treasury, with the priority going to support military efforts to retake Jerusalem.

61 Kettell, *Personal Narrative*, 159.

62 Lardicci, *A Synoptic Edition*, DB 87, section 17, 99.

63 Fuson, *The Log of Christopher Columbus*, 149. This is another instance of congeniality that Columbus worked hard to spread on each island he visited, albeit with ulterior motives. The reader should consider the preponderance of evidence provided in the various accounts of the first voyage as an indicator of true behavior.

64 Markham, *The Journal of Christopher Columbus*, 131. Confusion must have now entered Columbus's mind as to the exact geographic location of *Cibao*. Were the two Indios referencing another island to the east, a coastal zone, or an interior area? Constant frustration over language exchanges must have added to the emotional

stress that Columbus dealt with as disappointment after disappointment over the lack of finding gold and indicated islands.

65 Thacher, *Christopher Columbus*, 623. This statement makes one curious as to what exactly Columbus meant by writing this entry. All Indigenous peoples must have felt threatened upon encountering the Europeans, basing much of that fear on previous ongoing violent raids by marauding bands of Caribs.

66 Juan de la Cosa, owner of the *Santa Maria* and Master of the vessel, most likely allowed the boy to assume the helm. Morison gives the best sequence of events leading to the shipwreck and believes that Columbus had already given orders that the helm should only be attended by one of the approved pilots, not the ship's boys. Ferdinand Columbus defended his father vigorously concerning this incident, placing the blame solely on the de la Cosa, stating, "I had prohibited throughout voyage, telling them [pilots and captains] that with or without wind they should never trust the tiller to a ship's boy." Lardicci, A Synoptic Edition, *Historie*, FH 90, sections 5–6, 161.

67 See the La Navidad & Guacanagarí Village map in Chapter 10 for a precise location.

68 Kettell, *Personal Narrative*, 166.

69 This figure is probably a little short of the actual distance, based on the previous calculation from the shore party that visited the village on the previous Saturday. This author suggests the distance to be closer to 6 miles, depending on the agreed-upon site for the wreckage of the *Santa Maria*, which is still undergoing investigation in 2021.

70 Lardicci, *A Synoptic Edition*, *Histoire*, FH 90, sections 38–39. Ferdinand goes on to relate in superlative language how Columbus admired the Taíno people for their hard work and open hospitality.

71 Markham, *The Journal of Christopher Columbus*, 135. If these quotes from Las Casas are correct, it is difficult to imagine Columbus considering making them slaves, servants of the King and Queen, such as Columbus was himself, yes, but slaves, no, not at this point; something needed to occur to change his mind. Lardicci, *A Synoptic Edition*, DB 90, section 40, 103.

10

A TIME FOR DECISIONS

December 26 to January 15, 1493

> Today at sunrise the King [cacique] of this country came to the *Niña*, where I was, and almost in tears told me not to be dismayed because he would give me whatever he had.
>
> —Christopher Columbus, *Diario*, December 26, 1492

Columbus and Guacanagarí

December 26, Wednesday

Columbus slept aboard *Niña* Christmas night and awoke today with a visit from the cacique, the native chief telling the Italian not to worry; "everything" would be provided, such was the generosity of the Indios. The cacique told Columbus that two more houses had been made available to room and board many of the *Santa Maria*'s crew. In the middle of this conversation, another canoe arrived from a different village. These Indios, standing in their canoes alongside *Niña*, displayed small pieces of gold and made sounds mimicking bells ringing; the word was out, the Spaniards desired gold, and these Indio traders wanted hawk's bells. Watching all this, the cacique from the deck of *Niña* asked Columbus to save some bells; he would be back the next day with gold "the size of a man's hand." Columbus "rejoiced" on hearing the eagerness to trade gold, especially larger pieces than they had seen before. Sailors returning from shore also commented on how the villagers displayed gold as a trading item, eager to exchange for anything, especially bells.

The Cuban and Guanahani interpreters did not run off the previous night, remaining and assisting in a discussion between the cacique and Columbus about the specific location of the "gold mines." However, recall that the Cuban

DOI: 10.4324/9781003464143-15

and Guanahani Indios spoke a slightly different dialect from those in Haiti—Lucayan vs. Taíno dialects. Despite this possibility for further misunderstanding, Columbus heard the cacique mention *Cibao*, which Columbus had already internalized geographically as Cipangu (Japan). Falling deeper into an oblivion of misunderstanding, the interpreters relayed that more gold existed deep in the interior of where they were now, *Bohio* (La Española to Columbus), in the province of *Caritaba*. The chief made the promise to bring much gold because "it is so abundant that it is of no value."

Columbus now offered the cacique to take a brief meal onboard *Niña*. In appreciation, the cacique invited Columbus to his village to participate in a veritable feast, offering the Italian a huge meal consisting of three kinds of yams, shellfish, game, and bread made from the cassava plant.[1] After eating, the cacique invited Columbus to a grove of trees where, in a clearing, the former wearing only the shirt and gloves given to him by the explorer, a thousand of the villagers attended, watching as the cacique described something of this particular landscape, possibly showing a crop or how they used the land; nothing else is written about the activity at the grove.

Upon returning to the beach, the two leaders observed an archery demonstration instigated by Columbus. Selecting one of his best archers, Columbus had the man show the bow and arrow to the cacique and then shoot an arrow toward a distant target. Columbus knew that the Carib raiders that harassed and kidnapped the cacique's people attacked with bows and arrows; he had heard this before, but the cacique verified it again at this time. One can assume that Columbus wanted to impress the cacique and his advisors with the power the Spanish possessed, and possibly also to have them understand how to make and use the weapon themselves (Figure 10.1).[2]

Columbus and crew were fortunate that a large Indigenous village, En Bas Saline, was located onshore, only a short distance from the tragic wreck of the *Santa Maria*. The local cacique, Guacanagarí, graciously offered to help recover food, tools, and other items from the quickly sinking vessel.

At this point, several crew members loaded a Lombard cannon that had been on the *Santa Maria*, and with several hundred villagers watching, Columbus gave the order to shoot at a distant target. The loud explosion of gunpowder sent most villagers, including the cacique, dropping to their knees or flat on their stomachs, shocked by the noise and smoke. Now, Columbus or his interpreters gestured and spoke about how the Spanish would protect the village from any Carib attacks, noting, "...and bring them all prisoners with their hands tied." This is an important reference to Columbus's future action against the Caribs during subsequent voyages. While he had not yet stated an intention to enslave any Taíno or peaceful peoples, he would use force against any violent action by the Caribs upon either his men or Taíno islanders.[3] Lardicci translates an interesting section at this point where Las Casas wrote, "The conversation [between Guacanagarí and Columbus] came around to the Caribs, who

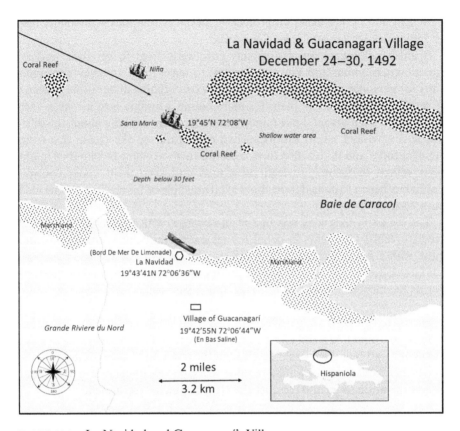

FIGURE 10.1 La Navidad and Guacanagrí's Village

infested those parts."[4] This historical reference supports the recent archaeological excavations validating the existence of Carib settlements on Hispaniola at the time of contact.[5] This is a significant point, as all previous Columbus writings assumed that Carib raiders raided Hispaniola from other islands, more specifically Puerto Rico and the Lesser Antilles.

Awed by the military demonstration, the cacique gave a large mask of gold, highly decorated, and other pieces of "jewels" to Columbus, placing it on the explorer's head and neck. Las Casas now wrote that Columbus felt great friendship with the cacique and came to believe that the sinking of the *Santa Maria* was an ordained act of God for some higher purpose; Columbus thought about how this should change his voyage plans and overall goals. He knew he could not house everyone on the *Niña*, so some men needed to stay, along with most of the Indios he originally planned to take to Spain. He decided to build a fort, staff it with volunteers, and leave provisions and other supplies to sustain them. From the remains of the *Santa Maria*, they would secure timber to build the fort and a tower, naming the encampment Villa de La Navidad; men would dig a ditch around the perimeter for protection, despite Columbus's confidence that no Indios would dare attack his Spaniards.[6]

Spanish volunteers desiring to stay constantly tried to get their leaders' attention (Columbus and Vincente Pinzón) to select them; they saw the possibility for personal gain if the gold fields did exist, arguing under some pretense of serving their monarchs' plans for maintaining a trading post in "Asia." No doubt, some men also did not mind remaining when thinking about the difficult return voyage, as no European had ever traversed the *Ocean Sea* from these latitudes and in this direction; there was a good chance Columbus might never return to Spain.[7] To lead these men and keep them under control, Columbus began to consider the most loyal and able of his crew and some men from *Niña*.

The log entry for today was one of his longest, with Columbus feeling the need to record the events in detail for review by the Spanish monarchs and those with a financial interest in the *Santa Maria* and the voyage in general. Las Casas, desiring to drive home the point that Columbus felt divine intervention as the mover of events for the past two days, wrote,

> He trusted in God that, when he returned from Spain, according to his intention, he would find a ton of gold collected by barter by those he was to leave behind, and that they would have found the mine, and spices in such quantities that the Sovereigns would, in three years, be able to undertake and fit out an expedition to go and conquer the Holy Sepulchre (Jerusalem).[8]

Switching quickly to the first-person narrative Las Casas quotes Columbus as stating,

> Thus, I protest [declare] to your Highnesses that all the profits of this my enterprise may be spent in the conquest of Jerusalem. Your Highnesses may laugh, and say that it is pleasing to you, and that, without this, you entertain that desire.[9]

December 27, Thursday

Worried about his temporary guests, the cacique came to the *Niña* telling Columbus that he had ordered gold to be found and delivered before the Europeans departed; he also begged Columbus to stay longer. Now an amazing event occurred in which the cacique requested a private meal with Columbus. The explorer consented, and then the Cuban or Guanahani interpreters indicated that the cacique's brother and another family relative would join in the taking of food. Columbus noticed that his Indio guests appeared nervous, as if they wanted to say something important. Looking at Columbus, the cacique pointed to himself, his brother, and the family relative, then pointed to Columbus, and then pointed to one or more of the Cuban and/or Guanahani Indios. The gesture was clear; all three of them wanted Columbus to take them to Spain! Interestingly, few scholars point to this episode as deferential evidence that some of the Indios with the Spaniards did not consider themselves "captives." Instead, as the cacique implies, it was an honor to be selected to go. The trip would not mean permanent enslavement but rather an opportunity to see the land of the newcomers and meet the high chiefs that Columbus spoke of—King Ferdinand and Queen Isabella.

No doubt, the cacique based this request on his observations during the last few days on how Columbus and his crew treated the other Taíno guides and interpreters, allowing them to roam freely aboard the ship, swimming in the vicinity, and being housed as guests of the caciques. Imagine the reaction of the Cuban and Guanahani Indios who, just a few days ago, feared this part of the trip, thinking they would be victims of bloodthirsty Caribs or carted off to an unknown fate. Again, by this time, a certain trust factor was already built into the relationship between the Taíno and the Spanish; as we shall see later, some of them will not be given the chance to make the final transatlantic voyage to Spain; they will instead be left on La Española with an opportunity to return to their home islands.

During this event, another canoe pulled up alongside *Niña*, and an Indio hurried up the rope ladder and reported to the cacique that another "god-boat" had been spotted at the far eastern end of the "island" (Haiti). Columbus knew immediately that this was the *Pinta*, and he asked if one of his men could go in a canoe with some Indios to search for the ship. Columbus perked up, yet old feelings of anger arose in him as he once again relived the events of Martín Pinzón's "treachery" and departure. However, his feelings were temporarily assuaged when the thought now arrived that, with two ships, he could plan his return to Spain.

December 28, Friday

Today was a day of planning. Columbus went ashore, and one of the cacique's brothers escorted him to the largest house in the village, the house set aside for Spaniards. Inside, the brother pointed to a couch made of palms, where they sat down and waited for the cacique to arrive. When he walked into the hut, the cacique placed a "large soft piece of gold" around Columbus's neck, thereby honoring his pledge to bring gold to the explorer.[10] The rest of the day, Columbus stayed as the cacique's guest, and with the help of his Cuban and Guanahani interpreters, he discussed with the cacique plans he wanted to implement; no details were given on this day. However, it is a strong possibility that Columbus discussed the arrangements for leaving behind some of his men at the fort being constructed, assuring the Indio cacique of his good intentions for mutual understanding and help; the cacique helping the stranded Spaniards adjust to the island's environment, and the Spaniards helping protect the cacique's people from outside threats.

December 29, Saturday

Back on the *Niña*, Spanish sailors helped a young nephew of the cacique onto the deck; the Indio wanted to see Columbus. By signs and probably interpreters, the cacique's nephew referred to an island toward the east called Guarionex; then, without further prompting, he spelled out a list of other geographic candidates, calling them *Macorix*, *Mayonic*, *Fuma*, *Cibao*, and *Coroay*, all of which contained gold. As the words came out, Columbus wrote them down, spelling the Indio pronunciations as best he could. Hearing all these possible locations where gold might be found, Columbus believed the cacique had withheld the information to force the Spaniards to trade exclusively with him. While Columbus pondered this thought, the cacique sent another large gold mask, but this time he wanted something specific in return. It seems that when the cacique had dined aboard the *Santa Maria*, he had seen, in Columbus's cabin, a clay washbasin and jug. Columbus understood the request, as they had not seen anything similar to this in any Indio village; he consented and had the items delivered.[11]

December 30, Sunday

By now, word of the Spanish visitors had spread for miles in every direction, and on this day, five regional caciques arrived in the village. Columbus, going ashore to dine with the cacique, learned the name of his host, or at least wrote it down for the first time in his journal; his name was *Guacanagarí*. The five chiefs there that day all swore allegiance to Guacanagarí, wearing smaller crowns than those of the great chief, suggesting a political hierarchy of ceremony and geographical jurisdiction. Guacanagarí met Columbus on the beach, escorting him by the arm to the same structure they had met yesterday. Today, however, the house contained an elevated platform upon which several seats were arranged. Guacanagarí motioned for Columbus to sit in one of the seats, as did the other chiefs.[12] Then, in ceremonial decorum, Guacanagarí removed his crown from his head and placed it on Columbus's head. This gesture, a mark of admiration and recognition of superiority or, at least, equality, moved Columbus. Without hesitating, Columbus removed a "splendid" bead collar from his neck and "put it upon that of the king." If that was not enough, and to show his solemn appreciation for all the help he and his people provided in the rescue and securing of supplies from the *Santa Maria*, Columbus took off his "cloak of fine scarlet cloth... he clothe the king with it."[13] The explorer further deeply moved, had a pair of leather shoes placed on Guacanagarí's feet, and in a final act of appreciation, Columbus slipped an expensive silver ring on the cacique's finger.[14] Two of the lesser caciques each presented Columbus with a large gold plate. Guacanagarí's smile could not have been any greater that day; this was the highlight of friendly relations between the Indios and the Spanish during the first voyage.

During the ceremony, an Indio messenger arrived with more news about *Pinta*. The ship was only a two-day journey by canoe to the east. Columbus then returned to his ship, making plans for departure, anxious to rejoin the fleet and confront *Pinta*'s insubordinate captain. Vincente Pinzón from *Niña* boarded the *Santa Maria* and told Columbus that he had seen rhubarb at a harbor 18 miles from their present location, another possible trading item.[15]

Return to Spain or Continue Exploring?

December 31, Monday

Columbus was now determined to prepare for his return voyage to Spain, and to this end, the entire crew worked to gather wood and water. He wanted to notify the Spanish monarchs of all that he had experienced so that follow-up expeditions, more ships, and additional supplies could extend the discoveries and finally reach Cathay. However, he still pondered what route to take; any route needed to include more cruising along the coastline toward the east; at least that was his thinking, but without the *Pinta*, all could be lost if something should happen to the *Niña*. Much of Columbus's lamentations in this entry ride on the fact that reefs may predominate the rest of the harbors he might explore, after all, the demise of the *Santa Maria* caught everyone by surprise in an area where Columbus thought it safe; it was better to get home intact.

January 1, 1493, Tuesday

Desiring some of the rhubarb mentioned by Vicente Pinzón, Columbus sent a skiff boat back to gather specimens. A problem occurred when the men discovered how deep the plants' roots went into the ground; no one had brought a spade in which to dig; however, some plants were obtained. Meanwhile, an Indio canoe with one Spaniard onboard was sent to search for *Pinta*, but nothing was seen; it is possible a Cuban or Guanahani Indio also went as an interpreter. After a distance of 20 miles (Las Casas again incorrectly recorded leagues), the search party landed briefly when sighting a village. Not far from the beach, they saw a "king" with two large plaques of gold placed on his head. Either one of Guacanagarí's villagers or a Cuban or Guanahani interpreter communicated with the leader, who immediately removed the gold crown from his head. The unidentified Spaniard in the group noticed other villagers wearing or possessing "a great deal of gold."[16] At this point, Las Casas asserts that

Columbus thought Guacanagarí forbade anyone within his region of influence to trade the gold with the Spaniards, desiring to keep that favor for himself. According to Las Casas, Columbus brushed off this alleged insult from the powerful Haitian cacique, believing his men who would remain on the island would discover much gold and spices on their own without being forced to trade.

This is another interesting development, and it confirms that Columbus planned that every item was to be willingly traded by the Indios or found naturally by the Spaniards left behind. One could mock this idea, knowing how slight in value were the Spanish trading goods; however, the value was seen in the other traders, and the Indios, from Columbus's standpoint, appeared not only happy with their trinkets, but they desired more. Also, Columbus already sensed a growing sophistication in Indio trading strategies, wanting more for their tiny pieces of gold, as recently seen in Haiti.

In terms of spices found to date, Las Casas noted that Columbus held them in high regard as being "worth more than black and Malegueta pepper," with the explorer telling those men wishing to remain on Hispaniola to find as much as possible.[17]

January 2, Wednesday

It was time to say goodbye; Columbus was rowed ashore. On the beach, Guacanagarí stood anticipating this last meeting. As a final sign of appreciation for everything the Indio cacique had provided, Columbus gave one of his fine shirts to Guacanagarí. Knowing that he would be leaving upward of 40 men, some of those men, with orders from Columbus, provided another demonstration of Spanish power, igniting one or more Lombard charges; one of those charges was directed at what was left of the *Santa María*'s side. In the entry for today, Columbus made it clear that Guacanagarí was still worried that the Carib Indios might attack, killing and kidnapping his people and the stranded Spaniards. Columbus assured the cacique that the "cannibals" would be defeated by the men he would be leaving stationed at the fort. Las Casas added that Columbus's little military demonstration was to send an indirect message to Guacanagarí—fear the Spaniards as you fear the Caribs. This is quite possible, as Columbus understood that it would be months before he could return, and initial friendships might turn ugly. Next, everyone walked to the nearby village, where a prepared feast awaited all—Spaniard, and Indio.

On this day, the list of selected men to remain in the New World was released. To lead them, Columbus chose his good friend Diego de Arana, a cousin of Beatriz Enriquez de Arana, Columbus's mistress. Arana held final authority, and his advisors and assistants (lieutenants) would be Pedro Gutierrez, representatives of the Spanish monarchs, and Rodrigo Escovedo, Secretary of the Fleet. Thirty-six other unlucky souls would be under their command; none of them would ever see Columbus or Spain again. Their deaths would not be discovered until late that year, when Columbus returned, and this disaster would alter Columbus's perceptions of Spanish-Indio relations. These perceptions would derive from a one-sided, Indio version of the future demise of the fort and all the men.[18]

On their way back to the beach for the final farewell to the men he would leave behind, an Indio from the village spoke to one of the Cuban or Guanahani interpreters, describing how much affection Guacanagarí held for Columbus, so much so that the great cacique ordered gold found and brought to the village so that it could be melted and made into a life-size image of their heavenly friend, Columbus.[19]

At the beach, according to Las Casas in his book *Historia*, Columbus gathered the 39 men chosen to stay and said these words:

> First, that they should consider the great mercies which God had given them and all of them up to that time, and the benefits He had offered them, for which they must always give Him endless thanks, and recommend themselves much to His goodness and mercy, taking care not to offend Him and placing all their hope in Him, supplicating Him also for his own return, which with His aid, he promised them to try to have as speedy as possible, by which he was confident in God that all would be very joyful. Second, he begged them and charged them and ordered them on the part of their Highnesses, to obey the Captain [de Arana] as himself, as he was confident of his goodness and fidelity. Third, that they should greatly respect and reverence the King Guacanagarí and his Chiefs and principal men, or *nitaynos*, and other inferior chiefs, and they should avoid as they would death, annoying them or tormenting them, since they had seen how much he and they owed to them, and the necessity for keeping them contented, remaining as they did in their land and under their dominion. Fourth, he ordered them and begged them earnestly, to do no injury or use any force against any Indian, man or woman, nor take from them anything against their will; more especially, they should be on guard and avoid doing injury or using violence to the women, by which they would cause scandal and set a bad example to the Indians, and show the infamy of the Christians, of whom the Indians were certain that they came from Heaven, and were sent by the celestial virtues.[20]

While the above speech might sound contrived from a prejudiced Las Casas, hoping that Columbus did say these words, the intent of action by Spaniards toward Indios is compatible with Columbus's actions up to this point. Las Casas went on with additional directives from Columbus for his men to follow, stating they were not to scatter themselves off in the interior and, under no circumstances, leave the island. He also told them not to "suffer their solitude." After all, they chose to stay; they should have no regrets as the days turned into weeks and weeks into months. He did ask them to investigate any claims by the local Indios of nearby gold mines, look for a better place to establish a trading post, barter fairly, and sequester the gold for proper distribution (meaning for the Spanish king and queen and Columbus's tenth), and finally to continually praise their king and queen, for if they were successful, great rewards would follow.

Before boarding the *Santa Maria*, a final check of all the necessary supplies left ashore occurred. Biscuits for a year, trinkets for trading, rope, nails, and a wide assortment of naval goods appeared sufficient for the men's survival, along with food obtained through bartering with the locals, fishing, and gathering. He expected them to sow the seeds he left and harvest the crops. Among the men staying behind included a "good gunner" for the one Lombard left behind, a carpenter, a caulker, a cooper, a tailor, and most importantly, a physician; Columbus noted they were all "seamen." Boarding the skiff boat, he left the shore and his men behind.[21]

January 3, Thursday

The entry today begins with a discussion of the Cuban and Guanahani Indios. Apparently, since the destruction of the *Santa Maria*, they had been housed in Guacanagarí's village, apparently unattended, as the preceding statements relate. Three of the group, probably from the Guanahani group of five, came to the *Niña* during the night, volunteering to return to Spain with Columbus, telling him that the other Indios, from Cuba, would be coming along but wanting to wait until sunrise; this implies free choice. This may be evidence that the Cuban and Guanahani Indios, at least some of them, chose to go with Columbus, while most were determined to stay—apparently, a discussion among the Cubans and Lucayans occurred. No one is sure how many were returned, as numerous authors cite numbers as low as six and as high as twelve; most focus on the lower figure, citing six or seven. Carol Delaney, in the most recent research, stated, "He took six Indians aboard on the return voyage to Spain, and he [Columbus] says that even more wanted to go."[22] If this is correct, the kidnapping charge for the transoceanic return trip should be questioned. We know no children and few women, or no women, were presented in Spain, so most likely, all the Cuban Indios remained in Haiti. This makes sense, as Haiti was close to Cuba and easily reached via canoe. Therefore, the most likely scenario is that three of the remaining five Guanahani Indios and the two Haitian Indios who volunteered to serve as guides on December 24 returned with Columbus—none of them against their will. This puts five Indigenous men on *Niña*.[23] However, two Indios remained on board the *Pinta* with Martín Pinzón and would soon reunite with Columbus, making a total of seven. However, as we shall see on January 15, Columbus brought on four men from eastern Hispaniola; this would make a total of nine Indigenous peoples making the ocean crossing on *Niña*, with the strong possibility that the two individuals on the *Pinta* had no choice. From a total of eleven men being transported, five of them agreed to go, while four did not, all on the *Niña*, while two remained on the *Pinta*.[24]

Sebastian Munster, writing a few decades after the event, noted,

> Which he [Columbus] took with him from the same Island [Indies] into Spain to use them as interpreters. Of which seven died by change in the air [humid and hot to dry and cold] One of them was permitted by the Admiral to depart, when the navy [ships coming over on the second voyage] came near to his country [Hispaniola]. The rest stole away privately and swam to the land [Hispaniola].[25]

Peter Martyr, who served in Rome as a teacher and scholar, journeyed to Spain in 1487, remaining there in service to the Spanish monarchs while writing extensively. His *Decades de Orbo Novo*, also known as *Decades*, a compilation of eight books (official reports), provided accurate information regarding the discovery and early colonization of the Americas. Regarding Columbus and the first voyage, he wrote, "He took with him six islanders thanks to whom all the words of their language have been written down with Latin characters."[26] The wording here is quite persuasive, indicating a willingness on the part of the Indigenous people on board Columbus's ships to share their language and knowledge, suggesting mutual understanding and cooperation. Ferdinand Columbus noted in his writing that Indios from Guanahani continued to remain onboard, where they helped with interpretation for subsequent island contacts, such as the incident on January 13 at Samaná Bay.[27] Las Casas, writing later in his *Historia*, remembered seeing the Indios in Seville but did not recall their number. He did say that according to the "Portuguese *History*," the number of Indigenous peoples seen in Lisbon was 10–12 individuals.[28]

The sea remained rough that day, and Columbus waited to depart the next day. The skiff boat did not go ashore, and no canoes approached the ship. In the meantime, he worried about Martín Pinzón and the *Pinta* reaching Spain ahead of the *Niña*. Thinking Pinzón was capable of duplicity, Columbus could see and hear the lies that Pinzón and his men would write and speak to the authorities. Then and there, Columbus was determined to make haste in his return.

The Voyage Home Begins

January 4, Friday

Finally, with the sunrise, the crew pulled up *Niña*'s anchor and carefully sailed NW, using the larger of two channels, running 18–60 feet in depth, lying just south of the 12-mile-long reef that protects Baie de Caracol (Caracol Bay).

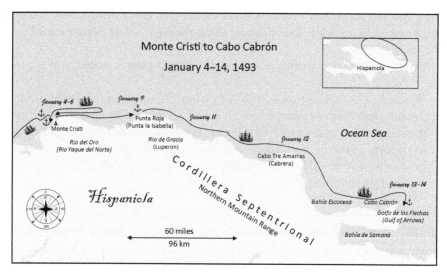

FIGURE 10.2   Monte Cristi to Cabo Cabrón

The crew measured only 50 feet of depth, 1 mile out (north) of Cabo Santo (Point Picolet), while inside the cape, submerged rocks dominate. The entry noted the proliferation of beaches, with a lush lowland extending inland, up to 4 miles, where the topography rises to vast mountains; this he described as he now sailed eastward along the northern coast of Hispaniola, sighting a mountain (El Morro de Monte Cristi) that connects to a wide level plain that reaches inland a great distance. Columbus noted a wide gulf running to the southeast for miles, determining that this coastline contained shoals and reefs for much of its length. In this, he relied on the report from several days prior given by the sailor who had gone in the Indio canoe, seeing several rivers but only one that might host a ship. In this area, Columbus anchored for the rest of the day and evening. In ending his entry for this day, Columbus concluded that Monte Cristi should serve as the directional focus for future visits to La Navidad, taking bearing readings and watching depth (Figure 10.2).

Reunited with Martin Pinzón and the crew of the *Pinta*, Columbus prepared for the voyage home. However, first, he wanted to skirt the northern coastline of Hispaniola to check its size and disposition.

January 5, Saturday

Starting again at daybreak, the *Niña* quickly ran into headwinds as they attempted to sail east, so Columbus decided to take refuge in the harbor south of Monte Cristi, eventually maneuvering the ship safely in between the small offshore island, Isla Cabra, and Monte Cristi. On an impulse, Columbus and some men explored Cabra, finding "fire and signs that fishermen had been there."[29] They also found beautifully tinted stones sea-washed to a perfect shine. Columbus thought they might adorn church edifices; he noted that they looked similar to the stones found in San Salvador. From the island, a panorama of low bushes and open fields spread out to the southeast, with a large river (Yaque del Norte River) flowing into a delta area.

In the other direction, to the east, Columbus noted a prominent cape, which he named Cape of Becerro (Punta Rucia). Between that point and Monte Cristi, the land appeared low with wide beaches fronting the ocean, while in the distance, mountains reached high into the sky, a reminder of the diversity of the land.

January 6, Sunday

The inner bay harbor at Monte Cristi proved shallow at 18–24 feet but provided the necessary protection from wind. Moving on this day, the fleet sailed east, noticing many shoals and reefs. By the afternoon, with the wind again coming from the east, a sailor climbed the mast to look for a suitable anchorage. Squinting, he spotted the *Pinta*. Shocked and relieved, Columbus first turned around and headed back 10 miles toward Monte Cristi. Once there, Martín Pinzón came aboard *Niña* in what must have been a cold reception. Columbus expected excuses, and Pinzón provided many, saying first that he did not want to separate from the fleet, further explaining that the Guanahani Indio onboard had pointed the way to the island of *Babeque*, where gold was believed to lie about in great quantities. Pinzón saw this as an opportunity to help Columbus, knowing that *Pinta* maneuvered more ably in the shallow waters near the coastline.

Columbus inwardly resented all excuses Pinzón made during the meeting, as Kettell concluded, "The Admiral concealed his resentment, that he might not aid the machinations of Satan in impeding the voyage, as he had hitherto done."[30] Still upset, Columbus learned that Pinzón and crew found no gold on *Babeque* and so were determined to return to Hispaniola and rejoin the fleet. However, once on the big island, Pinzón, like Columbus, traded for gold in substantial quantities.[31] Boldly, Pinzón told his men that whatever gold was obtained in trading, half of its value would go to him. When Columbus discovered this fact, he spilled out his frustration in the log entry by pointing to divine intervention that allowed him to be more successful than Pinzón with the establishment of the settlement at La Navidad. He wrote, "Thus I perceive, Sovereign Princes, that it was a providence of our Lord in suffering the ship to be cast away here, it being the best place in the whole island for a settlement and nearest to the gold mines."

Attempting to dismiss the misadventures of his insubordinate captain, Columbus learned from his Indio guides, probably the Cubans or Haitians, of another island south of Cuba called *Yamaye* (Jamaica), where gold lies in streams the size of beans, the distance from Cuba being only a 10-day canoe voyage or about 60 miles, and that people on this island go about with clothing. More stories came out as Columbus listened more and more to his now-remaining Indio guides as they told stories of an island to the east inhabited only by women—a new, trusting relationship formed.

January 7, Monday

Columbus and crew spent the day caulking the *Niña*. Going ashore in search of wood, a shore party reported seeing vast amounts of aloes and mastic. Columbus wanted to keep reminding the Spanish monarchs of the value of non-gold commodities as an alternative profit-making product.

January 8, Tuesday

Releasing his built-up frustration with Martín Pinzón, Columbus noted that he intended to continue the voyage of discovery along the entire island of Hispaniola but feared additional disobedience and possibly another episode of abandonment from the *Pinta*'s captain. And, for the first time, Columbus names Vincente Pinzón as another person he does not trust, stating that the brothers "had a party attached to them, the whole of them had displayed great haughtiness and avarice, disobeying his [Columbus's] commands, regardless of the honors he had conferred upon them."[32] The reader may find this statement from Las Casas and credited to Columbus confusing when considering that at no earlier time had Las Casas noted that Columbus had trouble with Vincente Pinzón. In fact, Vincente kept the *Niña* with Columbus when his brother sailed off to search for gold.

Columbus knew the majority of men under the service of the Spanish monarchs remained loyal, yet he wanted to take no further risks and preferred to return as soon as possible to Spain. The idea of disloyalty among the crew is important to remember when looking at future events on subsequent voyages, where self-serving *hidalgos* (members of Spanish nobility) and other fortune-seekers eagerly sought to undermine Columbus's administrative rules and protocols concerning the seeking of gold and relations with Indigenous populations of Hispaniola. As an Italian-born explorer, Columbus encountered on voyages two, three, and four crews offering split loyalty, often with episodes of jealousy, indifference, insubordination, and outright rebellion from his Spanish-born crews and settlers, particularly the *hidalgos*.[33]

Putting aside the above thoughts for a moment, Columbus decided to take a small crew and row up a nearby river (the Yaque del Norte River). It is from this river that men obtained fresh water only a short distance inland. As the depth lessened at the mouth of the river, crew members pointed to sparkling grains of yellow sand; excitement rose. Columbus looked, and he too spotted gold particles and noticed some larger specimens, as large as "horse-beans." Many large pieces of gold were collected. They filled their water casks with fresh water and returned to the *Niña* to find more fine particles clinging to the bottom of the water casks. Columbus smiled and named the river the Rio del Oro (River of Gold). Surely, much more gold existed upstream, many miles inland, in the foothills, piled in clumps where each turn in the river collides with the riverbank.

Thinking that several other rivers seen recently ran wider and deeper than the *Rio del Oro*, Columbus reasoned the possibilities of mining this area on future trips. As Las Casas recorded this thought from the original text, he also noted that Columbus was now, more than ever, anxious to return to the Court of Spain with the news of the discovery and "to get rid of the evil company that was with him, whom he had always said were a mutinous set."[34]

Along the Coast of Northeastern Hispaniola

January 9, Wednesday

The wind cooperated today, and the fleet of two ships headed ENE for a distance of 40 miles, where they encountered a point of land in the late afternoon naming this location, Punta Roja (today Punta La Isabella). Fearing reefs, neither the *Niña* nor the *Pinta* came close to shore. Columbus noted in this entry the beauty of the landscapes he had seen all that morning and early afternoon, citing the lush, green appearance of low-lying fields and numerous river mouths. He would remember this area, and later, on his second voyage, he would establish his trading post and supporting town, La Isabela, in this area.

In noting the wildlife of the region, Las Casas wrote that the crew saw many large turtles at Monte Cristi with oversized eggs lying about in abundance. Yesterday, Columbus recalled seeing three mermaids (sea cows) rise above the water, displaying vibrant colored skin, and "to some extent, they have the form of a human face."[35] Again, Las Casas claims that Columbus vented his anger at the Pinzóns when he ended this day's journal entry with these words: "I will not suffer the deeds of evil-disposed persons, with little worth, who, without respect for him to whom they owe their positions, presume to set up their own wills with little ceremony."[36] One can feel the passion and urgency that Columbus now exuded to return home before the Pinzón brothers. At this point, Columbus is thinking that a plan has been hatched between the two brothers to return home, claim some or all the glory of discovery, and obtain royal recognition, thereby establishing, through financial rewards, monies enough to sustain themselves and their families, including written agreements for future profits. Clearly, Columbus was covetous of "his" discoveries, resentful of past actions by the Pinzóns, and suspicious of what they might do next. Lardicci's translation of Columbus's feelings at this point states, "I will not suffer, he says, from the deeds of evil persons [Martín Pinzón] of little virtue, who, opposing the one who granted them such honor, presume to do what they wish, with little respect."[37]

January 10, Thursday

Setting sail that morning, the fleet made little progress by evening, traversing only 3 miles to another river and harbor. Columbus named the river Rio de Gracia; today, the town of Luperon sits at the southern end of this short bay. Exploring the river and bay in the skiff boat, men found the river shallow and full of shipworms; the *Pinta* had anchored here earlier for 16 days and now "suffered very severely from them."[38]

Las Casas, in this entry, now recounts Columbus's explanation of how Martín Pinzón traded for gold in this very port and learned from local Indios that Columbus was nearby to the west. Further, Las Casas wrote that Columbus believed the Martín had lied to him about how long he remained in the area, having his men swear they were in the vicinity for only six days. Continuing, Columbus decided that Pinzón's deceit was so prevalent, "he [Martín] could not hide it." Martín, according to Las Casas, forced his men to agree to give their captain half of all the gold traded or found. Before leaving this area, Martín "took four Indian men and two young girls by force, whom the Admiral ordered given clothing and that they should be returned to their country so that they might go to their houses."[39] Why would Columbus reveal this act of heroism if he was intent on bringing back captives against their will?

In the original old Spanish, Las Casas used the verb forms *tomo* and *fuerca* to clearly establish that Pinzón took these Indios by force, against their will. In the previous incidents that involved Columbus, Las Casas only used forms of the verb *tomar* (to take), leaving open, as has already been shown, the possibility that the Indios, after the January 3 incident, chose to return with Columbus. To bring home the point, Columbus, in the first-person narrative, concluded,

> Which [says the Admiral] is for the service of your Highnesses, because men and women all belong to your Highnesses [as citizen-servants] on this island especially as well as on the other islands. But here where your Highnesses already have a settlement [La Navidad] honour and favour must be shown to the people, since there is so much gold on this island and such good lands and so much spice.[40]

In other words, Columbus is attempting to set up a social-commercial environment in which the local population would become citizen-vassals of Spain, not slaves, under the jurisdiction of Spain, working with future Spanish settlers clustered in trading posts along the coast of "La Española" (Hispaniola). This societal arrangement would not be the same as that occurring in the Canary

Islands. For a comparative analysis of Columbus's vision and that concurrently evolving on the Canary Islands, see Appendix V. However, to be sure, according to Las Casas's version of the logbook, Columbus did force the Guanahani Indios to come with him as well as the Cubans. It suggested then that Columbus changed his mind on this issue, especially considering he did not trust Martín Pinzón to take his cargo of gold and captives ahead of the *Niña* and seek the glory of returning first to Spain. The question remains as to how many Indios Pinzón had on *Pinta* before he departed from Columbus to seek gold on his own. As noted earlier, that number may have been two or three individuals.[41] Using this rendering of the Indio captives, the final tally may well have been ten or eleven Indigenous peoples returning to Spain, seven with Columbus on the *Niña* and two or three on the *Pinta*. As already noted, this matches Peter Martyr's account.

January 11, Friday

The wind picked up at midnight, so Columbus ordered both ships to weigh anchor. The coastline of Hispaniola, after 9 miles, dropped to the southeast, with the fleet adjusting course accordingly, remaining at a respectable distance from the shore.[42] Columbus recorded a series of capes, rivers, and mountains. As the ships cruised along, Columbus carefully observed the landscape and recorded his admiration for the environment with such statements as "Between this Cabo del Angel (Puerto Plata)[43] and Monte de Plata is a gulf, bordered by a most charming country, consisting of lofty and beautiful fields extending far into the land."

   At this point, Las Casas, once again, describes an "opinion" of Columbus, stating, "In the Admiral's opinion, [it] contains fine streams of water and much gold." How Columbus could make that assumption from a distance as he sailed by in the *Niña* certainly suggests a non-interest issue with Las Casas, preferring to paraphrase it quickly and move on. If Columbus was so specific about both issues, "fine streams of water" and "much gold," why did he not use the first-person narrative? Now Las Casas names specific capes before summarizing the day's events, concluding that the fleet of two ships "made great progress," although no overall mileage was reported. Fearing coastal reefs, the ships remained well out to sea.[44]

January 12, Saturday

With the sunrise, Columbus anxiously pressed the crews to get underway, making 20 miles quickly, then another 24 miles, later observing at a distance a large landmass projecting directly east, the Samaná Peninsula. During the latter half of this voyage this day, the ships cruised past Cabo Tre Amarras (Cabrera) as they now headed SE, spotting impressive mountains and small harbors. After sailing past the modern-day town of Nagua, the coastline dramatically turned due east, initiating an introduction to the Samaná Peninsula, abounding with jutting headlands and short, shallow harbors, offering an impressive mountain background stretching from Las Terrenas to the end of the peninsula, Cabo Cabrón.

Finally, the headland gave way, and Columbus and crew observed a large, quickly opening bay, Bahia Escocesa (Scottish Bay), and an opposing peninsula standing distant at 6 miles. Anchoring near the shore in deep water (70 feet) in the inner bay, Bahia del Rincon, Columbus sent crews ashore in search of fresh water. As usual, nearby Indios disappeared. The last comment this day focused on Las Casas believing that Columbus was "astonished at the great size of the island." This leads to the possibility that the explorer entertained various geographic theories concerning the true size, shape, and relationship of the island landmass to the Asian mainland. Or was this Cipangu? Recall that Columbus, already impressed with the extent of the northern coast of Cuba and now the northern coast of Hispaniola, remained perplexed as to the geographic relationship between these two large islands and the mainland of Asia (Figure 10.3).

Hispaniola's coastline seemed to go on forever, as Columbus observed one bay and one river after another as he sailed eastward. As with Cuba, his mind played with the idea that Hispaniola might be part of the Asian mainland, or maybe this was Cipangu.

January 13, Sunday

Today, Columbus wanted to search for a closed harbor, which might offer him the opportunity to observe the predicted conjunction of the Sun and the Moon

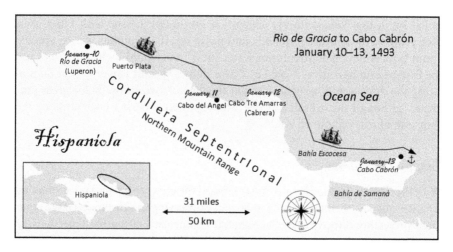

FIGURE 10.3   Río de Gracia to Cabo Cabrón

and Mercury with Jupiter.[45] This reveals Columbus's genuine interest in all things astronomical and his curiosity about how the natural world works.

However, he remained at anchor, sending another shore party in search of *ajes* (roots, potatoes). The group of explorers found Indios willing to exchange in trade. One Indio agreed to return to the *Niña*. Once onboard the ship, Columbus earnestly studied the native, offering a detailed description, as per Las Casas's understanding:

> This man was of a more unpleasing appearance than any that had yet been seen; his face was smutted all over with charcoal, though in all parts they are accustomed to paint themselves with a variety of colors. His hair was long, gathered and tied behind, and adorned with parrot's feathers. He was totally naked.[46]

Columbus, peering intently at his guest, assumed, at first, that the Indio came from a Carib tribe. Gesturing proved useless, but slowly the conversation, with the help of Guanahani and Cuban interpreters, Columbus learned that his guest came from the east, possibly from another island not too distant from Hispaniola. When shown a sample of gold, the Indio referenced the word *tuob* and pointed east.[47] Columbus pressed for more information, and the Indio seemed to believe that one island lying close remained populated exclusively by women and contained "much gold." Another island was mentioned: *Goanin* (unknown) and *Cariba* (Puerto Rico).

At the mention of *Cariba*, Columbus, through Las Casas's transcription, described the ongoing peril that Indios constantly feared: Carib attacks. The passage hit upon the now-accepted sequence of events of marauding Carib bands in canoe fleets, plying the waters of the Caribbean, seeking new victims, and eventually capturing helpless men, women, and children. As prisoners, the fate of the captured persons was determined later in a Carib village—slavery or, worse, being devoured physically during ritualistic ceremonies.

With the conversation over, the Indio and Columbus "feasted," with the latter giving beads and "pieces of red and green cloth." In return, Columbus asked the man to seek out and bring back whatever gold he could find. Then the Indio slipped into the *Niña*'s skiff, and sailors rowed him ashore. There, the Indios peered at the European ships, over 30 of them brandishing bows and arrows, an indication they might be Caribs. Jumping from the skiff, the Indio convinced his compatriots that the Spanish offered no threat. Next, a short trading exchange occurred with Spanish sailors attempting to buy all the bows and arrows, an obvious attempt to disarm the natives. After giving up a couple of their weapons, the Indios became suspicious and ran to pick up more weapons. As usually happens during a military escalation, a misinterpretation of a perceived action leads to a reaction; that is what happened next. Some Spaniards noticed several Indios carrying long, strong cords, assuming that their purpose was for "binding their prisoners."[48] Not to be captured, the few sailors, seven in number, decided to take the offense, charging the leading group of Indios with brandished swords and aiming their already loaded crossbows. This first violent encounter between Europeans and Indigenous peoples ended with no injury to the Spaniards; the Indios suffered a few sword cuts and punctures from crossbow bolts in the breast.

At first, the skirmish appeared to be an even fight, and the Indios held their ground. However, eventually, they retreated. As they did so, several Spanish men wanted to give chase but were held back by their senior commander. When the men reported back, Columbus at first felt angry that a battle had taken place, desiring to leave all Indios with a good impression of Spanish intentions. When he learned of the facts—that it appeared to be Caribs, or neighbors of the Caribs, with the possible intention of capturing the seven Spaniards as prisoners, he changed his opinion. Now Columbus solidified his belief that all Caribs were not to be trusted and thus should be treated as enemies of Spain and the Taíno and Lucayan peoples.[49]

January 14, Monday

Convinced that local Indios belonged to one or more Carib groups marauding eastern Hispaniola, Columbus decided, according to Las Casas, to "make prisoners of some of the Indians" and planned to send some men ashore for this purpose. When his shore party reached the beach, a large band of Indios peacefully surrounded the Spaniards. One lone Indio stepped forward, the same man who had visited Columbus the day before and presented various beads in an effort to establish a friendship. Then the cacique, who had now arrived, agreed to step into a skiff and meet Columbus.

Once again, Columbus treated a visiting Indio cacique as a guest, offering biscuits and honey. After the meal, the cacique accepted a red cap, beads, and cloth. The cacique's entourage received similar gifts, and a short discussion ensued, with Columbus's Indio interpreters able to ascertain information. The visiting cacique promised, as he moved to leave, to return with a golden mask. Las Casas noted the cacique and his elders went ashore, "well contented."[50]

As the day moved on, Columbus received reports from his crew about small leakages on the *Niña*, as did Martín Pinzón on the *Pinta*.

January 15, Tuesday

Realizing further contact with local Carib tribes would be futile, Columbus planned to sail to the island of *Carib* (Puerto Rico), where his interpreters had relayed that a bountiful amount of gold lay waiting to be traded and mined. He also considered another island mentioned in the translations, *Matinino*, where it was believed copper existed, an island dominated exclusively by women.[51]

In short order, he changed his mind, and instead, a plan evolved in his mind to skip *Matinino* and sail directly to Carib, where he might capture some female natives. Why he would want to do this is unexplained. He already had several willing Taíno and Lucayan "guests" on board; there was no need to forcibly take Caribs, even though existing Spanish law allowed the enslavement of war prisoners or people participating in inhuman (cannibalistic) behavior. There exists the possibility that he thought representatives of the Caribs, along with his Lucayan and Taíno interpreters, would provide a more cosmopolitan social representation of the Indies.

To see if the cacique would honor his promise to bring a gold mask for trade, Columbus sent a boat ashore. The cacique did not show, but he sent a gold crown, abundant cotton, bread, and tubers, all carried by a large number of armed men. A peaceful trade commenced, ending with both sides satisfied. As the shore party returned to the *Niña*, Columbus noticed a canoe approaching. Four young Indios climbed the rope ladder and stood on deck, immediately engaging in conversation with the Cuban and Lucayan interpreters. On hearing the translation, which includes glowing stories of easy access to gold in Carib, Columbus, according to Las Casas, was determined to "take them along with him." Dunn & Kelley again agree, translating this incident as an indication that Columbus desired to have them onboard as guides to "all those islands to the east, on the same route that the Admiral was to follow, that he decided to take them to Castile with him."[52] It is quite possible that the four young Caribs believed they would only be hitching a ride to the island of Carib (Puerto Rico) and disembarking for an eventual return to Hispaniola, with Columbus admitting that precise communication proved difficult.[53] The total number of Indios onboard the two ships now most likely totaled eleven: three Lucayans from Guanahani, two Taíno from Hispaniola (Haiti), and four young Caribs from his location today at the eastern end of Hispaniola, all on the *Niña*. The *Pinta* held two, possibly both Lucayans.[54]

Part of Columbus's diary focuses on traded Indio weapons. Impressed with the size and construction of the native bows, he drew a comparison with those currently in existence in France and England: long and powerful. Equally of note, the length of the accompanying arrows further impressed Columbus, specifically pointing out that the arrows were "very straight." He went on to write about "the very fine and long" cotton fibers and the abundant mastic. One item, *aji* (chili pepper), received considerable space in this journal entry, with Columbus seeing the trade item as "valuable." He conjectured that it would take many caravels exclusively employed to carry the food item to Spain each year.

The last portion of this entry connects seaweed seen on the outward voyage as being abundant at this harbor. From here, Columbus estimated that the distance to the Canary Islands from his current position must therefore be around 400 leagues (1,200 miles) (Figure 10.4).

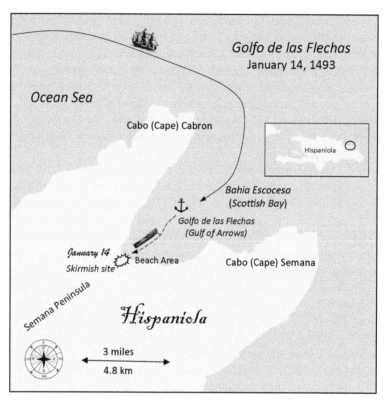

FIGURE 10.4 January 14: Bay of Semana

Known today as Scottish Bay, Columbus called it the Gulf of Arrows for the brief but intense armed skirmish with local Indigenous people, quite probably Carib, as they were skilled with the bow and arrow.

Notes

1 Sometimes called manioc or yucca, the root sections are edible, pounded, and worked into a meal bread. Columbus was impressed so much that Las Casas spelled out the specific foods eaten.
2 There is no mention that Columbus gave the cacique a bow and arrow from which Indios might begin making their own designed weapon. Certainly, the Indios could learn from observing the weapon and how it functioned. It is known that the Caribs of the Lesser Antilles used the weapon effectively against Taíno warriors and, later on, against Columbus's men during later voyages.
3 While out of the scope of this book, Columbus felt completely comfortable taking prisoners of war, as was the custom in most of the world. Later events, such as the attack and massacre of his men at La Navidad, gave Columbus the rationale for the enslavement of Caribs, not Taínos. As explained earlier in this book, new archaeological evidence confirms extensive Carib settlement in Hispaniola, opening the possibility of such expansion into Jamaica, Puerto Rico, and Eastern Cuba, which

helps explain the constant warfare going on between Caribs and Taíno, and why Columbus later believed it was the Caribs who killed all his men. Kathleen Deagan and José María Cruxent in their book, *Columbus's Outpost Among the Taínos* explained, "The tragedy at La Navidad was to have far-reaching consequences, not only for the establishment of La Isabela but also, more profoundly, for the growth of the mutual distrust that pervaded the attitudes of the Taíno Indians and the Spanish toward each other from that time on." 22.

4 Lardicci, *A Synoptic Edition, Historia*, LC 91, section 22, 263.
5 As discussed earlier, see Ann Ross, "Faces Divulge the Origins of Caribbean Prehistoric Inhabitants."
6 For a full account of the events of this day, read Lardicci's extended translation from the *Historia*, 262–3.
7 In making his selection, Columbus chose a calker, a carpenter, a gunner, a cooper, and others with special skills.
8 Markham, *The Journal of Christopher Columbus*, 139. As Carol Delaney noted in her book, Columbus's prime goal was not personal wealth or wealth for his family but to take back the holy city of Jerusalem, which was then in the hands of the Ottoman Turks. Also, Juan Gil wrote extensively about Columbus's ultimate goals in such writing as *Mitos y utopias del descubrimiento*.
9 Ibid. Lardicci and Dunn & Kelley closely agree with this translation.
10 Lardicci, *A Synoptic Edition*, DB 93, sections 11–12, 106. This translation describes how the cacique "began to run to the admiral," indicating a growing attempt to honor Columbus, as mentioned earlier in this day's entry.
11 Ibid., Lardicci has Las Casas quoting Columbus, "But there is so much of it [gold], in so many places… that it is a wonder," sections 6–7, 107.
12 Taínos called these carved seats *duhos*, reserved for chiefs and "other persons of high rank." Rouse, *The Taínos*, 9
13 Kettell, *Personal Narrative*, 177.
14 Several Indios had reported that these "gods" wore a brilliant band of metal around their fingers and had attempted to trade for the item with some members of the crew, to no avail. Metals, beaten into jewelry, became a prized trading item for Indigenous peoples, who admired their brilliant luster and durability.
15 Vincente Pinzon must have previously seen the rhubarb plants on the island of Amiga.
16 Thacher, *Christopher Columbus*, 631. As noted earlier in this work, Indigenous peoples of high social rank wore small, quite small, ear and nose gold pieces pressed into the flesh.
17 Dunn & Kelley, The Diario, 299. Dunn & Kelley note that they are unsure where *Malegueta pepper* comes from. One idea is that it is native to the west coast of Africa, and the other notion is that it is a derivative of ginger; see page 299 for references.
18 The entire contingent of Spaniards was missing or dead when Columbus returned; subsequent discussions with Guacanagarí and other Indios described how "Carib" or other Taíno warriors from the interior arrived in large numbers and quickly dispatched the Europeans, usually when the Spaniards went forth looking for gold in small groups. The resulting Indio versions of how this happened varied but tended to regard Spanish abuse of natives as the cause of retribution. However, this claim came from Taíno peoples friendly to Columbus; Carib accounts, who purportedly remained responsible for the killing, do not exist. Two interesting versions of the episode can be seen by looking first at Ferdinand Columbus's account in his father's biography, *The Life of the Admiral Christopher Columbus*, Chapters 49–51 in Keen, 117–21. To balance the perspectives, see Morison, *Admiral of the Ocean Sea*, 424–9. Las Casas also wrote about the incident; see *Las Casas on Columbus, Repertorium Columbianum*, 95–96.

19 It is not clear if the statue would remain in the village square as a commemoration of Columbus's visit or a gift for the explorer to take with him to Spain, with the first option seeming more likely. It is ironic to consider, based on events now occurring in the United States, that the leader of the Indigenous peoples for this region of Hispaniola would build and erect a statue of Columbus.

20 Taken from Thacher, *Christopher Columbus*, 632. Bernaldez believed the number of men left equaled forty, 366–7. Much of this is taken from Las Casas's *Historia de las Indias*, which Thacher used as a source. The Columbus speech is not provided by Las Casas in his *Diario*. See Lardicci, *A Synoptic Edition*, LC 98, commentary, 660.

21 See Markham, page 145, for a complete list of men left behind.

22 See Delaney, *Columbus and the Quest for Jerusalem*, 268, note 11.

23 Las Casas, for his part, as a young man, recalled seeing the Indios in Seville, Spain, but he did not recall their number.

24 See the January 16, 1493, entry.

25 Eden, *The First Three Books*, 29. The intent here is to show that Columbus made good on his promise to return any of the Indigenous peoples that accompanied him to Spain. It is interesting to consider the comment about "died by change of the air," as this could refer to the climatic differences between the humid regions of the Caribbean and the dry climate of Spain or reference the impact of disease, such as influenza. Columbus returned to Spain in March, and all seven or ten Indios were alive when they stepped onto dry land. They remained in Spain until September from the port of Cádiz. The moderate summer and fall temperatures, along with dryer humidity, should not have affected the health of any Indigenous persons.

26 Martyr, *Decades de Orbe Novo, Volume 1*. Martyr, on at least two occasions, declared a friendship with Columbus that might impact his impartiality. However, Martyr maintained an honorable reputation for accuracy and honesty throughout his tenure in Spain. Martyr provided a few examples of words derived from Columbus's men working with the Indigenous guides and interpreters, including *tueri* (heaven), *boa* (house), *cauni* (gold), and *Taíno* (virtuous man), the term *Taíno* now accepted by archaeologists as the term describing the Indigenous peoples occupying much of Cuba and coastal Hispaniola. Martyr also wrote *Opus epistolarum*, a compilation of hundreds of letters he wrote to various Italian and Spanish persons of interest.

27 Ferdinand Columbus, *The Life of the Admiral*, 88–89.

28 Lardicci, *A Synoptic Edition*, *Historia*, LC 98, last section, 272. This estimate, 10–12 Indians, appears the best approximation. I would suggest the following: Three Lucayans and two Cubans on *Niña* with Columbus from Hispaniola, two Lucayans on *Pinta* with Pinzon, and four to be abducted on the

29 Thacher, *Christopher Columbus*, 636. Indigenous peoples could have used the fires for cooking purposes, or, as has been noted by some scholars, as signals to alert local populations of arriving visitors, welcome or otherwise.

30 Kettell, *Personal Narrative*, 187. Martín Pinzon's act of duplicity infuriated Columbus, and it seems improbable that the latter did not, at least privately, unleash his emotions of displeasure. On the other hand, he understood the reality of the situation where many of his crew served with Pinzon on previous voyages, lived in close proximity to him in Spain, knew his family, and trusted him. For more on the ongoing tensions between Columbus and Martín Pinzon, see Carrillo, *Oviedo on Columbus*, Repertorium Columbianum, 52.

31 During the subsequent *Pleitos* lawsuit, Manuel de Valdovinos in 1515 swore under oath that Martín Pinzón took leave of Columbus at the island of Guanahani [incorrect], and from the Indigenous guides onboard *Pinta* found his way to *Hayani* [Hispaniola] and once there found "much gold." Wadsworth, *Columbus and His First Voyage*, 102.

32 Kettell, *Personal Narrative*, 189. This is an interesting psychological development, as Columbus now reportedly trusted his Indio guides more than his two subordinate captains, yet precise language exchanges remained difficult between Columbus and his native interpreters, with no one to completely trust—only himself.

33 For more on the backgrounds and actions of the *hidalgos* during subsequent voyages, see Delaney, *Columbus and the Quest for Jerusalem*, 135–6, 142–3; Bergreen, Columbus: *The Four Voyages*, 258–9; Morison, Admiral of the *Ocean Sea*, 435–6.

34 Markham, *The Journal of Christopher Columbus*, 153.

35 Ibid., 154. Sea Cows or Manatees present a long and flattened face described on a large head, with two small eyes set wide apart. Columbus noted that he had seen some of these creatures before, off the coast of Africa.

36 Ibid. Markham writes this as a direct quote from Columbus and included by Las Casas.

37 Dunn & Kelley, *The Diario*, 321; Lardicci, *A Synoptic Edition*, DB103, sections 9–10, 114. Las Casas also wrote that Columbus wanted no trouble with Pinzón, preferring to return and report to the Spanish monarchs.

38 Thacher, *Christopher Columbus*, 640. Martín Pinzon explored the north shore of La Española while attempting to rejoin the expedition.

39 Ibid., 641. Also see Lardicci, A Synoptic Edition, DB 104, sections 10–14, 114. The Thacher and Lardicci translations are nearly identical.

40 Ibid. The key terms used here, "honour" and "favour," speak directly to Columbus's future social interactions with Indigenous peoples, although one does pause as the full context of this quote attempts to connect these good intentions only to islands where gold and spices abound.

41 The January 6 entry of the logbook stated that "one of those Indians whom the admiral had entrusted to him, along with the others whom he was carrying aboard his vessel." Lardicci, *A Synoptic Edition*, DB101, section 15, 111–2. The others, most likely, were the Indios Pinzón picked up in Hispaniola, leaving two or three from Guanahani or Cuba on the *Pinta*.

42 An extended reef runs along the north coast of this section of Hispaniola, jutting menacingly outward one-half mile.

43 *Bahia de Cafemba* (Puerto Plata).

44 Some of the places, usually capes, he named Belprado, Cabo del Angel, Punta del Hierro, Punta Seca, Cabo Redondo, Cabo Frances, and Cabo Tajado. Las Casas noted that Columbus claimed the areas visited today were "densely populated." How could he know this without going ashore? See Lardicci, *A Synoptic Edition*, DB105, sections 7–10, 114–5.

45 He must have referenced this astronomical date and event in published scientific tables that he carried on board. The search for a closed harbor would afford him the opportunity to observe the planetary conjunction.

46 Kettell, Personal Narrative, 197. Ferdinand Columbus, in *Historie*, adds that "everyone in those regions went about like that." Lardicci, FH 107, section 14.

47 Las Casas notes that the Indio terms are *caona* and *nozay*, with the latter term used by the Guanahani Indios.

48 Columbus had learned from previous conversations with Cuban Indios that the binding of prisoners was a common practice before loading up their captured men, women, and children for transport.

49 This becomes an important factor during the second voyage as Indio and Spanish relations deteriorate. Columbus is clearly attempting to differentiate between "good Indios and bad Indios," Taíno from Carib.

50 Lardicci, *A Synoptic Edition*, DB 108, section 8, 117.

51 Historians have questioned where this island existed geographically, with no agreement as to its suggested location. Las Casas notes that Columbus believed his

interpreters, that women exclusively inhabited Matinino, and the "ferocity of the inhabitants." Lardicci, *A Synoptic Edition*. It is recommended to read all of DB 107, pages 116–7, for the crisp description of these Indios and the first violent act of the voyage.

52 Dunn & Kelley, *The Diario*, 339. In this incident, Fuson translated, "I [Columbus] have decided to take them with me to Castile." The translation cannot verify the use of force. It is interesting that the account relates how eagerly these four Caribs gave "good accounts" of the regional geography, hinting that they offered the information freely, leading to the possibility that they may have agreed to go. The dialect differences between Carib and Arawak-speaking peoples (Taíno and Lucayan) are sufficient to afford considerable misunderstanding, possibly explaining this situation. Las Casas, writing in his *Historia*, pronounces this act of taking the four Caribs as "a most unworthy thing to do," pressing the issue further and damning the action as "a violation of natural law," something that cannot "be committed without great sin." Lardicci, *A Synoptic Edition*, LC 109, *Historia*, 284.

53 Recall that new archaeological evidence points to substantial Carib population enclaves in eastern Hispaniola at the time Columbus voyaged to the island. Regular Carib canoe voyaging between Hispaniola and Puerto Rico is assumed due to the already established geographic spread of migration routes and ongoing trade and cultural contact between the two islands. Significant language differences existed between Carib (Arawakan) dialects and those of the Lucayan and Taíno traditions, making it difficult to see how these four young Indigenous men were Carib when considering they "seemed to the admiral to give such a good account of all these islands." Lardicci, A Synoptic Edition, DB 109, sections 10–11, 118. While Columbus believed them to be Carib, they were more likely eastern Taínos.

54 This estimate is derived directly from the various logbook translations, and scholars ranged the numbers to be anywhere from six to ten—most scholars do not explain the breakdown of Indios between Columbus and Pinzón, preferring to mention only Columbus. There is no surviving account from Martín Pinzón after he left the fleet on November 21 and until he rejoined Columbus on January 6, 1493; we do know that Columbus sent one Indio to the *Pinta* earlier; see Lardicci, DB 58, sections 6–7, 72.

PART V

Return Voyage, Accolades, and a Promise of Colonization

Knowing his pre-voyage planning of the ocean's winds and currents, Columbus heads north, looking to pick up the easterly winds and currents that will bring him to the Azores and home to Spain. Storms ravage both ships, eventually separating them once again. On route, Columbus continues his log entries, detailing the difficulties of the return voyage. Once they reach one of the Azores Islands, Portuguese settlers distrust the Spaniards, capturing and imprisoning some of the crew. Columbus negotiates and gets his crew released, quickly leaving the islands and heading due east. The first European land sighted was Portugal, which Columbus did not desire, yet he desperately needed supplies.

Columbus meets with King João II, sends off a letter to the Spanish monarchs, and allows the Portuguese residents in and around Lisbon to see the several Indigenous peoples he had onboard. In short order, Columbus sails out of the Portuguese harbor, heading for Spain, and arrives exactly where he started at the port of Palos de la Frontera. News spread like wildfire throughout Castile and Aragon that the Genoese adventure completed a western voyage to the Indies. Flocking crowds accompanied Columbus and his entourage as they made their way to Barcelona, where Ferdinand and Isabella currently held court.

It was a day to remember—a day Columbus certainly never forgot. He had achieved the unthinkable, an act of courage many thought unachievable—a mid-Atlantic crossing of untold miles, weeks of endless ocean vistas as if a doorway had opened to a "new world." Excited masses of people packed in to see the explorer and the seven captured *Indios*. The Spanish monarchs honored their new *Admiral of the Ocean Sea*, allowing him to sit in their presence and

DOI: 10.4324/9781003464143-16

retell adventures. Columbus did not disappoint; he hyped his successes and downplayed his failures, promising tenfold in gold and spices—from what he laid out before the court. Believing everything he said, the monarchs agreed to quickly raise the funds, ships, and men for a return to the Indies. Columbus would come again to the Indies on a second voyage, much bigger than the first, portending a new overseas frontier, an economic–commercial empire monopolized by the Spanish monarchs, run by Columbus and the men that he would appoint. For the Lucayan and Taíno, and yes, the Carib peoples, the future would hold a more uncertain outcome.

11

THE VOYAGE HOME

January 16 to March 15

> I am not able to delay because of the danger with the leaking caravels.
> —Christopher Columbus, *Diario*, January 16, 1493

Columbus Knows the Route Home

January 16, Wednesday

In the early morning hours of the pre-dawn sky, both ships sailed east by north, hoping to find the island of Carib. Las Casas paraphrased Columbus's writing to include a comment concerning the belief that all Lucayans and Taínos remained at risk, these peoples fearing constant raiding threats from Caribs. One of the Carib "guests" on board the *Niña* eagerly served as a guide, pointing constantly eastward as the ships made progress, changing his mind after covering 64 miles; the course was changed to the SE.[1]

Then something happened on board both ships. Las Casas wrote: "The crews began to despond at leaving their course homeward, on account of the leaky state of the vessels." Now, Columbus felt pressure to change his plans of visiting Carib Island. Instead, he gave in and ordered a course change to the NE, sailing 48 miles that day. The Carib Indios gestured and explained that this course would bring them close to the island of *Matinino*. Again, Las Casas interjected that Columbus wanted to "carry five or six of the inhabitants to Spain." This further evidence shows that Columbus desired to take back Indigenous peoples from the represented unique geographic regions of his voyage: the Bahamas, Cuba, Hispaniola, Carib men, and now, Carib women.

Upon further consideration and more crew reports of leaky planks, Columbus determined his Carib guides did not know the correct location of either

DOI: 10.4324/9781003464143-17

Carib or *Matinino*. He took the opportunity to explain Carib cannibalistic practices, laying out a sequence of raiding innocent peoples transporting them to Carib or villages on Hispaniola, and preying especially on male children, "but keeping the females themselves."[2] Thinking *Carib* and *Matinino* lie to the SE, he did not want to reverse course; he remained on a course heading of E by N.

January 17, Thursday through January 21, Monday

These journal entries summarize sailing events and summarize the progress, in miles, made on this day. Interestingly, they reported pelicans landing on both ships and encountering large masses of seaweed, followed by large groups of small birds. However, this is the time span when Columbus reveals his route to return home. Knowing his approximate latitude and his preconceived understanding of the Atlantic Ocean gyre, he calculated a general N by E, then a NE heading. This maneuver angled the fleet closer to the high latitude of 38 degrees north, the latitude of the southern Azores islands of São Miguel and Santa Maria. However, Columbus still did not know if the local winds and currents that he sailed would remain strong and constant, like their eastern counterpart, the Portuguese Current. In his mind, the most important consideration centered on the hope that the higher in latitude he sailed, the stronger the easterly flowing winds and currents would prevail—completing the gyre. So far on the outward voyage, his gamble paid off, and the meteorological puzzle fell, more or less, in line with expectations. Yet, the return voyage held the most unknown calculations. For example, did the winds and currents slacken between his present location and 38 degrees north within a becalmed region as one sailed east? He knew from experience that this phenomenon occurred west of the eastern Atlantic islands of Porto Santo and Madeira; could it be the same for the western portion of the *Ocean Sea*?

January 22, Tuesday

Today proved interesting. Variable winds turned calm later in the day, and Columbus allowed his Indio passengers to swim. Why would he do this? If this event is true, and again, we must question this episode, then it does not make sense. If the purpose was to allow them to wash themselves, he could have had his crew haul up buckets of seawater. It is true that the Indios could not escape as the ships on this day were far from any land, but why would someone interested in enslaving his captives allow the freedom to jump overboard and carouse in the water? A more likely scenario supports that Columbus conceded to a request from the Indios, who were not, in any way, restrained on the Spanish ships. Columbus wanted the Indios to be in a good mental and physical state when he presented them to the Spanish monarchs. Las Casas described this episode as if it were something of a usual procedure, also noting the presence of tropical birds and seaweed.³

January 23, Wednesday

Pressing on, the two-ship fleet struggled to make progress as winds vacillated, then picked up after changing direction, frustrating Columbus. Furthermore, he noticed Martín Pinzón's *Pinta* making even less progress than *Niña*. Curious, he ordered *Niña* to take down sail and observed *Pinta*'s mizzen sail flapping wildly. Columbus blamed this on the leaning and creaking mast, remarking that Pinzón needlessly did not take advantage of the fine woods in the "Indies" to cut himself a new mast. Despite this drawback, the fleet slugged forward toward the northeast. Mileages stated included 84 miles from the night before and 30 miles in the daytime.

January 24, Thursday

The wind continued shifting, a little stronger, allowing the ships to make 44 miles on an ENE course.

January 25, Friday

From midnight to sunrise, progress accelerated, gaining 33 miles, then 28 miles before sunset. Running short of food, remaining supplies dwindled to stale bread and "ajes." Crew members aggressively and successfully hunted a tuna and shark, sharing the kill among crew and Indios on both ships.

January 26, Saturday

The fleet in the darkness of this morning traveled east by south, churning ahead and making a respectable 56 miles, then another 40 miles after sunrise, followed by another 24 miles in the afternoon.

January 27, Sunday

Another day of good weather allowed both ships to make five miles an hour for 13 hours from last night, steering NE and then ENE, completing another 33 miles from dawn until sunset.

January 28, Monday

Holding steady, Columbus drove the ships onward, covering 36 miles from midnight and another 20 miles from sunrise, all heading in the ENE direction.

He noted a gentle, "soft" breeze with many tropical birds appearing overhead and much seaweed throughout this area.

January 29, Tuesday

The distances sailed now added up, adding 39 more miles from midnight to dawn, with an additional 24 miles from dawn to dusk. Las Casas noted, "The air is mild, as in Castile in April, and the sea smooth. Many dories[4] leaped on board."

January 30, Wednesday

The wind held as expected, blowing the ships in an eastward direction. Columbus compensated slightly by ordering the steersman to hold an ENE course. Happy with 21 miles covered from midnight, Columbus simply noted in his journal that the ships scurried on covering almost 40 miles during the daytime.

January 31, Thursday

The wind picked up, allowing the ships to complete 65 miles from sunset the previous day, and then another 40 miles from sunrise to sunset. Columbus noted that more tropical birds followed the ships for much of the day.

February 1, Friday

East Northeast remained the course, with the ships covering 135 miles between night and day sailing. Pleased with the favorable strong wind, Columbus is quoted as ending the entry with "Thanks be to God."

February 2, Saturday

The strong wind continued pushing the little fleet homeward, 117 miles toward the ENE. Seaweed thickened.

February 3, Sunday

Las Casas transcribed the entry for today to declare that Columbus sailed an incredible 168 miles throughout the day and night. He attempted a latitude reading with an astrolabe or quadrant, but the ship pitched and rolled too much for an accurate reading (Figure 11.1).

Columbus knew he would need to steer his two-ship fleet north to pick up easterly flowing winds and currents. However, he was not sure at what latitude he should do this. Common sense suggested a latitude equal to that of the Azores Islands, a sea region he knew well.

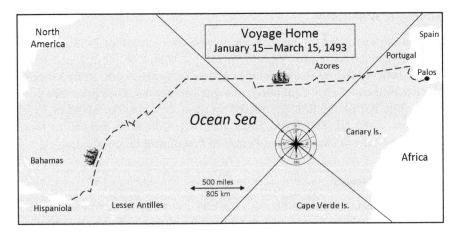

FIGURE 11.1 Voyage Home

A Change of Course for the Azores

February 4, Monday

Changing course, Columbus ordered a new heading toward the east by north. Under full sail, the fleet made 130 miles during the nighttime hours, a record. Then, thinking he was nearing the latitude of the Azores Islands, he altered course, sailing directly east, adding another 77 miles during the day for a total of 207 miles. If this entry is correct, Columbus now sensed his understanding of Atlantic geography was about to be challenged. He must have attempted a few latitude readings without the use of mechanical aids and estimated an approach zone for reaching the Azores. This is understandable in geographic terms, as he knew the miles sailed on his Palos to Canary Islands leg of the voyage, covering the distance in a relatively short time and noting latitudinal lines crossed. Using his knowledge of the Atlantic gyre, he knew, with some certainty, where he was and the likelihood of prevailing winds, allowing him to project an accurate course and plan for time to the Azores.

With cloudy skies above, intermittent rain, and increasingly colder air, Columbus began to feel confident that his pre-voyage planning was about to pay off.

February 5, Tuesday

Having reached the latitude he preferred, Columbus continued to steer the fleet due east, making a remarkable 11 miles an hour and covering 54 miles during the evening hours. Gaining even more speed, the fleet made 14 miles an hour, covering 110 miles. Petrel birds appeared, and floating sticks drifted by, increasing by the hour—a sign that land might be near.

February 6, Wednesday

The two ships continued a due-east course with a record run of 74 leagues (222 miles). In consultation with Vicente Pinzón on *Niña*, Columbus learned that Vicente believed the Azorean Island of Flores lay to the north, while Madeira Island was ahead if they continued on a due east course. The apprentice pilot on the ship, Bartolomè Roldan, offered his ideas, believing the island of Fayal bore toward the NE and Porto Santo due east. Columbus listened to these ideas, observed a thickening of seaweed, and continued his course east.

February 7, Thursday

The easterly course was maintained, making 130 miles at night and then 88 miles during daylight. Constantly conferring his charts, sighting the latitudes; and watching for floating debris, Columbus estimated the fleet now sat some 225 miles south of Flores Island in the Azores. Pedro Alonzo, the first pilot of *Niña*, disagreed, suggesting they were located on this day between the islands of Terceira and Santa Maria, near São Miguel. A different kind of seaweed appeared, reminding Columbus of similar sightings on previous trips to the Azores.

February 8, Friday

Not quite sure of his exact position, Columbus gambled today, first sailing east for a few hours, then abruptly changing course to the SE, then at sunrise, SSE covering 90 miles.

February 9, Saturday

Again, not sure of his position, Columbus jockeyed his headings, first continuing SSE, next NE, and finally to the east. The fleet went 51 miles.

February 10, Sunday

Sailing onward to the east, Columbus reached a distance of 130 miles through the night with a strong driving wind. With sunrise, strong sailing conditions continued, adding 99 more miles to their effort. Constant conversations between Columbus, Vicente Pinzón, and *Niña*'s pilots occurred, with everyone guessing their current location.[5] One opinion placed the fleet already to the east of Santa Maria Island, the last land of the Azores when sailing west to east. Columbus believed the island of Flores lay somewhere to the north, at not too great a distance, yet he feared his latitudinal position equaled that of North Africa. For his part, Columbus attempted to compare his current situation with the mileage calculations from the outgoing voyage. According to his figures, he sailed 263 leagues (789 miles) from the Canary Islands before sea-weed. Laying out that distance on one of his charts, he must have reversed the calculation using the daily distances covered once he accepted a due east course.

February 11, Monday

A constant, supportive wind, along with its accompanying current, drove the fleet onward to the east for 168 miles.

The Ocean Fury Unleashed

February 12, Tuesday

The fleet enjoyed the good weather until today. A high sea erupted, and the tempest continued throughout the day, sending the crew to shuttle down most sails and secure loose equipment. Columbus did not mention the status of his Indio passengers. With *Niña* and *Pinta* leaking, everyone worried the ships might not survive the storm, but Columbus felt the overall condition of the fleet was still good and the crew competent as the ships struggled for another 106 miles.

February 13, Wednesday

Today was crazy. The storm continued all night and into the early morning hours. Columbus lowered all sails and was still driven along, covering 52 miles. Then, with the morning sun, the wind dropped off. Columbus ordered some sails raised, and the fleet made another 55 miles. The waves reached new heights, slamming the sides of the ships and sending people and equipment flying first in one direction, then another. It is uncertain how the Indios responded; certainly, they had experienced stormy seas during canoe voyages in the Caribbean.

February 14, Thursday

Any hopeful thought for the storm to abate disappeared as the wind and rain not only continued but intensified, with waves coming in from "contrary direc-tions."[6] The ships, helpless to fight the wind and waves, became simple match-sticks in a vast, turbulent lake, sliding up one wave, then down another wave, pushing the fleet apart momentarily. The *Pinta* disappeared despite Columbus's attempt to keep candlelights at both ends of the ship.[7] The *Niña* went 54 miles during the night before sunrise. When the sun came up that day, the wind con-tinued. Now, the crew and Columbus himself became quite alarmed that *Niña*, stout as she is, might not survive. Calling the crew together, Columbus offered a divine suggestion; he called for a spiritual pilgrimage should they make it through the storm. Las Casas recalled the event from Columbus's writing in the following transcription.

> He ordered that a pilgrimage should be vowed to go to Santa Maria de Guadaloupe and a wax candle weighing five pounds should be carried and that everyone should vow that whoever was elected by chance should fulfill the pilgrimage. For this purpose, he ordered as many peas brought as there were persons on the ship [not counting Indios] and one was marked by a knife with the sign of the cross, and they were well shaken and placed in a cap.[8]

By sheer luck or otherwise, Columbus drew the pea with the marked cross. Further along and into this entry, other pleas and promises were made for additional pilgrimages to traditional Catholic sites.[9] A consensus arose that all surviving crew members would "go in their [penitential] shirts in procession to pray in a church under the invocation of Our Lady."[10] On top of this, many of the crew members prayed individually, making their own vows of penance and religious commitment.

As they finished this solemn event, the storm worsened, reaching "hurricane" levels of winds and waves. Columbus now took account of his situation. The low level of countering ballast now became apparent as the *Niña* pitched and rolled dangerously. At this point, Las Casas inserts comments that may not have been written by Columbus; the Dominican priest noted the deficiency of food, water, and wine due to Columbus's negligence to store up sufficiently, preferring instead to "husband his time in making discoveries, and expected to take in ballast at the isle of the women, which he [originally] intended to visit."[11] Lardicci translates this section, stating, "The remedy he [Columbus] undertook for this lack was—with seawater; and with this, they were relieved in their need."[12]

Now, Las Casas returns to the danger at hand, recounting how Columbus, knowing he might now perish, became "anxious" about losing the opportunity to return to Spain with his important discovery and redeem his ideas of a western route to the Indies. Las Casas claims that Columbus always worried that the smallest of challenges might interfere with his great Enterprise to the Indies, and to counter this apprehension, the explorer concluded his faith was insufficient. This rings somewhat true, as Columbus, a devout Catholic, sought divine intervention for each challenge encountered, interpreting the outcome as ascribed to God. To this end, Columbus doubted his commitment to his faith, and he was distressed that he might not see his sons again, "whom he had in school in Córdova."[13] As he struggled on, Columbus recounted the dangers of the outward voyage, the near mutiny, the possibility of missing islands or running out of food and water, and, of course, encountering a storm such as the one he now endured. For some of these life-threatening moments, Columbus's mind drifted to his sons and their situation in Spain, not wanting them to be orphans in a foreign land.

Columbus continued to struggle with his faith convictions as the hours of tempest continued; he wavered. Suddenly, Columbus decided to act; he was determined to write about his experiences in the Indies. This seems like an unbelievable task. How could Columbus write a full account of his voyage as the *Niña* rolled and bounced under the watery onslaught? This sounds like another case of Las Casas misreading the original text. Most scholars now agree that if Columbus did anything, he rolled up some of his notes from the daily journal entries, sealed them in a barrel using hot wax, and threw it overboard, the crew thinking it was some act of devotion.[14] Lardicci translated this section as "So that the monarchs might have news of his voyage if her were lost at sea—and so that they might learn… he took a parchment and wrote on it everything he could about all that he had found."[15] Ferdinand Columbus recorded that his father worried the barrel might not reach shore, so the explorer wrote another copy of his travels, placing it "high on the strencastle," with the hope that if the ship went down, the barrel would still float.[16]

The storm raged on, pushing little *Niña* forward under a now-tattered foresail. Constant downpours of rain soaked everyone and everything. One only wonders how the Indios reacted during this harrowing time.

The Azores Sighted and His Men Imprisoned

February 15, Friday

The wind abated, beginning early in the dark morning hours of this day. With a huge sigh of relief, Columbus set sail and ordered a course, ENE, about four miles an hour. At sunrise, land appeared. Straining their eyes, crew members on *Niña* suggested they were looking at the coastline of various islands, including Madeira, with one person suggesting they saw the "rock of Cintra near Lisbon."[17] Columbus, having visited various islands of the Azores previously, believed the sighting represented one of the southern Azores, such as Santa Maria, São Miguel, or Terceira.

February 16, Saturday

Sailing directly into the wind, Columbus hoped to reach the island, with the coastline slowly growing larger as the *Niña* tacked vigorously to gain miles. By sunrise, they had passed the island, so the pilots "hove to" and moved south. As they did this, they spotted another island (São Miguel) but continued to the first island sighted.

February 17, Sunday

Clouds enshrouded their view of the island, but crew members in the evening saw a light. Now everyone, including Columbus, could rest. This was the first land sighted in many weeks, and the entire crew, while trying to relax, remained anxious; for his part, Columbus had not slept for days, and Las Casas referenced how the explorer appeared "exceedingly lame from exposure to the cold, waves, and little food."

The land sighting appeared, then disappeared; late that night, something appeared again, with no one recognizing the coastline or being able to identify the island. They sailed around the island looking, as best they could, for a safe landing site.

February 18, Monday

In the early morning hours, when it was still dark, Columbus attempted to drop an anchor, but it became snagged, and then detached, resulting in a need to retire out to sea. Drifting to the north end of the island by sunrise, Columbus ordered another attempt at anchoring; this time, the anchor held. Excited, a shore party quickly surveyed the immediate area of the island, determining they had found the island of Santa Maria. Local Portuguese inhabitants helped Columbus locate a small nearby harbor. In discussions with these people, the crew told Columbus that the recent storm proved to be one of the most destructive seen in many years.

While the Portuguese in Santa Maria heard that Columbus had discovered the Indies, they were impressed, hardly believing the Spaniards had survived the storm.[18] At this point, Las Casas recounted how Columbus felt vindicated, with the explorer happily confirming that the plotting of the outgoing and return voyage routes proved correct. This, in a way, helps provide evidence that Columbus did understand the full extent and layout of the North Atlantic gyre and that he could rely on its winds and currents to take and return him successfully. Interestingly, Las Casas, in summarizing Columbus's abilities on this voyage, believed that the explorer excelled over his captains and pilots in determining the correct course to follow due to not falling asleep as much as his crew and misleading them on leagues sailed (Figure 11.2).[19]

Battered by a previous storm and in need of water and victuals, Columbus decided to approach the Azorean island of Santa Maria. He hoped that Portuguese officials on the island would honor his Spanish appointment and help his crew.

February 19, Tuesday

During the day, the crew gathered water and searched for wood. Just after sunset, three islanders stood offshore and asked to come onboard. The men brought with them "fowls and new bread with other things" as a gesture of

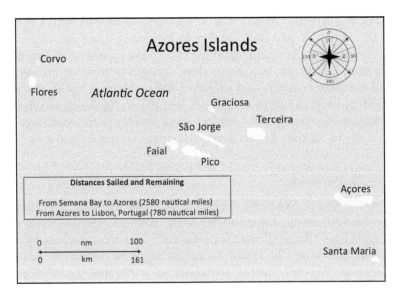

FIGURE 11.2   Azores Islands

help from Juan de Castañeda, administrative captain of Santa Maria. Interestingly, Castañeda, according to Las Casas' writings, claimed he "was well acquainted with the Admiral." This is evidence that Columbus did indeed visit the Azores islands prior to his 1492 voyage.[20]

Desiring to honor his pledge to visit a church dedicated to the Virgin Mary, Columbus sent half of the crew to a nearby "hermitage." In the middle of a short prayer service, armed Portuguese, led by Castañeda, appeared and arrested the Spaniards; some of the attackers approached on horseback. Later, Columbus worried when his men did not return. Hours went by, and Castañeda appeared with several other mounted soldiers and a group of accompanying armed men, demanding that Columbus come ashore. Columbus looked to see if any of his men stood among this group as prisoners, but none were visible. Sensing a trap, Columbus did not agree to come ashore; then, thinking quickly, the explorer invited Castañeda to come aboard *Niña*, but the Portuguese leader refused.

Now, Columbus shouted out, asking why he was being treated in such a hostile manner; he wanted to know what he or his men had done to offend the king of Portugal. Smartly, Columbus described, from personal experience, how King João always treated Spaniards and other foreigners, such as himself, with respect—free and safe as if residing in Lisbon. Castañeda hesitated, and Columbus continued to declare that he held certain letters of support from King Ferdinand and Queen Isabella and that he would present them on demand. Las Casas now stated that Columbus declared that he was now Admiral of the *Ocean Sea* and Viceroy of the Indies, referring to the *Santa Fe Capitulations*. However, this is incorrect. Columbus had not yet returned to Spain to receive official approval of his contract.[21]

Castañeda remained uncertain as to what should happen next. Columbus sensed this hesitation and declared that he had enough men on *Niña* to continue to Spain, where he would report the Portuguese actions taken against him and his men. Castañeda, needing to show strength in front of his men, discounted Columbus's letters and supposed titles and, once again, threatened action. More back-and-forth accusations brought no resolution to the armed confrontation. The entry ends with Columbus retiring to his anchorage position, needing to consider further action to retrieve his imprisoned crew.[22]

February 20, Wednesday

Knowing the Azores, Columbus decided to sail to the island of São Miguel, 52 miles to the NNE. Before raising anchor, work crews attempted to repair storm damage and have "the pipes filled with sea-water for ballast, because he was in a very bad harbor and he feared his cables might be cut, and it was so."[23] Remembering that the Azores contained no well-protected harbors, the self-proclaimed admiral felt frustrated and contained. Columbus looked over his remaining crew and discovered that only three of the men "who knew the sea," referencing their lack of maritime experience during storms.

February 21, Thursday

Again, the sea rose and the winds blew, making passage northward difficult. Everyone onboard tried their best to hold against the sea, but Columbus could see a growing danger, despite the fact that surging crests of waves came from only one direction. Fearing further danger, he decided to return to Santa Maria, wait out the storm, and negotiate for the release of his men, still imprisoned.

Las Casas noted this day how Columbus recounted good weather during his entire stay in the Indies, claiming, "For one hour alone he did not see the sea so that he could not navigate well."[24] Adding an interesting side note next, Las Casas wrote that Columbus, in his previous experiences in this sea region, never encountered rough seas once sailing "past" (west) of the Azores. This indicates that Columbus was somewhat acquainted with the immediate western waters west of the Azores. We do know that he sailed in here at least once when returning from his voyage to West Africa and possibly during episodes as a Genoese trading representative in Portugal.[25]

Las Casas connotes a comparison with the temperate areas that Columbus just experienced in the Indies with traditional religious convictions, thinking that Paradise (the Garden of Eden) must be located somewhere in the Indies "because it [Paradise] is a most temperate place."[26] Columbus melded his logic between weather and religion to assume that the lands he just discovered were, in fact, the "end of the Orient."[27]

February 22, Friday

Back in the same harbor he left yesterday, Columbus pondered what to do next. Suddenly, a man shouted from nearby rocks, asking for them to stay put and that representatives of the Portuguese were coming to discuss certain matters. Not long after this, a boat did appear with several men. One of them was a priest, and another was an *escribano* (notary). The group of men asked for security, and Columbus assured them of their safe return to the coast. With this promise, the Portuguese boarded *Niña*. Being late in the day, the visitors spent the night onboard. Then, the first thing the next morning, the leader of these men demanded Columbus show them his royal contract from Ferdinand and Isabella. At first, Columbus felt that his words were sufficient, but he relented and allowed the group to inspect the voyage authorization papers.[28] Satisfied, the men left and reported to Castañeda the genuine nature of Columbus's venture. Castañeda now changed his mind on holding the rest of *Niña*'s crew; he let them go. Columbus, through one of his returned crew members, learned that had Castañeda been able to capture Columbus, they would all have been held as prisoners indefinitely (Figure 11.3).[29]

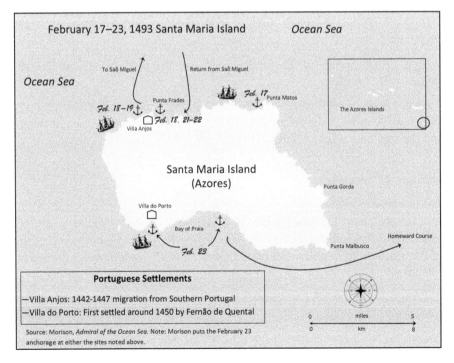

FIGURE 11.3 Santa Maria Island

Not welcome at first, Portuguese officials finally released some of Columbus's crew that had been detained. Columbus, not sure where Martin Pinzón was with the *Pinta*, was now determined to head home quickly.

A Run for Mainland

February 23, Saturday

Happy to leave Santa Maria, Columbus raised anchor and skirted the island in search of wood and stone for ballast. However, a change in wind direction tempted Columbus to set sail immediately for Spain.

February 24, Sunday

From midnight until sunrise, *Niña* covered 46 miles, then another 66 miles during daylight hours.

February 25, Monday

Going five miles per hour from midnight to sunrise, Columbus made 48 miles then made another 48 miles after sunrise to sunset. Interestingly, an eagle landed on *Niña*.

February 26, Tuesday

They continued to sail east, but this day a strong wind scurried them along, allowing 100 miles to be covered. Then the wind dropped to almost nothing, and the ship only went 24 miles.

February 27, Wednesday

Sensing he was getting close to Portugal and Spain, Columbus despaired as another onslaught of "great waves and high sea" ensued. Using one of the many charts at his disposal, he calculated Cape St. Vincent (southwestern tip of Portugal) to lie 75 miles distant, with the island of Madeira more distant at 240 miles.[30]

February 28, Thursday

While winds pounded *Niña* from all sides, Columbus tried to steer east, instead veering south and southeast, then dramatically changing to the NE and finally ENE—no mileage figures were recorded this day.[31]

March 1, Friday

From midnight to sunrise, he went 36 miles to the NE. During daylight hours, *Niña* plowed ahead 69 miles in the same direction.

March 2, Saturday

Pre-dawn winds remained strong, allowing Columbus to close out 84 miles and another 60 miles during the daylight hours.

March 3, Sunday

Just when he thought the worst was over, a hurricane struck, splitting his sails after sailing 60 miles. Columbus worried, as he had done before. With good mileage in the last few days, he was on track, sailing east toward home. Why did a last storm need to strike? Yet Las Casas described how Columbus remained nervous but confident that God would not let him fail at this point in the voyage. To reveal their religious commitment, the crew followed Columbus's lead, promising another pilgrimage, this one to Santa Maria de la Cinta in Huelva, Spain. Again, Columbus drew the responsibility to complete this bold penitence. The crew, for their part, promised to fast the first Saturday after returning safely, eating only bread and drinking only water.

Later in the day, some crew members believed they had sighted the Portuguese coast; word spread, and excitement grew.

Portugal Sighted and Contact with King João

March 4, Monday

A short weather reprieve dissipated when another gale blew forth that carried into the dark morning hours. Little *Niña* bounced like a cork in a violent bathtub, first dragged upward, then thrust dangerously downward as each new wave crest rolled along. As daylight approached, someone spotted land. This brought little happiness to Columbus and the crew; they had to worry about surviving the last vestiges of the current storm, close but not home. Acting conservatively, Columbus knew he could not approach the shore in his present situation, so he held to a location several miles off the coast, praying for salvation. Las Casas now related the outcome, writing, "Thus God guarded them until day, and he [Columbus] says that it was with infinite labour and fright."[32]

Amazingly, Columbus's prayers were answered. As the sun rose in the eastern sky, everyone clearly recognized the shoreline, having sighted the Rock of Cintra, near the entrance to Lisbon's harbor. With few options left, Columbus decoded reluctantly to dock *Niña* into King João's capital city, undoubtedly wondering how he would be welcomed. Columbus knew João was aware of his expedition and the somewhat disagreeable terms on which the former had left Portugal. Anchoring for a short time at the town of Cascaes, near the entrance to the harbor, several skiff boats came out to greet the Spaniards. These Portuguese visitors, shocked to see *Niña* survive the hurricane, described how they too had prayed for the crew. Later, Columbus moved his ship deeper into the harbor, anchoring at Rastelo, near Lisbon. Here, these residents stood in wonderment that Columbus remained alive, believing "there was never a winter with so many tempests, and that twenty-five ships had been lost in Flanders and others there that had not been able to go out four months."[33]

Columbus now penned a letter to João, then residing in Vale de Paraíso, 27 miles distant, asking for permission to anchor formally in Lisbon and to seek repairs and supplies as needed to complete his voyage. Interestingly, Las Casas wrote that one purpose of the letter was to inform the Portuguese king that Columbus was returning from the Indies, not Guinea (West Africa).[34]

March 5, Tuesday

An interesting visitor approached the *Niña* this morning; it was the explorer Bartolome Dias, whose ship lay in anchor at Rastelo, not far from Columbus. Diaz came alongside and demanded that Columbus accompany him and give "an account of himself to the stewards of the king."[35] Columbus did not hesitate to reply, stating that he represented the king and queen of Castile and was under no compulsion to provide information to foreign dignitaries. Digging in further, Columbus declared his determination to stay onboard and use force, if necessary, to stop anyone from boarding his ship.

Dias then asked for a designated crew member to give an account; again, Columbus demurred, providing a bit of historical context that Spanish ship captains never surrendered themselves or their men to foreign inspection or questioning unless agreed to by that captain. Dias relented and next asked to see Columbus's royal authorization papers. Columbus agreed, and Dias's captain, Alvaro Dama, climbed *Niña*'s rope ladder and stood on deck as he was officially received with a drum beating, a trumpet blast, and pipes. Impressed after reviewing the royal Spanish papers, Dama returned to Dias; the latter was then satisfied with Columbus's intentions. Dias made haste to the royal palace in Lisbon to inform his king.

March 6, Wednesday

A huge throng of Lisbon citizens crowded the docks to get a glimpse of *Niña* and its crew. By now, gossip and stories ran through the streets with some truth and some exaggeration that Columbus had indeed discovered a western route to the Indies. Rumors that Columbus brought Indigenous peoples with him made the tense atmosphere highly anticipatory—everyone wanted to get a look at humans from the antipodes (the other side of the world).[36] Conjectures by these onlookers about the Indio's appearance must have ranged from a variety of background knowledge from previous book readings (such as Marco Polo) and stories absorbed about the color and personalities of these people from *otro mundo*, another world. Ferdinand Columbus noted that many Portuguese citizens crowded onto the deck of the *Niña* "to see the Indians that he brought back," crowding around the caravel personal rowboats maneuvered to get close to Columbus's ship.[37]

Las Casas wrote that Columbus today thanked God for this widespread interest by the Portuguese, believing his strong faith was beginning to grant him the accolades and attention he deserved. Nothing else is written into the journal account for this day, discussing if any Portuguese dignitaries visited Columbus or if he, or any of his crew, disembarked and interacted with the townspeople. Surely, the Indios remained in clear view on the deck, to the delight of curious onlookers close enough to view them clearly.

March 7, Thursday

Today, royal representatives did appear. In fact, Las Casas described a "multitude of people" including knights and two "stewards" from João's court. Praise rang high as all visitors marveled at the Indios and the stories told by Columbus and the crew. Everyone praised Columbus for his unique contribution of opening a route to the Indies that would surely initiate "the advancement of the Christian religion."[38]

March 8, Friday

One, Martín de Noronha, representing João, came aboard carrying an official letter from the king, requesting a royal appearance.[39] A few seconds of hesitation, again due to his previous "doings" with João, dissolved as he understood his current desperate situation, needing water and supplies; he replied that he would be happy to meet and talk with the king and his officers.

Columbus reluctantly left his ship. Royal knights accompanied Columbus to the town of Sacanben (Sacavém), 6 miles north of Lisbon, on the shore of the *Mar da Palha*. It is not clear if anyone, Indios or crew, from *Niña* accompanied Columbus. The entry states that the king ordered his stewards to see to the needs of the crew, free of charge, and to grant anything Columbus needed on his journey. A close reading of this entry assumes that no Indios or crew members accompanied Columbus, although surely João would have wanted to see the Indios and some trade items obtained in the Indies.[40]

March 9, Saturday

Moving slowly through a rainstorm, Columbus and his Portuguese escorts journeyed 30 miles north to the town of Val do Paraíso. King João received the explorer "in the most honorable manner," providing a royal audience with many Portuguese nobles and ladies. In anticipation of hearing about the Genoese travels, the king insisted that Columbus be seated, a rare honor, so as to be more comfortable giving a full account of the expedition. Not long into Columbus's retelling of his voyage, João referenced the Treaty of Alcáçovas (1479) prohibiting Spanish exploration south of the Canary Islands. The king insisted that lands south of 28 degrees north latitude that resided in the *Ocean Sea* remained reserved for Portuguese exploration and exploitation, especially the concept of monopolistic trade zones and corridors.

Columbus, pretending not to understand the legal guidelines set out in the treaty, entreated João that his only instructions from the Spanish monarchs excluded his maneuvering of ships to the east, including no contact with Guinea (West Africa) or points south along the African coast. Of particular note, Columbus was told not to put into the port of São Jorge de Mina, the center of Portuguese trade on the Guinea coast. Columbus relaxed somewhat when João appeared to believe the explorer's words, with the latter stating that Columbus need not provide geographic proof of territories explored.

It is not certain how much information Columbus divulged concerning his 4-month voyage about the geography, physical, and social knowledge of the Indies. The Portuguese king surely pressed Columbus on the Indios and the items he discovered and now possessed, and those would shortly be presented to the Spanish monarchs. Yet, nothing further is included in this entry except that Columbus sat through a party given by a Portuguese person, the Prior of Crato; this was a traditional title bestowed on a noble as head of the Order of Knights (Hospitaller) in Portugal.[41]

March 10, Sunday

Today, Columbus and João attended mass and then met again in a conference setting. The Portuguese king may have been pressed to probe more deeply Columbus's exact route through the Indies, stressing the need to know the latitude sightings, size, and type of islands and/or mainland visited, contacts made with kings or dignitaries of these locations, and notification of any official trade agreements or political treaties enjoined. The entry speaks of João first assuring Columbus that provisions are available and assistance in any repairs or maritime supplies needed to make *Niña* seaworthy. Then the king's tone turned serious and suspicious. Columbus immediately became defensive, repeating his official charge of exploration, including geographic limitations and commercial contacts. While the meeting ended on a positive note, however, doubt about Columbus's actual route and contacts remained a mystery, suggesting the Spanish explorer was withholding important information concerning possible geographic violations of the Treaty of Alcáçovas.

Las Casas, in *Historia*, describes this session between Columbus and João as tense, even accusatory, with the Portuguese king showing "great anger and ill-feeling," believing that the lands Columbus visited "were within the seas, and the boundaries, of his [João's] dominions in Guinea." This interpretation reveals how João may have been encouraged by his advisors to change his "happy" feelings about Columbus's success and seek detailed information as to the location of the islands visited.[42]

March 11, Monday

This morning Columbus briefly met João, and the explorer thanked the king for his hospitality and offer of help. The Portuguese king presented Columbus with a sealed letter and asked that it be given to Ferdinand and Isabella upon his return to Spain. After a dinner sponsored by Don Martín de Noronha, knights Columbus were escorted in the direction of St. Anthony's monastery near Villafranca. Here, the queen, Eleanor of Viseu,[43] lived and she desired to see and talk with Columbus. Columbus reportedly paid his respects, kissing her hand and recounting some general stories of his adventures; this was an official visit in the presence of other nobles. He left the monastery and traveled into the night to the town of Llandra.

March 12, Tuesday

Leaving early the next day and anxious to get to his ship, Columbus was intercepted before starting out with a message from King João offering a carriage and housing for an overland trip back to Spain. Columbus declined immediately and hurried on toward Lisbon, arriving after dark.

Palos and Home

March 13, Wednesday

With the sun just rising, Columbus set sail for Spain, expertly using a northwest wind to move *Niña* on a course for home despite heavy seas.

March 14, Thursday

This morning, gratefully, everyone sighted Cape St. Vincent, signaling a change in course east to Spain.

March 15, Friday

Arriving off the coast of Saltes,[44] they were now in Spanish waters and excited about reaching home. By noon, Palos appeared, and Columbus anchored *Niña*. The voyage, arguably the most impactful voyage in history, was over.

The journal ends with Columbus learning that the Spanish monarchs now resided in Barcelona, and he wished to proceed there via ship as soon as possible. In summarizing his voyage, Columbus expressed his thanks for divine guidance and help through all he had seen and witnessed.

> For although he believed without scruple that the Almighty created all things good, that all is excellent but sin, and that nothing can be done with his permission, "yet" he observes, "it has been most wonderfully manifested in the circumstances of this voyage, as may be seen by considering the many signal miracles performed throughout, as well as the fortune which has attended myself, who passed so long a time at the court of your Highnesses, and met with opposition of so many of the principal persons of your household, who were all against me, and ridiculed my project. The wish I hope in Our Lord will prove the greatest honour to Christianity ever accomplished with such ease."[45]

Notes

1 Lardicci uses the plural "some of those four." Lardicci, *A Synoptic Edition*, DB110, section 5, 119. Markham agrees; see *The Journal of Christopher Columbus*, 165. Dunn & Kelley also agree, *The Diario*, 343.
2 Kettell, Personal Narrative, 205. This practice ensured female concubines for the purposes of slavery and procreation.
3 Lardicci quotes, "The Indians went swimming," DB113, section 5, 121; Dunn & Kelley agree, 351. Markham noted, "The Indians swam about," 168.
4 Dory fish are found in both the Pacific and Atlantic, typically brightly colored or diversely patterned with a thin body and high dorsal fin. Several species are known for their jumping abilities.
5 Ferdinand Columbus reported that "in the pilots' opinions," the ships remained well south of the Azores, while Columbus believed they were 150 leagues [450 miles] from the islands. Lardicci, *A Synoptic Edition*, *Historie*, FH 118, all, 167.
6 Thacher, *Christopher Columbus*, 654. "Contrary" waves are a result of two distinct wind systems pressing into an ocean area at perpendicular angles. This can also occur when wave swells from different sea regions travel a long distance, entering the impact area of swells emanating from a different direction, sometimes referred to as a "cross sea."
7 This is the last reference to Martín Pinzon and the fate of the *Pinta*. Most scholars believe that Pinzon arrived in Palos shortly after Columbus had arrived at his home port and left for Seville. Delaney, *Columbus and the Quest for Jerusalem*, 271. See Lardicci for the original Spanish transcription, part of which is "Desapareçió la Pinta," see P119, 667, for full English translation, 125, full Spanish original, 414–5, 667.
8 Thacher, *Christopher Columbus*, 655.
9 Two sites that were mentioned were Santa Maria de Loreto and Santa Clara de Moguer.

10 Ibid.
11 Kettel, *Personal Narrative*, 217–9. Kettell notes that Columbus was fortunate to have sailed late in the year. If the voyage had commenced a few months prior to October, the outgoing voyage may have encountered a severe hurricane.
12 Lardicci, *A Synoptic Edition*, DB 120, section 32, 126.
13 Ibid., section 39, 127. Diego and Ferdinand were serving as pages for the Spanish monarchs.
14 A moderate position on this event might entertain the idea that Columbus began writing his summary of voyage encounters before the storm began, anticipating the need to summarize his journal entries.
15 Lardicci, *A Synoptic Edition*, DB 120, sections 40–43, 127. This attempt to write in all he could certainly appeared to be a difficult task amid the physical and mental stress of the situation on February 15. The wooden barrel containing Columbus's frantic recounting of his voyage is lost to history.
16 Ibid., *A Synoptic Edition*, *Historie*, FH 120, section 45b, 169.
17 Dunn & Kelley, *The Diario*, 373.
18 The Portuguese inhabitants appeared quite surprised to hear that Columbus survived the storm, "considering the very violent storm that had lasted for fifteen days." Lardicci, *A Synoptic Edition Historie*, FH 123, all, 169.
19 Lardicci, *A Synoptic Edition*, *Historia*, LC 123, 292.
20 All the translations use the term "very well" for describing Castañeda's knowledge of Columbus, but none venture to explain how this might be a fact.
21 Of course, Las Casas wrote this entry decades after the event and assumed the reader knew that Columbus was subsequently confirmed with the titles he requested. For Ferdinand Columbus's take on this confrontation, see Lardicci, *A Synoptic Edition*, *Historie*, FH 124, all, 169–71. At one point, Columbus tells the Portuguese captain that any overt action might cause an incident that would start a war between Spain and Portugal.
22 Ferdinand Columbus noted that at this point, his father had "three sailors and a few cabin boys" to sail the ship, the others being the Indios and men with no maritime skills. Ibid., FH 125, section d. 171. The *Historie* also has a section where Columbus, frustrated with the deliberations, threatens to come ashore and capture scores of Portuguese settlers as prisoners and bring them back to Spain. This is either a massive exaggeration by Ferdinand, as his father at the time only had a handful of men, or a revelation about Columbus's short temper. FH 124, section 32.
23 Thacher, *Christopher Columbus*, 660. Thacher's translation here for "pipes" refers to the empty sea casks that *Niña* carried.
24 Ibid., 661.
25 This could have been directly from Lisbon, but more likely when returning from Porto Santo or Madeira Island to Lisbon.
26 Dunn & Kelley, *The Diario*, 383. The term *temperate* may have alluded to climate, meaning a place where there are neither extremely cold nor hot environments. It is interesting to consider that Columbus visited the Caribbean in the late fall and winter months, a time of relatively mild humidity, despite a temperature warmer than that of Spain at the same time of year.
27 Ibid. It is quite unusual for the weather in the Caribbean during the months extending from mid-October through February to remain temperate and storm-free. Columbus, of course, sees this as a true sign of God's power to withhold adversity, allowing him to "discover" the Indies and experience the environment of Paradise.
28 See Lardicci, *A Synoptic Edition*, *Historia*, LC 127, 296–97.
29 Some of Columbus's men reported that, as prisoners, they heard that an official order from the Portuguese king decreed that if Columbus attempted to anchor in any of the Azores Islands, he and his men were to be captured. Ibid., FH 127, section 12.

30 See Lardicci, *A Synoptic Edition, Historia,* LC 133, 298 for Las Casas's dramatic account of this storm.
31 According to Giorgio Bazzurro of the Istituto Idrografico Della Marina, Columbus had mastered the ability to track the variations in wind direction, enabling him to make constant course deviations. *L'Eredita dei Colombo,* 54.
32 Thacher, *Christopher Columbus,* 663.
33 Ibid.
34 While Columbus had visited the west coast of Africa, as a Portuguese and later as a Spanish resident, João was well aware that Columbus had sailed the previous October from Palos, the Portuguese king having sent a small fleet to intercept Columbus from dropping below the agreed upon latitude of the Canary Islands. See Lardicci, *A Synoptic Edition, Historia,* LC 133, 299.
35 Kettell, *Personal Narrative,* 232. The stewards normally included members of King João's advisors.
36 Pietro Martire de Anghiera, also known as Peter Martyr, reported upon Columbus's safe arrival in Spain, "There has returned from the Western Antipodes one Christopher Columbus of Liguria." The use of the term *antipodes* suggested a new, unknown land, not Asia. The debate over what Columbus discovered by Ferdinand and Isabella and other contemporary Europeans, especially Florentine Simone del Verde's view that the discovery was "the other world opposite our own," see Fernández-Armesto, *Columbus,* 106–10.
37 Lardicci, *A Synoptic Edition, Historie,* FH 135, all, 173–5. Ferdinand adds that the crowds of curious onlookers remained high throughout the day.
38 Ibid., 234. It is interesting that no mention was made of the commercial possibilities that Columbus's actions now make possible. This is especially significant as the Portuguese always placed financial gain high on their list of desired goals in their decades-long search for a route to the Indies. Certainly, many of the knights and other persons of Portuguese notoriety that came aboard this day desired to see the wealth items stored below deck, yet there is no mention of gold, spices, or any other trade item that Columbus had on board.
39 Columbus was related by marriage to the Noronha family; his wife's niece was Isabel de Noronha, married into Portugal's powerful Bragança extended family.
40 Las Casas also does not mention if anyone accompanied Columbus on his short trip to see the Portuguese king. Lardicci, *A Synoptic Edition, Historia,* LC 136, 300. Later in LC 138, he noted that João appeared "happy" to hear about the people and geography of the Indies as told by Columbus, believing that Columbus only had to travel a short distance and it would have been easy to bring along "some Indians," 301.
41 At this time, Diogo Fernandes de Almeida (son of Lopo de Almeida, Count of Abrantes) most likely held this position.
42 See Lardicci, *A Synoptic Edition, Historia,* LC 139, 302.
43 Queen Eleanor, fearing an ongoing epidemic in and around the city of Lisbon, fled to the convent, seeking shelter and isolation. Before this event, her relations at that time proved challenging, and she no longer shared the same residence as the king. Caraci, personal communication, July 22, 2023. For more information on Columbus's visit with Eleanor, see Caraci, *Three Days in May,* 796.
44 The Saltes is a small island. An accompanying inlet allows ships to enter the port near the towns of Palos de la Frontera and Huelva, Spain.
45 Kettell, *Personal Narrative,* 237–8. Las Casas related a slightly different version of Columbus's last entry; see Lardicci, *A Synoptic Edition, Historia,* LC 140, 303.

12

SPANISH ACCOLADES AND FUTURE PLANS

> This voyage has miraculously proven this to be so, as can be learned from this writing, by the remarkable miracles which have occurred during the voyage…
>
> —Christopher Columbus, *Diario*, March 15, 1493

Triumphant Return at the Palace of Ferdinand and Isabella

Excited local townspeople ran through the streets of Palos to welcome home their men; elated, the crew returned. Many of them gave up hope months prior, thinking all of them were lost in the depths of the great *Ocean Sea*. Incredibly, no one had died. It is assumed that this means Indios as well as Spaniards. Columbus went further, describing no sickness except for minor complaints. For him, God had thrown a mantle of divine protection over everything he did and everywhere he journeyed; Columbus genuinely believed his voyage to be predestined as a success. However, as he stepped onto the pier at Palos, he may have glanced west, worried about his 39 men garrisoned on Hispaniola, knowing he needed to report his findings to Ferdinand and Isabella and seek permission for another expedition.[1] He also wondered, or worried, about Martín Pinzón's location and the men of the *Pinta*. As he scanned the small harbor, he saw no sign of Pinzón. The people of Palos shook their heads in the negative when asked about the *Pinta*, then shrugged their shoulders, admitting ignorance of the ship's whereabouts. Ironically, Pinzón arrived hours later. Despondent beyond belief, he did not beat Columbus to Palos and did not wait for *Pinta* to dock; using the skiff, he went ashore and straight to this home. He died there inexplicably, a few days later.[2]

DOI: 10.4324/9781003464143-18

For now, Columbus kept the Guanahani and Cuban Indios on board *Niña*, along with his cargo of gold trinkets and samples of plants and spices he believed validated his visit to the Indies. Immediately, news spread to the nearby towns of Moguer and Huelva and beyond. Curious Spaniards pressed Columbus for a view of his Indian guests and at some point, in the first few days, the Guanahani and Cuban peoples remained onboard *Niña* for a few days, then were possibly housed at the La Ràbida monastery.[3]

Columbus secured humble housing for himself, and he quickly dispatched the two letters written previously.[4] Learning that the monarchs now resided, hundreds of miles distant, at the palace in Barcelona, he wanted them to know he had safely returned, ready to present himself, his Indio guests, his traded goods, and his collection of plant specimens. Morison noted how *bodas y banquestes* (parties and banquets) abounded in and around Palos during the following days.[5] For 2 weeks, Columbus waited for a letter giving him permission to come before the Spanish majesties. He spent time with Fray Juan Pérez at the nearby monastery of La Ràbida. Local citizens, excited about Columbus's triumph, carried him in a celebration procession to the monastery. In this interim period, it is suggested by Margarita Zamora that Columbus worked with Juan Pérez to review, conceptualize, and write the letters mentioned previously to members of the Spanish court announcing his discovery.[6] One letter went to Luis de Santángel (Keeper of the Royal Privy Purse) and the other to Rafaél (Gabriel) Sánchez (General Treasurer), both serving as finance advisors. Santángel had persuaded Isabella, at the last minute, to recall Columbus and sponsor the voyage. Zamora, after studying both letters, conceded, "The versions differ from each other," noting that both letters appeared to be written after the March 4 letter that Columbus wrote to the Spanish monarchs, then declaring that the "February letter was at least substantially revised, if not completely composed, by someone other than Columbus."[7] This is another piece of evidence that suggests Columbus's Castilian writing skill left something to be desired, as was suggested earlier concerning the *Diario* transcription by Las Casas; if true, one must challenge historical written documents attributed to Columbus.[8]

On the journey to Barcelona, Columbus stopped in Seville, reconnecting with Genoese merchant friends and city officials. Everyone wanted to meet him and glance at the people from the Indies. Morison believes there were ten Indigenous peoples in attendance, of whom there is no account of their actions in Spain.[9] The city erupted upon seeing the Indios, pushing to get closer to the strangers and shouting their astonishment and curiosity. Francisco Gómara later wrote of the festive, excited atmosphere, believing Columbus's feat to be the "greatest event since the creation of the world, save the incarnation and death of Him who created it."[10]

While in Seville, Columbus received his official request to present himself and his native guests to Ferdinand and Isabella; it is unknown if any of his crew received a royal invitation. After 2 weeks, he set out on the overland journey to Barcelona, accompanied by his six to seven Indigenous interpreters. Little is known about this journey; surely, he met hundreds, if not thousands, of curious Spaniards, wanting to see the explorer, wish him well, and gaze upon the people from the Indies, for up to this point, word spread that Columbus had indeed sailed to and returned from numerous islands near faraway Asia. The dusty, long trip went by quickly, with Columbus and company arriving in Barcelona on Palm Sunday, March 31, 1493.

There is some suggestion that crowds awaited his grand entrance through the city gates and followed him to the Monastery of Las Cuevas, while Morison noted that the Indios resided in a lodging house near the "Gates of Imágines." During these first few days in Barcelona, a young Bartolome de las Casas caught a glimpse of both Columbus and the Indigenous peoples he would one day so valiantly defend.[11] No doubt, Columbus reveled in the moment. Religious events crowded the daily calendar, encouraging the explorer to remind himself that his mission's success derived from divine guidance and support. Throngs of visitors entered the city, now motivated to attend sacred services, revel in the pomp of religious processions, and seek out Columbus—word of the explorer's arrival now circulated miles from the city. Columbus socialized with many of his previous friends, some Genoese, and financial backers, such as the Duke of Medinaceli. As far as we know, the Indios did not participate in any of these gatherings.

After the Easter celebration, Ferdinand and Isabella sent an official letter requesting his immediate presence. Morison detailed the salutation opening words, "Don Cristóbal Colón, their Admiral of the *Ocean Sea*, Viceroy and Governor of the islands he hath discovered in the Indies."[12] One can imagine the look and reaction of Christopher Columbus upon reading these words. He was vindicated, and rightfully rewarded for his long years of conceptualizing, and implementing the first Enterprise to the Indies. Of course, the ultimate recognition was about to come.

Columbus's son, Ferdinand, a page in the Court, recorded the events that followed.

> All the court and the city came out to meet him, and the Catholic Sovereigns received him in public, seated with all majesty and grandeur on rich thrones under a canopy of cloth of gold. When he came forward to kiss their hands, they rose from their thrones as if he were a great lord and would not let him kiss their hands but made him sit down beside them. After he [Columbus] had given them a brief account of the voyage and its success, they permitted him retire to his lodgings, in which he went accompanied by the whole court.[13]

Imagining this scene in Barcelona helps a reader understand the mental metamorphosis now occurring in Columbus's mind. From a Genoese boy raised with limited life opportunities to a young trading representative helping Genoese merchants in the Mediterranean and later along the Atlantic coastline get rich, he was now an instant national hero and soon a European hero. He had served God and his sovereigns; the first phase of his mission stood completed. His status continued for the next few days as he appeared in public with Ferdinand and Isabella. Again, Ferdinand, Columbus's son, recalled the special, almost unique, favoritism now heaped on his father.

> So much did their Highnesses favor and honor him that when the King rode about Barcelona, the Admiral rode on one side of him...never before had anyone been permitted to ride with the King, save his very close kinsman, the Infante.[14]

In considering Columbus's relations with the Indigenous peoples he encountered, Bergreen admitted, "His initial contacts with the inhabitants of the New World were tentative and respectful, even heartening."[15] This is an interesting, if not wholly accurate, estimation. From Columbus's point of view, his actions, tentative momentarily, resulted in a consistent firm desire to continue the search for Cipangu and Cathay, hoping to secure permission to establish a trading post, accompanying town, and future political connections. Respectful, he was, although, as you have read, many scholars believe he purposely kidnapped Indigenous peoples and forced them to serve as guides and interpreters. This book has presented evidence that at least some of the Indios agreed to go to Spain after the *Santa Maria* was shipwrecked.

One of the few eyewitness observers present at the welcoming ceremony, Fernández de Oviedo, recalled that momentous day and remembered watching the Indio visitors, claiming, "I saw the admiral Chripstól [sic] Colom there with the first Indians." He was careful to suggest the Indigenous peoples "went or were taken."[16] This remark suggests his own doubt as to whether the "Indians" went willingly or were forced.

One prime source to view Columbus's immediate post-voyage views on Spanish/Indio relations is his letter to Luis de Santangel, written as he arrived in Spain. He wrote, "They firmly believe that I, with my ships and men, came from heaven, and with this idea I have been received everywhere, since they lost their fear of me."[17] Columbus does suggest that he did take his interpreters and guides by force, as he wrote, "*Yo entendia harto de otros Indios que ya tenia tomados...* (I heard from other Indians I had already taken...)."[18] Columbus goes on to explain in the letter that

> I had to win their love, and to induce them to become Christians, and to love and serve their Highnesses and the whole Castilian nation, and help to get for us things they have in abundance, which are necessary to us.[19]

Of course, all of this is what Columbus wanted to believe as he tried to convey positive interactions between the Indigenous peoples and his actions, with the hope of securing a second voyage.

Plans for Voyage Two

Historians usually name the time from April 15, a Saturday, as his date of arrival in Barcelona. No one is sure when he stepped before the Spanish monarchs for official recognition, but the happy occasion occurred sometime before April 20, 1493, at the palace in Barcelona (Placa de Rei). Meanwhile, news of Columbus's successful voyage began to spread, first throughout Spain, then slowly and intermittently throughout Europe. Columbus's previous benefactor, Luis de la Cerda, the Duke of Medinaceli, heard of the return while Columbus remained in Lisbon and wrote a letter announcing the explorer's return.[20] During Columbus's overland trek from Seville across Spain, copies of the explorer's letter to Luis de Santángel arrived in Italy, were translated, and printed in substantial numbers. Within months, copies of the Latin version found their way to capitals and major cities as far north as Antwerp. The name Cristóbol Colón became known in all major political courts in Europe. For Old World Europe, Columbus was not the discoverer of a New World, but the discoverer of a western route to the Indies.

Yet not everyone appeared impressed with Columbus's accomplishments. Recall the royal councils and committees of learned men who insisted that the feat could not be done. Add to this group members of the Spanish Royal Court who believed Columbus had not discovered Asia but only a few isolated islands located in the vast *Ocean Sea*. Cecil Jane studied letters written at this time and remarked, "Their [royal officials'] original skepticism had been justified and that the discovery of a few islands and an unknown race of savages was an inadequate return for the investment made..."[21]

In a discussion with Ferdinand and Isabella, Columbus encouraged the monarchs to ask Pope Alexander VI to officially recognize the geographic claims he made, declaring each island he visited a Spanish sovereign territory. Isabella thought this was a good idea and did not hesitate to send out such a request to Rome immediately. Ferdinand, too, did not question the right of Spain to claim newly discovered lands despite the fact that significant human habitation already existed in the region. One might think that the Spanish monarchs might question their right to claim islands that might be under the dominion of East Asian political leaders, including the fabled island kingdom of Cipangu. Or one might chastise Columbus and the monarchs for thinking they possessed some justified basis for claiming islands currently inhabited. Were there any limitations to these geographic claims? What about the existing Indigenous populations?

From this lack of political sensitivity, the basis for limited colonization in the Americas sprouted. The rationale for this philosophy lies in Columbus's understanding that he detected no signs of outside political domination, except for the frequent mention of Carib raiders. At first, Columbus may have thought the Caribs represented armed enforcers of an Asian ruler, but that thought evaporated as the voyage moved to Hispaniola. He was certain that local *caciques* held all the political power. This is an interesting point to ponder. Had the Caribbean islands been under the yoke of a Central or South American kingdom, such as a vibrant, strong Mayan kingdom, plans for the second voyage may have worked out differently.

Considering the 15th-century philosophical mindset of Spanish nobility, indeed, the country at large, flush with victory over their former Moorish overlords, it is easy to arrive at a religiously ordained right of cultural superiority for any heathen (non-Christian) kingdoms encountered. Pope Alexander, himself born and raised in Aragon, held the same cultural-political philosophical foundation. In fact, Alexander did not hesitate, and during the first week of May 1493, his protective declaration, known as the *Eximiae devotionis* gave Spain the religious authority to claim the newly "discovered" lands. In consultation with Columbus, the Spanish monarchs wanted a definitive geographic line recognized as the operative boundary for Spain's new claim to the Indies. Columbus advised Isabella and Ferdinand that he had previously assigned his Atlantic frontier line 100 leagues west of the Azores, extending that line north to Icelandic waters and south to waters west of the Cape Verde Islands, conceptualizing this as the boundary between the Old World and the unknown *Ocean Sea*.

Without conferring with their usual committees of experts, the Spanish monarchs agreed and asked the pope to issue a special bull or declaration ascribing Spanish dominion on all lands, islands, and Asian mainlands that have or will be "discovered" as within the new geo-political realm of Spain. The pope again agreed and sent forth his *Inter caetera*; it was official, despite immediate objections from King João II in Portugal. However, the pope's decrees extended only to Catholic kingdoms; later, Protestant monarchs and entrepreneurs openly challenged Spain's New World hegemony.

At the end of May, King Ferdinand and Queen Isabella agreed to officially recognize Columbus's rights and privileges put forth in the *Santa Fe Capitulations*.[22] Thus, on the 28th day of that month, Fernan Alvarez, Court Secretary, and Pedro Gutierrez, Chancellor, witnessed the signing of the document (*Royal Authorization of the Second Voyage*) along with Alonso Perez, holder of the official seal.[23] Columbus, elated, read through the document carefully to ensure all points of concern appeared addressed. One area that may have caused him hesitation referred to the granting of administrative privileges over all the "islands and mainlands" he had discovered. The problem here was that the Admiral, his new official title, did not discover any Asian mainland.[24] Columbus, at this point in the adventure, did not fully understand or remotely grasp the geographic extent of his first voyage experiences. He had mapped the route and noted approximate latitude and longitude positions (based on Ptolemy's hours west of the Canaries), but the true geographic location of his discoveries within the "Indies" remained unresolved.

The official authorization contains a turning point, a major shift in overseas policy, leaving as a secondary goal the setting up and maintaining one or more trading posts. The key deviation is hinted at in the following statement: It reads,

> And in order that in the country of the said islands and mainland which have been in from hence forth shall be discovered in the said *Ocean Sea*, in the said region of the Indies, *the settlers of the whole of it* [emphasis by author] may be better governed, we give you such power and authority that you may be able as our viceroy and governor, to exercise by yourself and by your lieutenants…The civil and criminal jurisdiction high and low and that you shall be able to remove or withdraw the set officers…[25]

Notice that "islands" is plural, while "mainland" is singular. In the *Santa Fe Capitulations*, the designation was plural for both geographical areas. Columbus seemingly convinced his Spanish sponsors that his island resided close to only one mainland, Cathay. The more telling phrase is "the settlers of the whole of it," revealing an intent not for a small, isolated trading post with an accompanying town, and for acquiring permission from local warlords or chiefs for trading rights. No, this was for the "whole of it," suggesting commercial and political control over all regions of said islands—colonialism. The question then is raised: Did Columbus suggest this policy change, or did royal advisors insist on complete hegemony? Or, did the idea originate with the king or queen? Let's probe a little deeper before tackling this question.

For this second voyage, King Ferdinand and Queen Isabella ordered Columbus to collect "fees" to support the administrative staff to run the various governmental offices supporting Columbus, now officially known as Viceroy and Governor. Fees mean taxes, monetary or otherwise established by the office holders. This meant any "settler" coming to the Indies became obliged to pay the determined fee, and the frequency and duration of these fees were determined by island officials, including Columbus. Was every European subject planning on joining the second voyage aware of this requirement? The answer is maybe, as it was a long-standing political reality in Spanish-held territories of the Iberian Peninsula prior to and after the *Reconquista* that all subjects paid at least two levels of taxes, local and kingdom-wide. However, since this was a new land far from the homeland, that expectation may not have been considered. But it will be later enforced by Columbus, and he would use his authority to "tax" the Indigenous peoples, whom he now considered "subjects" of Ferdinand and Isabella—with him acting as royal proxy and enforcer.[26]

There is an ongoing debate by historians and archaeologists as to the concept of pre-Columbian tribute among the Lucayan, Taíno, and Carib cultures. Moscoso (2003) and Siegel (1997) put forth the idea of a village collective tribute, where members of the tribe were dominated by the wishes of the local and regional caciques, including the production quotas and redistribution of goods.[27] Opposing that view are arguments espousing a voluntary "potlach-type" tradition of sharing food and other products as needed and at designated times (Cassá, 1992).[28] Keegan noted that in excavations at the En Bas Saline site (Hispaniola), the proposed location for Guacanagarí's village, one researcher reported specific areas reserved for the production of food and other products; this led Keegan to theorize that the cacique's household "was involved in the same activities as other households in the village."[29] Archaeologist Peter Siegel maintained that the Taíno polities ascribed traditional social distinctions and the idea of tribute from lower to higher levels of status. He further suggests that the location of regional caciques' villages tended to be near the geographical center of their territory, allowing for more efficient control of their hinterlands, that is, social and commercial tribute and compliance with given political directives.[30]

Ferdinand and Isabella specifically delineated the categories of subjects. "We command all residents, sojourners, and other persons who are or shall be in the said islands in mainland, to obey you as our Lord admiral of the said ocean."[31] This statement seemingly refers to "residents" as the legitimate (approved) persons granted permission to sail to the Indies. The next term "sojourners" implies those persons unauthorized by crown-appointed officials (e.g., Columbus), hinting at possible non-Spanish encroachment, particularly Portuguese. Again, the last term in this series of nouns refers back to the phrase "[the] whole of it," with a nondescript phrase, "other persons," which apparently directly implicates Indigenous peoples inhabiting geographic areas claimed by Columbus. Excepting this royal interpretation and command, Columbus, as we have seen, preemptively declared, as noted in his logbook, believed that "taking possession" of one island gave Spain the legal (royal) authority to claim all islands in the region—might makes right.

Knowing the above, Ferdinand and Isabella agreed to allow Columbus an avenue to extract unwanted "settlers" and others from the said islands and return them to Spain. No doubt the intent here centered on unruly, criminal, or otherwise undesirable new Spanish immigrants, but Columbus may have read this as a command—and to include non-Spanish Europeans and Indigenous peoples. This section reads,

> It is our will and pleasure that if you should consider it expedient for our service and the execution of our justice that any persons who so ever you are and shall be in the said in these in mainland should depart from them and should not enter nor be in them, and should come and present themselves before us, you may command it in our name, and make them depart there from.[32]

Going a step further, the Spanish monarchs demanded, "We command such persons by these presents [this declaration] to do so at once." Analyzing the above official instructions reveals the administrative pressure Columbus felt as he prepared for the second voyage. From commanding 90-plus men on the first voyage to having responsibility for over 1,000 people, including a wide swath of the Spanish social order, this must have played heavily on the Admiral. He had commanded men and ships before, but only in a limited capacity. Now, his all-encompassing power, defied all previous Spanish authorizations; he would have the power, but would he exercise that power effectively to please his royal patrons? More importantly, would he exercise his new-found authority fairly with the Spanish colonizers and Indigenous peoples? Before the voyage began, Columbus may have had second thoughts about demanding administrative control of his new island domains. If he did not act strongly, law and order might cause chaos; if he acted too strongly, especially since he was a Genoese foreigner commanding mostly Spaniards, mutiny, leading to a full-scale revolt, might occur. Recall what happened on the first voyage: mutinous threats from the crew and Martín Pinzón's act of maritime disobedience, setting off on his own search for gold. Logic called for a balanced approach that met the needs of everyone involved and that best served his ends; we will see him attempt this strategy as problems erupt on Hispaniola early on during his landing on the large island in late 1493. Did Columbus already know, before he sailed for the second voyage, that his mind and thoughts lie on the *Ocean Sea*, not on land? Later events proved that idea as true; he would attempt to delegate municipal and judicial authority on Hispaniola to others, such as his brother, Bartholomew, while he searched for the mainlands he missed on the first voyage— Cathay, or any part of the Asian shoreline; these destinations served as his ultimate maritime goal.

Columbus queried the Spanish monarchs before going to Barcelona in a memorandum, providing his insights for the next voyage and subsequent actions. He suggested no more than 2,000 persons be allowed on Hispaniola, declaring only those "residents who take up residence there" be authorized to secure gold mining rights. Presumably, this suggestion was intended to cut down on nomadic gold mining in unauthorized areas—this became a major problem almost immediately. To further control the entire settlement process, Columbus argued that only he, or his designated official, issue binding gold licenses, ensuring the proper amounts of gold taxes go to Ferdinand and Isabella.[33]

In comparing his suggestions for settlement with the already-described royal declarations, we see some differences enacted. On the issue of an overall settlement, it is not clear if Columbus premeditatively wanted to initiate colonization of the entire island, opting instead to initiate the original 1492 agreement of discovery and setting up a few trading posts, accompanying towns, and gold mining sites. In truth, Columbus wanted to limit European settlement on Hispaniola to "three or four towns" located "in the most suitable places" and that the "colonists go there be distributed among the said places and towns."[34] This socio-political setup limits geographic expansion and does not necessarily end in full island colonization. Under this system, the Indigenous peoples retain most or all their existing village sites and cacique-established kingdoms. Evidence for this statement is again given with Columbus declaring, "None of the colonists be permitted to go and gather gold save with the license of the governor (Columbus)."[35] Of course, limiting colonization as we now know it, especially in potential gold-bearing areas, was nearly impossible based on historical precedent in European economic-political expansion, yet this concept may have still functioned for Columbus. Under this government system, he only controlled the seaports (trading posts), a few accompanying towns, and access to gold mines.

Reading Columbus's letter to Luis de Santángel reveals key opinions about the explorer's vision for Spain's future involvement in his discoveries. First, Columbus makes it clear that he recognizes that he holds "them [islands] for their Highnesses, who can command them as absolutely as the kingdoms of Castile." The point is clear: King Ferdinand and Queen Isabella will determine the extent of future participation or colonization between Spain and the new discoveries, not Columbus. Second, Columbus suggests that participation might include working the gold mines, all of which are located in the interior region of Hispaniola (Cibao), the idea being that Spaniards would work these minds, not the native population. Third, and most importantly, Columbus notes that his discovery will allow "all commerce with the mainland on this side [Spain] or with that of the great Khan [Cathay], on the other, with which there would be great trade and profit." The presumption here suggests the development of trading posts, operating from large seaports, gathering commercial commodities through mining, and trading with Indigenous populations. As supporting evidence that Columbus favored, at least for the time being, limited settlement or colonization of the Caribbean, he declared that he had already begun the process by taking "possession of a large town, which I have named the City of Navidad."[36]

However, as we have seen earlier in the declarations of intention for the second voyage, Ferdinand and Isabella commanded Columbus to "take the whole of it," clearly meaning the entire island of Hispaniola and, by assumption, all the islands in the Caribbean region. Advisors to the Spanish monarchs may have urged their sponsors to include this statement so that there would be no misunderstanding—the crown retained authority over future involvement, that is, colonization, of any lands discovered by Columbus. This regional hegemony also deprived Portugal, or any other European or Asian power, of claiming political rights. For all practical purposes, Columbus's options for developing his version of colonialism dropped low on his priority list, posing a dilemma, a dilemma exacerbated by actions soon to be encountered on his second voyage. Whatever friendly thoughts and plans he currently held and now considered for the Indigenous peoples he encountered on the first voyage, Columbus needed to place the wishes of the Spanish monarchs as his top priority, everything else was secondary. Columbus had been too good a salesperson; royal expectations, the expectations of the Spanish people, and the notoriety he now possessed in other European political states raised greater expectations of him and the second voyage; the pressure of leadership loomed as his greatest future challenge.

Furthermore, the Spanish monarchs demanded harsh punishments for any colonists found violating rules or expectations laid out in their royal instructions decreed on May 29, 1493. In discussing the ensuing Indigenous and Spanish relationship, they stated, "And if some person or persons should maltreat the said Indians in any manner whatsoever, the said Admiral [Columbus], Viceroy and Governor of Their Highnesses, shall punish them severely."[37] Following this, Ferdinand and Isabella spelled out 18 specific points of concern, mostly relating to the collection of gold and other trade items, managing provisions and weapons, the appointment of lower officials, how to barter, the conversion of the Indians, and who may or may not come back to Spain. This may appear as a helpful political foundation for Columbus to establish his authority; it may also be seen, more appropriately, as a political straitjacket, restricting and regulating his interpretations and his soon-to-be administrative responsibilities— one wonders how Columbus reacted to the royal instructions.

Meanwhile, Columbus, enthralled with his newfound fame and anxious to return to Hispaniola and relieve the 39 crew members now stranded at La Navidad, left Barcelona for Seville, dreaming, and no doubt worrying, of things to come.

Notes

1 Bergreen, *The Four Voyages*, 119. Columbus placed his responsibility to rescue his men as a top priority.
2 Many stories have surfaced as to what happened to Martín Pinzon after arriving in Palos. See Morison, 352; for more on the life and death of Pinzon, see "Pinzón, Martín Alonso," by William Lemos, pp. 546–8. Bergreen notes that syphilis may have been the captain's undoing. *The Four Voyages*, 113.
3 Morison, *Admiral of the Ocean Sea*, 353–4.
4 There remains a debate as to the date of writing and dispatching of the two letters. Some scholars believe the letters were sent from Lisbon, but this seems counterintuitive as Columbus would not want to risk the letter falling into the hands of Portuguese officials. See de Lollis, "Notes on the Documents," cxxxi–cxxxix.
5 Morison, *Admiral of the Ocean Sea*, 353.
6 Jane disagrees with this and suggests that Columbus utilized an *amanuensis* [copyist] to write the February 15 letters, meant for members of the royal court, while attending to his shipboard duties much earlier. See pp. cxxxiv–cxxxv. Jane agrees with historian Caesar De Lollis that the letters were written between January 17 and February 11 during good sailing weather on the return trip. The postscript dated February 15, according to Jane, may have been the date it was sealed on board the *Niña*.

7 Zamora, *Reading Columbus*, 6. Zamora's findings are backed by Demetrio Ramos Pérez, who believes, as does Zamora, that the letters were edited and rewritten to serve as the official royal announcement of the discovery. To read Zamora's full analysis of the letters, see UC Press E-Books Collection, 1982–2004, online. https://publishing.cdlib.org/ucpressebooks/

8 Ilaria Caraci has written extensively on this subject, including the *postils* or notes attributed to Columbus, written in the margins of books he read and later referenced.

9 Delaney and this author believe that number to be six. See Delaney, 118. Recall that the Cuban peoples on board did not reboard the *Niña* on Hispaniola. Las Casas recorded seven Indigenous persons, while Andrés Bernáldez wrote that ten Indians came back with Columbus, four were left in Seville, and six journeyed to Barcelona with the Admiral. Las Casas added that some had died on the voyage to Spain, which is not recorded in any other document. Columbus, of course, maintained that no one died, Spanish or Indigenous, during the first voyage. See Davidson, *Columbus: Now and Then*, 285; and Bernáldez, 369. Gonzalo Fernández de Oviedo believed only six had arrived in Barcelona. See *Oviedo on Columbus, Reportorium Columbianum*, 53. One of the earliest accounts describing Indigenous peoples brought to Spain is by Sebastian Munster, a 15th-century German cartographer and cosmographer. Writing in his popular *Cosmographia* (1544), Munster simply stated, "But he, [Columbus], hoisting up his sails, directed his voyage toward Spain, bringing with him ten men of the said Island [Indies], so that in the end that they might learn the Spanish tongue, which they might easily do, because all the words of their language may well be written with our letters." Eden, *The First Three Books*, 29. Peter Martyr also noted that Columbus returned with "ten of their men." *Selections from Peter Martyr*, 48. One eyewitness on the voyage, Manuel de Valdovinos, serving on the *Niña*, stated in 1515, as part of his testimony in the Columbian lawsuits, that "they had taken interpreters from the Indians there" without designating a number. Wadsworth, *Columbus and His First Voyage*, 102.

10 Taken from Delaney, 112. Gómara recalled this event in his 1552 publication *Historia General de las Indias*.

11 Morison, *Admiral of the Ocean Sea*, 354. There is little detailed information about these glory days as Columbus prepared for his official visit. Morison conjectured about the monastery stay for Columbus, basing this on previous evidence that the monastery is where Columbus had stayed on special visits. But that should be challenged, noting that fame which Columbus carried into the city, knowing that it was not uncommon for visiting high-ranking officials to obtain temporary residence somewhere on or near the *Placa del Rei* (palace), a short distance from the waterfront.

12 Ibid.

13 Keen, *The Life of the Admiral*, 101.

14 Ibid. The Infante was Ferdinand's and Isabella's second child and their only son, Juan (John). He was born in June of 1478 and was 13 years old at the time.

15 Bergreen, *Columbus: The Four Voyages*, 114. The overriding geographic and social aspects of the encounter caused Columbus confusion and suggested a reason for being, as Bergreen wrote, "tentative." He expected more highly advanced civilizations technologically, and his ports of call were, one at the same time, what he expected Asia to look like, yet not aligning with his prior reading experiences from Marco Polo's book.

16 Davidson, *Columbus Then and Now*, 285. Original source: Fernández de Oviedo, *Historia general*, chapter VII, 28.

17 Historic Documents, English translation of *The Letter of Columbus to Luis De SantAngel Announcing his Discovery*, USHistory.org

18 Rosenbach, *The Spanish Letter*, 11.

19 Wadsworth, 84. Wadsworth's translation here is quite generous toward Columbus's intentions for understanding how the Indigenous peoples projected the amazement of the newcomers to one in which they wanted to serve the Spanish monarchs and become Christians.

20 The Duke of Medinaceli wrote the letter on March 19, 1493, from his home at Cogolludo to the Grand Cardinal of Spain, describing how he helped encourage Columbus to solicit the queen for royal backing and that Columbus had "now made good discovering such wonderful things." He went on to exhort the Spanish majesties, "I beg you to believe what he says [concerning all he discovered]." Morison, *Journals and Documents*, 20. The entire letter is included in this source.

21 Jane, *The Four Voyages of Columbus*, xiv. Jane further explained that a recent heavy tax decree impacted everyone in Spain, along with the realization that monies were in short supply. Recognizing this financial situation, persons within the court questioned the monarch's decision to finance a second voyage.

22 Later, Columbus's son, Diego Colón, began a lawsuit to re-establish the full terms of the capitulations; a 1511 verdict only partially satisfied both parties, and the lawsuit continued. During various testimonies, some of the crew from the first voyage provided evidence for the court to consider. The complete Spanish version of the lawsuit proceedings, known as the *Pleitos colombinos*, can be read and studied. See *Colección de documentos ineditos*. Selected portions of the transcript are published in English; see Wadsworth, *Columbus and His First Voyage*.

23 Keen, *Life of the Admiral*, 108. To read the full authorization of the contract, see Keen, 105–8.

24 On his second voyage, Columbus, frustrated in his attempt to find the Asian mainland, cruised along the Cuban coastline, believing it to be a peninsula of Asia, later forcing his men to swear to that effect.

25 Ibid., 106. The monarchs prescribed their new area of political hegemony as "commences by a limit or line, which we have caused to be marked, and which passes from the Azores to the Cape Verde Islands, from north to south, from pole to pole, in such a manner that all which is beyond of the said line to the westward is ours and belongs to us."

26 At first, Columbus ordered the taxing [tribute of gold] of Indigenous peoples as a limited geographic policy, inclusive of peoples living in the Cibao, or mountainous regions of central Hispaniola. Those living in coastal areas could substitute cotton "spun or woven." See Bergreen, *The Four Voyages*, 203–4. The western provinces of Hispaniola also agreed to pay tribute with cotton or food. See Keegan, "Pacification, Conquest, and Genocide," 533.

27 Also supporting the concept of intervillage pre-Columbian tribute is May Jane Berman, who believes tribute is one of many social, commercial, and political commodities exchanged, with other items being trading, raiding, and gift-giving. "Good as Gold," Chapter 7, *Islands at the* Crossroads, 104.

28 Taken from Keegan, *Taino Indian Myths*, 117. For original sources, see the bibliography.

29 Ibid. This assumption provides support for both theories of top-down authoritative control of tribute and a community-wide sharing of produced resources. Keegan referred to Ensor (2003); see bibliography. Berman and Gnivecki reported an archaeological determination that none of the indigenous pottery unearthed at this site displayed Spanish influence in shape or decoration, "Colonial Encounters," 33. Other sites throughout Hispaniola, especially those further inland, reveal European influence.

30 "Competitive Polities and Territorial Expansion in the Caribbean," 210–11.

31 Ibid., 107. These royal commands are declarative in the sense that Columbus was now expected to follow them explicitly as the governing authority of the Indies.

This may explain his perceived harsh treatment of the Spanish settlers that came with him on the second voyage. Any indication that he refused to uphold these commands would be deemed a break in the bilateral contract and grounds for dismissal. During the second voyage, scores of unhappy "settlers" returned to Spain, castigating Columbus for being too harsh and unbending in his stated rules and requirements. The Spanish monarchs listened to these complaints but continued to support Columbus as he followed the instructions laid out in the pre-second voyage documents.

32 Ibid.

33 Ibid., 284. In effect, Columbus now faced a "no-win" scenario. Even the friendships he had established with Indigenous caciques would be tested.

34 Morison, "Columbus's Memorial to the Sovereigns," *Journals and Other Documents*, 200.

35 Ibid. Columbus goes further in suggesting to the Spanish monarchs to allow him to limit the number of colonists to 2,000 and to only permit sojourns into possible gold fields at certain times of the year, encouraging the implementation of harsh penalties for violators, 201. All of this points to a carefully controlled, population-limited, economically based bartering system of shoreline contact with brief gold hunting trips into the interior, not full-scale island settlement and political domination.

36 All the quotes in this paragraph come from Wadsworth, *Columbus and His First Voyage*, 85. The interpretations of Wadsworth's translations are my beliefs.

37 Morison, "Instructions of Sovereigns for Second Voyage," *Journals and Other Documents*, 204. This explains why Columbus, during the second and third voyages, disciplined a good number of Spaniards on Hispaniola, in some cases hanging several individuals. This also explains why, despite the complaints of returning colonists to Spain, the monarchs continually supported Columbus in the Admiral's ongoing, incessant problem of suppressing wayward colonists from taking advantage of Indians, mistreating them, and running off looking for gold. It is always interesting to see scholars so quickly blame Columbus for poor administrative abilities under the social, economic, and political situation found in early Hispaniola.

AFTERWORD

Despite the writings of various authors concerning Columbus's belief that he had discovered lands near Cathay, India, Cipangu, and the "Indies," the new Admiral of the *Ocean Sea* had doubts. Contradictory evidence exists that points in two directions. On October 13, 1492, his second day in San Salvador, Columbus appeared anxious that he had only "discovered" a small island somewhere in the western *Ocean Sea*. He said, "But in order not to waste time, I wish to go and see if I can strike the island of Chipangu [Cipangu]."[1] The overall geographic size and location of the islands apparently led him to believe these lands resided on the eastern fringe of the Asian continent. Cuba, for example, displayed a southeast-to-northwest orientation, tricking Columbus into thinking the island's landmass matched the cartographic depictions shown on Martín Behaim's map and subsequent globe for the Mangi (southern China) peninsula. This map, being the most contemporary to 1492, may have influenced Columbus's thinking.[2] Yet his summarizing letter, written later as the voyage neared its end, reveals that he thought Juana (Cuba) was mainland Asia. He expected to see "great cities or towns." Excited, Columbus followed the coast only to find, "At the end of many leagues, seeing that there was no change and that the coast was bearing me northwards..."[3] Thinking the great cities and towns might be located inland, he sent two men in search of a "king or great cities." After three days, the men returned with reports of seeing only "small hamlets and people without number, but nothing of importance." Frustrated, Columbus queried his Guanahani interpreters, who disclosed the sad truth that Cuba was an island.

Anticipation ran high as Columbus crossed over to Hispaniola, but the same small, empty villages greeted his arrival at each new north shore location.

DOI: 10.4324/9781003464143-19

Surely, he thought, Hispaniola must contain the sophisticated, advanced civilization of Cipangu. However, as Ilaria Caraci reminds us, "Their [Indigenous peoples] nudity, the simplicity of their customs, and the lack of precious ornaments did not agree with what Columbus knew of the sovereign [Great Khan of China] and his kingdom."[4] Working through the logic of what he saw and experienced, Columbus then believed these islands resided on the periphery of the east coast of Mangi and Cathay. However, he saw no direct evidence of Asian overlords, only the mention of the term *Cami* [Khan] while on the island of Cuba. He imagined the Cuban Indios at war with the forces of the Khan, offering a perplexing conundrum: If he helped the Cuban Indios, he risked contracting good relations with Asian rulers. If he did not, the local caciques might reject his friendly overtures.

While Columbus's dual personality sought new, unexplored experiences, that is, new geographic data, he constantly desired a rapid synthesis, a grounding confirmation, reconciling preconceived ideas and theorems, hoping for a believable, practical explanation. This mind-functioning process derived from his years of searching out new markets as a Genoese trading representative; success for him was the only option. When the geographic and social observed facts did not agree with his pre-voyage understanding, Columbus's confusion worried him, but he knew he could not report that confusion to Ferdinand and Isabella. To this end, Columbus wrote in his letter to the Spanish sovereigns that "Española [Hispaniola] is a marvel." He wrote of the vast mountains, broad, fertile plains, rich soil, and "rivers, many and great, and of good water, the majority of which contain gold."[5] The Admiral then praised the Indigenous peoples as "very marvelously timorous," in which they "all go naked, men and women," possessing "no iron or steel or weapons." These facts contradicted the colorful descriptions of Marco Polo—descriptions he came to expect on Cipangu or any mainland destination. But the contradiction did not matter, desiring instead to illuminate the geographic and social realities of the first voyage.

Columbus's mistake then, his precursor to disaster for the second voyage, evolved from a contrived twisting of the "discovery" facts of the first voyage to appear appealing to his royal sponsors. The Admiral, in essence, arranged for his own failure. However, as has been shown earlier, Ferdinand and Isabella, despite reservations from royal advisors, decided to accept Columbus at his word and go all out in extrapolating the geographic facts, economic possibilities (gold mining), and the social and demographic situation on the islands, which led inevitably in the direction of comprehensive colonization.

The interim events between the first and second voyages changed the path of history for Spain and the Indigenous peoples of the islands Columbus visited, and eventually all islands of the Caribbean and mainland regions of North and South America. Columbus's initial goal at the beginning and at the end of the first voyage was neither hemispheric hegemonic control nor enslavement of Indigenous peoples. His goal centered on obtaining gold, spices, and any other commodities to inflate Spain's financial position, enabling domestic economic stability and funding military expeditions to push back Muslim advances in eastern Europe and North Africa, eventually reconquering the Holy Land. He would do this by setting up negotiated trading posts, settling small towns nearby, and arranging through local caciques access to gold mines and river panning regions.

For certain, Columbus would try his limited colonial policy, but he eventually failed. Not so much on what he did or what he did not do, but on what the Spaniards and others who accompanied him on the second voyage did. Some blame is also shared by a few of the Indigenous caciques who reacted aggressively, killing small groups of Spanish gold hunters in defense of the women and land. Columbus, knowing the royal expectations given to him "to take the whole of it," now came sharply into focus. He had to control the situation, especially since initial gold mining produced limited amounts of the precious mineral, discouraging at first and then fomenting rebellion among the newly arrived 1,500 colonists. The pressure was on him to act decisively. This he would do, offending Spaniards and Indigenous people alike. It would be a no-win scenario, escalating into hanging some of his own settlers and enslaving rebellious Indios, men, women, and children.

In considering Columbus's decisions and actions during the first voyage, one gets the sense he witnessed tremendous anticipation, almost knowing his success meant Spain's success. As a Genoese native, akin, in many ways, to the likes of Marco Polo, Columbus's ambitions became Spain's ambitions, and later, Europe's ambitions. Little did he understand, or did he, that his enterprising experiences from October 1492 through March 1493 played out with too many uncontrollable human and geographic factors, promising Spain's recognition as Europe's premier political nation-state, yet setting up the foundation from later voyages and other Spanish, English, and French incursions for colonial domination of a "New World," irretrievably destroying existing Indigenous peoples, their homes, their culture, and their freedom.[6]

Columbus had indeed possessed uncanny maritime and navigational skills, allied with a healthy dose of propitious good luck. These capabilities, if he had satisfied himself with seagoing voyages of discovery and peaceful trading exchanges, as exhibited during the 1492 voyage, would have procured for himself and his family the little fame and fortune that he so desperately sought, but in view of the fact that he was hopelessly ambitious, devoutly religious, and prone to believing the impossible, the Genoese risk-taker gambled for it all; he won and, at the same time, he lost. We have made him an enduring historical figure who is, at one and the same time, hated and admired.

In a way, Columbus appears as an enigma, a distorted collection of conflicting qualities—enterprising and ambitious, convivial and suspicious, trusting and wary, determined and irresolute—a 15th-century human. Or is Columbus's story untrustworthy, partly fiction, partly historical truth, brought forth in historical documents, transcriptions, and translations from the 15th and 16th centuries, susceptible to significant author bias and preconceived ideas that disrupt an accurate analysis?

Notes

1 Cohen, J. M., *The Four Voyages of Christopher Columbus*, 129.
2 See Arthur Davies's remarkable article, "Behaim, Martellus, and Columbus," 451–9. Davies suggests a map by Bartholomew Columbus may have been the inspiration, even copied, for Behaim and Martellus. Behaim began work on this map in 1489, giving Columbus ample time to have possibly seen prototypes of the finished map gores, or that Davies is correct, and the Columbus brothers already had a similar copy, having produced it years earlier. Recall that the 1491 Martellus map also depicted the Mangi Peninsula; this map was widely available in Spain and Portugal.
3 Jane, *The Journal of Christopher Columbus*, 192.
4 Caraci, *The Puzzling Hero*, 38.
5 Jane, *The Journal of Christopher Columbus*, 194.
6 With Columbus's discovery, other European nations desired a piece of the action, seeking out cartographic sources that soon appeared throughout the continent. For more information on the cartography produced during the critical period shortly after Columbus's death, see Simonetta Conti, "La scoperta del Nuovo Mondo in alcuni Tolomei a stampa, dal 1507 a 1540," in *Geostorie*, 2015, 141–55.

APPENDIX I

History and Methodology of Columbus's Landfall

On October 12, 1492, at 7:01 a.m., the sun appeared from behind the anchored fleet. Columbus sent orders to the Pinzón brothers to prepare to land; the crew remained excited yet tense. However, where did they land? That question has perplexed geographers and historians for over a century. Let us begin with Las Casas's journal entry, which contains a frustratingly brief comment—a comment that only contains this description:

> The vessels were hove-to, waiting for daylight; and on Friday they arrived at a small island of the Lucayos, called, in the language of the Indians, Guanahani. Presently, they saw naked people. The Admiral went on shore in the armed boat, and Martín Alonso Pinzón, and Vicente Yañez, his brother, who was captain of the *Niña*.[1]

To guide us through the possibilities, it is necessary to understand that there are two levels of dispute. The first level is on a broad geographic scale, seeking to identify the Caribbean island of Guanahani. Robert Fuson, in his book *The Log of Christopher Columbus*, details the many landfall theories scholars have elucidated and professionally proposed. Fuson begins by stating the obvious: The Caribbean covers a huge swath of ocean, the Bahamas alone contain many islands spread over 30,000 square miles, and most of the islands contain similar flora and fauna, making Columbus's elaborate descriptions somewhat unhelpful.[2]

Geographically, three island groups comprise the Caribbean: the Bahamas, the Greater Antilles, and the Lesser Antilles. We will focus on the Bahamas as the most likely candidate for Columbus's first landfall. The Bahamas' sea region stretches from Grand Bahama and the Abacos Islands in the north to Inagua and the Turks and Caicos Islands in the south.[3] Columbus never visited Grand Bahama or the Abacos Islands; had he done so, natives may have tipped him in on the proximity to mainland North America. For our purposes, we will limit the approach latitudes for his first voyage somewhere between San Salvador and Samana Cay; this leaves four candidates for first contact: San Salvador, Rum Cay, Cat Island, and Samana Cay. For decades, historians and geographers have passionately debated the pros and cons of each island candidate.

The first recorded mention of the first landfall occurred in 1625, with support for Cat Island, located west and slightly north of San Salvador. For the next 168 years, no other extant accounts surfaced. Then, in 1793, Juan Muñoz received a task from the King of Spain, including writing a general history of the Americas, mapping the geography of conquest, and determining the first landfall of Columbus. Knowing the prior support for Cat Island from learned European history and geography professors, Muñoz surprised his readers by naming Watlings Island as the preferred site. In response to this announcement, a deluge of 19th-century theories sprouted, beginning with Fernández de Navarrete in 1825. Navarrete shocked the academic world by pointing to Grand Turk, an island 240 nautical miles south of Cat Island. On the surface, his ideas seemed far-fetched, but American historian Samuel Kettell followed suit 2 years later.

The "Landfall Wars" continued with an influential American writer, Washington Irving, wanting to debunk Navarrete and firmly believing Las Casas's written navigational directions and distances, publishing a well-received biography of Columbus.[4] Irving supported the original selection of Cat Island. Then, in the late 1830s, Alexander Von Humboldt, a leading German geographer,[5] joined the fray, seconding Cat Island. The back and forth on landfall islands moved by the mid-19th century to Watlings Island. However, in 1882, Gustavus Fox, former Secretary of the Navy for Abraham Lincoln and an accomplished mariner, declared a new island, Samana Cay, as the most logical first landing location. Henry Harrisse, an American historian born in Paris, later in his career became fascinated with the discovery of the Americas, logically reviewed previous landfall theories, and decided that Fox was right in naming Samana Cay (1892). A few years later, former New York State Senator and later an active Columbus scholar, John Boyd Thacher, wrote an influential two-volume biography of Columbus that gained much notoriety. Along with this publication came his decision to promote Watlings Island.[6]

As the 20th century began, more inquisitive historians and geographers jumped into the debate; however, everything changed when Samuel Elliot Morison entered the landfall arena. Morison lent his prestige as an admiral in the United States Navy and winner of the Pulitzer Prize for his biography of Christopher Columbus, naming Watlings Island as "the" San Salvador.[7] His arguments appeared indisputable; He spent years reading background books and articles, sailing the Caribbean on several occasions, plotting the effects of winds and currents in the Atlantic Ocean, and estimating the effect of magnetic variation along ocean longitudes.

Morison's gravitas prevailed, despite a few scholars offering Caribbean alternatives such as East Caicos, Concepción, and Plana Cays. Italian scholar Paolo Taviani, later renowned for his comprehensive biography of Columbus, accordingly, announced his support for Morison in 1972, keeping Watlings Island in the spotlight for European readers. Yet historians, geographers, and mariners—professional or amateur—opened the seemingly endless floodgates of intellectual response, spilling forth more geographical theories and more island possibilities, such as Plana Cays and Grand Turk, including a new candidate, Egg/Royal; retired aerospace engineer Arne Molander suggested these last two tiny, uninhabited islands. Robert Fuson, already naming East Caicos as the spot in 1961, switched to Grand Turk in 1982, right after Molander's announcement.

Two newcomers, Oliver Dunn and James E. Kelley, working separately, backed Morison's Watlings Island. However, Joseph Judge, an editor at the National Geographic Society, collaborating with explorer and writer Luis Marden, decided to try a team approach, recruiting specialists from a variety of study fields, including historians, geographers, navigators, and technicians working on the most advanced computers of the mid-1980s. The goal centered on pinpointing the landing site and announcing the results in Judge's popular *National Geographic* magazine.[8] The outcome startled scholars and the public alike, attempting to disrupt the broadly accepted Watlings Island scenario. Accompanying their written comments with excellent maps and photographs, the team declared Samana Cay as the true "San Salvador." Robert Fuson published his highly acclaimed Las Casas translation of the journal the next year, declaring in an appendix his support for Samana Cay.

Interestingly, scholars supporting Samana Cay hoped National Geographic's publication would change public opinion and end the debate. The debate did not end. With the quincentenary of Columbus's landing approaching quickly, Philip Richardson and Roger Goldsmith reviewed National Geographic's findings in 1987. Citing disagreement with Marden's calculations for wind and current correction, the researchers gathered an array of data and "applied corrections consistently along the whole track of the *Santa Maria*."[9] The result vindicated Morison. Running the track numerous times with varying wind and current data sets for September and October, the endpoint of contact for the night of October 11, 1492, remained within a 25-km (15.5 nautical miles) distance from Watlings Island—out of a total voyage of 5,500 km (3,417 miles).

The authors, Richardson and Goldsmith, also posited data for magnetic variation. Their two main sources included suggested variation modeling by W. Van Bemmelan (1889).[10] Van Bemmelan used the three Columbus journal entries in September to construct a model for the Western Atlantic. The model reveals NE variation from the Canary Islands to approximately 30 degrees west longitude—the Atlantic frontier line. Then, with intensity, the NW magnetic variation increases to over 6 degrees at 45 degrees west longitude (September 23), the area where Columbus makes his first course adjustment, bearing NW. A slow gain of NW variation continues until 55 degrees west longitude, reaching a peak of 7.5 degrees near October 1. From there until landfall, variation decreases to 0 degrees at landfall.[11]

While Richardson and Goldsmith's scientific results generated scholarly interest, the results confirmed and supported Morison and Watlings Island. Yet, upon further consideration, Richardson and Goldsmith, in 1992, decided the data factors used in their 1987 study needed modification. The pair of scholars reduced the previous length of the Columbus league and dramatically increased magnetic variation at landfall.[12] The overall impact of these changes resulted in a new, more southerly landfall near the Turks and Caicos Islands.

As interesting as the above 1992 study appears, Richardson and Goldsmith's studies reveal that magnetic variation may have played a significant role in determining Columbus's track across the *Ocean Sea*, yet the uncertainty of the transatlantic magnetic field in 1492 remained. To show the effect of different values for magnetic variation, the authors calculated, as they had in their initial 1987 study, that Watlings Island needed an endpoint value of 7.0 degrees W, while Samana Cay needed 9.2 degrees, and Grand Turk Island required 13.5 degrees. The 7.0 degrees of variation fits nicely into Morison's calculations.

The 1992 study did verify a suspicion this author raised concerning the impact of the Gulf Stream current. The effect of leeway, or the angular drift from course heading, is accentuated as a ship approaches the Bahamas, driving a vessel NW beginning in the zone about 65 degrees west longitude and intensifying as the ship travels west. At 70 degrees west longitude, the angle of drift is NNW.[13] This extreme drift angle occurred between October 8 and the 11 and was due to the northward turn of Gulf Stream winds. Richardson and Goldsmith calculated a drift totaling 8 km in their 1987 study and 11 km to the NW in their 1992 report. This author has modified their adjustment to take into account a more northerly (NNW) drift for the final three days, pushing the landfall sighting 11 km (from the 1992 study) closer to the southeast coast of Watlings Island. The Final Landfall Map highlights Richardson and Goldsmith's 1987 location with a 1992 leeway correction, Morison's 1942 sighting point, and this author's estimate.

The many unknown variables play havoc with fine-tuning the eventual landfall sighting on October 12 at 2:00 a.m. For example, this author's October 10 course heading would need a slight correction for NNW drift to accommodate the 5–6 miles discrepancy between my projected point and the actual location. In either situation, the case can be made that Columbus and crew sighted the SE coastline of San Salvador near the 24 degrees north latitude line and the 74°36′ west longitude, providing support for Morison's estimation.

William F. Keegan, using the Dunn and Kelley translation, decided in 1992 to start with the one well-described island, La Isabella (today Crooked, Fortune, and Acklins islands), the fourth island visited by Columbus, and work backward in an attempt to discover the true San Salvador. Keegan is believed to have found an important Indigenous city mentioned in the log, noted by Columbus's Indio guides as large and ruled by a powerful cacique. According to Keegan, the dig site revealed a village six times the size of most Lucayan settlements. With this site confirmed, Keegan found 31 Lucayan sites on La Fernandina (Long Island), with at least two of the sites matching noted locations in the log and locating the pond noted by Columbus, making this the third island visited. The second landfall, Santa María de la Concepción, Keegan concluded must be Rum Cay, explaining the incorrect size reported in the log as either a change of measurement by Columbus or an error by the transcription scribe or in Las Casas's translation. This is the weakest argument in Keegan's case, yet he continued to expound the merits of San Salvador based on Charles Hoffman's extensive and ongoing excavations, at the Long Bay site on Watlings Island (San Salvador) beginning in 1983, identifying green and yellow glass beads, brass belt buckles, and pieces of Spanish pottery, all items typically traded during Columbus's run through the Bahamas.[14]

The historical underwriting for Watlings Island is significant. A. B. Becher, a member of the Royal Geographical Society and Assistant Hydrographer for the Royal Navy, began researching the Columbus transatlantic track and arrived at a decision in 1856 using Navarrete's log translation, scoring each daily entry data on a map. Becher found the log descriptions led to Watlings Island; course tracks and distances accurately transcribed the transatlantic crossing and subsequent island visits. It is interesting that Becher allows for a full degree of magnetic variation of the compass for the final leg on October 11.[15]

Noted geographer R. H. Major, writing in 1883, confirmed his earlier opinion that Watlings Island was indeed the first Columbus landfall. His shortwritten defense, only two pages long in a leading geographic publication, brushed aside Gustavus Fox's assertion that Samana Cay was the site. Major named three sources he used to determine the landfall location: Columbus's log, Columbus's detailed description of Guanahani, and evidence from the earliest extant maps. Focusing on the last two items, Major correctly reestablished that Watlings Island contains the only large interior lagoon (lake) in the middle of the island. He further states, "Captain Fox also supplies a map of Samana [Samana Cay], which contained no lagoon whatever." For the third point, Major references a 1601 map crafted by the official 17th-century Spanish historiographer, Antonio de Herrera y Tordesillas. The map shows a reasonably accurate representation of Spanish Caribbean islands, clearly labeling the island where San Salvador is today as *Guanahani*. On these points, Major rests his case.[16]

The following year, 1884, American naval officer J. B. Murdock affirmed Becher's choice of Watlings Island. However, Murdock found "grave defects" in Becher's analysis of certain data. Murdock's arguments persuaded Sir Clements Markham, in 1892, to declare in favor of Watlings Island. As the 400th anniversary of Columbus's voyage approached, some scholars decided simply to summarize the various landfall theories, allowing the reader to make a final judgment. As the 20th century began, Filson Young published a biography of Columbus, asking the Earl of Dunraven to write an appendix section on landfall theories. According to a later analysis, Dunraven assumed Watlings Island but refused to eliminate other candidates.[17]

H. C. F. Cox, Attorney-General of the Bahamas in 1926, stifled an attempt by residents of Cat Island to change their island's name to San Salvador, believing it to be the landfall site. Cox referenced that most "writers," scholarly or not, historically agreed that Watlings Island is the correct location, firmly suggesting, "It has been definitely proved that the landfall of Columbus in the New World was on that Island of the Bahamas commonly called Watlings Island but by Columbus named San Salvador."[18] To make this a final official announcement, Cox declared the island should henceforth be called San Salvador.[19]

One of the most convincing and thorough investigations followed the next year, 1927, when R. T. Gould published, and later read his work titled "The Landfall of Columbus: An Old Problem Re-Stated," arguing through a process of elimination that Watlings Island stood above all other island candidates. Gould analyzed previous theories, pointing out errors or unwarranted assumptions, assumptions on inconsistent logbook distances, and descriptions of island physical features, including interior water bodies. He pounced on other assumptions where the logbook has Columbus sighting islands—land sightings clearly beyond the ability of the human eye.[20] Errors in the logbook are unreconciled, which makes it tempting for historians to simply blame the logbook distances as incorrectly transcribed, or placed down originally by Columbus, or more likely by Las Casas, in error. Gould gives much of the credit to Murdock in issuing "an impartial statement, unshaken in essentials by later criticism, of the reasons which go to show that in all probability Watlings Island is the true Guanahani."[21]

Using miles and league measurements from Samuel Kettell's *Personal Narrative of the First Voyage of Columbus to America* and adjusting distances with Morison's and Fuson's calculations, this author laid out a transatlantic course with the United States Geological Survey National Map—Advanced Viewer, using a standard of 3.0 nautical miles per one mile recorded in the logbook. Morison had calculated that figure slightly higher (3.18) but argued that Columbus regularly overestimated speed and distance; Fuson averaged the low and high estimates and decided to use 3.0 miles per league. Morison's longer miles per league resulted in a destination of Watlings Island, while Fuson, using the shorter miles per league, concluded that Samana Cay was the first landfall. The separation between the two landfall candidates is 65 nautical miles. Morison, as you recall, accounted for assumed magnetic variation and drift; Fuson did not.

Running the transatlantic crossing several times on the computer mapping software noted above, using slightly modified data for the magnetic variations estimated by Richardson and Goldsmith (1987) and Morison (1942), and averaging their differences, and accounting for the average angular drift of the Gulf Stream current for that time year and day, this author concluded that Watlings Island is, indeed, Guanahani (San Salvador).

This author's computer-run analysis of Columbus's route, using distances sailed as noted in Las Casas's summarized version of the admiral's logbook, points to San Salvador as the island first sighted. My landfall location is just south of Morison's computation and north of the points noted by Richardson and Goldsmith.

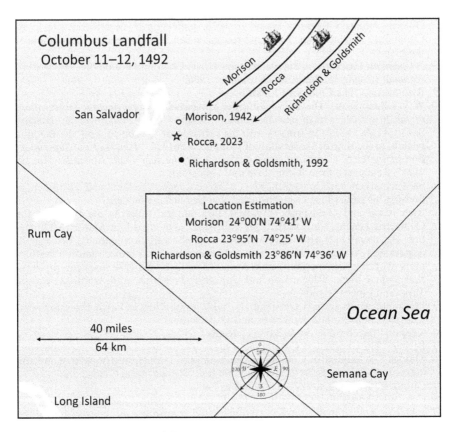

FIGURE I.1 Columbus Landfall

Notes

1 Thacher, *The Journal of Christopher Columbus*, 103. The "armed boat" refers to the men being armed.
2 The Bahamas and the Greater Antilles are considered by geographers as part of the North American continent, so in reality, Columbus did land in North America.
3 Politically, the Turks and Caicos Islands are not part of the Bahamas; geographically, they are.
4 Navarrete, following Irving's influential publication of *A History of the Life and Voyages of Christopher Columbus* (1828), responded [1829] by praising the style of writing but questioned its accuracy: writing, "Mr. Washington should rectify some facts or opinion that, taken from original sources, still lack the certainty and punctuality which are required to approach perfection." *Coleccion de los viages y descubrimientos*, XIV, translation by author.
5 Humboldt conducted expeditions to Spanish America, the United States, and Russia. He was one of the first to theorize that South America and Africa fractured from one larger continent. His book *Kosmos* (1845–47) consolidated much of his field and theoretical research into a multivolume classic on geography and nature.
6 Thacher's book, *Christopher Columbus, His Life, His Works, His Remains, together with an Essay on Peter Martyr of Anghera and Bartolomé de las Casas, the first Historians of America* (two volumes, 1903), produced an acceptable translation of Las Casas's abridgment of Columbus's journal.
7 Officials renamed Watlings Island in 1926, preferring to declare the site to be Columbus's San Salvador. Today, we recognize San Salvador as the official name of the island.
8 *A Columbus Casebook*: A Supplement to "Where Columbus Found the New World," *National Geographic Magazine*, November 1986.
9 Richardson, "The Columbus Landfall," 4.
10 W. Van Bemmelan, "Die Abewichung der Manetnadel," *Supplement to Observations of the Royal Magnetical and Meteorological Observatory at Batavia 21, Bataiva.* Schott, C. A. 1881. "An Inquiry into the variation of the compass off the Bahama Islands, at the time of the landfall of Columbus in 1492." *Report of the Superintendent of the U. S. Coast and Geodetic Survey for the year 1880.* Appendix No. 19, 412–7. Referenced from Richardson and Goldsmith.
11 See Richardson and Goldsmith, *The Columbus Landfall*, 6. Apparently, Morison, in deriving his landfall location, also used Van Bemmelan's model.
12 Richardson and Goldsmith employed 2.67 nautical miles as the basis for the Geometric League, while in their previous study, they used Luis Marden's 2.81 figure. The researchers arbitrarily assigned magnetic variation amounts between 10 degrees and 20 degrees W and recorded several tracks to project landfall destinations. Working with materials from Josiah Marvel and his 1988 magnetic variation chart course tracks, Richardson and Goldsmith's research led to landfalls near the Turks and Caicos Islands.
13 Prevailing winds were determined (in 2021) using Google Earth Pro-designated wind directions for late September and early October.
14 Keegan, "Beachead in the Bahamas," 46–50.
15 Becher, "The Landfall of Columbus," 190.
16 Major, "The Landfall of Columbus," *Proceedings*, 42–43. He also noted that Samana (Samana Cay) is correctly located and that it is "distinct" from Guanahani.
17 Gould, R. T. "The Landfall of Columbus," 407.
18 Cox, "The Landfall of Columbus," *The Royal Geographical Journal*, 338–9.
19 Ibid. Cox argued that a wireless station neared completion on the island "and the name of the island on which the station is erected should be finalized." 339. He also

suggested that the name Watlings be carried forward in official records to protect previously named title deeds and other documents.

20 The line of sight for most individuals is 2.4 miles, standing at 6 feet in height at ocean level. In the case of San Salvador (Watlings), standing in the masthead of the *Santa Maria* at 60 feet from the ocean, a mariner may see up to 9 miles of ocean in the distance; the distance would increase as the object sighted increased in height. For example, a mariner could spot a 140-foot hilltop up to 14 miles (23 km) away.

21 Gould, "The Landfall of Columbus," 425.

APPENDIX II

Anchorage and Beach Landing Site

Surprisingly, few scholars have spent effort on determining the actual beach or coastal location where Columbus and his crew first stepped ashore in the New World. The geographic problem, if it is to be entertained for scholarly study, needs to consider oceanographic factors (winds and currents) and physical geography (reefs and shoals) and a close reading of the journal entry for October 11–12. For purposes of this study, San Salvador (formerly Watlings Island) is the subject of investigation. Traditionally, three anchorage and landing sites currently hold high recognition from scholarly analysis: the leeward coast (west side) of San Salvador midway up Long Bay (Morison), the northeast side at the south end of Green's Harbor (Becher), and the south coast in the middle of French Bay (Murdock). This author believes the first landfall location is situated on the leeward side (west) at the north end of Fernandez Bay (Bamboo Point).

This study will focus on comparing Morison's Long Bay location with northern Fernandez Bay. The key physical factor in determining anchorage and landing sites is reef location. There are many reefs surrounding San Salvador. One might believe that a lower sea level in 1492 might be significant. In this case, sea level rise does not play a significant factor in discerning potential landing sites. Between 1500 and today, sea level has risen only 11 cm (4.3 inches).[1]

In considering currents and wind direction, contemporary meteorological data reveals prevailing winds to the NW, typical of mid-October. Wind direction in this scenario supports all four theories of approach. As far as the journal goes, nothing is written concerning the intervening time from October 12, when land was sighted at 2 a.m., and Columbus landing. Samuel Kettell's translated description reads:

> At two o'clock in the morning, the land was discovered, at two leagues distance; they took in sail and remained under the square-sail lying to till day, which was Friday, when they found themselves near a small island [one of the Lucayos), called in the Indian language Guanahani.[2]

As Columbus approached Guanahani on the morning of the 12th, he quickly realized a significant reef structure encircled the entire island, or at least the southeast portion of the island. While the day before, he recorded "heavy seas," Columbus noted nothing about the weather on the 12th, so we may assume the heavy seas had abated; otherwise, he necessarily would have waited another day to land. However, even on a calm sea day, 15th-century mariners sought a safe harbor, and for Columbus, a safe harbor from the SE blowing winds existed on the leeward or west side. Morison agrees and has Columbus spend the morning tacking slightly in a due west direction, staying a mile or two off the southern coast. By 10 a.m., he rounded the southwest peninsula of Guanahani and turned NE, following the coast, and searched for a break in the reef. Approximately 5 miles up the coast, spotters on the ships indicated a break and a dangerous reef. To "break a reef" (find a path through), Columbus ordered Vicente and Martín Pinzón to probe closer to the reef, carefully maneuvering *Niña* and *Pinta* while taking depth soundings constantly. Experienced and brave, the Pinzón brothers, knowing their ships' draft at around 6 feet, sought an area with a sounding of 5–6 fathoms (25–35 feet), ensuring a safety factor in unknown waters.[3]

Depth reading data helped this author narrow the area where the three ships possibly anchored that historic day.[4] From this safe anchorage, skiff boats, one on each ship, paddled were lowered and crew members rowed in toward the beach, searching as they went for rock outcroppings. The beach extension covers 50–70 feet and rises gently to a level area encroached with low-lying vegetation and a forest of trees. This matches Columbus's description. In addition, less than a mile away to the south, a small Lucayan village existed, with another settlement a quarter of a mile farther south and still another 1.5 miles to the north of his landing site.

Supporting the Morison location theory is Charles Hoffman's archaeological investigation findings reported in 1986. Citing evidence such as colored glass seed beads, green glass fragments, a bronze D-ring (buckle), a copper grommet, and a Spanish coin dating to before 1492, this was the first physical evidence that matches Columbus's descriptions of traded items during his landing at San Salvador. Hoffman noted that the field exaction site, believed to be one of several villages on the west coast of the island, was near Morison's proposed landing location and just over 100 meters from the beach.

While the Morison landing site appears practical and is currently the preferred location for Columbus's first footprints, there are other options, and Hoffman himself preferred a landing site further north, just above Bamboo Point. He wrote, "Columbus could have anchored his three ships in 30 meters of water, away from the reefs, yet only a few hundred meters from the beach; if he did so, it was in the vicinity of Bamboo Point near present-day Cockburn Town."[5] Despite his exciting finds at the south end of Long Bay, he points to several other digs that uncovered pre-historic artifacts, concluding that "there may have been a series of occupation or activity areas of varying intensities" all along the west side of San Salvador, including the north end at Bamboo Point.[6]

Lying 2.25 miles north along the coast from Morison's site is another attractive alternative, eliminating nearby surface reef outcroppings and allowing a closer anchorage-to-shore distance. Located at Bamboo Point, the site offers the best deep-sea approach and, most importantly, no surface rocks or underwater obstructions. This location occupies a reef-free zone, the largest in San Salvador, with the nearest reef structure, above or below the surface, at 2,500 feet wide, running north to south. At 1,000 feet out, a ridge drops off to deep water, but at 900 feet distance from shore, a shelf appears leveling to 32 feet, a good depth for the fleet's anchorage. Using the skiff boat, Columbus and crew only needed to row 800 feet to the beach.[7] This site today is just south of the main town, Cockburn (pronounced Coburn). At least one Lucayan village existed at or just north of the suggested Columbus landing site at Bamboo Point. Not more than a few hundred feet from the beach, an extensive forest of trees pervaded that area, which still exists today, and extended inland into the large interior lake called today, Great Lake. Michael Craton, in *A History of the Bahamas*, has Columbus first landing at the Morison site, then moving up to Bamboo Point late on October 12 and remaining there until 14.[8]

For decades, most historians and geographers have accepted Morison's determination for Columbus's first voyage landing site in San Salvador. However, my reef analysis in 2021 revealed that an equally attractive anchorage is located 2.4 miles north of the current Columbus monument, near the present-day town of Cockburn Town.

In terms of population proximity, apparently near the landing sight according to Columbus's journal entry for October 12–14, both Long Bay and Bamboo Point supported small but thriving village populations. Jeffrey Blick, in his zooarchaeological study, estimated Guanahani's Indigenous population at between 500 and 1,000 persons at the time of European discovery. His study results point to native populations accessing and exploiting both land and sea resources. Blick's study examined site SS-3 on the northwest coast, north of Bamboo Point, and SS-4 on the northeast coast (see Guanahania Map in Chapter 6); Columbus and some of his men rowed, using their skiff boats, near

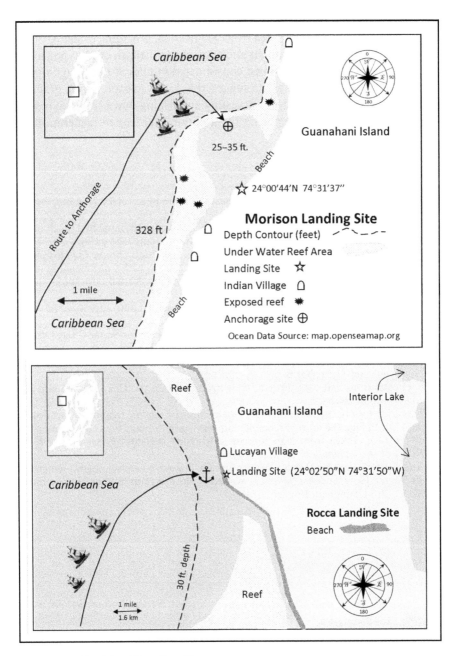

FIGURE II.1   Combined Landing Site

the SS-3 site on October 14.[9] Working a 5 × 5-meter excavation, Blick acquired animal vertebrate specimens dated from 963 to 1426, providing evidence of the types and quantities of fish, caught and consumed. Shellfish of all types, along with many species of fish remained consolidated in piles at the village site. In conclusion, Blick stated, "The data suggest that Lucayan exploitation practices were unsustainable, and by over-harvesting and fishing down the local marine food web, they were compromising the ability of subsequent generations to meet their needs."[10]

Notes

1 Timmer, "Recent sea level rise is the fastest since 800 BCE," *ARS Technica*, online.
2 Kettell, *Personal Narrative*, 33–34. The reference to the Lucayos was added by Kettell. The Lucayan people, a branch of the Taíno peoples, inhabited much of the Bahamas, speaking the Taíno language (the Arawak language group). The Taíno resided mostly in Cuba and Hispaniola (Haiti). The Taíno phrase, *Lukku-Cairi*, is transferred in Spanish as *Lucayan people of the islands*, with *Cairi* meaning island or *Cayo* (Cay). Lardicci and Dunn & Kelley mirror the Kettell translation almost exactly.
3 See Morison's detailed analysis for his selected beach landing site, *Admiral of the Ocean Sea*, 226–29.
4 All sonar soundings are estimated from the Navionics Online Sonar Chart (2021).
5 Hoffman, "Archaeological Investigations at the Long Bay Site," 238.
6 Ibid. For more information on archaeological work in the Bahamas, see Berman, "Lucayans and Their World."
7 Reef extensions and ocean depths were acquired from the U.S. Coast Guard and NOAA online charts.
8 This is interesting, as Columbus made no mention of moving to another location on the 12th. In fact, the journal recounts him leaving in the skiff boats on the morning of the 14th. Taken from map sources in Michael Jackson's *Preservation and the Future of the Bahamian Past*, 22.
9 Archaeologist enthusiast Ruth Wolper initially discovered archaeological remains at SS-3 in the 1950s, and several others worked in the area prior to Blick's involvement.
10 Blick, "Pre-Columbian Impact," 181.

APPENDIX III

Las Casas and Columbus on the Future of the Indigenous Peoples: A Comparison to the Portuguese Experience in São da la Mina

Las Casas's transcript of the *Diario* leads translators and then writers using that translation to jump to conclusions about Columbus's attitude toward Indigenous peoples. Let's take a look at several translations to see how different authors interpreted this important section of the December 16, 1492, logbook entry of Christopher Columbus. You have already read Lardicci's translation in the daily entry earlier in this work, and let's dispel one point that keeps coming up in Las Casas's attempt to reveal Columbus's attitude about Indio courage. Las Casas writes the adjective phrase "muy cobardes" which in most modern translations can mean *cowardly*; however, the *Real Academia Española Diccionario* lists the first line translation as meaning *pusillanimous* (without value for facing unknown or dangerous situations). This implies *timidity*, not cowardice. Did Las Casas incorrectly interpret Columbus's assertion in this case? Being afraid of the unknown is a human trait and not a negative social slight. As has been shown over and over, on this first voyage, the Indios, once they met and interacted on an initial trading exchange, became less timid, trading freely and even freely swimming or canoeing out to the ships for a visit or more item exchanges. By December 16, Columbus knew this fact well, so the argument can be made that he was setting up a later suggestion that because the Indios were a timid people, subsequent Spanish operations, that is, setting up a trading post and town, would be unopposed.[1]

Another key term here is *mandar* (send), as in the original, "y así son Buenos para les mandar y les hazer trabajar." This is translated by Lardicci as "and so they are good for being given commands and being made to till, to plant."[2] The Spanish translation from the *Real Academia Española Diccionario* does not use *mandar* for *command* except in the singular number; in the plural, *mandar* refers to *we sent*, and *they send*. The context of the sentence refers to *they* so the primary meaning for *mandar* is *send*, not *command*. Sending some-one or some people to complete a task may be interpreted as a request, not an order. Nowhere during the first voyage did Columbus order (command) groups of Indios to complete a task. He did send his Guanahani interpreters ashore on occasion, but again, there is no indication they were forced to go. On the contrary, as has already been argued, forcing a kidnapped prisoner to go ashore and translate an important message, alone or only accompanied by one or two men, stretches the imagination.

The December 16 entry is highly suspected of philandering, as Las Casas moves in and out of the first-person narrative. Why would he do this? The entry begins with a third-person description of an Indio apparently drifting in a canoe. Las Casas writes that Columbus picked up the lone occupant and the canoe, gave him some trinkets, and brought him safely to shore. In short order, the Indio paddled to shore and gave a positive account of his experiences with the odd-looking strangers. Then, without reason, Las Casas moves into the first person, with Columbus purportedly declaring that he hoped the Spanish monarchs would Christianize them and make them subjects of Spain, adding, "For I consider them yours [already]."[3]

Inserting Columbus's quote in this particular location is interesting in that it tells us much about what Columbus and Las Casas hoped for Indigenous peoples. But is it a reliable representation of Columbus's opinion? Are these really the words and thoughts of Columbus? He held no authority to consider anyone encountered during the first voyage as a subject of Spain. That only became a goal when stated in the royal declarations for the second voyage. Recall that the first voyage recognized that Columbus would become "Viceroy and Governor" of "discovered islands and mainlands" related to any trading post or supporting town that might be set up, not entire Indigenous popula-tions. While Columbus previously wrote concerning his hopes for the Indige-nous peoples becoming willing Christians, he never expressed that desire as official Spanish policy, acting as Viceroy and Governor. However, Las Casas, writing 30 years later, decided, that in the middle of describing an exchange between a group of Indios onboard the *Santa Maria* and Columbus, to switch to the first-person narrative. A writer would only do so for an important rea-son, or maybe two possible reasons. First, Las Casas wanted to reveal the ori-gins of Spanish intentions to Christianize Indigenous peoples, which he thought was an appropriate, even a necessary, religious calling if carried out without force. Second, once Christianized, Indigenous peoples became sub-jects for Spain, but only if they desired such an outcome. Having Columbus state this policy as a representative of Spain in the first person established an official beginning to Spanish policy, a policy approved by Las Casas.

The point here is that one may suggest that Las Casas wanted to reveal that since Columbus was given authority to act as Governor and Viceroy of islands and mainlands discovered, he had the authority to establish policy relations between the Indigenous peoples and Spanish settlers. If Las Casas is correct in inserting Columbus's true intentions, then Las Casas and Columbus saw a future where people living in areas now claimed by Spain would become willing subjects (vassals), not slaves, and willing Christians.[4] A close read of the passage does not suggest coercion or military domination, implying an important distinction that needs to be made. From their viewpoint, Las Casas and Columbus were helping Indigenous peoples move into a more modern world—a European world. These new subjects would be clothed and shown how to farm new crops and tend cattle, sheep, and goats. They would receive protection from Carib slaving raids and other Europeans attempting to infringe on Spanish lands. They would learn new trades and how to work metal and fashion tools. They would learn to speak Spanish and learn to write—all the attributes of a Spanish subject. Most of all, the Indigenous peoples would learn of the one and only true god, the Christian god, a god that promised them eternal life.

The above-noted cultural and economic transition might be appealing to Las Casas and Columbus, and probably also to the Spanish monarchs, but did it occur in other pre-existing colonial outposts, such as the Spanish-controlled Canary Islands or Portuguese-dominated Azores, the Cape Verde Islands, or at São Jorge da Mina—Portugal's West African trading colony? If it did, then Columbus entertained these experiences as a model to follow; if not, then Columbus would be implementing a wholly new socioeconomic colonial system.

For practical purposes, we will only consider systems in place during spring-summer 1493—the interlude between the first and second voyages and those regions already possessing Indigenous populations. We can eliminate the Cape Verde islands, as they were found to be uninhabited by Genoese and Portuguese explorers in the mid-1400s. The same holds true, at present, for the Azores, discovered by Portugal in 1427.[5] On the other hand, São Jorge da Mina, situated on the Gulf of Guinea, was not on an island but rather on a small peninsula of mainland Africa. This geographical reality influenced, not determined, from the start, that European contact and ongoing presence would remain limited and defined geographically. Mariana Boscariol, a scholar at the University of Lisbon, explained the situation, stating that the trading post was on "a limited and well-defined portion of land where the Portuguese could stay with full control, resulting from an agreement with the terms stipulated by the local authorities."[6] The key here is that São Jorge da Mina resulted from political and economic negotiations between Portuguese officials and local African leaders. Boscariol offers a look at how the trading post began.

First, the construction of a fortress was not well received by the locals, who were in general resistant in letting the Portuguese to move forward with their plan. Second, Pereira mentioned that the fortification was expected to serve not only as an accommodation or for trade but also for their defence.

This meant their own physical protection but also of their goods (*fazendas*), and not only in relation to the locals but also in the imminent possibility of other Europeans to reach the territory.[7]

The African scenario may have represented what Columbus had in mind in constructing La Navidad, leaving men to carry on the good relations that the Admiral initiated. However, there is a critical difference in that Columbus gave permission to his men to leave the immediate area and search for the gold mines, which he hoped to work and exploit with Spanish (not Indigenous) labor when he returned. It is interesting to consider the alternative outcome had he never given that permission. In La Mina, the opposite situation ensued, with Portuguese merchants and traders, rarely journeying inland in search of gold or other valuable products. In fact, Pereira reported,

> These people were gentile and some of them were already made Christians, this I say for the inhabitants of the land in the same place where the castle is, because the merchants come from far away and do not have many conversations with us as those who are our neighbors.[8]

Notice that African traders came willingly to the Portuguese trading post expressly to exchange wares of value from locations apparently of significant distance. Also, as in the case of Columbus, Portuguese influencers attempted to convert local Africans and were somewhat successful. It is interesting that Pereira describes the local Indigenous peoples as gentle and willing to interact peacefully. Comparing the Portuguese situation on La Mina to the instructions Columbus gave to the 39 men left at La Navidad, we see almost an identical situation for the establishment and growth of a colonial trading post, understanding that European territorial control was limited, and social and economic interaction was voluntary.

Columbus did give Indigenous islanders the opportunity to bring their wares to him and his men. His logbook is full of day-long festivities of curious natives coming and going, men and women, swimming or canoeing out to the Spanish ships, eager to trade various articles of food or plants. Often, these Indigenous traders sported gold adornments pierced into their skin or on their person. Columbus noticed, and his men certainly focused on this, and it was a tempting allure, beckoning them to find the source of all this potential wealth.

On Hispaniola, Columbus realized that gold in sufficient quantities would not be forthcoming from local villages, at least not in the quantities he wanted to bring to Spain. This forced him, early during his second voyage, to send a search party into the interior of Hispaniola, basing this decision on numerous stories told by shoreline villagers. There, in the interior, Alonso de Hojeda and his men committed abuses against the Indigenous people living in an area known as Cibao. Meanwhile, back in La Navidad, Columbus continued to give gifts to the local friendly Taíno cacique, Guacanagarí. Columbus knew from his experience in La Mina that gifts served as an introduction to obtaining trading rights. Boscariol noted this as a tool used from the very first days of La Mina's creation: "Giving gifts to the merchants, representatives, local authorities, and their relatives became a common strategy during the Portuguese rule in Mina."[9] Columbus appeared impressed with the Indigenous chief; he was naked and noble, humble and magisterial, an initial enigma, and later a trusted friend and ally.

Clearly, Columbus desired to instill good relations with these people as future trading partners. However, Columbus needed to find a proper location for his trading post—a La Mina in the Indies. There were two obvious choices: Cipangu and/or Cathay (somewhere in mainland Asia). Just as La Mina resided on the west coast of Guinea, monopolizing West African trade, Columbus's trading post would dominate East Asian trade. By establishing friendly relations, these off-the-mainland island people he met on the first voyage would participate in an ongoing economic exchange, coming to his trading post enthusiastic about trading their goods.

Three key goals or actions desired by Columbus and Las Casas but missing from the Portuguese-African trading post at La Mina are now noted. First, Columbus and Las Casas desired to introduce religious conversion as a goal for the entire Indigenous population, whereas the Portuguese saw this as a secondary, almost peripheral goal. Second, Columbus not only claimed Spanish sovereignty over the beaches and harbors he visited but over the entirety of each island's regions at least that is what Las Casas wrote in his abridged version of the logbook; the Portuguese, by choice, restricted territorial claim to their immediate trading post.[10] Third, the Spanish monarchs, despite Columbus's intention of initially restricting colonization inland, issued declarations commanding the Admiral to colonize "the whole of it," expanding Spanish political control to all regions of every island and making the Indigenous peoples, de facto, subjects of the mother country.[11] The Portuguese, on the other hand, realized early on that any attempt to expand territorial control would meet with concerted multi-tribe military retributions from large, powerful tribes, damaging future trading agreements. They not only recognized tribal social-political control over adjacent villages, but they continually respected Indigenous autonomy.

In this manner, Columbus carried two visions for the future of Indigenous peoples. The first vision, learned and developed by initial friendly contact with islanders during the first voyage, aligned more closely with experiences already established by the Portuguese in West Africa, such as Arguin and La Mina.[12] However, as the first voyage continued, Columbus became suggestive of reimagining the Indigenous peoples as good, gentle Christian subjects. King Ferdinand and Queen Isabella engrained in the royal commands for the second voyage that Columbus now added cultural and political control to the priority, setting up a trading post. The fix was in, and it is suggested that Columbus understood that the Portuguese model of colonialism on São Jorge da Mina no longer functioned as an operative final goal; a trading post and supporting town concept became the first objective, a preliminary step toward a still-unknown process of settlement expansion—island-wide colonialism.

Notes

1 Columbus's letter to Luis de Santangel confirms the Admiral's use of the expression *termerosos sin remedio*, "fearful with remedy." *The Spanish Letter of Columbus to Luis de Sant'Angel: Dated 15 February* 1493, reprinted in reduced facsimile, and translated by Johann Rosenbach, April 1493. See for full text 1–7. Internet Archive.
2 Lardicci, *A Synoptic Edition, Historia*, LC 80, section 30, 248.
3 Dunn and Kelley, *The Diario*, 231. The bracketed comment is from Dunn and Kelley.
4 Delgado, Book review, *Journal of Latin American Studies*, 571–3.
5 There has been recent archaeological interest in pursuing a search for Indigenous peoples on a few of the islands with one paper suggesting Northern European migration to the Azores 700 years before the Portuguese arrived. See *Climate change facilitated the early colonization of the Azores Archipelago during medieval times*, by Pedro M. Raposeiro et al.
6 Boscariol, "São Jorge da Mina and Macao: A Comparative Reappraisal of European Encounters," Abstract.
7 Ibid., 39. Pereira was the captain (or Factor) of São Jorge da Mina from 1519 to 1522. In effect, he held powers similar to the Spanish titles of Viceroy and Governor. Columbus visited the area at least, maybe more, and saw firsthand the colonial political hierarchy of this extra-Portuguese colony (trading post/fortress)
8 Ibid., 40, quoted from, Brásio, A. (ed.) (1952), Monumenta Missionaria Africana, vol. 1 (Lisboa, Agência Geral do Ultramar).
9 Ibid., 41. Columbus, during his first voyage, gave gifts on every island he visited. Though considered trifles by Spaniards, local Indigenous peoples found them desirable.
10 As the Portuguese explored, trading zones were established by Portuguese monarchs, and acquired goods were "publicly auction[ed] in Lisbon." Accordingly, winning merchants paid a yearly fee to the king and received exclusivity in running trade operations. One of the first Portuguese trading zones set the model for further trading extensions, located at Arguin, an island off the coast of modern-day Mauritania, where an appointed governor, controlled trade with the nearby West African coast. A *factoria* (trading post) and a supporting fort represented the extent of the Portuguese settlement. See Ijoma, "Portuguese Activities in West Africa," 137–8.
11 Columbus did declare Spanish sovereignty over all the islands he visited during his first voyage. He did this, not knowing the future plans Ferdinand and Isabela might have for his claims, although he soon learned that the Spanish monarchs desired him to administer all the islands and people therein, Spanish and Indigenous. Keen, The *Life of the Admiral*, 106. Personally, as he claimed later, he was more interested in continuing his discovery voyages than in administering large geographical territories such as Hispaniola.
12 For more on Arguin as a Portuguese colony, see, Ijoma, "Portuguese Activities in West Africa," 137–8.

APPENDIX IV

Columbus's Vision for Spanish-Indio Relations on La Española (Hispaniola) in Comparison to the Existing Slave Conditions on the Canary Islands, circa 1492

Historian Philip Morgan declared in "Origins of American Slavery," "No European nation embarked on New World ventures with the intention of enslaving anyone."[1] This is certainly true of Columbus's first voyage but is open for debate on subsequent Spanish expeditions to the Americas. Morgan connects the rise of slavery to the practical economic conditions encountered. One of the first examples of this economic need can be seen in the Canary Islands. Here, Portuguese and Spanish colonizers attempted to conquer each island with the expressed desire to use the Guanche population as workers in the burgeoning sugar industry. Let's explore how this developed and compare its conception and implementation to Columbus's intentions for the Caribbean islands.

Anthony M. Stevens-Arroyo argued that analyzing Spain's experience and practice in colonizing the Canary Islands is more profitable than looking at subsequent conquests of Mexico and Central America. Certainly, a Spanish colonization presence existed for decades before 1492. This economically driven expansion included the Mediterranean Sea (Balearic Islands) and the Atlantic Ocean on the Canary Islands.[2] For purposes of this investigation, we will confine our study to the Canary Islands.

Following the initial observation of comparative analysis by Las Casas, Stevens-Arroyo agrees that the jump from the Canary Islands to Columbus's exploration of the Caribbean emerged as an ongoing, natural desire for territorial expansion, with the Canaries serving as a "halfway house" between the homeland of the Iberian Peninsula and the Americas.[3]

When Portuguese and Spanish explorations first arrived in the Canary Islands in the 14th century, they immediately noticed the small geographic size of each island. Gran Canaria, one of the largest islands in the group, is 602 square miles, while Tenerife is 785 square miles in geographic extent. In comparison, Cuba is over 42,000 square miles, and Haiti and the Dominican Republic combined (Hispaniola) total nearly 30,000 square miles. Also, the Canary Islands are a relatively short distance from their homeland, Spain, approximately 800 miles, whereas Cuba lies over 4,000 miles away. Knowing these geographic facts, one might believe that the exploration, conquest, and colonization of the Canary Islands might begin and end in a shorter time span and with great ease due to the proximity of homeland support and smaller land area.

What is missing here is the fact that everything changed with Ferdinand's and Isabella's final victory over the Moors at Granada (January 1492). Whereas, before this time, the Spanish monarchs poured their money and effort into the *Reconquista*. This also partially explains why Columbus needed to wait for final monarchial approval to launch his voyage.

During the years before the *Reconquista*, an evolving victor-vanquished mentality emerged with conquering Spaniards seizing land from the Moors, then partitioning the population for work and servitude to *grandees* or *hidalgos*—Spanish nobility or soldiers who had distinguished themselves in military service.[4] The geo-social concept became known as *repartimiento*—distribution (land and people). One must understand that this system of reward allowed for continued Spanish motivation in carrying on the fight ever southward on the Iberian Peninsula, climaxing with the siege and surrender of the last Muslim stronghold at Granada. Recall that Columbus was present at this final stage of the war and understood all too well how service to his majesties might result in social and financial gain. With Spanish lands consolidated and secure, the time had come to expand Spanish influence, both economic and religious.

Conflicting claims by Portugal and Spain of the Canary Islands ended in 1479 with the Treaty of Alcàçovas. Alfonso V, King of Portugal, formally recognized Spain's claim to all the Canary Islands, with Ferdinand and Isabela recognizing Portugal's hegemony over the Azores, Cape Verde Islands, and Madeira Island. In addition, Portugal retained exclusive rights to navigating, conquering, and trading in the waters and coastlines south of the Canary Islands.[5] Isabella and Ferdinand now "entertained contradictory notions about what should be done with the natives."[6] The main concern centered on the question of how the native peoples, the Guanche, should be treated. The Spanish monarchs wanted to establish peaceful trading posts and settlements, but the native islanders were not Muslim, Jewish, or Christian, so their religious status needed consideration. Considering their lack of technological advancement, most Spaniards saw the natives of the Canary Islands as inferior and, as such, felt free to treat them as such. Frequent armed clashes forced the Spanish monarchs to consider a new administrative approach.

To maintain control, the Spanish monarchs inserted official governors on the islands. This, in turn, called into question the rights of the original settlers and inherited holders of *repartimiento* charters.[7] In an attempt to bring order to the constant warfare between Guanche resistors and Spanish settlers, Spain sent military leaders and rapidly subdued the remaining Guanche resistance in Gran Canaria and Tenerife.[8]

Alice Carter Cook, as far back as 1900, understood the unfortunate experiences of the Guanche people. She wrote,

> In the guise of Christianity, they [the Guanche people] received slavery; for civilization, extermination; while their simple, strong, and wholesome life was superseded by the empty pomp and groveling superstition of the invaders.[9]

By the time the Spaniards arrived on the scene, native Guanches lived in seven of the Canary Islands: Lanzarote, Fuerteventura, Gran Canaria, Tenerife, La Palma, Gomera, and Hierro. Scholars are not sure if regular communication occurred between the islands that make up the Canaries, but we do know that regular contact pre-1492 was firmly established in the Caribbean. We do know that Canary Islanders practiced a unique form of hieroglyphic writing, as samples have been found on at least five of the islands.[10] For livelihood, Guanche men and women fished and grew limited crops such as wheat, corn, and legumes. Political affiliation demanded service to a local chief, who enlisted men to help fight the ongoing pre-European intra-island conflicts over land and authority. Cook estimates that 5,000 Guanche men became involved in local wars when Spanish explorers visited the islands, fighting only with traditional weapons, stones, and sticks. This is much the same situation that Columbus discovered in the Caribbean.

The Guanche people fought valiantly against Spanish incursions beginning in 1402. As each Spanish adventurer claimed control of one of the Canary Islands, the Spanish monarchs rewarded their actions with an official *capitanía*. First begun by Portuguese monarchs, the Spanish version contained many of the same rewards and responsibilities. The title *donatàrio* gave the Spanish leader control over a portion of land, or, in some cases, the entire island. Responsibilities included caring for the European and Indigenous peoples living within the boundaries of the grant, promoting, or in many cases, demanding, the labor of local peoples in farming or other commercial activities, and providing religious guidance and conversion.[11] By the time Columbus left for his first voyage, Spanish control pervaded every island except Tenerife and La Palma.[12]

The socio-political system evolving at that time in the Canary Islands is described by James L. Parsons as a precursor, a testing ground for Spanish authorities on how to administer acquired lands outside the Iberian Peninsula. He noted that a governmental policy developed from existing regional Spanish laws and traditions and was then adapted and modified as new Spanish monarchs and local *donatàrios* attempted to implement their own interpretation of control—colonialism. By 1492, the system had functioned in the following accepted manner: The crown appointed governors, who then granted lands and peoples to Spaniards and others who had provided distinguished service to the crown. Local *donatàrios* formed regional governing bodies, *cabildos* (councils), that "regulated every phase of life through a complex structure of regulations, fines, and taxes."[13]

Those Guanches who resisted Spanish conquest and subsequent colonization, for the most part, became slaves, whereas those who did not remained free in name only. Interestingly, beginning with Columbus's second voyage, free Guanches joined the fleet when the ships stopped in Gomera for supplies. One of these native conscripts distinguished himself on the island of Guadeloupe when he successfully outraced a fleet-footed Carib fleeing into the jungle. The incident, recorded in the log of the second voyage, received praise from Columbus and the crew who witnessed the event.[14]

With the onset of the sugar industry in the Canary Islands, owners of *fazendas* (large estates) employed paid Spanish help and Guanche slaves.[15] The number of slaves per estate averaged 30–35 persons, limited due to the relatively small acreage employed, compared to those that arose later in the Americas, where sugar mills regularly employed over 100 native-American and black slaves.

Columbus knew quite well the slave system in operation in the Canary Islands at the time of his August 1492 visit to Gomera. Yet he made no statements about interacting with slaves or slave owners at that time. We can only guess his predisposition for slavery during his first voyage; interestingly, he never owned a slave.[16] Certainly, he had no directive from the crown to do so, as the *Santa Fe Capitulations* made no mention of slavery. It can be argued that honoring him with the title of Viceroy and Governor of new lands discovered inherently allowed for this option to be employed.[17]

As already argued in the main body of this work, he wrote about the Spanish monarchs and that the Indios were timid and easily controlled, easily manipulated into a docile servant class. Theoretically, Indio servants would have the same rights as any Spanish citizen, but as seen in the Canary Island scenario, any non-compliance with stated Spanish regulations and local laws could result in being considered a hostile, rebellious act and therefore enslaved—social expectations included docility, conformity, and a lifetime of productivity. More often than not, the only slaves transported from their home islands, coming out of the Canary Islands and from the Caribbean, during Columbus's first two voyages were those Indigenous peoples, mostly men, who took up arms against the Spanish explorers and colonizers. It is important to distinguish between explorers and colonizers. Columbus technically enslaved no one during his first voyage, yet he wrote about how they would become vassals (servants) of his majesties, working productively within a Spanish-controlled geographic environment—baptized, clothed, and enjoined to Spanish society, albeit at a lower social level—a 15th-century paternalism.

However, an argument might be made that he wanted only to establish a limited colonial *factoria*, with the intention of implementing and maintaining social, political, and economic control over specific and limited geographic locations. These locations would include a designated seaport, its accompanying town, and the gold mining areas of central Hispaniola—a region called *Cibao* by local Indigenous peoples. A well-maintained road, cut through the dense brush and rising topography, would link the gold mines to the town. The described geographic area is then the *factoria*, and as Columbus prepared for his second voyage, his plans for colonization resided within this limited geographic boundary. Additionally, Isabella and Ferdinand made it quite clear that Columbus and his men must:

> treat the said *Indios* very well and lovingly and abstain from doing them any injury, arranging that both people hold much conversation and intimacy, each serving the others to the best of their ability should maltreat said Indians in any manner whatsoever, the said Admiral, as viceroy and governor of their highnesses, shall punish them [Spanish settlers] severely by virtue of the authority vested in him by their majesties for this purpose.[18]

Tragically, during the second voyage, everything changed with the discovery of his massacred men at La Navidad. This was a turning point for Columbus, but he did not take military action, preferring to relocate his trading post and town eastward a short distance, naming the new settlement La Isabella. Shortly thereafter, Spaniards sent to the mountainous areas of central Hispaniola, built a small fort (Santo Tomás), and spent their time searching for gold to mine or trading trinkets with local Taíno for small gold pieces. Columbus soon learned that Caonabó, the Taíno, possibly Carib, cacique assumed to be the one responsible for the massacre at La Navidad, now planned to attack Santo Tomás. Columbus sent Alonso de Hojeda and 400 men to reinforce the small fort, relieving the existing Spaniard in charge, Pedro Margarit. Margarit's new orders commanded him to explore parts of southern and eastern Hispaniola, areas unknown to Columbus. Columbus issued strict orders to Margarit to "suffer [Indios] no harm, and that nothing is taken from them against their will, instead, make them feel honored and protected."[19] Margarit and later Hojeda began disobeying Columbus's prime directive to establish and keep good relations, stealing food and gold from interior tribes, Taíno, and Carib, reversing initial good relations. As this occurred, Columbus decided to set sail westward, seeking Cathay or Cipangu, which he believed to be close, leaving his son, Diego, in charge, shortly joined by Bartholomew Columbus, Christopher's brother. This was a transforming mistake on the part of Christopher Columbus; his absence hastened the breakdown of law and order on Hispaniola, with bands of

Spaniards splintering off to seek gold, women, and food. When Bartholomew attempted to punish these men, resentment grew among the colonists. For now, it was clear that the hidalgos and most of the other settlers only desired to get rich at the expense of the Indigenous populations.

The tension escalated when Caonabó rallied his people to attack the Spanish garrison at San Tomás and later move for an all-out assault on La Isabella. Columbus, now home from his voyage to Jamaica and Cuba, could no longer hold back, and the resulting Battle of Vega Real scattered the native army, later capturing Caonabó.[20] After this event, Columbus, considering Caonabó and his soldiers to be captured war prisoners, as was the custom of the time, was determined to send them to Spain, where the Spanish monarchs should decide what to do with them. This may have proved to be a difficult decision for Columbus, but he felt sure if the Caribs could be civilized and Christianized, "at least their souls would be saved."[21]

Columbus possessed some knowledge of the ongoing struggle between Spanish colonizers in the Canaries and the Guanche peoples, having visited the islands several times previously. Knowing that the Spanish policy allowed for the enslavement of prisoners of war, he transferred this policy to the Americas, but only as punishment for the La Navidad massacre (first voyage) and the native attack on La Isabella (second voyage). For our purposes here in investigating his actions during the first voyage, Columbus made no threat of enslavement resulting from any military action he might take. Of course, one may consider forcing the Indigenous peoples of Hispaniola to accept a political and social status of "subjects of Spain" as de facto slavery; the differences sometimes blur in practical application. Spaniards in the Caribbean later employed varied strategies and preferences for dealing with Indigenous peoples without consultation or involvement of the Spanish crown or native populations, freelancing their own version of political control. This concern became a problem for Columbus on the second voyage. His strong hand in dealing with rebellious Spaniards, partly derived from the native mistreatment those men inflicted, earned resentment from his settlers. Columbus had to deal with increasing episodes where large bands of Indios attacked, robbed, and sometimes killed individual or small groups of Spaniards. The conflict occurred as a matter of action-reaction; in one incident during the second voyage, several Indios stole clothing articles from Spaniards in the mining district of *Cibao*, resulting in retribution by the captain in charge, Alonso de Hojeda. Despite firm instructions to treat the Indigenous peoples well, Hojeda "cut off the ears of one of the Indians and sent the chief [the local cacique], his brother, and a nephew back to Isabella [town] in chains to be executed."[22] Columbus, furious over Hojeda's punishment, freed the captives, but the incident revealed the difficulty of controlling men bent on personal gain, no matter the cost; it would only get worse from here.

Columbus's vision of socio-political hegemony thus evolved, similar to what existed in the Canary Islands, and included the following sequence of actions: First, he would make contact and initiate friendly ties with political leaders (local chiefs, regional caciques), then establish one or more temporary trading posts. Second, on successive voyages, he would set up permanent trading posts and support towns, housing volunteer Spanish migrants. Third, depending on local cooperation, Columbus would extend his political control by expanding his geographic boundaries and assimilating Indigenous peoples. Fourth, geo-political expansion would continue until the entire island became under his rule—a sequenced recipe for colonialism. Columbus imagined, coming from a paternalistic European paradigm, a happy contingent of Spanish settlers, digging and panning for gold, growing, and tending acres of mastic trees and various spices. Working alongside them, even happier Indigenous workers would carve out a new life, buoyed by the protection Columbus would provide from Carib raiding, thankful for being shown the one and only true God, and excited for new economic opportunities the Europeans might provide. Columbus appeared to sum up his vision by stating in his letter to Isabella and Ferdinand "that they might become Christians and be inclined to the love and service of their highnesses and of the whole Castilian nation and strive to aid us…"[23] This is what Columbus believed—leading Spaniards and Indigenous peoples to a social and economic commonality of purpose, considering his view, a myopic view, as the only alternative. He did not see colonialism as a negative outcome; neither did many 15th-century Europeans, especially Spaniards.

The above-theorized action sequence is what occurred initially, more or less, on the Canary Islands but quickly devolved disastrously for the Guanche people. Trading posts (seaports) such as San Sebastian on Gomera did spring up. As we have seen, *fazendas* arose on Gran Canaria, Gomera, and other islands as the influx of Spanish adventurers grew. Local feuds sprang up between colonists infringing ever more on Guanche-inhabited areas, resulting in captured Indigenous fighters forcibly thrust into slave environments, often sold to other landowners on nearby islands. And so it would be in the Caribbean, with Columbus unable to contain the excesses of his men, especially the *hidalgos* (men of wealth and position), and his questionable administrative actions.

Another major factor in considering the differences between slavery developing in the Canary Islands compared to the Caribbean is the sheer number of potential slaves, with the Indigenous population of the Caribbean many times greater than the combined Guanche population.[24] This demographic relationship held for the early years of exploration and settlement 1492–1520, after that time, population decline from European diseases and abuse culled the remaining Indigenous survivors down to a small percentage of the pre-contact population.[25] At the end of his voyage, when he wrote his experiences for the Spanish monarchs, Columbus did suggest enslaving some of the Indigenous peoples, noting how mastic and "aloe wood" could become profitable commodities. Then he added, "and slaves, as many as they [Ferdinand and Isabella] shall order to be shipped and who will be from the idolaters."[26] This declaration of limiting slavery would change and expand during Columbus's second voyage as he faced open rebellion among Hispaniola's Indigenous peoples.

Notes

1 Morgan, "Origins of American Slavery," 52.
2 Stevens-Arroyo, "The Inter-Atlantic Paradigm," 515. Stevens-Arroyo believes there remained significant differences in the method and manner in which colonization and its accompanying enforced servitude and slavery developed between the Spanish-controlled islands of the Canaries and Columbus's early attempts in the Caribbean. Both regions were certainly formed as a product of medieval thinking informed by religious and economic considerations. See p. 516 for his explanations of key elements that played significant roles in the thought formation of Spanish officials.
3 The quote is from Fernàndez-Armesto, *Before Columbus*, 1987: 212–3 and taken from Stevens-Arroyo, 517.
4 For more information on Spanish Grandees, see Ayán, "Spaces of Power of the Spanish Nobility (1480–1715)," 13–14.
5 Columbus worried that he might infringe on waters south of the Canaries during his 1492 and later voyages.
6 Stevens-Arroyo, "The Inter-Atlantic Paradigm," 521.
7 This would happen in the Caribbean, where Christopher Columbus and later his sons conducted legal challenges to the Crown's usurping administrative power on Hispaniola.
8 Interestingly, among the Spanish soldiers who took part in these final campaigns were Hernán Cortés and Francisco Pizarro. Note how the dates of conquest for Gran Canaria (1483) and Tenerife (1496) lie within the period of time when Columbus sailed and formulated his policy of colonization and eventual conquest. See Stevens-Arroyo, "The Inter-Atlantic Paradigm," 523–4 for more information concerning "the tug of war between medieval repopulation and an imperialistic pattern of subjugation…"
9 Cook, *The Aborigines of the Canary Islands*, 451. Cook asserted that the physical and socio-cultural destruction was so thorough that anthropologists and other scientists have difficulty identifying a comprehensive, accurate picture of their pre-invasion existence.
10 Ibid., 457. Apparently, the samples discovered differed considerably in form and extent.
11 It should be noted that Spanish authority to force Indigenous peoples to work in any capacity was not originally given to *donatàrios*, foretelling a similar experience in the Americas and highlighting the difficulty in providing a uniform code of behavior over local authorities.
12 Parsons, "The Migration of Canary Islanders to the Americas," 448.
13 Ibid., 447. Parson explained that Ferdinand and Isabella understood the governmental structure that appeared to be working on the Canary Islands. The assumption here is that the same model would also work well on the newly acquired islands of the Indies.
14 Ibid., 451. As the years moved on and the Spanish presence grew in the Americas, more Guanche, *criollos* (Spaniards born in the Canary Islands), and *isleños* (Spanish-Guanche mix) departed for opportunities on the new frontier. Between 1492 and 1506, no less than twelve fleets, heading west, stopped in the Canaries for supplies

and added Guanche and others as passengers. Some of the fleet commanders agreeing to accept Canary Islanders included Columbus, Ojeda, Vespucci, and Ovando. 452.

15 Guanche slaves were shipped to the nearby islands of Madeira and Porto Santo and were in residence there during the time Columbus lived there. "Vieira, Sugar Islands," 58. Later, enslaved Blacks from West Africa joined the Guanche labor force. There is no evidence that, at any time in his life, Christopher Columbus owned slaves.

16 Certainly, the Indigenous peoples he brought back during the first voyage were not slaves, as Susan Ramírez wrote in her book *A History of Colonial Latin America*, 3, and as suggested by Delaney, *Columbus and the Quest for Jerusalem*, 268, n. 11.

17 Las Casas wrote later that Columbus understood and honored the papal decree of *motu proprio* (proper motion), giving the Spanish monarchs "supreme rulers, as sovereign emperors, over all the kings and princes and realms throughout the Indies, both islands and mainlands already discovered and yet to be discovered." Griffin, *Las Casas on Columbus, Repertorium Columbianum*, 76.

18 Hinckley, Clark, B. *Christopher Columbus*, 119–20.

19 Delaney, 145. See pages 144–6 for a full account of this critical episode, fully changing the dynamics of Spanish/Indio relations.

20 Caraci believes that Taínos made up most, if not all, of the Indigenous warriors at the Battle of Vega Real. Personal Communication, July 22, 2023.

21 Ibid., 154. For an excellent summary of the treachery of Margarit and Hojeda, and Columbus's reaction and subsequent actions, see Delaney, 152–6.

22 Ibid., 129–30.

23 Jane, *The Four Voyages of Columbus*, 8.

24 Caribbean population estimates by Las Casas and others, historically and recently, spread from a low estimate of 300,000 to more than five million, while the Canary Islands Guanche by 1492 most likely ranged between 40,000 and 60,000 persons.

25 Much of the loss was due to the two devastating epidemics: influenza in 1493 and smallpox in 1518. Untold numbers of people died from the hard work forced on the inhabitants. See Reséndez, Andrés, *The Other Slavery*.

26 Jane, *The Four Voyages of Columbus*, 16. Idolaters, at this point, meant the Caribs and others that practiced cannibalism as described by the Lucayan and Taíno peoples.

APPENDIX V

Slavery in the Pre-Columbian Americas

Slavery existed throughout the known world at the time of Columbus, as it had for time immemorial. David Eltis noted that despite the temporary decline in Euro-African-Asian slavery due to the fall of the Roman Empire, human bondage or forced servitude rose steadily during the Middle Ages. In Europe, the Iberian Peninsula, recovering from Roman and Visigoth occupation, endured centuries of Moorish military campaigns of geographic expansion, resulting in thousands of captured combatants and civilians transformed into forced slaves, typically working at agricultural tasks and increasingly taking on domestic chores in burgeoning Arab towns such as Granada or Màlaga. As Christians battled back, regaining territory, a reversed enslavement escalated, with Muslims forced into laboring the same type of work; each side understood the social-religious connection, allowing conquering armies the right to subjugate military enemies and non-believing peoples.[1] This practice represents a form of *faith slavery*.[2]

Columbus saw this personally during his extended time in Spain, joining King Ferdinand and Queen Isabella at the newly erected military encampment at Santa Fe. Rumors for decades suggested that Columbus may have joined in the intense fighting during the summer and fall of 1492. On January 2, 1492, as the Moorish leader Boabdil capitulated, Christian forces, including Columbus, entered the Muslim city of Granada for a final triumph. This signaled to all present a powerful religious conviction: God was on the side of the Christians.[3] Columbus became particularly moved. He wrote,

I saw the Royal Standards of Your Highnesses placed by force of arms on the towers of the Alhambra, which is the fortress of the said city; and I saw the Moorish King come out to the gates of the city and kiss the Royal Hands of Your Highnesses.[4]

It is clear from the above accounts that slavery remained linked to religious conversion, and it is this mindset that Columbus would bring to his encounters in the Americas. But what type of slavery, if any, existed in the Americas as he prepared his ships and men for their first voyage in the summer of 1492?

Eltis admits that slavery "had long existed in the Pre-Columbian Americas."[5] He cites examples from the "complex" Aztec social milieu to the unsophisticated, yet persistent, cannibalistic Brazilian tribe of the Tupinambà. In both situations, the precursor to slavery was war. The fate of captured prisoners depended wholly on the current situation and the whims of the victorious leader. Aztec prisoners, those spared death from sacrificial slaughter, found life an arduous daily exercise in mental and physical stamina, working in agricultural fields in and around the capital city of Tenochtitlan or constructing causeways within the urban center. As is well known, Aztec religious festivals culminated with human sacrifice to a variety of gods, such as Huitzilopochtli (war) or Tlaloc (rain and fertility). Dozens of victims climbed the steep steps of the Temple of Mayor as thousands of worshipers watched in silent prayer below. Priests performed a brief religious ceremony, offering the living heart of the victim in return for favorable outcomes—victory in war, adequate rain, and prosperous crops. The severed victims' heads, thrown to the crowd, signaled an end to the violent episode. Bernal Diaz del Castillo, a witness to the final Spanish assault on Tenochtitlan, recalled the screams of victims from atop Temple Major, some Spanish, some Indian allies—Tlaxcalans, among the unlucky prisoners. Indigenous allies from former Aztec vassal territories, such as Cholula, Huexotzingo, Texcoco, Chalco, and Tlamanalco, avenged years of forced Aztec slavery and killing during the final siege and conquest of Tenochtitlan by entering the city, murdering unarmed priests, women, and children, and destroying personal homes, warehouses, and causeways.[6]

In Central America, Mayan civilization remained in decline, albeit with slavery intact. Other tribal nations in the region not only used warfare to obtain slaves but also inculcated non-warfare methods of obtaining and maintaining a slave class. This system occurred "internally through a judicial process, indebtedness, or deprivation."[7] Often, these people obtained some degree of freedom, depending on the local traditions and length of service.

Interestingly, the Incas of South America used a system of mandatory assignment of work. Known as the *Mit'a*, local leaders required family members to help build roads, construct buildings, and work in agriculture not owned by your family. The idea here was to force the person to work, but only for limited periods, to benefit the overall progress of community and state development.[8] The Tehuelche people of the Argentina-Chile region, a hunting-gathering culture that roamed the grasslands of Patagonia and the foothills of the Andes, engaged in intra-regional conflict as the constant search for food and supplies pressured individual tribal families. Resulting battles determined victors and newly acknowledged boundaries of operation. Defeated tribes suffered partial or full enslavement.[9]

Scholarly investigations into pre-Columbian North American slavery have accelerated in recent years, with local and regional studies leading the way. At least one comprehensive effort by Christina Snyder attempted to study native slavery in the American South, reporting on tribal traditions for warfare, resulting in captive-taking, assimilating "outsider" captives, recognizing Indian racial slavery, and discussing instances of Indian enslaving Blacks. For Snyder, Indigenous slavery followed war-related activities, admitting a constant state of war existed alongside enslavement, stating, "Conflict constantly simmered and regularly boiled over into war."[10] Powerful chieftains initiated aggression as an effort to "enhance the power of their own ruling lineages." If this sounds familiar, consider one main reason Columbus demanded certain rights and privileges guaranteed to him and his lineage: He wanted to provide wealth and power to his two sons. Slave trading among these Southern tribes involved individual slave exchanges or entire groups. Native American slave trading often involved the selling of persons for goods and/or services, such as food, hides, or weapons. Also, temporary wartime alliances might see an agreement with one party promising captured prisoners.

In a recent online publication titled "Warfare in Aboriginal Societies," the Canadian government announced, "Despite the myth that Aboriginals lived in happy harmony before the arrival of Europeans, war was central to the way of life of many First Nations cultures." Admitting that the causes of the inter-tribal conflicts were numerous, citing personal disagreements that offended the honor of the tribe or encroachments on recognized boundaries. New archaeological evidence points to the fact that Indigenous nations such as the Huron, Petun, and Iroquois worked constantly to build "timber palisades," fortifying their people from the ongoing threat of attack.[11] The taking of prisoners for slavery or punishment ranked high among the motivations for warfare. As a sign of bravery, it was not uncommon for warriors to seek out captives, return to their village, and publicly torture the prisoner. Praise from the village chief, elders, and other warriors followed and helped raise the prestige of that warrior's social status. Sometimes, the village chief awarded captured prisoners to the wives of lost warriors—securing a personal slave, albeit with certain freedoms and responsibilities. Once Europeans, French, and English settlers arrived on the scene, Canadian Indigenous peoples were eager to engage in slave trading, selling captives or their scalps for money or supplies.[12]

The Northwest Coast tribes, in what is now the United States, constructed a somewhat rigid social structure determined by family ties, the possession of desirable goods, and the status of parents at the time of the child's birth. Wealth determination varied from tribe to tribe, some honoring the creation or implementation of spiritual songs or ritual dances as valuable as the number of animal skins, precious stones, and other physical items owned by the individual.

The exception to the above statement included the successful production of a village potlatch, a giving festival in which the host honored fellow clan members by presenting gifts, a sign of new wealth. Demonstrating physical bravery also provided an opportunity for social advancement, as highlighted by the once-a-year whale hunt. At other times, distinguishing your actions during inter-tribal warfare allowed the victor to secure one or more slaves from the vanquished, male or female. Anderson-Córdova cited a reference that acknowledged Taíno involvement in the raiding and kidnapping of women, a separate occurrence from random Carib raids.[13] One American scholar described a three-tiered system of social status with nobility at the top, followed by commoners, and finally, slaves. Most often, when a village raided a neighboring area, slaves, including women and children, became fair game. Social tradition additionally allowed for the purchase of slaves from the same village or other tribes; at other times, one might obtain a slave "received as gifts, or who were the offspring of a man of high rank and a slave woman." Ultimately, "Because of the stigma attached to being a slave, they had no status and virtually no hope of ever gaining any."[14]

Peter Siegel, in his "Competitive Polities and Territorial Expansion in the Caribbean," declared, "In the case of Caribbean pre-Columbian chiefly polities, we see the full spectrum of feuding, ranging from small-scale rivalries to battles of subjugation and conquest."[15] The results of these intertribal conflicts resulted in the acquisition of new territory and human subjects. Siegel noted how predatory expansion of group territories is "well documented ethnographically," and goes on to cite numerous specific sources.[16]

In reviewing warfare and slavery in the Caribbean, a good place to start is the destruction of the Ciboney people by subsequent invasions by Taíno tribes migrating northward from the Lesser Antilles and South America. The Ciboney were simple people with no identifiable social structure other than membership in small tribal clans. They occupied gullies and caves for protection from enemies and severe weather. Their hunter-gatherer lifestyle did not include any attempts at agriculture, not even cassava. Operating independently in nomadic bands, they moved constantly without residing in established villages.[17]

Beginning around 250 AD and accelerating around 1000 AD, experienced seafarers, known today as the Arawak-speaking (Taíno and Lucayan) people, daringly crossed over from the Venezuela-Trinidad area to islands in the Greater Antilles, especially Hispaniola, Puerto Rico, and Cuba. Upon contact, competition for available land and sea resources initiated aggression and eventual warfare. While there is little evidence to detail the extent of each island's conflicts, the Taíno soon dominated, leaving Ciboney tribes retreating inland to remote locations, avoiding contact whenever possible. By the time Columbus arrived, "the Ciboney were completely displaced, marginalized, and weakened in Cuba, Hispaniola, Puerto Rico, and, to a lesser extent, the Bahamas."[18] This process of Indigenous conquest and territorial acquisition occurred hundreds of years before Columbus.

The Taíno, with extensive seafaring experience, worked migration routes from the main islands to neighboring small islands in the Bahamas. On Hispaniola and Cuba, they formed large villages and a complex social structure that differed slightly from region to region. Two cultural Taíno groups included the Saladoids and Barrancoids, identified by their distinct pottery creations, settling in large numbers in varied geographic environments, including open, raised grasslands, forest enclosures, interior valleys, and along protected beaches.

Established in greater numbers than the Ciboney, the Taíno held control over most of the landscape of the Greater Antilles of Caribbean territory by 1492. However, just as the Ciboney suffered conquest and displacement from the Taíno, other migrants, the Caribs, threatened established Taíno settlements from the south. Moving up about the same time as the Taíno, the Caribs island-hopped from the Lesser Antilles, adding islands to their territorial conquests. Using the island of Guadeloupe as a home base, they conducted initial forays to Puerto Rico, then into Eastern Hispaniola. As experts with the bow and arrow, they soon devastated unprotected smaller Taíno tribes. Fearing death or abduction, by the 15th century, Taíno villages grew in size as there was relative safety in numbers. To protect themselves, Taíno caciques (chiefs) established formal territorial *cacicazgos* (kingdoms). Wielding total power, caciques organized their lands economically and politically; one source noted, "They had forces able to carry out military activities, but they did not have standing armies."[19]

Taíno peoples lived in distinct geographic areas, *cacicazgos* dominated by a chief (*cacique*), male or female, more often than not isolated on Hispaniola by the centrally dominating mountain terrain. The center of a cacique's influence usually coalesced with a lowland river valley, with at least one exception, that of Caonabó within the central plains of the island.

Irwin Rouse, a noted archaeologist of the Caribbean region, believed that warfare remained a constant phenomenon throughout the Greater Antilles and Bahamas. Most violent interactions occurred during Carib raids and "disputes over hunting and fishing rights, or to force a chief who had received a bride [they were polygamists] price to deliver the woman purchased."[20] The cacique seeking retribution organized a fighting group of villagers, the size of which depended on the threat. Bearing homemade weapons such as wood-sharpened clubs and spears, the warriors attended a pre-fight religious event, painting themselves with red and black pigment and adorning their necks or heads with shell-carved images of various *zemis* [gods].[21] Rouse added that Taíno tribes living in the northeastern region of Hispaniola and Puerto Rico evolved into fierce warriors as a result of the ongoing push of Carib incursions.

Not given Columbus's European intervention, increased wars, growing ever more destructive, may have taken place, especially on Hispaniola, where Carib raiders began to settle in larger numbers within interior valleys. For the time

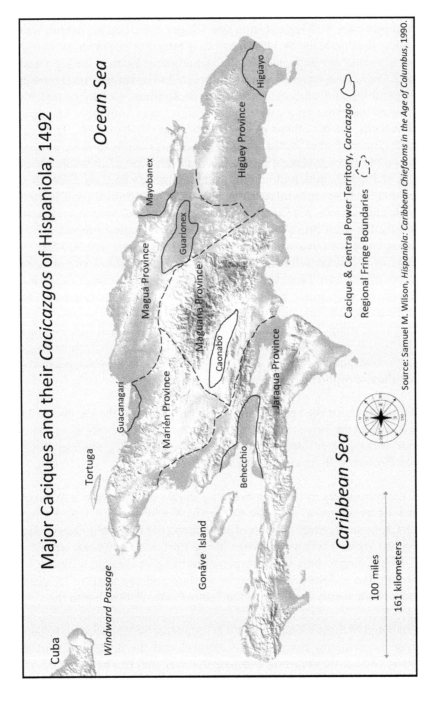

FIGURE V.1 Major Caciques and Their *Cacicazgos* of Hispaniola, 1492

being, aggressive Caribs restricted their warlike actions to irregular raiding adventures, intending to strike fear in the Taíno villages while confiscating goods and prisoners. Striking out from new villages in Eastern Hispaniola and Puerto Rico, Carib raiders, by 1492, found easy targets of opportunity among the small islands of the Bahamas. Recall Columbus's notation in the log about the men of Guanahani covered with what appeared to be battle scars. Through physical gesturing and unrecognizable vocal declarations, Columbus and his men surmised that these people were under serious threat from other islanders.

Until recently, the hypothesis of Carib settlement on Hispaniola, Jamaica, and Cuba remained unvalidated, despite Columbus's claim to the contrary. Ann Ross and others, investigating the facial morphology of pre-Columbian Lucayans of the Bahamas, announced two breakthrough findings. First, they reported that the Lucayan skull structure more closely resembled peoples from Hispaniola and Jamaica, not Cuba—the closest large island. Second, and more dramatically, the team provided extensive evidence indicating support for "a Carib invasion of the Greater Antilles beginning around the year AD 800."[22] Purposely using the term "invasion" suggests a large, warlike expansion by Carib tribes into former Taíno territory, not just for the intention of capturing prisoners but for subjugation and colonization—does this sound familiar? The Taíno did it to the Ciboney, and now, in the 15th century, the Caribs were in the process of completing their conquest. The report concluded that wide-ranging efforts by "Carib invaders" focused on expanding their territorial control over Hispaniola.[23] Weighing in on the issue, Hugh Thomas, in his comprehensive survey of the rise of the Spanish empire, concluded,

> Had it not been for the Spanish invasions, it is likely that the Caribs would have destroyed the Taínos as the Taínos destroyed the Ciboneys. Some have written of the ancient Caribbean as if it had been Elysium [paradise]. But it was an Elysium with savagery in the wings.[24]

One of the researchers in the path-breaking study noted above was William Keegan, long recognized as a top pre-Columbian Caribbean expert. Reporting his results, Keegan declared, "I've spent years trying to prove Columbus wrong when he was right: There were Caribs in the northern Caribbean when he arrived. We're going to have to reinterpret everything we thought we knew."[25] In discussing the widespread practice of warfare and cannibalism, Keegan admitted it was a possibility, likening the Taíno–Carib relationship to the

> Hatfields and McCoys's kind of situation, suggesting back and forth constant fighting. Interestingly, Keegan sees Columbus and the Spanish monarchs thinking, 'Well, if they're going to behave that way, they can be enslaved.' All of a sudden, every native person in the entire Caribbean became a Carib as far as the colonists were concerned.[26]

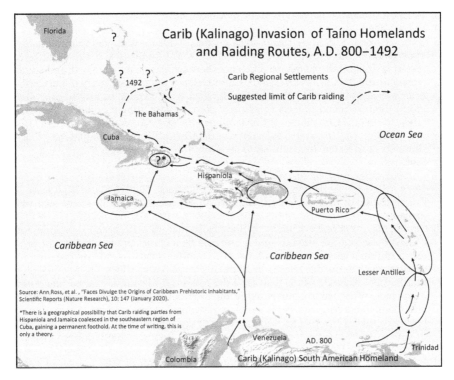

FIGURE V.2 Carib (Kalinago) Invasion

Until recently, historians believed that Columbus misinterpreted Taíno stories about wild tribes that raided their villages, stories that suggested an invasion-like onslaught. Evidence now points to Columbus's later belief that Carib (Kalinago) people had been, and were currently (1492), engaged in a systematic invasion of the Caribbean, moving north and west, stealing property, and women and children.

Notes

1 Eltis, "Slavery," *Christopher Columbus and the Age of Exploration: An Encyclopedia*, edited by Silvio A. Bedini, New York: De Capo Press, 1998. For information on slavery from the Italian city-states and the Ottoman Empire (Mamluk Sultante) see Barker, Hannah. "Societies with Slaves: Genoa, Venice, and the Mamluk Sultanate." In *That Most Precious Merchandise: The Mediterranean Trade in Black Sea Slaves*.

2 While faith slavery remained a de facto socio-military policy during the Reconquista on the Iberian Peninsula, Pope Pius II issued a bull in 1462 connecting the concept to extra-Iberian colonization. The ruling sent to the Spanish court concerned the treatment of natives in the Canary Islands. The decree stated that converted natives could not be enslaved; however, if they did not convert, they could be enslaved. Delaney, *Columbus and the Quest for Jerusalem*, 141. Thus, this became official church policy, with expectations for enforcement by Catholic monarchs.

3 Delaney, *Columbus and the Quest for Jerusalem*, 65.

4 Fuson, *The Log of Christopher Columbus*, 51.

5 Eltis, "Slavery," 632. More recent archaeological evidence continues to increase our knowledge of the extent and complexity of social bondage and class structure, revealing similarities and unique differences between the mainland (North and South America) and the Caribbean Islands. Carol Delaney noted that slavery in the Caribbean was already in effect throughout the area when Columbus arrived. She also linked the conversion process to eventual slavery, should the encountered peoples refuse to become Christians, see *Columbus and the Quest for Jerusalem*, n. 62, 275.

6 See Castillo, *The Discovery and Conquest of Mexico*, Book 2, Chapter XI. Water causeways connected Tenochtitlan to lakefront towns and villages.

7 Ibid.

8 Canseco, *History of the Inca Realm*, 63.

9 Helle, "Slavery," see section on the Pre-Columbian era. The Tehuelche experience is similar to that of the nomadic tribes of North America, such as the Comanche and Pawnee.

10 Snyder, *Slavery in Indian Country*, 4. She admits that tribes engaged in hostilities for endless reasons, sometimes to simply enhance their status, often to enlarge or protect traditional geographic boundaries (i.e., hunting grounds), and on occasion to revenge previous outside attacks by aggressive neighboring tribes. The one constant that Snyder acknowledges is that while the reasons for hostilities varied, the result often, most often, led to captive-taking and eventual slavery. It is interesting to note how Columbus's critics decry his use of employing the same motives on Hispaniola, revenging the La Navidad massacre, and his desire to claim and work the gold fields of Cibao (central Hispaniola) without harassment from regional Indigenous tribes.

11 "Warfare in Pre-Columbian North America," Online.

12 Ibid. The research concludes that scalping, the cutting off of the top layer of head skin along with the hair, existed well before Europeans came to the Canadian region. British settlers learned of the practice, first as victims, then later incorporated scalping as a common response when seeking revenge for a previous Indian assault or family massacre. For more information on scalping on the North American continent, see Miller, "Evidence for Prehistoric Scalping in Northeastern Nebraska," 211–9; Bamforth, Douglas B., "What Do We Know about Warfare on the Great Plains?" 8.

13 Anderson-Córdova, *Surviving Spanish Conquest*, Chapter 5 notes, 206. The reference is to Jalil Sued Badillo, *Los Caribes: Realidad o fábula: Ensayo de rectificación histórica*, Editorial Antillana, Rio Piedras, Puerto Rico, 1978, 58–64.

14 Daugherty, "People of the Salmon," 65–66. Daugherty also points to the aggressive Tupinamba tribe, whose paternalistic social structure and warlike behavior called for the village leaders to live apart in a large hut from the rest of the people. "He slept there with one or more of his wives and with his captive female slaves and a young boy or two who performed various services," 195. The same holds for the Skagits tribe in Washington State, where wealthy men might own one or more slaves. Daugherty relates the story of one such village leader who captured a young girl from another village and sold her to another tribe. He also suggests slaveholding increased with village locations closer to the coast. 318.

15 In *Islands at the Crossroads: Migration, Seafaring, and Interaction in the Caribbean*, chapter 10, 196.

16 Ibid., 193. Siegel alludes to the ongoing violence between "intruders and residents," suggesting a continuing struggle for caciques to maintain political hegemony within their existing controlled territory and pressures to expand and/or defend themselves from outside threats.

17 Rouse, *Taíno*, 20. The Guanahatabeys sourced local shellfish for their main suste-
   nance; interestingly, no prehistoric pottery has ever been found in their territory of
   western Cuba. Some evidence presented suggested that at least three small surviving
   tribes of Ciboney continued to live on the western shores of Hispaniola (Haiti) at
   the time of contact. See Fernandez, "The Forgotten Innocents," 246.
18 Beckles, "The Indigenous Caribbean People," 4–5.
19 DuBois & Turits, *Freedom Roots*, 17. Columbus witnessed the ability of caciques to
   quickly mobilize villagers for protection from Carib and others raiding isolated villages or infringing on shoreline regions. This is similar to how American militias
   were used so effectively in colonial America. The authors also note that women
   could attain leadership as a cacique. In 1503, one woman, Anacoana, fought the
   Spanish in a one-sided affair and died defending her *cacicazgo*. Columbus's replacement, Nocolás Ovando, trying to mop up Indigenous resistance on Hispaniola,
   ordered local caciques to be captured.
20 Rouse, *The Taínos*, 17.
21 Ibid., for more information on the role zemis (also spelled *cemís*) played in Taíno
   culture, see Rouse, 13–14. The author also discusses the Spanish reaction to finding
   zemis, 148–49. See also, Deagan & Cruxent, "Reluctant Hosts," 32. An excellent
   summary of zemis as part of their belief system, as well as other common rituals,
   can be read in Guitar & Estevez, "Taíno," 121–4. On the relationship of zemis to the
   natural environment, see Dubois & Turits, "The Indigenous Caribbean," 18.
22 Ross, et al. "Faces Divulge the Origins of Caribbean Prehistoric Inhabitants,"
   abstract. As a side note, the report noted that no observable similarities in skull
   structure appeared when comparing pre-Columbian specimens from the Bahamas
   with those from southern Florida, suggesting little or no migration from mainland
   North America southward to the Bahamas.
23 The authors of the report cite that they need more specimens and evidence to solid-
   ify their claims, but they feel confident in their findings. On the issue of Cuba, they
   need more Cuban specimens from the eastern region and along the southern coast,
   the areas nearest already established Carib settlements on Hispaniola and Jamaica.
24 Thomas, Hugh. *Rivers of Gold*, 115. The central message here suggests ongoing
   interisland warfare with the intent to conquer, occupy, and subjugate the inhabiting
   population—the same accusation usually reserved for Columbus. At the time of
   Thomas's writing, he was unaware of the archaeological evidence confirming a
   strong Carib presence north of the islands of Guadeloupe and Martinique. Indeed,
   Carib penetration deep into Hispaniola and the eastern coastline of Cuba supports
   the concept of Indigenous conquest and colonization.
25 Van Hoose, Natalie, Research News. Florida Museum of Natural History. January
   10, 2020.
26 Ibid. However, the last statement is not true, as Guacanagarí and his Taíno subjects
   remained friendly with the Spaniards throughout Columbus's explorations.

APPENDIX VI

Latitude and Longitude Estimates for Daily Sailing Locations

Find below estimates of latitude and longitude positions for the end of each day of sailing. The author ran multiple computer distance calculations using the United States Geological Survey's (USGS) National Map—Advanced Viewer. Distance miles (leagues) originated from Robert Fuson's translation of the Las Casas *Diario* using a ratio change of between 2.67 and 3.2 nautical miles, with these figures being averaged lower to three nautical miles per stated league. In Chapter 4, a calculation for magnetic variation is noted in the section titled "The Difficulty Measuring Latitude at Sea and Magnetic Variation" and in the notes beginning with the September 17 log entry; the gradual increase in magnetic variation affords an equal change in compass bearing, intensifying as they neared land. Additionally, this author used slight directional changes based on seasonal wind patterns as the ships entered the main Trade Winds zone and as they neared the last several days of the journey, entering the Caribbean/Gulf Stream effect. The intent here is not to provide exact locational positions but to allow the reader to sense approximate, end-of-day locations. The reader can input latitude and longitude coordinates into any online mapping service such as Google Earth, USGS National Map Viewer, or National Oceanic and Atmospheric Administration's (NOAA's) National Geodetic Survey Data Explorer to locate Columbus's position on any given day; with the latter, one can use their cursor to skim across the map to zero in on their coordinates and place a marker. Should the reader be interested in checking the location of contemporary offshore reefs for the final anchorage site and other island anchorages, use the Navionics Chart Viewer, available online to the public. While reefs can change, their growth rate is quite slow, at only a few centimeters a year.

Ship Location: End of Day

August 3, 1492	7°22′W 35°47′N	24	45°55′W 29°27′N
4	8°30′W 34°38′N	25	46°54′W 28°55′N
5	10°12′W 32°53′N	26	48°49′W 28°53′N
6	11°28′W 31°33′N	27	49°91′W 28°67′N
7	12°32′W 30°35′N	28	50°76′W 28°63′N
9–11	In Transit to Gomera	29	52°14′W 28°58′N
12	07°28′W 28°03′N	30	52°90′W 28°46′N
September 6	17°02′W 28°03′N	October 1	54°28′W 28°42′N
7	10°08′W 27°58′N	2	56°42′W 28°31′N
8–9	drifting in area	3	59°24′W 28°17′N
10	23°17′W 28°03′N	4	62°55′W 28°05′N
11	25°35′W 28°02′N	5	66°10′W 27°47′N
12	27°25′W 27°58′N	6	68°26′W 27°37′N
13	29°18′W 28°00′N	7	69°58′W 27°22′N
14	30°26′W 28°04′N	8	70°32′W 27°06′N
15	3°158′W 28°02′N	9	71°03′W 26°41′N
16	34°00′W 28°00′N	10	73°25′W 24°38′N
17	36°45′W 28°00′N	11	74°26′W 23°57′N
18	39°52′W 28°03′N	12 (anchorage)	74°31′54″W 24°02′42″N
19	41°18′W 28°02′N		
20	41°44′W 28°04′N		
21	42°28′W 28°15′N		
22	44°05′W 28°49′N		
23	45°02′W 29°27′N		

BIBLIOGRAPHY

Allen, Alexander. "Credibility and Incredulity: A Critique of Bartolomé de Las Casas's *A Short Account of the Destruction of the Indies*," *The Gettysburg Historical Journal*, Vol. 9 (2010), Article 5. https://cuploa.gettysburg.edu/ghj

Altman, Ida. *Life and Society in the Early Spanish Caribbean*. Baton Rouge: Louisiana State University Press, 2021.

Alvares, Claudia. "New World Slavery: Redefining the Human," *Annali d'Italianistica*, Vol. 26, Humanisms, Posthumanisms & Neohumanisms (2008), 131–153. https://www.jstor.org/stable/24016277

Anderson-Córdova, Karen. *Surviving Spanish Conquest: Indian Fight, Flight, and Cultural Transformation in Hispaniola and Puerto Rico*. Tuscaloosa: University of Alabama Press, 2017.

Axtell, James. *Beyond 1492: Encounters in Colonial North America*. Oxford, England: Oxford University Press, 1992.

———. "Babel of Tongues: Communicating with the Indians in Eastern North America," In *The Language Encounter in the Americas, 1492 to 1800*, edited by Edward G. Gray and Norman Fiering, 7–60. New York: Berghahn Book.

Ayán, Carmen Sanz. "Spaces of Power of the Spanish Nobility (1480–1715): Introduction," *Renaissance and Reformation / Renaissance et Réforme*, Vol. 43, No. 4 (2020), 9–18. https://www.jstor.org/stable/27028212

Azorin-Molina, Cesar, Melisa Menendez, Tim R. McVicar, Adrian Acevedo, Sergio M. Vicente-Serrano, Emilio Cuevas, Lorenzo Minola and Deliang Chen, "Wind Speed Variability Over the Canary Islands, 1948–2014: Focusing on Trend Differences at the Land-Ocean Interface and Below-Above the Trade Wind Inversion Layer," *Climate Dynamics*, Vol. 50 (2018), 4061–4081. https://link.springer.com/article/10.1007/s00382-017-3861-0

Bamforth, Douglas B. "What Do We Know about Warfare on the Great Plains?" In *Archaeological Perspectives on Warfare on the Great Plains*, edited by Douglas B. Bamforth and Andrew J. Clark, 3–34. University Press of Colorado, 2018. https://doi.org/10.2307/j.ctvgd21w.3

Barbie, Bischof, Arthur J. Mariano, and Edward H. Ryan. "The Portugal Current System," Surface Currents in the Atlantic Ocean. https://oceancurrents.rsmas.miami.edu/atlantic/portugal.html

Barker, Hannah. "Societies with Slaves: Genoa, Venice, and the Mamluk Sultanate." In *That Most Precious Merchandise: The Mediterranean Trade in Black Sea Slaves, 1260-1500*, 61–91. University of Pennsylvania Press, 2019. http://www.jstor.org/stable/j.ctv16t6ckk.7

Bartoski-Velez, Elise. "The First Interpretations of the Columbian Enterprise," *Revista Canadiense de Estudios Hispánicos*, Vol. 33, No. 2 (2009), 317–334. http://www.jstor.org/stable/27764260

———. *The Legacy of Christopher Columbus in the Americas*. Nashville: Vanderbilt University Press, 2014. (Google Books is in full version)

Bazzurro, Giorgio. *L'Eredita dei Colombo: dal "Libro de Conto" de Cristoforo e da quello del Fratello Bartolomeo*. Istituto Idrografico della Marina, Genoa, 2020.

Beasley. "The French Conquest of the Canaries in 1402–06," *The Geographical Journal*, Vol. 25, No. 1 (1905), 77–81.

Becher, A. B. "The Landfall of Columbus on His First Voyage to America," *The Journal of the Royal Geographical Society of London*, Vol. 26 (1856), 189–203.

Beckles, Hilary. "Kalinago (Carib) Resistance to European Colonisation of the Caribbean," *Caribbean Quarterly*, Vol. 54, No. 4 (2008), 77–94. http://www.jstor.org/stable/40654700

Beckles, Hilary and Verene A. Shepherd, "The Indigenous Caribbean People," *Liberties Lost: Caribbean Indigenous Societies and Slave Systems*. Cambridge, England: Cambridge University Press, 2004.

Bergreen, Laurence. *Columbus: The Four Voyages, 1492–1504*. New York: Penguin Books, 2011.

Berman, Mary Jane, and Perry L. Gnivecki. "Good as Gold: The Aesthetic Brilliance of the Lucayans," In *Islands at the Crossroads: Migration, Seafaring, and Interaction in the Caribbean*. Tuscaloosa: University of Alabama Press, 2011.

———. "Colonial Encounters in Lucayan Contexts," In *Material Encounters and Indigenous Transformations in the Early Colonial Americas: Archaeological Case Studies*, edited by Corinne L. Hofman and Floris W.M. Keehnen, Vol. 9, 32–57. Brill, 2019. http://www.jstor.org/stable/10.1163/j.ctvrxk2gr.8

Berman, Mary Jane, Perry L. Gnivecki, and Deborah M. Pearsall. "Plants, People, and Culture in the Prehistoric Central Bahamas: A View from the Three Dog Site, an Early Lucayan Settlement on San Salvador Island, Bahamas," *Latin American Antiquity*, Vol. 11, No. 3 (2000), 219–239.

———. "New Perspectives on Bahamian Archaeology: The Lucayans and their World," *Journal of Caribbean Archaeology*, Vol. 15, 2015, 3–22.

Berman, Mary Jane, Perry L. Gnivecki, Deborah M. Pearsall, and Charlene Dixon Hutcheson. "Impressions of a Lost Technology: A Study of Lucayan-Taíno Basketry," *Journal of Field Archaeology*, Vol. 27, No. 4 (Winter, 2000), 417–435.

Berman, Mary Jane, Perry L. Gnivecki, Deborah M. Pearsall, Charlene Dixon Hutcheson, and Deborah M. Pearsall. "At the Crossroads: Starch Grain and Phytolith Analyses in Lucayan Prehistory," *Latin American Antiquity*, Vol. 19, No. 2 (2008), 181–203.

Berman, Mary Jane, Perry L. Gnivecki, Deborah M. Pearsall, Charlene Dixon Hutcheson, Deborah M. Pearsall, April K. Sievert, and Thomas R. Whyte. "Form and

Function of Bipolar Lithic Artifacts from the Three Dog Site, San Salvador, Bahamas, *Latin American Antiquity*, Vol. 10, No. 4 (Dec., 1999), 415–432.

Berman, Mary Jane, Perry L. Gnivecki, Deborah M. Pearsall, Charlene Dixon Hutcheson, Deborah M. Pearsall, April K. Sievert, Thomas R. Whyte, and Perry L. Gnivecki. "Chapter 2: Colonial Encounters in Lucayan Contexts," *Material Encounters and Indigenous Transformations in the Early Colonial Americas: Archaeological Case Studies*, edited by Corinne L. Hofman and Floris W.M. Keehnen. Leiden: Brill, 2019.

Bernáldez, Andrés. *Historia de los reyes católicos D. Fernando y Doña Isabel*. Gabriel y Ruíz de Apodaca, Fernando de, 1828–1888. Written 1513? Published, 1870. Archive. com: https://archive.org/details/historiadelosrey00bern

Bigelow, Allison Margaret. "Seasons of Gold," In *Mining Language: Racial Thinking, Indigenous Knowledge, and Colonial Metallurgy in the Early Modern Iberian World*, 79–102. University of North Carolina Press, 2020. http://www.jstor.org/stable/10.5149/9781469654409_bigelow.9

Blick, Jeffrey P. "Pre-Columbian Impact on Terrestrial, Intertidal, and Marine Resources, San Salvador, Bahamas (AD 950–1500)," *Journal for Nature Conservation*, Vol. 15, No. 3 (2007), 174–183.

Boscariol, Mariana. "São Jorge da Mina and Macao: A Comparative Reappriaisal of European Encounters," *Journal of the British Academy*, Vol. 9, supplementary issue 4 (Global Border Making and Securitisation in the Early Modern World, Abstract, 2021.

Boucher, Phillip P. *Cannibal Encounters: Europeans and Island Caribs, 1492–1763*. Baltimore: John Hopkins University Press, 1992.

Bourne, Edward G. (Eds.) "Articles of Agreement Between the Lords the Catholic Sovereigns and Cristóbal Colon," *The Voyages of Columbus and of John Cabot*, New York: Charles Scribner's Sons, 1906.

———. "Title Granted by the Catholic Sovereigns to Cristóbal Colon of Admiral, Viceroy and Governor of the Islands and Mainland That May Be Discovered," *The Voyages of Columbus and of John Cabot*. New York: Charles Scribner's Sons, 1906.

Bradford, Ernle. *Christopher Columbus*. New York: Viking, 1973.

Campbell, I. C. "The Lateen Sail in World History," *Journal of World History*, Vol. 6, No. 1 (Spring, 1995), 1–23.

Canseco, María Rostworowski de Díez. *History of the Inca Realm*. Cambridge: Cambridge University Press, 1999.

Caraci, Ilaria. *Columbus and the Portuguese' Voyages in the Columbian Sources*, Instituto de Investigação Científica Tropical, 1988. Access through Google Books.

———. *Columbo Vero e Falso: La Construzione delle Historie Fernandine*, Sagep Editrice, 1989.

———. *The Puzzling Hero: Studies on Christopher Columbus and the Culture of His Age*. Translation from Italian by Mayta Munson. Roma, Italia: Carocci editore, 2002.

———. *Three Days in May*. Translated by Barbara R. Cochran, 2019.

Carr, Robert S., William C. Schaffer, Jeff B. Ransom, Michael P. Pateman. "Ritual Cave Use in the Bahamas," *Sacred Darkness: A Global Perspective on the Ritual Use of Caves*. Louisville, Colorado: University Press of Colorado, 2012.

Carrillo, Jesús. *Oviedo on Columbus, Repertorium Columbianum*, Vol. IX, UCLA Center for Medieval and Renaissance Studies, Belgium: Brepolis Publishers, 2000.

Cassá, R. *Los indios de las Antillas*. Madrid: Editorial MAPFRE, 1992.

Castillo, Bernal Días del. *The Discovery and Conquest of Mexico*. Kingsport, Tennessee: Farrar, Straus and Cudahy, 1956.

Catz, Rebecca. "Columbus in Portugal," In *Christopher Columbus and the Age of Exploration*, edited by Silio A. Bedini. New York: Da Capo Press, 1998.

Cervantes, Fernando. *Conquistadores: A New History of Spanish Discovery and Conquest*. New York: Viking, 2021.

Cohen, J. M. *The Four Voyages of Christopher Columbus*. London: Peguin, 1969.

Colección de documentos ineditos relativos al descubrimiento, Conquista y organización de las antiguas posesiones españolas de ultramar, Madrid, Est. tip.: Sucesores de Rivadeneyra, 1885–1932. https://archive.org/details/coleccindedocume56452gut

Collis, John Stewart. *Christopher Columbus*. London: MacDonald and James Publishers, 1976.

Columbus, Christopher. *Letter of Christopher Columbus to Rafael Sánchez (May, 1493)*. Chicago: W.H. Lowdermilk Company, English translation, 1893.

Columbus, Ferdinand. *The Life of the Admiral Christopher Columbus*. Translated by Benjamin Keen. Brunswick, New Jersey: Rutgers University Press, 1992.

Conti, Simonetta. *Portolano e carta nautica: Confronto Toponomastico*, IX Convegno Internzionale di Storia della Cartografia, Pisa e Roma, 1981.

———. "Towards the unknown. Columbus and the great navigators," In *Civilization of the Sea. The Great History of the Italian Navy*, 162–187. Editorial Project editions, 2015.

Cook, Alice Carter. "The Aborigines of the Canary Islands," *American Anthropologist*, Vol. 2, No. 3 (1900), 451–493. http://www.jstor.org/stable/658963

Covarrubias Orozco, Sebastián de. *Tesoro de la lengua castellana, o Española*, 1611 edition, Madrid: Sánchez, 1873. https://archive.org/details/tesorodelalengua00covauoft

Cox, H. C. F. "The Landfall of Columbus," *The Royal Geographical Journal*, Vol. 68, No. 4 (1926), 338–339.

Craton, Michael. *A History of the Bahamas*, 3rd ed. Waterloo, Ontario, Canada: San Salvador Press, 1986.

Cummins, John. *The Voyage of Christopher Columbus: Columbus' Own Journal of Discovery*. New York: St. Martín's Press, 1992. https://archive.org/details/in.ernet.dli.2015.87337

Curet, L. Antonio, and Mark W. Hauser, editors *Islands at the Crossroads: Migration, Seafaring, and Interaction in the Caribbean*. Tuscaloosa: University of Alabama Press, 2011.

Curet, L. Antonio. "The Taíno: Phenomena, Concepts, and Terms," *Ethnohistory*, Vol. 61, No. 3 (2014), 467–495.

Daugherty, Richard D. "People of the Salmon," In *America in 1492: The World of the Indian Peoples Before the Arrival of Columbus*, edited by Alvin M. Josephy, Jr, 49–84. New York: Alfred A. Knopf, 1992.

Davidson, Miles H., *Columbus Then and Now: A Life Reexamined*. Norman, Oklahoma: University of Oklahoma Press, 1997.

Davies, Arthur. *The Geographical Journal*, Vol. 143, No. 3 (1977), 451–459.

De Booy, Theodoor. "Lucayan Remains on the Caicos Islands," *American Anthropologist*, New Series, Vol. 14, No. 1 (1912), 81–105.

———. "Lucayan Artifacts from the Bahamas," *American Anthropologist*, New Series, Vol. 15, No. 1 (1913), 1–7.

Deagan, Kathleen "Colonial Origins and Colonial Transformations in Spanish America," *Historical Archaeology*, Vol. 37, No. 4 (2003), 3–13. http://www.jstor.org/stable/25617091

Deagan, Kathleen, and José María Cruxent. "Reluctant Hosts: The Taínos of Hispaniola," In *Columbus's Outpost among the Taínos: Spain and America at La Isabela, 1493–1498*, 23–46. Yale University Press, 2002. http://www.jstor.org/stable/j.ctt1np8rz.6

Delaney, Carol. *Columbus and the Quest for Jerusalem*. New York: Free Press, 2011.

Delgado, Mariano. Book Review, *Journal of Latin American Studies*, 40, 571–618. Daniel Castro, *Another Face of Empire: Bartolome´ de Las Casas, Indigenous Rights and Ecclesiastical Imperialism* (Durham, NC, and London: Duke University Press, 2007)

Dilke, O. A. W. "Toscanelli, 'Paolo Dal Pozzo'", In *Christopher Columbus and the Age of Exploration*, edited by Silio A. Bedini. New York: Da Capo Press, 1998.

Dubios, Laurent, and Richard Lee Turits. "The Indigenous Caribbean," In *Freedom Roots: Histories from the Caribbean*, 9–52. University of North Carolina Press, 2019. http://www.jstor.org/stable/10.5149/9781469653624_dubois.5

Dugard, Martín, *The Last Voyage of Columbus*. New York: Little, Brown and Company, 2005.

Dunn, Oliver and James E. Kelley, Jr. *The Diario of Christopher Columbus's First Voyage to America, 1492–1493*, Vol. 70. (American Exploration and Travel Series), Norman, Oklahoma: University of Oklahoma Press, 1991.

Durlacher-Wolper, Ruth G. "Columbus's Landfall and the Indian Settlements of San Salvador," *The Florida Anthropologist*, Vol. 35, No. 4 (1982), 203–207.

Dyson, John. *Columbus: For Gold, God, and Glory*. New York: Simon & Schuster, 1991.

Eatough, Geoffrey. Editor and Translator, *Selections from Peter Martyr, Repertorium Columbianum*, Vo'. V. Belgium: Brepols, 1999.

Ehrenberg, Ralph E (Editor). *Mapping the World: An Illustrated History of Cartography*. Washington, DC: National Geographic Society, 2006.

Elbl, Ivana. "The Volume of the Early Atlantic Slave Trade, 1450–1521," *The Journal of African History*, Vol. 38, No. 1 (1997), 31–75. http://www.jstor.org/stable/182945

Eltis. "Slavery," *Christopher Columbus and the Age of Exploration: An Encyclopedia*, edited by Silvio A. Bedini, New York: De Capo Press, 1998.

Ember, M. "The Conditions that May Favor Avunculocal Residence," *Behavior Science Review*, Vol. 9 (1974), 203–209.

Ensor, B. E. Crow-Omaha Marital Alliances and Social Transformations: Archaeological Case Studies on the Taino, Hohokam, and Archaic Lower Mississippi Valley, Ph.D. dissertation, University of Florida, Gainsville, 2003.

Fayer, Joan M. "African Interpreters in the Atlantic Slave Trade," *Anthropological Linguistics*, Vol. 45, No. 3 (2003), 281–295. http://www.jstor.org/stable/30028896

Fernandez, Augustine. "The Forgotten Innocents: Caribbean Aborigines and their Fate," *Southwest Review*, Vol. 55, No. 3 (Summer 1970), 238–252.

Fernández-Armesto, Felipe. *Columbus and the Conquest of the Impossible*. London: Weidenfeld and Nicolson, 1974.

———. *Columbus on Himself*, Indianapolis: Hackett Publishing Company, Inc., 2010.

—*1492: The Year the World Began*. New York: HarperCollins, 2009. (In Google Books full text—see p. 59 for description of natives)

Ferro, Gaetano. "Columbus and his Sailings, According to the 'Diary' of the First Voyage: Observations of a Geographer," *Proceedings, First San Salvador Conference: Columbus and His World*. 1986.

Fitzpatrick, Scott M. "Seafaring Capabilities in the Pre-Columbian Caribbean," *Journal of Maritime Archaeology*, Vol. 8, No. 1 (2013), 101–138. http://www.jstor.org/stable/23747327

Forbes-Pateman, V. et al. "A Population History of Indigenous Bahamian Islanders: Insights from Ancient DNA," *American Journal of Biological Anthropology*, Vol. 8, No. 1, (2022), 1–14.

Ford, Paul Leicester (Editor). *Writings of Christopher Columbus: Descriptive of the Discovery and Occupation of the New World*. New York: Charles L. Webster & Co., 1892. [online] https://archive.org/details/writingsofchrist00colu/page/n10/mode/1up

Fox, Gustavus. *Methods and Results: An Attempt to Solve the Problem of the First Landing Place of Columbus in the New World*. Washington Government Printing Office: United States Coast and Geodetic Survey, 1882. https://archive.org/details/attempttosolvepr00foxg/mode/1up

Fuson, Robert H. *The Log of Christopher Columbus*. Camden, Maine: International Marine Publishing, 1992.

Gierloff-Emden, H.G. "Columbus' Navigation: Navigation and Oceanographic Conditions of the First Discovery Voyage of Columbus," *GeoJournal*, Vol. 26, No. 4 (April 1992), 454–464.

Gil, Juan. *Mitos y utopías del descubrimiento*, Colección "Alianza Universidad," Alianza Editorial, Madrid, 1989.

Godfrey, P.J., D.C. Edwards, R.R. Smith, and R.L. Davis. 1994. Natural History of Northeastern San Salvador Island: a "New World" Where the New World Began, Bahamian Field Station Trail Guide. 28pp. Accessed: James St. John. Inland Lakes & Ponds on San Salvador Island. Professor, Ohio State University. http://jsjgeology.net/San-Salvador,Bahamas-inland-lakes-and-ponds.htm

Goldsmith, Roger A., and Philip L. Richardson. "Numerical Simulations of Columbus' Atlantic Crossings," Technical Report, Woods Hole Oceanographic Institution, February 1992.

Gómara, Francisco López de. *Historia General of the Indias*, 1552.

Gould, R. T. "The Landfall of Columbus: An Old Problem Re-Stated," *The Geographical Journal*, Vol. 69, No. 5 (1927), 403–425.

Graßhoff, Gerd, Florian Mittenhuber, and Elisabeth Rinner. "Of Paths and Places: The Origin of Ptolemy's Geography," *Archive for History of Exact Sciences*, Vol. 71, No. 6 (2017), 483–508. http://www.jstor.org/stable/45211928

Griffin, Nigel. *Las Casas on Columbus: Background and Second and Fourth Voyages*, *Repertorium Columbianum*, Vol. VI, UCLA Center for Medieval and Renaissance Studies, Belgium: Brepolis Publishers, 1999.

Guerrero, M. Montserrat León. *Mujeres Que Ayudaron al Plan Descubridor de Colón*, Universidad de Valladolid, 2017. https://dialnet.unirioja.es/ejemplar/465729

Guitar, Lynne, Jorge Estevez, and Joyce Leung. "Taínos," In *The Encyclopedia of Caribbean Religions: Volume 1: A-L; Volume 2: M-Z*, edited by Patrick Taylor, Frederick I. Case, and Sean Meighoo, 1014–1029. University of Illinois Press, 2013. http://www.jstor.org/stable/10.5406/j.ctt2tt9kw.113

Gyory, Joanna, Arthur J. Mariano, and Edward H. Ryan. "The Canary Current," *Ocean Surface Currents*. https://oceancurrents.rsmas.miami.edu/atlantic/canary.html

Harlow, George E. "Pre-Columbian Jadeitite Artifacts from San Salvador Island, Bahamas and Comparison with Jades of the Eastern Caribbean and Jadeitites of the Greater Caribbean Region," *Journal of Archaeological Science: Reports*, Vol. 26, 2019.

Heathcote, N.H. de Vaudrey. "Christopher Columbus and the Discovery of Magnetic Variation," *Science Progress in the Twentieth Century* (1919–1933), Vol. 27, No. 105 (1932), 82–103.

Helle, Richard. "Slavery," *Encyclopedia Britannica*. Retrieved 16 August 2021.

Henige, David. *Numbers from Nowhere: The American Indian Contact Population*. Norman, Oklahoma: University of Oklahoma Press, 1998.

———. "Writings: Journal," In *Christopher Columbus and the Age of Exploration*, edited by Silio A. Bedini. New York: Da Capo Press, 1998.

———. *Historical Evidence and Argument*. Madison: University of Wisconsin Press, 2005.

Hinckley, Clark B. *Christopher Columbus: A Man Among the Gentiles*. Salt Lake City: Deseret Book Co., (2014).

Hoffman, Charles A. "Archaeological Investigations at the Long Bay Site, San Salvador, Bahamas," *Proceedings: First San Salvador Conference, Columbus and His World*, October 30–November 3, 1986.

Hudson, G. F. "Marco Polo," *The Geographical Journal*, Vol. 120, No. 3 (1954), 299–311.

Ijoma, J.O. "Portuguese Activities in West Africa Before 1600 The Consequences," *Transafrican Journal of History*, Vol. 11 (1982), 136–146. http://www.jstor.org/stable/24328537

Jackson, Christopher C. *Preservation and the Future of the Bahamian Past: A Case Study of San Salvador Island's Historic Resources*, M.A. Thesis, University of Georgia, 2010. https://getd.libs.uga.edu

Jane, Cecil, "The Opinion of Columbus Concerning Cuba and the 'Indies'," *The Geographical Journal*, Vol. 71, No. 3 (1929), 266–270. https://ui.adsabs.harvard.edu/abs/1929GeogJ..73..266J/abstract

———. "The Letter of Columbus Announcing the Success of His First Voyage," *The Hispanic American Historical Review*, Vol. 10, No. 1 (1930), 33–50.

———. *The Four Voyages of Columbus: A History in Eight Documents, Including Five Christopher Columbus, in the Original Spanish, with English Translations*, Foreword by L. A. Vigneras, New York: Dover, 1988, (One Volume). [online] Journal with translation by Cecil Jane.

Jos, Emiliano. "Las Casas, Historian of Christopher Columbus," *The Americas*, Vol. 12, No. 4 (1956), 355–362.

Karttunen, Frances. *Between Worlds: Interpreters, Guides, and Survivors*. Brunswick, New Jersey: Rutgers University Press, 1994.

———. "Interpreters Snatched from the Shore," In *The Language Encounter in the Americas, 1492 to 1800*, edited by Edward G. Gray and Norman Fiering, 215–229. New York: Berghahn Books, 2000.

Keegan, William F. "The Ecology of Lucayan Arawak Fishing Practices," *American Antiquity*, Vol. 51, No. 4 (1986), 816–825.

———. "Beahhead in the Bahamas: Landfall," *Archaeology*, Vol. 45, No. 1 (1992), 44–56. http://www.jstor.org/stable/41766288

———. "Lucayan Settlement Patterns and Recent Coastal Changes in the Bahamas," In *Paleoshorelines and Prehistory: An Investigation of Method*, edited by Lucille Lewis Johnson, Boca Raton, Florida: CRC Press, 1992.

———. *Taíno Indian Myth and Practice: The Arrival of the Stranger King*. Gainesville: University of Florida Press, 2007.

Keegan, William F., and Corrine L. Hofman. *The Caribbean Before Columbus*. Oxford, England: Oxford University Press, 2016.

Keegan, William F., and Morgan D. Maclachlan. "The Evolution of Avunculocal Chiefdoms: A Reconstruction of Taíno Kinship and Politics," *American Anthropologist*, New Series, Vol. 91, No. 3 (1989), 613–630.

Keegan, William F., and Steven W. Mitchell. "The Archaeology of Christopher Columbus' Voyage Through the Bahamas, 1492," *American Archaeology*, Vol. 6, No. 2 (1987), 102–108.

———. "Pacification, Conquest, and Genocide," In *Christopher Columbus and the Age of Exploration*, edited by Silio A. Bedini. New York: Da Capo Press, 1998.

Keehnen, Floris W.M., Corinne L. Hoffman, and Andrzej T. Antczak. "Material Encounters and Indigenous Transformations in the Early Colonial Americas," *Archaeological Case Studies, Material Encounters and Indigenous Transformations in the Early Colonial Americas: Archaeological Case Studies*, edited by Corinne L. Hofman and Floris W.M. Keehnen. Leiden: Brill, 2019. http://www.jstor.org/stable/10.1163/j.ctvrxk2gr.22

Kelley, James E. Jr. "The Navigation of Columbus on His First Voyage to America," *Proceedings, First San Salvador Conference: Columbus and His World*. 1986. [online].

Kettell, Samuel. (Translated from the Martín Fernandez de Navarrete 1825 Spanish version), Boston: Thomas B. Wait and Son, 1827. https://archive.org/details/personalnarrativ00colu

Kicza, John E. "A Synoptic Edition of the Log of Columbus's First Voyage [Review]," *Renaissance Quarterly*, Vol. 54, No. 1 (Spring, 2001), 280–282.

Lamb, Ursula. "Lawsuits (Pleitos Colombinos)," In *Christopher Columbus and the Age of Exploration*, edited by Silio A. Bedini. New York: Da Capo Press, 1998.

Lardicci, Francesca, "Introduction," *A Synoptic Edition of the Log of Columbus's First Voyage*, Volume VI of *Repertorium Columbianum*, UCLA Center for Medieval and Renaissance Studies, 1999.

Las Casas, Bartolomé de las Casas. *First Voyage of Columbus*. Translated from the Spanish by Thomas B. Wait and Son. Boston, 1825.

Lemos, William. "Pinzón, Martín Alonso," In *Christopher Columbus and the Age of Exploration*, edited by Silio A. Bedini. New York: Da Capo Press, 1998.

Lynch, James J. "the Maps of Discovery," *The North American Review*, Vol. 277, No. 5 (1992), 6–15.

Major, R. H. "The Landfall of Columbus," *Proceedings of the Royal Geographical Society and Monthly Record of Geography (New Monthly Series)*, Vol. 6, No. 1 (1884), 42–43.

Mann, Charles. *1491: New Revelations of the Americas Before Columbus*. New York: Vintage Press, 1997.

Manzano Manzano. *Los Pinzones y el descubrimiento de América*, 3 vols. Madrid: Ed. Cultura Hispánica, 1988.

Markham, Clements R. *The Journal of Christopher Columbus and Documents relating to the Voyages John Cabot and Gaspar Corte Real*, London: Hakluyt Society, 1893. [Live link] [based on Navarette 1825].

Martinell, Grife F. *Aspectos lingüisticos del descubrimiento y de la Conquista*. Madrid: E. Cultura Hispánica.

Martinón-Torres, Marcos, Roberto Valcárcel Rojas, Juanita Sáenz Samper, María Filomena Buerra. "Metallic encounters in Cuba: The technology, exchange and meaning of metals before and after Columbus," *Journal of Anthropological Archaeology*, Vol. 31, No. 4 (2012), 439–454.

Martyr. *De Orbe Novo, Volume 1*, reprinted as *The Eight Decades of Peter Martyr D' Anghera*, Francis Augustus MacNutt, 1912.

McIntosh, Gregory. "Martín Alonso Pinzón's Discovery of Babueca and the Identity of Guanahani," *Terrae Incognitae* (Academia), Vol. 24 (1992), 79–100.

Meinig, D.W. *The Shaping of America: A Geographical Perspective on 500 Years of History, Vol. 1, Atlantic America*. New Haven, Connecticut: Yale University Press, 1995.

Mercer, John. *The Canary Islanders: Their Prehistory, Conquest, and Survival*. Collings Publisher, 1980.

Miller, Elizabeth. "Evidence for Prehistoric Scalping in Northeastern Nebraska," *Plains Anthropologist*, Vol. 39, No. 148 (1994), 211–219. http://www.jstor.org/stable/256 69265

Miller, Joaquin. *The Journal of Columbus' First Voyage*. Washington, DC: The Inventors' Outlook, 1912. [Online: Internet Archive] https://archive.org/details/journalof columbu00colurich/page/2/mode/1up

Moody, Alton B. "The Nautical Mile," *United States Naval Institute Proceedings*, Vol. 75. No. 11, Annapolis, November 1949.

Morgan, Philip D. "Origins of American Slavery," *OAH Magazine of History*, Vol. 19, No. 4 (2005), 51–56. http://www.jstor.org/stable/25161964

Morison, Samuel Eliot. "Texts and Translations of the Journal of Columbus's First Voyage," *The Hispanic American Historical Review*, Vol. 19, No. 3 (1939), 235–261.

———. *Journals and Other Documents on the Life and Voyages of Christopher Columbus*. New York: Heritage Press, 1963.

———. *Admiral of the Ocean Sea: A Life of the Christopher Columbus*. Boston: Little Brown and Company, 1970.

Moscoso, F. "Chiefdoms in the Islands and Mainland: A Comparison," In *General History of the Caribbean, Volume 1: Autochthonous Societies*, edited by J. Sued-Badillo, 292–315, Paris: UNESCO Publishing., 2003.

Munster, Sebastian. *Of the Newe India, and Illandes in the West Ocean Sea*. 1544. Reprint, translated by Richard Eden, *The First Three English Books on* America, 1553. Online: Internet Archive. https://archive.org/details/firstthreeenglis00arberich/page/n5/mode/2up

Murphy, Patrick J., and Ray W. Coye. "Columbus: 'The Dawn of an Age'," In *Mutiny and Its Bounty: Leadership Lessons from the Age of Discovery*, 15–35. Yale University Press, 2013. http://www.jstor.org/stable/j.ctt32bhqq.8

Nader, Helen. "Writings: An Overview," *Christopher Columbus and the Age of Exploration: An Encyclopedia*, edited by Silvio A. Bedini. New York: De Capo Press, 1998.

Navarette, Martín Fernandez. *Coleccion de los viages y descubrimientos, que hicieron por mar los Españoles; desde fines del siglo XV, con varios documentos inéditos concernientes á la historia de la marina castellana y de los estableciementos Españoles en Indias; Viages menores, y los de Vespucio; Poblaciones en el Darien, suplemento al tomo II* (in original Spanish), Madrid en la Imprenta Real, 1829.

———. *Viajes de Colón*. Madrid: Calpe, 1922. Navarette's original translation circa 1825 of Las Casas's *Diario*.

Newson, Linda A. "African and Luso-Africans in the Portuguese Slave Trade on the Upper Guinea Coast in the Early Seventeenth Century," *Journal of African History*, Vol. 53, No. 1 (2012), 1–24. http://www.jstor.org/stable/41480264

Nield, David. Mysterious Text Suggests Europeans Knew of America Long Before Columbus Set Sail, October 12, 2021, *Science Alert*. https://www.sciencealert.com/ancient-texts-suggest-italian-sailors-knew-about-america-way-before-columbus

Nunn, George N. *The Geographical Conceptions of Columbus*, Thesis, University of California, American Geographical Society Research Series No. 14, W.L.G. Joerg, editor, 1924. https://play.google.com/books/reader?id=mNErAAAAIAAJ&pg=GBS.PP2&hl=en

O'Callaghan, Joseph F. "Treaty of Alcáçovas," In *Christopher Columbus and the Age of Exploration: An Encyclopedia*, edited by Silvio A. Bedini. New York: De Capo Press, 1998.

Olschki, Leonardo, "What Columbus Saw on Landing in the West Indies," *Proceedings of the American Philosophical Society*, Vol. 84, No. 5 (1941), 633–659.

Papal Encyclicals Online, Sicut Dudum, "Against the Enslaving of Black Natives from the Canary Islands," Pope Eugene IV, 1435. https://www.papalencyclicals.net/eugene04/eugene04sicut.htm

Park, Lisa. "Comparing Two Long-term Hurricane Frequency and Intensity Records from San Salvador Island, Bahamas," *Journal of Coastal Record*, Vol. 28, No. 4 (2012), 891–902.

Parsons, James J. "The Migration of Canary Islanders to the Americas: An Unbroken Current Since Columbus," *The Americas*, Vol. 30, No. 4 (1983), 447–481.

Peck, Douglas. "The Controversial Skill of Columbus as a Navigator: An Enduring Historical Enigma," *The Journal of Navigation*, Vol. 62 (2009), 417–425.

Phillips, William D. Jr., and Carla Rahn Phillips. *The Worlds of Christopher Columbus*. Cambridge, England: Cambridge Press, 1992.

Pons, Frank Moya. "Caribbean Trade," In *Christopher Columbus and the Age of Exploration: An Encyclopedia*, edited by Silvio A. Bedini. New York: De Capo Press, 1998.

Ramírez, Susan Elizabeth. *A History of Colonial Latin America from First Encounters to Independence*. New York: Routledge, 2022.

Randles, W. G. L. "The Evaluation of Columbus' 'India' Project by Portuguese and Spanish Cosmographers in the Light of the Geographical Science of the Period," *Imago Mundi*, Vol. 42 (1990), 50–64.

Raposeiro, Pedro M. et al., Proceedings of the National Academy of Sciences, 4-Oct-2021. https://www.pnas.org/cgi/doi/10.1073/pnas.2108236118

Reséndez, Andrés. *The Other Slavery*. Boston: Houghton Mifflin, 2016.

Restall, Matthew. *Seven Myths of the Spanish Conquests*. Oxford, England: Oxford University Press, 2003.

Richardson, Philip L. and Roger A. Goldsmith. "The Columbus Landfall: Voyage Track Corrected for Winds and Currents," *Oceanus*, Vol. 30, No. 3 (Fall 1987), 2–10.

Rickey, V. Frederick. "How Columbus Encountered America," *Mathematics Magazine*, Vol. 65, No. 4 (1992), 219–225.

Rocca, Al M. *Mapping Christopher Columbus: An Historical Geography of His Early Life to 1492*. McFarland, 2023.

———. "Mapping the Proposed Caribbean Zoonotic (Swine Influenza) Epidemic of 1493 as a Geographic Model of Infectious Virus Dispersion," *Terra Incognitae*, (pending: Spring, 2024).

Rojas, Roberto Valcárcel. "European Material Culture in Indigenous Sites in Northeastern Cuba," In *Material Encounters and Indigenous Transformations in the Early Colonial Americas: Archaeological Case Studies*, edited by Corinne L. Hofman and Floris W.M. Keehnen, 9: 102–123. Brill, 2019. http://www.jstor.org/stable/10.1163/j.ctvrxk2gr.11

Rosenbach, Johann. *The Spanish letter of Columbus to Luis de Sant'Angel*: dated 15 February 1493, Spanish translation reprinted in reduced facsimile, and trans. from the unique copy of the original edition (printed by Johann Rosenbach at Barcelona early in April 1493), Published in 1893, London: Quaritch, https://archive.org/details/spanishletterco01quargoog

Ross, Ann H., William F. Keegan, Michael P. Pateman, and Collen B. Young. "Faces Divulge the Origins of Caribbean Prehistoric Inhabitants," *Scientific Reports (Nature Research)*, Vol. 10 (2020), 147.

Rouse, Irving. "The First Repeopling," In *The Taínos: Rise and Decline of the People Who Greeted Columbus*. New Haven, Connecticut: Yale University Press, 1992. http://www. jstor.org/stable/j.ctt5vm4fn.8

Ruiz, Teofilo F. "Hernando de Talavera," *Christopher Columbus and the Age of Exploration: An Encyclopedia*, edited by Silvio A. Bedini. New York: De Capo Press, 1998.

Sale, Kirkpatrick. *The Conquest of Paradise*. New York: Alfred A. Knopf, 1990.

Sánchez, Luis. *Tesoro De La Lengua Castellana, O Española*. Madrid: Dirigido a la Magestad Catolica del Rey Don Felipe III, 1611.

Sauer, Carl. *The Early Spanish Main*. Berkeley: University of California Press, 1969.

Sears, William H., and Shaun O. Sullivan. "Bahamas Prehistory," *American Antiquity*, Vol. 43, No. 1 (1978), 3–25.

Siegel, P. E. *Ancestor Worship and Cosmology among the Taíno. In Taíno: Pre-Columbian Art and Culture from the Caribbean*, edited by F. Bercht, E. Brodsky, J. A. Farmer, and D. Taylor, 106–111. New York: Monacelli Press, 1997.

Snyder, Christina. *Slavery in Indian Country*. Cambridge: Harvard University Press, 2010.

Stevens-Arroyo, Anthony M. "The Inter-Atlantic Paradigm: The Failure of Spanish Medieval Colonization of the Canary and Caribbean Islands," *Comparative Studies in Society and History*, Vol. 35, No. 3 (1993), 515–543. http://www.jstor.org/stable/ 179144

———. "Juan Mateo Guaticabanu, September 21, 1496: Evangelization and Martyrdom in the Time of Columbus," *The Catholic Historical Review*, Vol. 82, No. 4 (1996), 614–636. https://www.proquest.com/central/docview/200016137/fulltext/D40FD0EF 971C4BFBPQ/25?accountid=25342

Stone, Erin Woodruff. "Slave Raiders vs. Friars: *Tierra Firme, 1513–1522*," *The Americas*, Vol. 74, No. 2 (2017), 139–170.

———. *Captives of Conquest: Slavery in the Early Modern Spanish Caribbean*. University of Pennsylvania Press, 2021. https://doi.org/10.2307/j.ctv18dvw1v

Taviani, Paolo. *Christopher Columbus: The Grand Design*, London: Orbis Publshing (English edition). 1985.

———. *Columbus: The Great Adventure, His Life, His Times, and His Voyages*. Translated from the Italian by Luciano F. Farina and Marc A. Beckwith. New York: Orion Books, 1991.

———. "Fernando Colón," In *Christopher Columbus and the Age of Exploration: An Encyclopedia*, edited by Silvio A. Bedini. New York: De Capo Press, 1998.

Taylor, Douglas R., and Berend J. Hoff. "The Linguistic Repertory of the Island-Carib in the Seventeenth Century: The Men's Language: A Carib Pidgin?" *International Journal of American Linguistics*, Vol. 46, No. 4(1980), 301–312. http://www.jstor.org/ stable/1264711

Thacher, John Boyd. *Christopher Columbus: His Life, His Work, His Remains*, 3 vols. New York: G. P. Putnam's Sons, 1903–1904. https://babel.hathitrust.org/cgi/ pt?id=hvd.32044009917428&view=1up&seq=391&size=125

"The Compass of Columbus," *The American Catholic Historical Researches*, New Series, Vol. 7, No. 1 (1911), 1–7. https://www.jstor.org/stable/44374849

Timmer, John. "Recent Sea Level Rise Is the Fastest Since 800 BCE," *ARS Technica*, n.d. online. https://arstechnica.com/science/2016/02/recent-sea-level-rise-is-the-fastest-since-800-bce/

Varela, Consuelo. "The Difficult Beginnings: Columbus as a Mediator of New World Products," In *Global Goods and the Spanish Empire, 1492–1824*, eds. Bethany Aram, Bartolome Yun-Casalilla, Camden, England: Palgrave Macmillan, 2014.

Vaudrey Heathcote, N. H. de. "Christopher Columbus and the Discovery of Magnetic Variation," *Science Progress in the Twentieth Century (1919–1933)*, Vol. 27, No. 105 (1932), 82–103. http://www.jstor.org/stable/43430760

Vieira, Alberto. "Sugar Islands: The Sugar Economy of Madeira and the Canaries, 1450–1650," In *Tropical Babylons: Sugar and the Making of the Atlantic World, 1450–1680*, edited by Stuart B. Schwartz, 42–84. University of North Carolina Press, 2004. https://doi.org/10.5149/9780807895627_schwartz.7

Vigário, Edgar. "Who Made Jácome de Bruges Disappear," Academia Online, September 2013.

Vogt, John L. "The Lisbon Slave House and African Trade, 1486–1521," *Proceedings of the American Philosophical Society*, Vol. 117, No. 1 (1973), 1–16. http://www.jstor.org/stable/985944

Wadsworth, James E. *Columbus and His First Voyage: A History in Documents*. London: Bloomsbury Academic Publishing, 2020. [in Simpson library: available e-book online with Simpson Library].

"Warfare in Pre-Columbian North America," Department of National Defense—military history. n.d. Online: www.canada.ca/

Washburn, Wilcomb E. "The Meaning of 'Discovery' in the Fifteenth and Sixteenth Centuries," *The American Historical Review*, Vol. 68, No. 1 (1962), 1–21.

Watts, Pauline Moffitt. "Prophecy and Discovery: On the Spiritual Origins of Christopher Columbus's 'Enterprise of the Indies'," *The American Historical Review*, Vol. 90, No. 1 (1985), 73–102. https://doi.org/10.2307/1860749

West, Delno C. West. "Christopher Columbus, Lost Biblical Sites, and the Last Crusade," *The Catholic Historical Review*, Vol. 78, No. 4 (1992), v–541. http://www.jstor.org/stable/25023872

———. "The Library of Columbus," *Christopher Columbus and the Age of Exploration: An Encyclopedia*, New York: D Capo Press, 1998.

Wilford, John Noble. *The Mysterious History of Columbus*, Vintage Books, 1992.

William, Gillett and Charles Gillett. "The Religious Motives of Christopher Columbus, *Papers of the American Society of Church History*, Vols. 4–5, 1892.

Wilson, Samuel M. *Hispaniola: Caribbean Chiefdoms in the Age of Columbus*, University of Alabama Press, 1990.

Wright, Thomas, *The Travels of Marco Polo, the Venetian*. Translated from the 13th-century Italian text. 1854 English Edition, London. (online)

Zamora, Margarita. "Todos son palabras formales del Almirante: Las Casas y el Diario de Colón," *Hispanic Review*, Vol. 57, No. 1 (Winter, 1989), 25–41.

———. *Reading Columbus*, Berkeley: University of California Press, 1993.

INDEX

Pages in *italics* refer to figures and pages followed by "n" refer to notes.

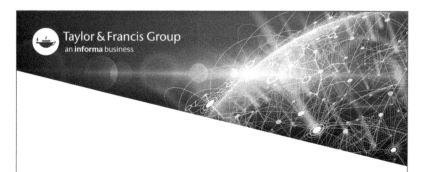